YOUR BEST ENTERTAINMENT

The Films of Hollywood's Golden Age

How they were made, why they were made, the people who made them, the way they were sold, the audiences who were thrilled by them, the escape they offered…

Charles Lee Jackson, II

I0446517

Strange Particle Press

Copyright © 2024 CLJII

All rights reserved.
ISBN: 9798865835851

This book is a journalistic reference work celebrating the era when movies were "Your Best entertainment". As such, the publishers believe its contents are protected under both the First amendment and the "fair use" laws.

The images used throughout this book are intended to deepen reader's appreciation of classic motion pictures and the phenomenon they created - and to preserve a record of them as they were seen in their own time.

12 GOLDEN AGE FILM MYSTERIES – DO YOU KNOW THE ANSWERS?

1. Which actor in *Casablanca* (Warner Bros., 1942) utters the famous line, "Play it again, Sam"- Humprey Bogart or Ingrid Bergman?

2. How did Universal Pictures explain Sherlock Holmes, consulting detective of the Victorian age, being alive to battling World War Two Nazis?

3. In *Devil Girl from Mars* (British Lion, 1954) an alien arrives seeking males to help repopulate her dying civilization, but what later film reversed her quest?

4. In how many motion pictures did Bela Lugosi portray Dracula?

5. Why did Michael Todd film *Oklahoma!* twice?

6. Where does the Laurel and Hardy 1935 M-G-M comedy *Bonnie Scotland* primarily take place? (Hint: it ain't Scotland.)

7. Who was the animated character who spoke not in words but in sound effects?

8. Why did Republic Pictures promote plainclothes cop Dick Tracy to a G-Man?

10. What box-office star and author appeared as himself in a film version of his war-time autobiography?

11. What documentary feature film caused Walt Disney to leave distributor RKO Radio and create his own releasing company?

In *The Mark of Zorro* (20th Century-Fox, 1940), Eugene Pallette played *Fray* Felipe, a valiant priest. The role was essentially the same as a part Pallette played in what previous adventure film?

You will learn the answers to all these questions as you read this book. Or skip to the last page and test your knowledge now...

DEDICATION

Nick Clooney
Who loves the history of Hollywood
And hopes to see it preserved and
appreciated

The author also wishes to thank Forrest J
Ackerman, Ned Comstock of the USC Film and
Television Archives, the staff of the Fairbanks
Center for Film Study, Academy of Motion Picture
Arts and Sciences, and all of the individuals (as
listed in "references" below) whose interviews and
conversations informed my understanding of the
picture business in those lauded years.

CONTENTS

FOREWORD

"Who are all those *old* people?"
"Why is it so *slow*?"
"If it was any good, it'd be in *color*!"

IF YOU'RE A fan of classic motion pictures, or B pictures, or short subjects, and you're a mom or dad or a grandparent, you've probably heard one or more of these remarks if you've tried to show your little ones the films you grew up with or learned to love from TV. If you're one of those youngsters who's discovered classic Hollywood for yourself and can't get your love across to your contemporaries, you may have heard these put-downs. Either way, here's a book to show them what you already know. In these days of fast action and instant gratification, it can be hard to catch the interest of a young person who's been weaned on "sci-fi" and "super-hero" movies, long on fights and explosions and short on plot development. Oh, there are still dramas being made, but their audiences have never been able to capture the kid in every movie-goer.

So here's a chance to show them what you love about pictures, good old motion pictures with Humphrey Bogart or Alice Faye or Roy Rogers or Buster Crabbe. In this book, you'll find explanations about the studios, films, and people; examples to share with that next generation or two.

i

For that matter, if you're just a long-time film-goer who misses those grand days and the movie-going experience that's faded from society, and just want to re-live your own happy days of yesteryear, you can dive into these pages as a guide to find more to love, and to heck with those who just don't get it.

This is also a book for the fan of a specific *genre* to use to learn about other types of films, to see what a favorite cowboy star, for example, has done in mysteries or musicals.

You see, most books on film take a "surgical" approach – they are focused on one person, one film, one *genre*, or one studio. Or they present some person's idea of what the "best" films of some category are.

This book takes a "scattershot" approach, covering a wide assortment of *genres* and a deep spectrum of quality. Drama, Science fiction, Musicals, and more; The greats, the average, the typical, the poor – any picture that amuses and entertains, even ones that do so only by virtue of their ineptitude. Only the bland, the disgusting, the boring are excluded.

At one time, the slogan, "Movies Are Your Best Entertainment" was a popular phrase in advertising, but it's unknown if anyone – including the person who coined it – realized the mild irony that it makes the acronym "MAYBE".

But there's no "maybe" that motion pictures are a fine story-telling medium as well as a window on history and society during their "golden years". So come on and take a peek through that window, and get an introduction to the many aspects of the motion picture.

INTRODUCTION

THE MOTION PICTURE was an almost inevitable step in the evolution of entertainment. Centuries of epic poems, novels, pictographs, and legends developed a language for story-telling, and the inventions and discoveries of Matthew Brady, Eadweard Muybridge, George Eastman, Thomas Edison and his staff, and William Friese-Greene provided the medium. J. Stuart Blackton, Georges Méliès, the *frères* Pathé, and others defined the parameters of cinema; D.W. Griffith, Cecil B. DeMille, and their contemporaries explored and expanded the techniques and artistry that became moving pictures, and Henry MacRae invented the way that pictures are made. The film industry as we know it now, in the United States, was built up mostly by men fleeing from the "patents trust" (which strangled expansion of the medium by thinking of picture as product, not art) to Hollywood, where they created many of the studios and distributors that still exist today. Sound on film, Technicolor, CinemaScope, stereoptical printing, all of these have enhanced the movie-going experience. From the "slices of life" shot by the Lumière brothers to the one-reel comedies of Mack Sennett, from 1912's *Cleopatra* The Romance Of A Woman And A Queen (United States Film Company) to this week's blockbuster, from Grauman's Chinese and the Radio City Music Hall to the Odeon or the local film society clubhouse, people all over the globe have, for over a hundred years, lived by the motto, "Movies Are Your Best Entertainment".

The history of the Motion Picture is a rich tapestry reflecting the history of Mankind, from pre-history to today's headlines. New viewers come to old pictures with varying degrees of understanding. Here are some useful bits of information to help you through this book.

SOME BASICS

First of all, the "B" in "B picture" is not a grade – despite what you may have read in reference books, there's no such thing as a "grade-B picture". I mean, think about it: in school, "B" means "above average", and yet critics decry the B picture as something very bad. How could it be above average *and* very bad?

No, the "B" in this case relates to marketing. In the days of 45-RPM records, a hit song would be issued as a single recording. But the vinyl disc had two sides, and not filling the reverse would be wasteful. So another song by the same artist, or an instrumental version of the hit, would be pressed onto that second side. The obverse, the hit, became the "A" side, the reverse the "B" side. (The designations were more recently resurrected for double-sided DVDs.)

In the days of the double-feature program, the main feature became known as the "A" picture; the second feature – the "flip side" of the bill – became the "B" picture. No inherent decree of quality, just a marketing distinction. However, the B pictures, being intended as lesser attractions, were shorter, less expensive, more subject to formulizing.

After 1933, the major studios, to ensure continuity of business (and to capitalize on a program begun by theatre owners, who'd found that, not surprisingly, two pictures brought in bigger crowds than single features), maintained full schedules of B-picture production, keeping casts and crews working and filling their captive chain theatres. This also kept people working through the Depression and kept money flowing to keep the studios alive (though much of that money would come from New York banks, ending the days of the truly independent producer). Minor studios concentrated on shorter features, offering them to neighborhood theaters as matinee fodder or as B pictures to accompany major-studio A pictures. Theaters benefitted another way: shorter films meant an extra intermission or two, which meant more opportunities for audience members to visit the snack bar, always a lucrative source of revenue, revenue that was not shared with the distributors.

Returning to the same subjects and characters offered the picture companies many built-in economies, and familiarity, it was determined, bred not contempt but content. Audiences wanted to see the next "Boston Blackie" or "Hardy Family" picture, kids waited to see the new Roy Rogers or "Durango Kid". The system supported itself for over 20 years, until television began to provide the same sort of entertainment as the B picture, in one's own home – and for free, after an initial investment. Studios either re-tooled their B units as television producers or simply closed them, leaving theaters to return to scrounging for second features.

But the legacy of the Bs was not just television. Today those old ephemeral films still catch the fancy of old fans and new, and provide a glimpse of Old Hollywood and entertainment that still, well, entertains.

You'll find in this volume ten *genres* and two formats that encompass the Hollywood product. A few things you *won't* find are "horror" pictures, exploitation films, and "nudies".

"Horror" was always a portmanteau label for any film with monsters, the supernatural, or the inexplicable. This meant that "horror" embraced fantasy, *outré* mysteries, dark dramas, and even science-fiction, which studio heads failed to distinguish from fantasy because it was all stuff they – and, to be honest, much of the audience – didn't understand. But, as an example, the Universal pictures *The Phantom of the Opera*, *Dracula*, and *Frankenstein* are all "horror", but the first is a drama, the second fantasy, the third science fiction. So here I have sorted out each "horror" picture by its primary focus, though you'll find many films mix and match fantasy and science fiction, and all have some drama element. (This mixing of *genres* is by no means singular to these two groups, as you'll see.) At least one has fallen into "adventure" as that is the overwhelming element in the picture. Gory modern-style "horror" films like *Night of the Living Dead* (Walter Reade Organization *et al.*, 1968) and its ilk are excluded.

Exploitation Pictures have been around through the whole history of the medium, from "Blaxploitation" pictures like *Dolemite* (Dimension Pictures, '75) and soft-core pornography (you need an example? OK, *Blazing Stewardesses* [Independent-International, '75]) to "public warning" productions. Films of this last collection tend to fall in one of the ten *genres* (as for example titles like *Reefer Madness* [originally *The Burning Question*, States' Rights, '36], which, while exploitative, would fit in the "Drama" chapter). But if they're too narrow of focus, too rarified, or just plain unpleasant, they've been left out.

"Nudies" and other focused-marketed pictures are outside the scope of this work (which is to say, I don't care for them and have not gone out of my way to research them), so someone else can write *that* book.

Regrettably, one category, the "Race Films", is not covered because of its exclusion from "mainstream" Hollywood and the politics of the period. Black performers were passed over for starring vehicles as much due to financial considerations as prejudice. Major studio heads knew that, in the Old South quadrant, pictures with African-American actors would simply not receive engagements, as the people there were viewed with unwarranted distrust and hatred, blamed for the cruel treatments inflicted upon them by Whites, who assumed reprisals. Black performers were thus relegated to supporting roles, usually as singers or dancers, domestics, or comedy-relief characters, though in these roles they could and did improve their image to White audiences. But at the same time, enterprising "Negro" promoters carved out the niche of "Race Films" for screening at Black-only movie-houses in the parts of the country still gripped by the evil of segregation. In these films, which Blacks who were supporting players in Hollywood justifiably became stars in the niche market. (Monogram Pictures even produced films for the "sepia circuit", but it was an unusual move for a major studio, even a small one.) Few of the pictures played major circuits, and to a great extent, the entire field was overlooked until recently. New authors and film historians have been rectifying the omission from Hollywood History, and an interested fan will have little difficulty finding books to fill in the story of Black participation in pictures.

You will note in these pages that films are identified with (distributor, year), rather than director credits. Until the rise of the *auteur* theory (that the director is the author of a film) any one of several people might be considered the creator of a motion picture, but it was more often than not the producer who defined what a picture would be, by his choice of writer, director, stars, and crew. In some cases, if the director came aboard the production early, or if the director was also the producer, of course, his influence was manifest – in fact this is the source of the *auteur* theory. Even if the Front Office of a studio selected the property or title, it was usually the producer who took up the creative process. If so, that person will be mentioned in the text. But it's the company that releases a film that gives one a better understanding of what to expect from a film, so the distributor – last link in the creative chain – gets the credit here.

Though the main emphasis of this text is on Hollywood product up to 1976, there are also examples of earlier and later pictures for context and comparison. The cut-off is simply defined: it's just before *Star Wars* (20th Century-Fox, 1977), which opened up a new era of adventure pictures that shifted science fiction, fantasy, and high adventure from the sidelines to the forefront at the box office, beginning the medium as we know it today.

Terms you won't find here are "silent pictures" and "talkies". Except for a brief period at the very beginning, pictures were never "silent" – they had some sort of aural accompaniment. Edison provided recorded cylinders with some films, and theaters usually had an orchestra pit with a few musicians or at least an organ or piano to provide mood music. Even the local store with a projector and a sheet for a screen had *some* sort of music. As the medium grew up, distributors provided sheet music geared to the ability of a theater to provide. DW Griffith, for example, constructed a full score to be sent out with *The Birth of a Nation* (Epoch Producing Corporation, '15). Music and even sound effects were part of the movie-going experience even before *Don Juan* (Warner Bros., '26). So, no "silent pictures". Pantomime pictures, perhaps, or, for the highfalutin, Mute Cinema or the Voiceless Screen.

(This, by the way, is part of the reason early talking pictures had little or no music [unless of course they were musicals]: music was viewed as "old hat", a remnant to be swept away and replaced with dialogue. That it also saved money was another strong point in favor of the policy, though it was soon found that audiences didn't question and even enjoyed the underscore – the background music – in a picture.)

Pictures were never called "silent" until they'd been talking for years, and then it was a term of derision. Likewise "talkies"; initially, the speaking films were called "all-talking" or, for brevity, "talkers". "Talkies" was the derisive term used by those who considered the new version of the medium a flash in the pan and a gimmick of which audiences would soon tire. So, taking the stand that talking pictures are here to stay (a safe bet, I think), here they are "talkers" – or just pictures.

(And by the way, though the term "movie" will be used here sparingly, that nickname started out as a "fan" term; industry insiders called them "pictures" or "shows" and used "movies" jokingly. It was the Movie Fan Magazines and the public [bless 'em, as Carl Denham once remarked] that used the term seriously. Today, "movie" has pretty much become the standard word for moving pictures, but in the double-feature era, they were still "pictures", so that's what they'll be here, unless the context requires otherwise.)

One other thing: Making and showing the films isn't enough; the audience needs to know the pictures are out there. And that was a combined effort by the distributor and the exhibitor, with posters, advertising "squibs", and "ballyhoo" (stunts and ideas for promoting a film) offered to theaters. Movie houses would display outside one-sheet (and larger) posters of the current program, and lobby cards – typically 11x14 "mini"-posters – of upcoming attractions in, not surprisingly, the lobby. Ballyhoo might include clubs offering, for example, a free screening of the last chapter of a serial if the kid had gotten his club card punched for each of the earlier chapters. Large lobby displays, or actors dressed as a film character, with a "sandwich board" emblazoned with the film title, could be hired to march along the boulevard. Press promotion books could have prepared newspaper articles about the film or one of the stars, pictures to color, quizzes to answer, all sorts of ideas to draw in the crowds. Of course, the most obvious promotion is the "trailer" (so called because it originally followed the feature) or preview of a coming attraction, a short film emphasizing the action or drama of a film "coming soon to this theater". A well wrought trailer would have the public lined up around the block.

A COUPLE OF technical notes: Many books make little if any distinction among the phases of the motion-picture business, because they're so thoroughly ingrained in the public mind these days. But for many years, the business had three distinct areas of operation: Production, Distribution, and Exhibition. The major studios encompassed two or all three of these, with production facilities and personnel that created the films; distributors that released the films and prepared publicity for them; and exhibitors, the individual and chain theaters that actually displayed the films to the public. M-G-M, Paramount, RKO Radio, 20th Century-Fox, Warner Bros., and Republic had all three; Universal, Columbia, Monogram, and PRC had only production and distribution; United Artists had only distribution and exhibition. Late comers to the game might have one, two, or three pieces of the pie, while the other old-timers who had only one piece teamed up with each other or one of the majors to get their product to the market.

PICTURE LENGTHS

1 reel = 10 minutes *(or more before projection speed was standardized at 24 frames per second)*

1 to 3 reels = short subject

4 to 5 reels = featurette or "streamliner"

5 to 7 reels = B feature

7 or more reels = A feature *(or, before 1933 and after 1962, just a feature)*

The dividing lines are fuzzy, and sometimes the categorization is determined by the content. Pictures in 6 to 8 reels can also be categorized as "program" pictures, suitable for distribution and exhibition as either an A or a B depending on the venue. The minor studios, without theatre chains, marketed extensively in this manner.

ABBREVIATIONS

Some of the distributors mentioned in the text are so well known, so ubiquitous, that the spelling out of their full names has become superfluous in texts of this sort. To save space, these names are abbreviated thus:

AA = Allied Artists (successor to Monogram)

A-I-P = American International Pictures

BV = Buena Vista, distributor of Walt Disney Productions from 1953

M-G-M = Metro-Goldwyn-Mayer (a Loew's, Incorporated, subsidiary)

PRC = Producers Releasing Corporation, later Eagle-Lion

UA = United Artists

Ufa = Universum Film Aktiengesellschaft (Universe Film Joint-stock Company)

U-I = Universal International, distributor of Universal Pictures 1946 to 1962

THE DISTRIBUTORS

THE MOTION PICTURE PATENTS COMPANY was the first film distributing company, formed by a consolidation headed up by Edison and Biograph, created to end squabbling among fledgling studios but which then enacted Draconian regulations upon its members. The "Patents Trust" viewed motion pictures as product, sold by the foot, not entertainment. They all but monopolized the three types of business (production, distribution, and exhibition), collecting fees from each operation. By 1910, this over-reach had caused filmmakers like Carl Laemmle, Adolph Zukor, and William Fox (names you'll see again) to break the Trust and make *their* films *their* way. In response, the Trust sent their new "enforcers", the General Film Company, to disrupt the actions of the wildcat studios – called "independents" in a derisive tone – by smashing or stealing equipment and product, disrupting screenings, anything to force the independents out of business. The wildcatters responded by fleeing the New York area, eventually to California, and the federal government, taking a dim view of the Patents Company's policies, brought action against it, declaring by court order in 1915 that it constituted an unlawful monopoly, ordering the Trust disbanded. In later years, while the independents were free to expand production at the behest of artists like D.W. Griffith, and films grew better looking and longer, and the studios developed the star system to attract regular viewers, the films of the Patents Company remained mostly unchanged, and Edison's unwillingness to adapt to changing times spelled the end of the Motion Picture Patents Company.

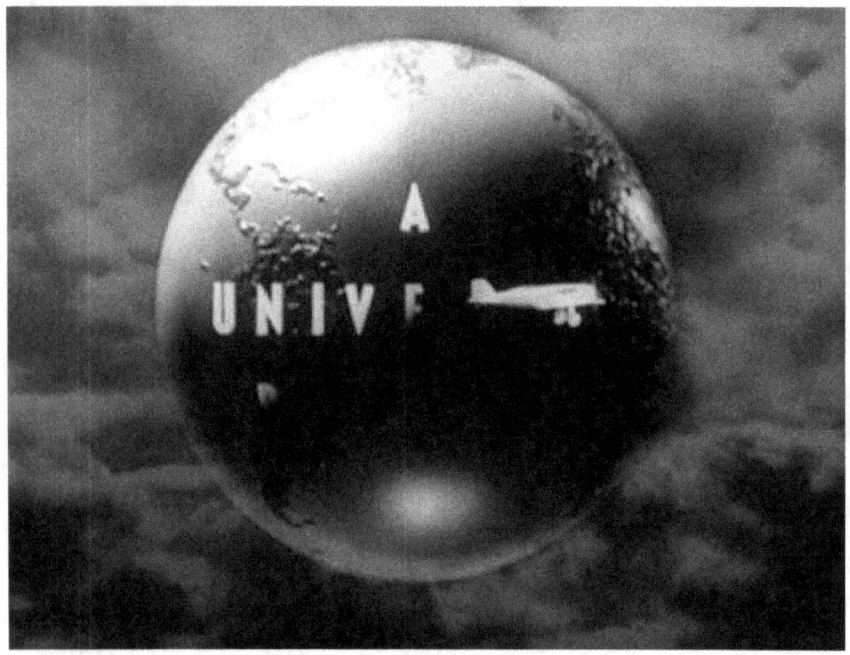

UNIVERSAL PICTURES developed in 1912 from Independent Motion Pictures (IMP), the creation of Jewish German immigrant Carl Laemmle, who had become enamored of the picture business but couldn't abide by the rules of "The Trust", the organization begun in 1908 by Thomas Edison to control all aspects of film production and exhibition. Opening Universal City at the north end of the Cahuenga Pass in the San Fernando Valley, Laemmle bought out all other participants to have a family-owned company. Geared to money-making, "Uncle" Carl even opened his studio to tourists – at a price – to watch pictures being made. Though this was phased out with the Talkers, later management re-instated the policy and today Universal City is a top tourist attraction. Though producing many good Westerns and comedies, the studio came for a time to specialize in Gothic-style horror, and even after the family was bought out, the new owners kept returning to monsters, top-lining Lon Chaney (Junior) as their big "monster" star and de-emphasizing mood for action. With no exhibition system, Universal held independent-theater loyalty through a program of shorts and especially serials, but lost ground when the studio was acquired by International Pictures, the policy of which was "all high-quality pictures", a policy that almost brought the studio to its knees. That meant many lay-offs among the staff and the closing of serial and B-picture units, which had been the life-blood of the studio. Having no theater chains to guarantee exhibition of their films, the company floundered until re-instating the series pictures that had sustained their predecessors. Later owners moved into TV production, and today, as NBC Universal, the company continues its programs of film and television production.

PARAMOUNT PICTURES began in 1916 from the merger of Adolph Zukor's Famous Players company with the Jesse L. Lasky picture company, and after briefly releasing as "Famous Players-Lasky" adopted the Paramount name (from a distributor Zukor had bought) and built new studios at Marathon and Melrose on the south side of Hollywood (where today it is the only major studio *in* the film capital). Winning the first "Best Picture" Oscar with *Wings* in '27, the studio continued on a steady course, with slick looking musicals and comedies, moody detective thrillers and solid dramas. Paramount was the home of Cecil B. DeMille and Preston Sturges; of Bing Crosby, Bob Hope, Alan Ladd, WC

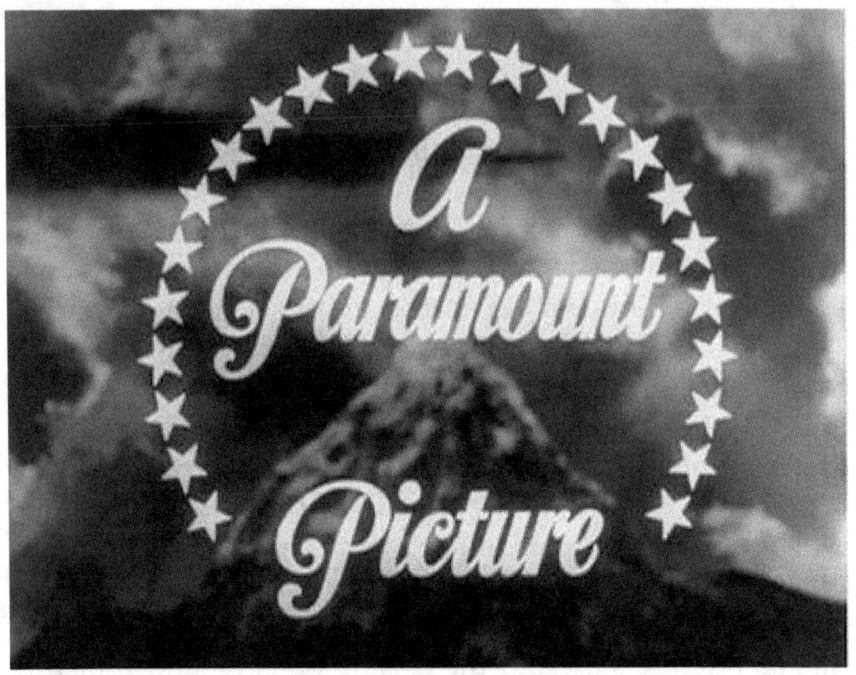

Fields, and the four Marx Brothers, of The "Road" pictures, Billy Wilder's *The Lost Weekend* ('45), and *Sunset Blvd.* ('50). In the television age Paramount became a part of Gulf + Western Industries, and acquired next-door neighbor Desilu, renaming it Paramount TV, and with it the profitable "Star Trek", which surprised the industry with its revival a generation later as both a successful feature-film series and a television dynasty. Now part of Viacom, Paramount controls a vast library of classic films and is affiliated with CBS and numerous cable-television outlets.

UNITED ARTISTS was the creation in 1919 of four top film-makers who were unhappy with studio politics and chiseling executives, intended as a company that would exist solely to release quality features by the principals (Douglas Fairbanks, Mary Pickford, Charles Chaplin, and D.W. Griffith) and other stars and producers who shared their ideals. Sadly, a shortage of such quality product limited

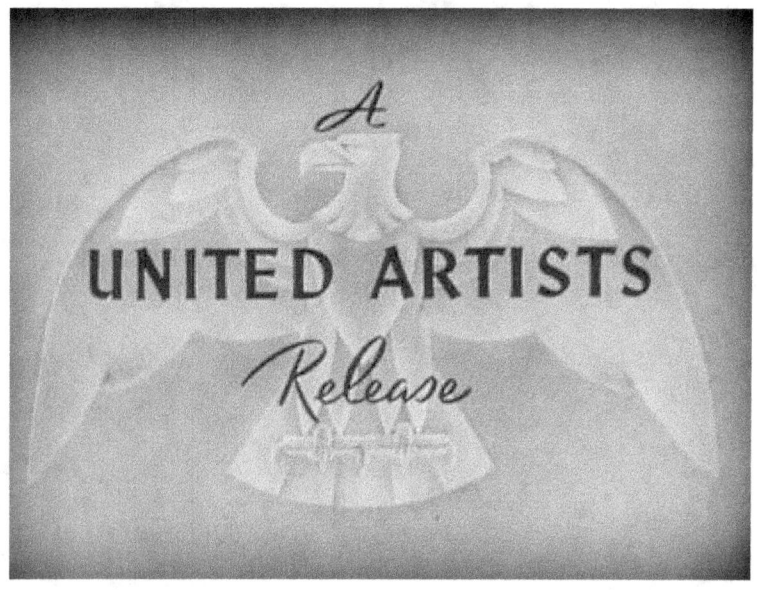

regular programs, and soon Fairbanks and Griffith dropped out, and Chaplin's product came so infrequently that the quality couldn't balance the slow returns. Other producers joined, and in-fighting, plus the necessity to distribute lesser films (including the popular but second-feature Hal Roach comedies and streamliners) compromised the original ideal. But producers like Samuel Goldwyn, Alexander Korda, Edward Small, and even Walt Disney brought superior product to them, and the company survived to become the distributor of the "James Bond" series. An eventual buy-out merged the company with mighty M-G-M, adding their catalogue of films to an already outstanding library.

WARNER BROS., started in 1923, built up from the Duquesne Amusement & Supply Company, a Pittsburgh-area exhibition company owned by the four Wonskolaser brothers. Their first big success was brought by a dog – but not just any dog: Rin-tin-tin, the veteran of the Great War who became a star of the Mute Cinema. In 1925, brother Sam

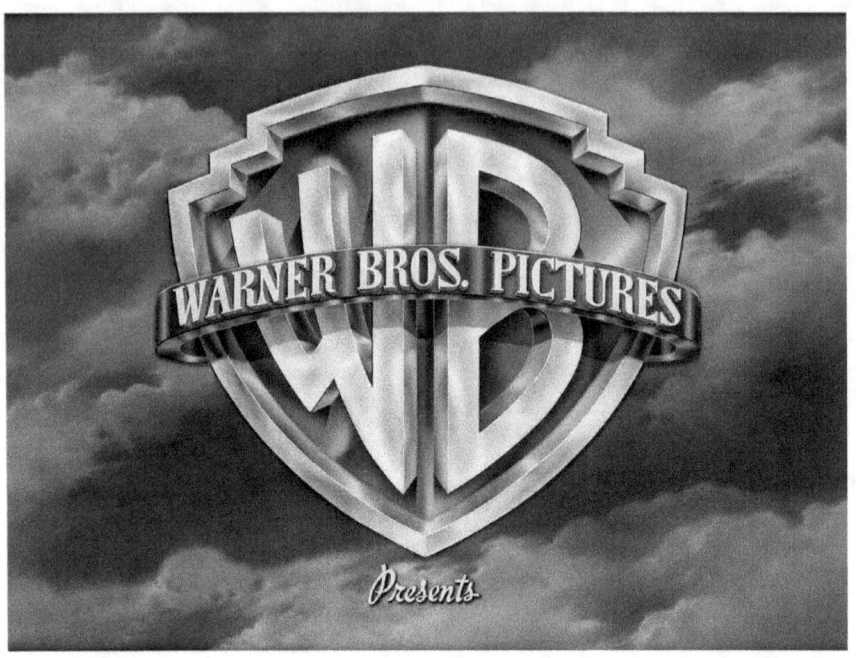

bucked the fears of the major studios and persuaded his brothers to partner with Western Electric to utilize the Vitaphone system – a sound-track on synchronized discs to accompany the film – in shorts and presently features (despite brother Harry's quip, "Who the Hell wants to hear actors talk?"). The picture saved the company from bankruptcy, and Warners moved into the '30s by acquiring rival First National and purchasing the Skouras theatres to provide the studio guaranteed exhibition venues. The studio established a gritty, moody look that perfectly suited a string of gangster pictures and even provided a distinctive background for musicals. The striking visuals of Busby Berkeley's choreography drew crowds, and the performances of James Cagney, Errol Flynn, Bette Davis, Humphrey Bogart, Jack Carson, and Doris Day – and the animated antics of Porky Pig, Bugs Bunny, Daffy Duck and their ilk – pleased audiences who were for the most part unaware of the back-stage battles between the stars and studio head, brother Jack. One of the first studios to engage television, Warner Bros., had hits like "Maverick" and "77

Sunset Strip", while continuing to release features. In 1969, the studio became part of the Kinney National Company, which also acquired DC Comics, home of Superman and Batman, leading to several big-budget "super-hero" pictures which continue to this day with Batman, Superman, Wonder Woman, and other famous names, in live-action features and animated features and TV episodes. Now a unit of Time-Warner, Inc., the studio has amassed a huge library of feature films, not only its own but the bounty of M-G-M/UA, RKO Radio, Monogram, and other producers through Time's acquisition of Turner Broadcasting and the collection of classic (and non-classic) pictures which had been accumulated by movie-fan Ted Turner.

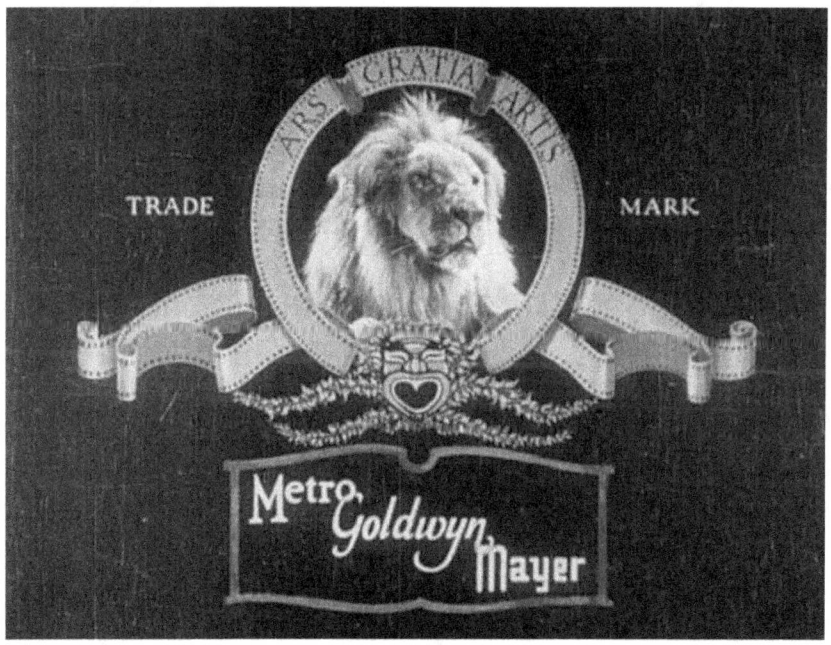

METRO-GOLDWYN-MAYER, making its debut in 1924, had its origins in Goldwyn Pictures and Marcus Loew's Metro Pictures. When the studios merged, Loew saw the need for an authoritative hand to run the operations, and signed Louis B. Mayer, whose decade-old picture company had made a strong showing. Beginning as Metro-Goldwyn, the company soon found itself adding a "Mayer" to its corporate name (though Loew's own company retained control of the organization for many years). M-G-M built itself into *the* outstanding studio in town, with Mayer and producer Irving Thalberg (brought in from Universal) demanding and getting perfection, re-taking scenes, changing casts and crews, even re-shooting pictures that showed poorly in previews. The influence of the talented, tasteful Thalberg was missed after his early demise in 1936, but the huge stable of stars ("More Than There Are in Heaven") and high production values kept the studio at the apex of Hollywood. Stars like the three Marx Brothers, Clark Gable, Norma Shearer, Gene Kelly, Judy Garland, Mickey Rooney, and Lionel Barrymore guaranteed big box-office receipts, and the lavish treatments of the films, many in Technicolor, kept M-G-M a top property. A later acquisition of United Artists led to M-G-M's purchase by Ted Turner, and today the films of the two companies – and several others – are the basis for the programming of the popular cable channel TCM.

COLUMBIA PICTURES CORPORATION of California was reorganized in 1924 from CBC Sales, in which the Cohn Brothers, Harry and Jack, had been partnered with Joe Brandt since 1919. CBC had been almost a joke in the Industry, its poverty-row productions earning it the soubriquet "Corned Beef and Cabbage", and Harry, now chief of the studio, was determined to improve the image of the company, starting with its logotype that now featured the liberty personification "Columbia", the lady with the torch. But the studio's films were still mostly bargain-basement, until the addition to the staff of Frank Capra, who pushed for and received better scripts and bigger budgets. It was Capra's *It Happened One Night* (1934) that garnered Columbia its first Oscar, and from then, though the studio output was mostly Bs, they released a few pictures every year, and better pictures every season.

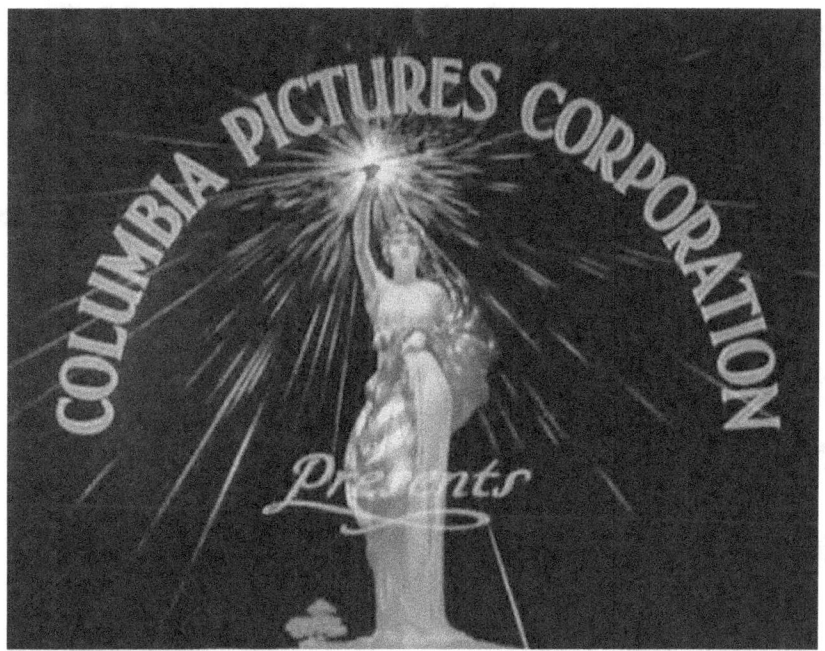

With series like "Blondie" and "Boston Blackie", shorts like the "Three Stooges", and contracted producers providing "the Durango Kid" and chapter plays for a solid income-base, big-budget specials like *Lost Horizon* ('37) and *The Jolson Story* ('46) eventually made Columbia a major studio. With no exhibition arm, Columbia relied on shorts and serials for continuity of product with theater chains, and prospered. After the death of Harry Cohn, the studio continued under diverse hands until being acquired by Sony, which retired the studio's famous name.

RKO RADIO PICTURES, an agglomeration of Radio Corporation of America with the Keith-Orpheum theatre circuit and Film Booking Office in 1928, was the first Hollywood studio created solely to produce Talking Pictures, using the "Photophone" sound system. FBO provided the nucleus for production and distribution, K-O provided the theatres, and RCA provided sound and supervision. The studio briefly releasing as "RKO-Pathé" (Joseph P. Kennedy

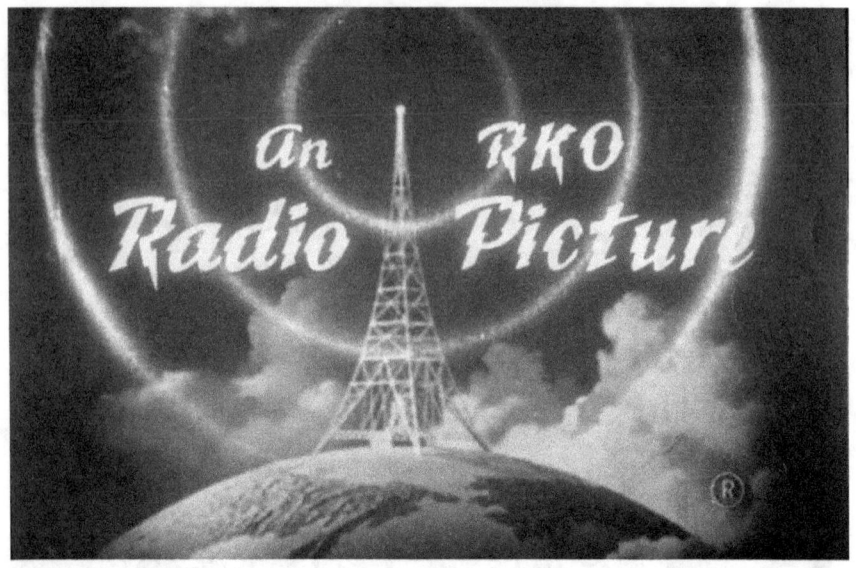

of FBO had arranged to sell his shares of Pathé as he withdrew from the picture business), then as "Radio Pictures" before settling on the same name for both production and distribution arms. The studio quickly found its niche, providing entertaining musicals (Astaire and Rogers), tough dramas, B westerns (with Tom Keene, Harry Carey, and Tim Holt), comedies (Leon Errol and the "Mexican Spitfire"), and mysteries (the Saint and the Falcon), then took a lead in film *noir* toward the end of the Second World War, with pictures like *Murder, My Sweet* (1944, which revitalized crooner Dick Powell as a tough guy). In the post-War era, under the leadership of magnate Howard R. Hughes, the company's fortunes, ironically, took a down-turn, and while affiliates and subsidiaries flourished, Hughes sold out to the General Tire and Rubber Company, which ran the operation as RKO-General, while selling its real property to the new Desilu Television company, concentrating on the distribution of its library until finally closing out permanently in 1957.

MONOGRAM PICTURES CORPORATION was formed from the merging of W. Ray Johnson's Raytone Productions

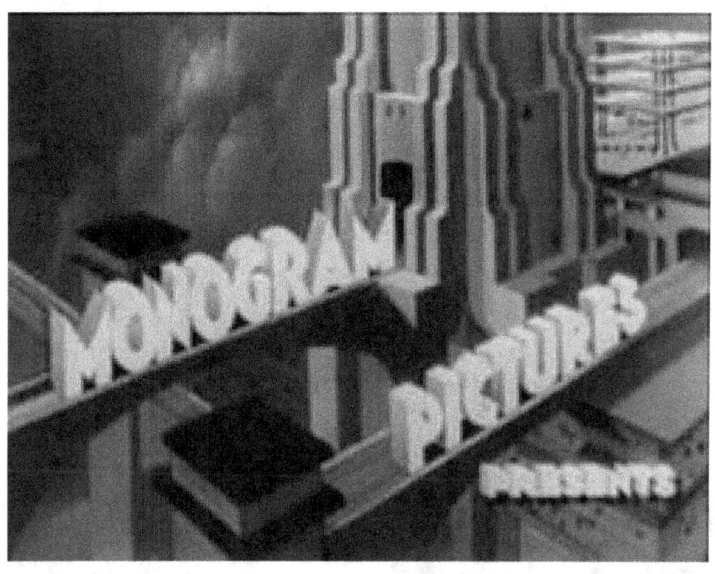

and Trem Carr's SonoArt and World Wide Pictures in 1931, and ran a steady program of inexpensive but quality pictures, mainly mysteries and Westerns, most of the latter directed by Robert North Bradbury and starring his son Bob Steele or young John Wayne. By 1935, Monogram was in hock to Consolidated Film Industries, the Hollywood lab run by Herbert J. Yates, who offered them a merger to settle the debt. Johnson and Carr agreed, but within two years, unhappy with the Yates regime, Carr sold out, and restarted Monogram, producing Westerns (Johnny Mack Brown), mysteries (Mr. Wong), and comedies (the Bowery Boys) through the '40s, until a re-organization of the corporation put Allied Artists, previously a subsidiary, in the forefront, releasing much the same kind of pictures – plus science-fiction thrillers – but also a line of quality productions.

20th CENTURY-FOX FILM CORPORATION was, as the name suggests, comprised of two companies. Fox Film had been the baby of William Fox, one of the pioneers of U.S. cinema; he had assembled his company by the merging of a production company with a distributor, and linking them with a chain of theatres, creating the "vertical" monopoly, and in the '20s invested in sound through the Fox Movietone system, which was substantially identical to RCA's Photophone, with sound track on the film itself. But by the mid-'30s, crushed by the stock-market crash and industry maneuvering, Fox himself had been pushed out, and the only way to save the company proved to be by merging with 20th Century Productions, which had been started in 1933 by Darryl F. Zanuck (late of Warner Bros.), Joseph Schenk, William Goetz, and Raymond Griffith, and which had been releasing quality productions through United Artists. The

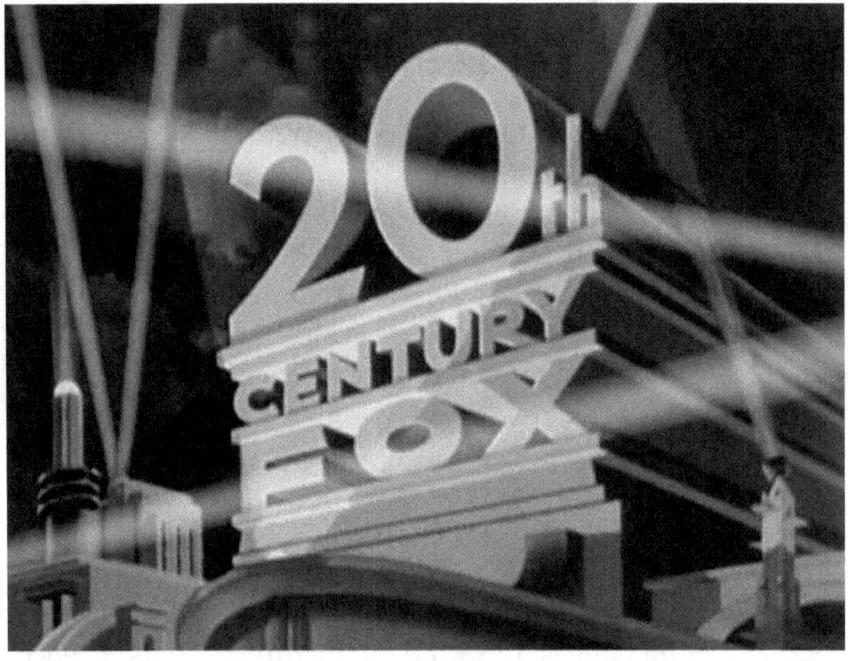

two companies merged in 1935, and to Fox's stars Alice Faye and Shirley Temple, Zanuck added Tyrone Power, Don Ameche, Sonia Henie, the Ritz Brothers, and Betty Grable, continuing the quality of product, releasing many fine biografilms and musicals, and B mysteries and comedies. In the '50s, the studio introduced CinemaScope to compete with television, and in 1977, signed a deal with the then new LucasFilms that gave them the distribution of a series of some of the medium's most profitable pictures – the "Star Wars" saga. Later becoming part of Rupert Murdoch's News Corporation (which re-named itself Fox), the studio is now incorporated into the Walt Disney organization.

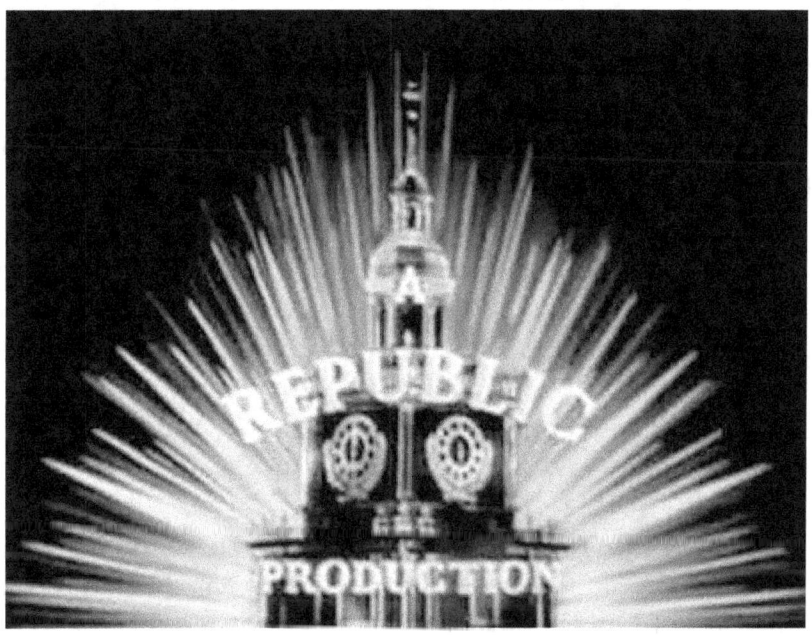

REPUBLIC PICTURES CORPORATION grew from rather dubious roots; Herbert J. Yates, head of Consolidated Film Industries, the town's leading film-processing laboratory, had extended credit to Monogram, Mascot, Liberty, and other producers, and then foreclosed, buying out some, merging all into his new production-distribution-exhibition company in late 1935. Mascot serials became Republic serials and Monogram westerns became Republic westerns, greatly benefitting from the change, and the company provided top, good looking entertainment for rural and kid audiences. Stars included Gene Autry, John Wayne, Bob Steele, and Roy Rogers, and though Republic specialized in Westerns and hick comedies, the studio produced some quite good mysteries and scary pictures as well, and distributed the occasional A picture of an independent producer. One *genre* viewed by critics as a stumbling block for Republic was the musical, for although many fine singing cowboy pictures were produced, so were less successful films starring Vera Hruba Ralston, ice-skating star but more importantly the wife of studio prez Yates. Today the studio is most fondly remembered for its good looking cliffhanger serials, a staple of the studio throughout its existence. Republic was the first studio to explore television production, but though one of its shows, "Stories of the Century", won an Emmy, the studio never really made a sufficient showing to stay in business. The lot became a rental facility, home of "Four Star Television" and later became "CBS Television Center" and "MTM", before becoming home to KCBS and KCAL television stations. Gone now over 50 years, Republic left a legacy of action and adventure to fans who continue to support it today.

PRODUCERS RELEASING CORPORATION. When a film "buff" speaks of "Poverty Row", he often overstates the case, lumping in humble companies like Republic and Monogram with the *really* low-budget independent producers. The *real* king of Poverty Row was PRC, the little studio established in 1940 by Sigmund Neufeld and his brother, who billed himself as Sam Newfield, after the demise of Producers Distributing Corporation, their previous employer. Sam, principal director for the studio, was so prolific that he directed under *three* different names. Bela Lugosi's vehicle *The Devil Bat* ('41) is a typical example of the quality of the studio's output: acceptable and interesting, but under-nourished. Their numerous Westerns starred performers like Buster Crabbe and Lash LaRue, with comedy often provided by Al "Fuzzy"

St. John, a former Keystone comic. A director of great style

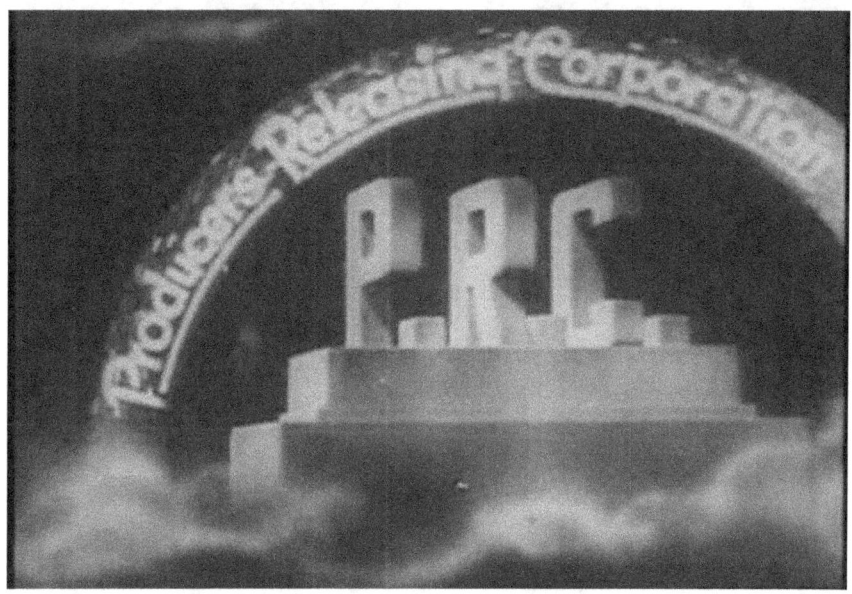

who joined the studio in 1942 was Edgar G. Ulmer, who was known as the "Capra of PRC" for his efficient but stylish output. The studio was acquired by Pathé Industries, and evolved into Eagle-Lion Films in 1946. Eagle-Lion distributed PRC's films thereafter, and in 1947 the PRC name was abandoned. Eventually the studio's catalogue of films came under the control of United Artists, and so is now part of the impressive list of Warner Bros. properties.

BUENA VISTA. Walt Disney had a long history of popular animated cartoons by the early 1950s when he opened his own distribution arm. He'd released through Columbia from the beginning of the "Mickey Mouse" series, but, tiring of the penurious production advances from Harry Cohn, had switched to United Artists in 1931; in 1936 a stupid squabble over distribution revenues and, of all things, television rights caused Walt to sign with RKO Radio. UA was particularly chagrined when, a year later, *Snow White And The Seven*

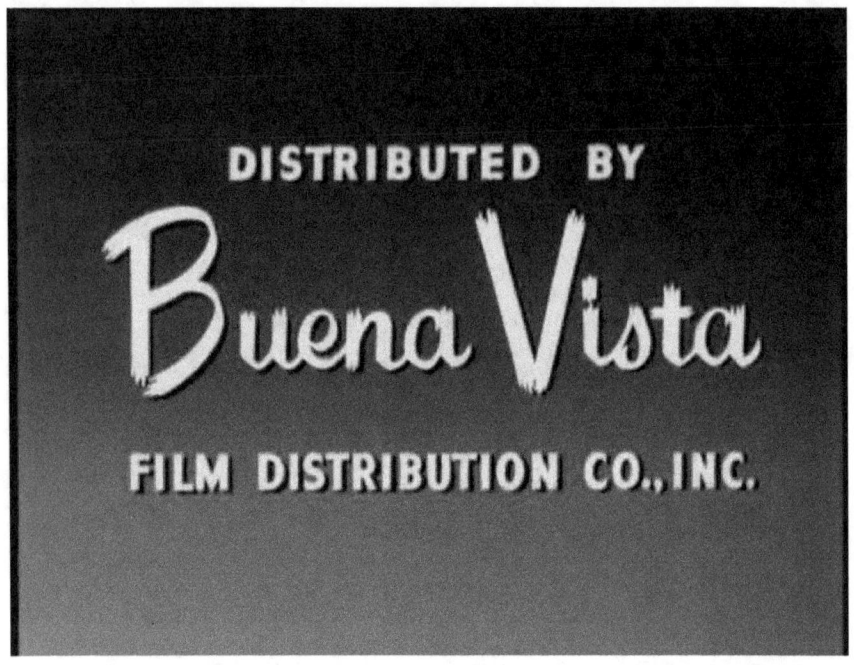

Dwarfs was a world-wide hit. Disney released many features and shorts through RKO Radio, but one series of shorts was viewed with disfavor by the distributor: the "True Life" featurettes. So when Disney planned *The Living Desert* (1953), a "True Life" *feature*, Disney avoided argument by creating his *own* distribution company, Buena Vista (named after the street on which the Disney studio is located). Its first major release was *20000 Leagues Under The Sea* ('54), and all Disney films since then have been released through Buena Vista, even when Disney spun off other specialized production companies like Hollywood Films, and even though a production-company logo headed the films. Eventually, Buena Vista was re-named Walt Disney Motion Picture Distribution.

AMERICAN INTERNATIONAL PICTURES was created in 1956 from American Releasing Corp. by James H.

Nicholson

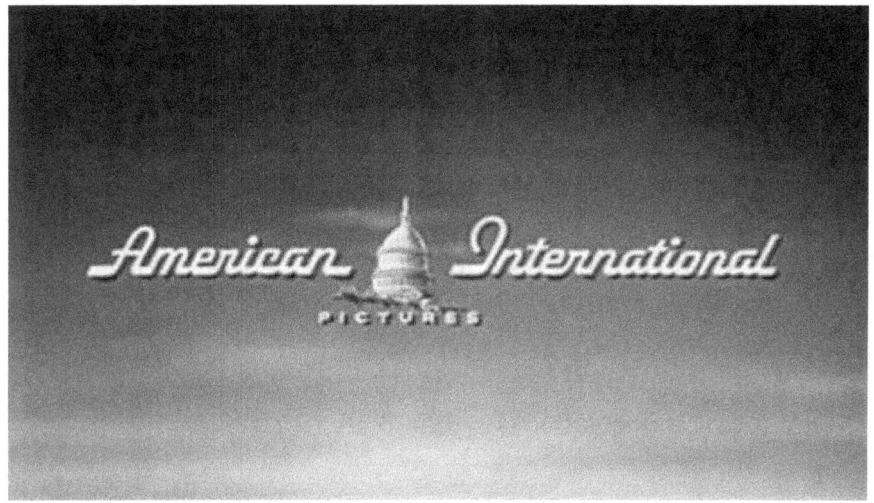

and Samuel Z. Arkoff, and was dedicated to producing and distributing inexpensive, exploitative entertainment for the youth market. And in the '50s that meant rock 'n' roll, crime, and science fiction, *genres* indicated by focus groups, a new (at the time) marketing technique in which audiences told the producer what they *wanted* to see. AIP's most prolific producer was Roger Corman, purveyor of films like *It Conquered The World* (1956) and *War Of The Satellites* ('58), but others contributed numerous titles that pulled in the kiddies and teens to drive-ins and hard-top theatres. In the '60s, Corman persuaded the bosses to make bigger-budgeted pictures, and for them did his "Edgar Allan Poe" series. Also popular in this period was the "Beach Party" series, with wacky humor and especially nubile beach bunnies and buff surfer dudes. (The studio even mixed the *genres* in pictures like '65's *Dr. Goldfoot And The Bikini Machine*.) Distribution of foreign films and expansion into TV and recording bolstered the company's fortunes, and when Arkoff decided to retire (briefly), the studio was sold in 1979 to Filmways, Inc, previously known for television shows like "The Beverly

Hillbillies". Filmways later became Orion Pictures, which eventually surrendered its interests to M-G-M.

These are the studios that made up the overwhelming majority of Hollywood product in the 20th century. Literally hundreds of "independent" studios – producers without distribution networks, that released films in States Rights arrangements (selling the films to local distributors who made their own deals with exhibitors and who made the real profits, if any) or by selling to one of the Majors – supplied the rest, and their growing market-share in the post-War era was part of what defined the B Picture for later generations; cheap, clumsy, often tasteless exploitation features that made younger audiences believe that B Pictures had always been that way.

As you'll see, in Hollywood's "Golden Age", a picture was a picture, and the Bs and their cousins the Matinee Westerns had as many good and bad productions as their big-budget brothers, the A pictures.

The leading "class" *genre* of American pictures was the most direct, straightforward type of film…

CHAPTER ONE: DRAMA

DRAMA IS SORT of the vanilla of movie flavors: savory and scrumptious by itself, but amenable to admixture with a panoply of tastes and textures, a base line and a background for all other *genres* of cinema. While comedy had been king before pictures talked, the opportunity to hear the express of emotions drew the drama to the top of the hierarchy in the '30s. Women's pictures, the so-called "three hankie" films or "weepers", with heroines beset by misery only to be rescued in the last reel, made a great distraction from the daily drudgeries. Biblical stories, classic novels, star vehicles were produced in profusion. Doctors Kildare and Christian and the Hardy Family, and later the exploits of Rusty the dog, provided familiar faces and serious situations laced with gentle humor; Torchy Blane and other reporters added the underworld to the mix. Modern classics like *This Gun For Hire* (Paramount, 1942) and especially *Gone With The Wind* (M-G-M, '39) thrilled audiences with complex characters caught up in the whirlwind of life. After the Second World War, *films noirs*, which hovered on the border with mystery, embraced drama with loners and anti-heroes, culminating in pictures like *Rebel Without A Cause* (WB, '55). Drama has continued to rule the Movies, and almost every *genre* uses drama as the medium to tell its tales of the west, of outer space, of costumed characters, because drama is the very force of life itself, the thousand little daily events against which the stories that capture us are told. Included in this broad assortment of pictures you may find a wealth of subjects and treatments, human interest and mild comedy, suspense and surprise.

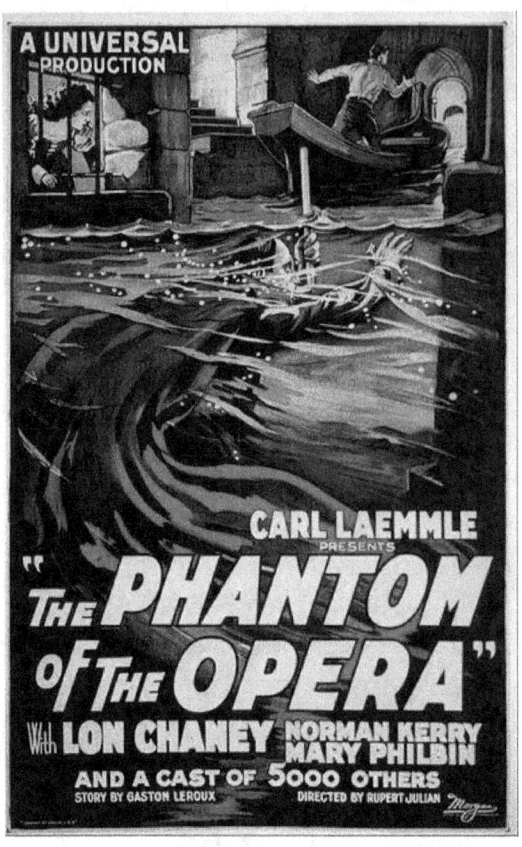

Lon Chaney – "The Man of 1,000 Faces" according to his publicity – was the biggest "character" star of the mute cinema, even though often one couldn't tell if it was really he, so extensive and versatile were his make-ups and characterizations. Years after his untimely demise in 1930, he was still being hailed, but mostly for two of his many films, both from Universal: the 1923 *The Hunchback of Notre Dame*, and 1925's *The Phantom of the Opera*, in which he portrayed Erik, the "ghost" of the Paris Opera, mad from years of self-imposed exile from society, brought about by his "supreme ugliness". Conceiving a great love for a minor singer (Mary Philbin), he uses his skills to secretly mold her into a star. But then he realizes he must have her – and her talent – for himself, and kidnaps her to his lair deep beneath the opera house. The scene in which, against his command, she removes his mask and reveals his face to the audience has gone down through film history as the greatest of shocks, despite greater horrors to come. Still a masterful work, even if usually seen only at Hallowe'en time, "Phantom" draws new audiences every year. Multiple re-makes and variations have benefitted from its reputation, including *Phantom of the Opera* (Universal, '43), called more opera than phantom, and Hammer's 1962 version, as well as the popular Broadway musical and film, even animated parodies like "Spooks", a 1930 Walter Lantz cartoon sparked by a re-issue of the original with a synchronized music-track.

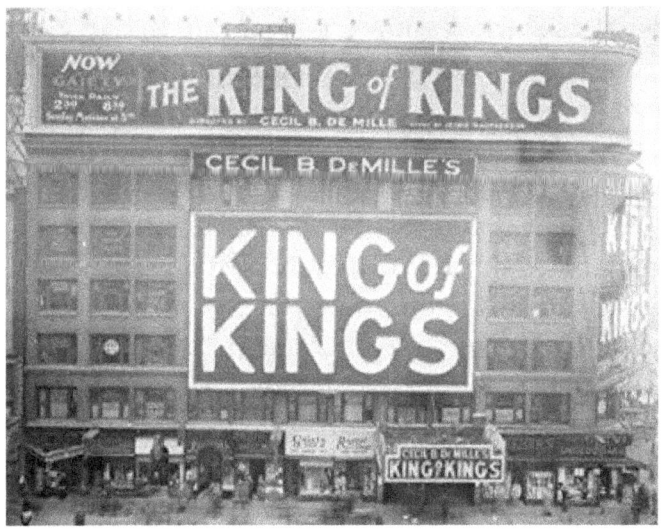

Cecil B. DeMille's very careful tightwire walk that showed reverence and yet down-played the Christ's miracles in favor of His kindness made *The King Of Kings* (Pathé Exchanges and Producers Distributing Corporation, 1927) a hit in its day and a classic in its future. With H.B. Warner as Jesus, Jacqueline Logan as Mary Magdalen, and Joseph Schildkraut as Judas Iscariot, it told the story of the life of Christ from the conversion of Judas to the Resurrection (depicted in two-strip Technicolor). Religious themes, handled carefully, could be counted on for big box-office receipts, and DeMille mined this vein several more times, culminating in his special-effects-bolstered *The Ten Commandments* (Paramount, '56). Other producers favored religious themes, often including miraculous events that propelled the pictures into the realm of fantasy. Straightforward biblical-period dramas, however, include the M-G-M epics *Quo Vadis* ('51) and *Ben Hur* A Tale of the Christ ('26, remade in '59).

For a rough, tough setting for a Man's picture, you can't beat a prison. Gangsters, fall guys, the convicted innocents, all crammed together behind bars (and frequently over-crowded), a place where everyone's miserable and where the slightest spark can ignite a powderkeg of hatred. It's a place many pictures start or end, or pass through, but a number of films spend nearly the whole picture inside those gray bars. *The Big House* (M-G-M, 1930) is an archetype of the sub-*genre*, as then-popular Chester Morris finds himself penned up with Wallace Beery (in a role intended for Lon Chaney) and other hard-timers. The drudgery, hopelessness, and desperation of the convicts are brought out, and the inevitable failure of prison-breaks are depicted, though the picture has a happy ending (well, for some people). The picture's brutality would never be matched during the "Golden Age", as it strained the bounds of the motion-picture Production Code. Though producers generally flouted the code in its first years (usually erroneous called the "pre-code" era), after 1934, when Joseph Breen took control of the Hayes Office of industry self-censorship, code rules were strictly enforced, ending scenes of murder and licentiousness. The picture was almost immediately parodied in Laurel and Hardy's *Pardon Us* (M-G-M, '31), but more serious followers included the aptly titled

Brute Force (U-I, '47), *House of Numbers* (M-G-M, '57), *Birdman of Alcatraz* (UA, '62), and *Escape from Alcatraz* (Paramount, '79).

Shamelessly playing on the adorable Jackie Cooper as young Dink Purcell, who idolizes his has-been, down-on-his-luck father, whom he still calls *The Champ* (Wallace Beery) in their 1931 release, M-G-M brought out a picture that would appeal to both men and women, as the Champ schemes to bring the boy into the orbit of his estranged mother (Irene Rich). Sentimental stories about kids re-uniting their parents (both successfully and not) were always good box-office, and Cooper in particular remained a popular youngster in several of these films, having proved himself in Hal Roach's "Our Gang" shorts. Cooper went on to a career as a teen, then faded briefly before scoring again as an adult in two television series, and moving into production. Other kid-and-companion pictures include Chaplin's *The Kid* (First National, '20), and *Sammy Going South* (Bryanston Films, '63; *A Boy Ten Feet Tall* [Paramount Pictures, '65] in US). For a different sort of relationship, consider Tatum O'Neal in *Paper Moon* (Paramount, '73).

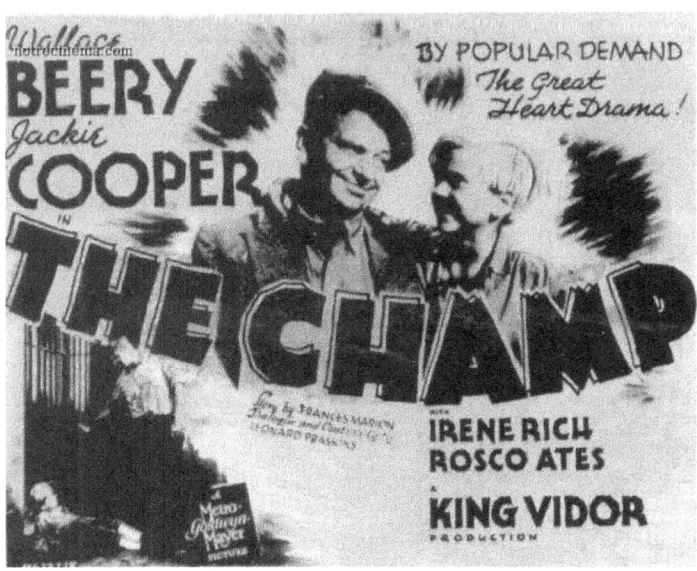

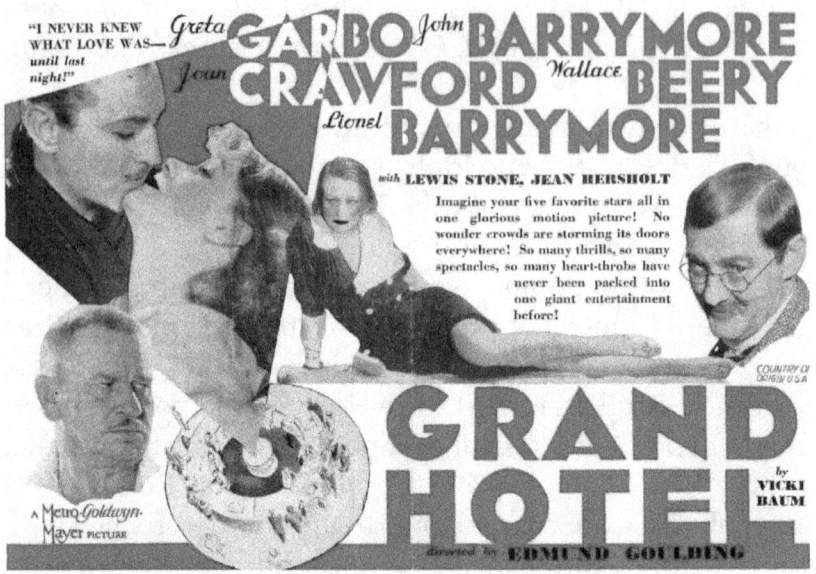

"People come, people go. Nothing ever happens," remarks Herr Doktor Otternshlag (Lewis Stone) about Berlin's greatest *caravanserai*, *Grand Hotel*, in the 1932 M-G-M extravaganza and Oscar winner based on the novel by Vicki Baum. But liquor has dulled his eye to the things that *do* happen, to and about Grusinskaya the dancer (Garbo), her jewel-thief lover Baron Felix von Gaigern (John Barrymore), *Fraulein* Flaemmchen, the ambitious stenographer (Joan Crawford), Wallace Beery, Lionel Barrymore, Jean Hersholt, and all the rest that make up a compelling cross-section of society within these confines. First and far from the last of the ambitious "all-star" story productions, it's the film in which the divine Garbo says, "I want to be alone. I think I have never been so tired in my life." Other similar all-star titles include *Dinner at Eight* and *Night Flight* (both from M-G-M in '33) and the later Hercule Poirot mysteries, such as *Murder on the Orient Express* (*Q.V. in Mysteries*) among others.

When John Wilkes Booth broke his leg fleeing from the

scene of his assassination of U.S. President Abraham Lincoln, he set in motion a tragedy of American history, and 70 years later Darryl F. Zanuck brought the story to the screen as the 20th Century production *The Prisoner of Shark Island* (UA, 1936) as directed by John Ford. Warner Baxter starred as Dr. Samuel Mudd, condemned to the penitentiary at Fort Jefferson, Dry Tortugas, for setting Booth's leg and thus facilitating his escape. Gloria Stuart, Harry Carey, and John Carradine (at his most menacing) also starred. Historical recreations were always popular screen subjects, including lives of politicians (*All the King's Men* [Columbia, '49] or *JFK* [Warners, '91]), disasters (like 20th Century-Fox's *In Old Chicago* ['38] or Metro's *San Francisco* ['36]), and valiant failures like Charlie Kane (*Q.V.* below). Historical dramas were always popular, some literal, some adapted (such as Republic's 1940 *Dark Command*, a work of fiction based upon the depredations of Quantrill's Raiders during the War Between the States).

The Raven (Universal, 1936) is a prime example of the "horror" film that is actually just an extreme form of the Drama. Bela Lugosi stars as Dr. Vollin, whose love of the works of Poe is only surpassed by his desire for pretty Jean Thatcher (Irene Ware), and who goes to unsurpassed schemes of villainy to secure her for himself, mutilating escaped convict Bateman (Karloff) and dooming the girl's father and friends to Poe-themed torments. The film was so gruesome that British censors ruled not just against it, but all US "horror" pictures for several years. Other films of this type, with no fantastic element to the scares, include *The Black Cat* (Universal, 1934, also teaming Karloff and Lugosi), *Horror Island* (Universal, 1941, with comic overtones and mystery) and *The Seventh Victim* (RKO Radio, 1943).

The Petrified Forest had been a smash on Broadway, and when Warner Bros. brought it to the screen in 1936, the star (Leslie Howard) of Robert E. Sherwood's play refused to appear unless his stage co-star, Humphrey Bogart, was also

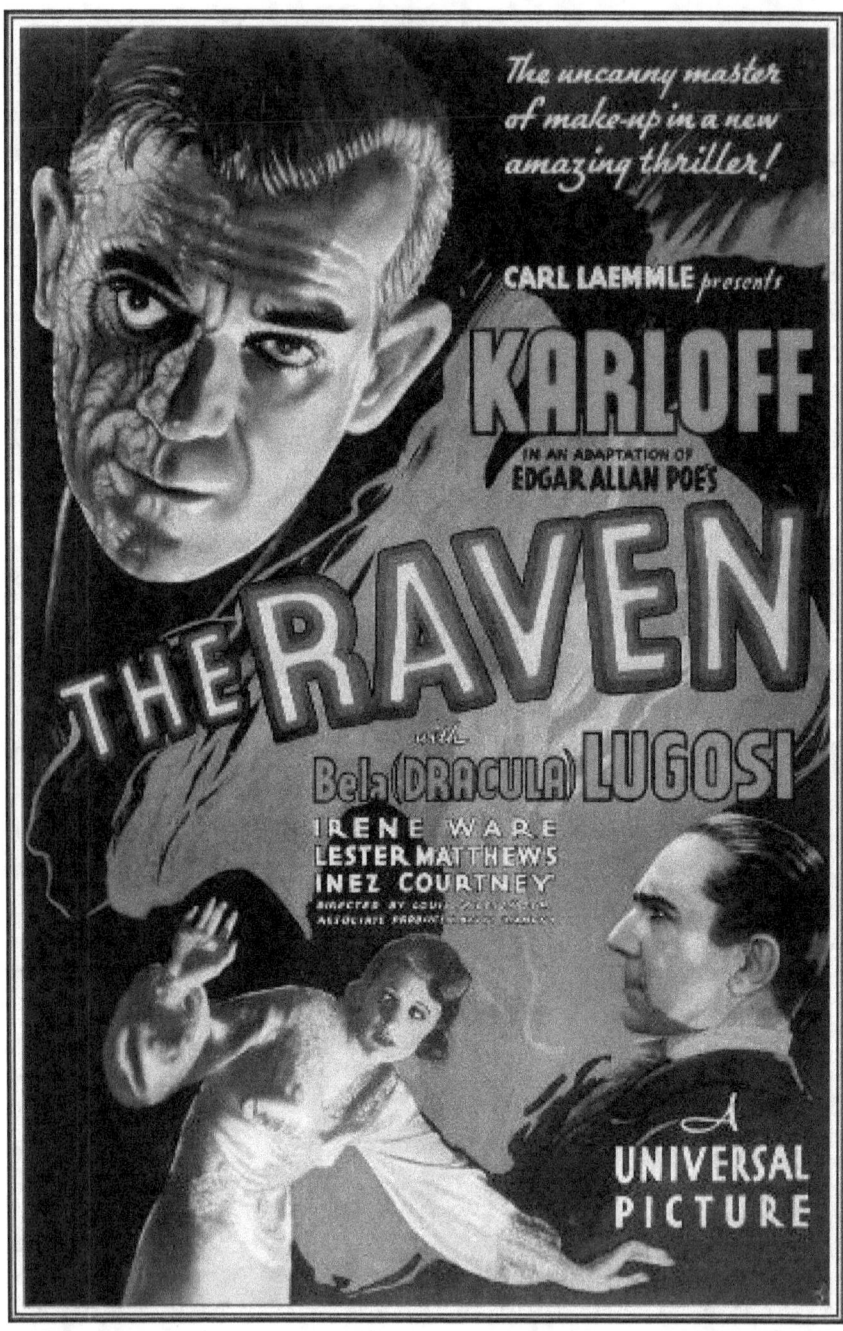

signed. For once, the "stagy" quality of the story enhanced the production, one in a long line of stage shows permanentized by Hollywood, as Duke Mantee (Bogey) attempts to terrorize the inhabitants of a little diner on the outskirts of the "forest", which is an expanse of desert dotted with trees so old they've turned to stone. Duke's efforts are blunted by the lackadaisical Alan Squire (Howard), who doesn't really care all that much about his life, except that his death might help others. Bette Davis, Dick Foran, Adrian Morris, and Joe Sawyer supported the stars in this powerful tale. Other stage hits brought to screen include titles as diverse as *Dead End* (UA, '37), *The Children's Hour* (United Artists, '61 [previously filmed as *These Three* by William Wyler for UA in '36]), and a host of musicals.

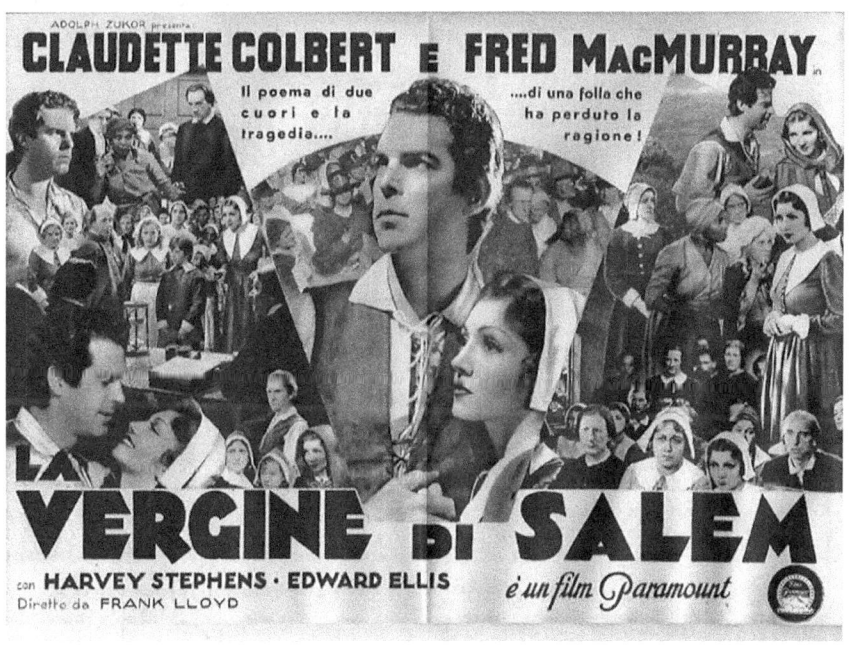

The disgraceful witch trials of Puritan Massachusetts in the 17th century formed the background for *Maid Of Salem* (Paramount, 1937), produced and directed by Frank Lloyd. Tying in a love story between Barbara Clark (Claudette Colbert) of Salem and Roger Coverman (Fred MacMurray), fugitive from Virginia's oppressive tax laws, the story sets

Barbara up for trouble when she covers up her clandestine affair with Roger. When curious Virginia Goode (Bonita Granville) is punished for stealing a slave's book of witchcraft, she blames her behavior on the slave (Madame Sul-te-Wan), and when Barbara comes to the woman's defense, she too is branded and sentenced to hang on Gallows Hill. Young Granville's role echoes her part in the previous year's *These Three* (UA), the adaptation of Lillian Hellman's play *The Children's Hour*. Also in the cast, Virginia Weidler, Donald Meek, and Gale Sondergaard (who made quite a good witch herself in other pictures). Later, playwright Arthur Miller made use of the same *milieu* in *The Crucible* (released as *Les sorcières de Salem* by UA in '56, and remade by 20th Century Fox in '96) to parallel the witch trials with the witch hunts of the McCarthy era.

Judge Hardy and family started out as the central characters of a film called *A Family Affair* (M-G-M, 1937) based on a play by Aurania Rouverol, with Lionel Barrymore and Spring Byington as the parents of a small-town family, as small towns and families were seen by studio head Louis B. Mayer. But brash young Mickey Rooney as their son really stole the spotlight, and the next year, with a bit of re-casting spurred by Barrymore's injuries (that put him in a wheelchair), the series took off for 14 installments over nine years, and one sentimental return, *Andy Hardy Comes Home* (M-G-M, '58), plus three appearances by cast members as their characters in Metro short subjects. The principal cast was comprised of Andrew Hardy (Rooney), dad Judge James K. Hardy (Lewis Stone), mom Emily Hardy (Fay Holden), and sister Marian (Cecilia Parker). The other regulars were Sara Haden as Aunt Millie and Ann Rutherford as Polly Benedict, Andy's steady girlfriend (except when the plot demanded otherwise). Up-and-coming starlets like Jean Porter, Kathryn Grayson, Martha O'Driscoll, Marsha Hunt, and of course Judy Garland frequented the episodes, testing their mettle. The series, pleasant dramas with comic overtones and the trademark "heart to heart" talks between the Judge and Andy, was emulated by other studios in similar family pictures, but it was the original that was awarded a special Oscar in 1942 for its achievement in "representing the American Way of Life". Most other "family" series tended toward the comic, but a late 'forties series from Columbia, starring young Ted Donaldson and Flame, a German Shepherd, beginning with *The Adventures of Rusty* ('45) emphasized the serious side of family life.

Smart Blonde (WB, 1936) began a series of nine crime/suspense pictures starring tough-guy Barton MacLane as cop Steve McBride and wise-cracking, tough girl Glenda Farrell as Torchy Blane, plus comic Tom Kennedy (brother of popular comic actor Edgar) as Steve's sidekick Gahagan. The series was based on a series of stories by Frederick Nebel, who in the '30s was touted as another Dashiell Hammett (though in the stories the "Torchy" character was a guy named Kennedy). Nebel, antipathetic to Hollywood, claiming they had chewed up his colleagues, simply took the money and ran, which is why none of the other pictures was based on his work. But the series inspired many more reporter pictures, though they hardly needed it: reporters, male and female, made ideal heroes, as their investigations could lead them into all kinds of trouble – actor Lee Tracy (in for example *Doctor X* [WB, '32]) and Farrell herself (in *Mystery of the Wax Museum* [WB, '33]) had all but invented the snoopy reporter in the early talker years. In subsequent pictures, Torchy, ever on the verge of marrying Steve if he doesn't strangle her first, visited Panama and Chinatown, ran for mayor, played with dynamite – and was portrayed by two other actresses: Lola Lane once and Jane Wyman once in the final entry. Consider also Lois Lane, a film character based on a cartoon-strip heroine distilled from the iconic picture reporter. (In fact, creator Jerry Siegel confirmed that the name was derived from "Torchy Blane" and Lola Lane the actress, though he had Farrell in time when he created the character.)

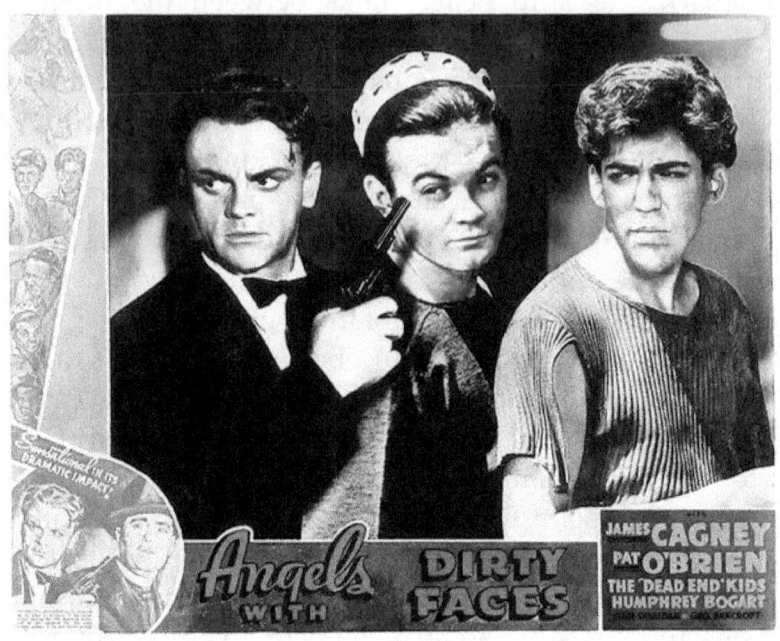

Warner Brothers especially, but really all the studios, proved that crime *did* pay – if you made a picture about it. From *Scarface* The Shame of a Nation (UA, 1932) to *Machine-Gun Kelly* (A-I-P, '58) and beyond, audiences have thrilled to the depredations and retribution of criminals. One Broadway play, *Dead End*, tied in criminals with the kids of the slums who idolized them. When it came to the screen in 1937, it introduced a gang of rough street kids who, signed to picture contracts, became the "Dead End" Kids (and later, the "Little Tough Guys", the "East Side Kids" and finally the "Bowery Boys" in different groupings and for different studios). Among the films that featured the original Kids was *Angels With Dirty Faces* (WB, 1938), in which the kids (Bernard Punsley, Gabriel Dell, Huntz Hall, Leo Gorcey, Bobby Jordan, and Billy Halop) have come to idolize gangster Rocky Sullivan (James Cagney) instead of good, upstanding Father Connolly (Pat O'Brien) the neighborhood priest. When Rocky is caught and sent to the electric chair, Connolly, a childhood friend of Rocky's, tries to persuade him to feign cowardice to crush the boys' hero-worship and turn them from the path of crime. The "Kids" continued in *The Angels Wash Their Faces* (WB,'39) and others, through to *The "Dead End" Kids "On Dress Parade"* (WB, '39). Having made heroes of criminals in the early '30s, Warners had balanced the scales of Justice both by allowing the actors who'd played gangsters to play G-Men, and by showing depths of character in the dastards. *From Little Caesar* ('30) to *The Roaring Twenties* ('39), Warners made hay from the underworld, even spoofing their successes in pictures like *A Slight Case of Murder* ('38).

The "Doctor Kildare" series was hugely popular in the late '30s and early '40s, so popular that it survived the loss of its star, Lew Ayres as Jimmy Kildare (who was fired from Metro due to his unpopular stand as a conscientious objector during the Second World War), and continued with the crusty-but-kindly older physician, Jimmy's mentor Doctor Leonard Gillespie (Lionel Barrymore). Before M-G-M began the series in 1938 with *Young Dr. Kildare*, the character had appeared the previous year in the Paramount picture *Internes Can't Take Money*, with Joel McCrea as the ambitious young doctor-in-training created by Max Brand (an author more famous for his Westerns). In the first ten films, Samuel S. Hinds co-starred as Jimmy's father, also a physician; in the six additional pictures, Gillespie worked with several new interns, testing them to see if one could be his new assistant, for once a series being used to prove young *male* performers like Van Johnson, Richard Quine (who became a director), Philip Dorn, and James Craig (formerly a minor cowboy star). The rather large supporting cast included Alma Kruger, Walter Kingsford, Nell Craig, Nat Pendleton, and Frank Orth, and the "Kildare/Gillespie" series led the way for several other "doctor" series and single pictures, though the genesis of altruistic physician films was *Men in White*, a 1934 Metro version of a popular play by Sidney Kingsley (also author of

Dead End) that starred Clark Gable and Kildare's dad-to-be Hinds. Country doctors, inspired by the real-life Dr. Dafoe (physician to the famous Canadian Dionne Quintuplets), included kindly old Doctor Christian, played by kindly old Jean Hersholt in half a dozen B-pictures (and a long running radio series).

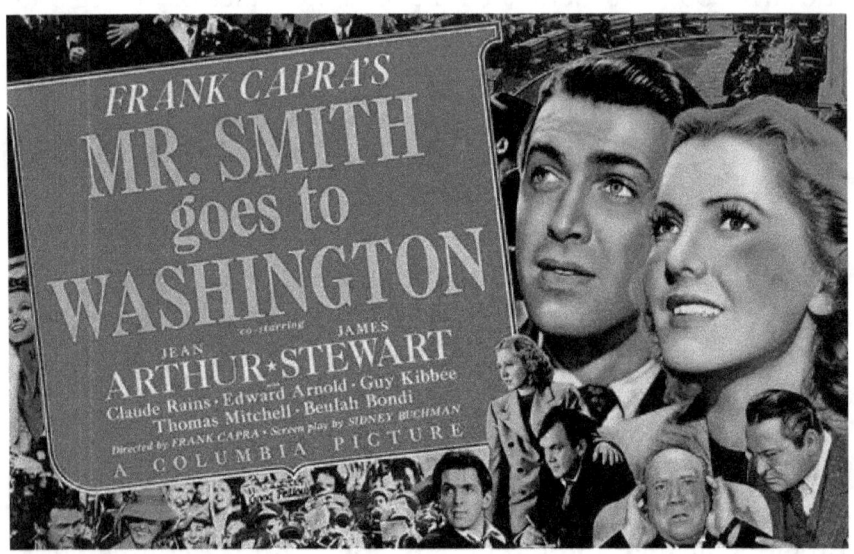

Mr. Smith Goes to Washington (Columbia, 1939) exemplifies all the corn-fed American values that audiences came to expect from producer-director Frank Capra. Corruption versus innocence, big-city influence versus small-town honesty, the story tells of young Thomas Jefferson Smith (James Stewart), appointed to fill the term of a junior senator, who arrives in the Federal City to learn that government just doesn't work the way it should, and that no one – not even his revered superior (Claude Rains) – is above being corrupted. Jeff's desperate filibuster on the senate floor, while outside his supporters are being beaten and quashed, is a masterpiece of film-making, and has a chilling resonance to later political eras. This drama was laced with comedy and romance, like other Capra efforts including *Meet John Doe*

(WB, '41), but we'll see Capra again under comedy and fantasy. Other political pictures of interest include *Abe Lincoln in Illinois* (RKO Radio, 1940) and *All The King's Men* (Columbia, '49).

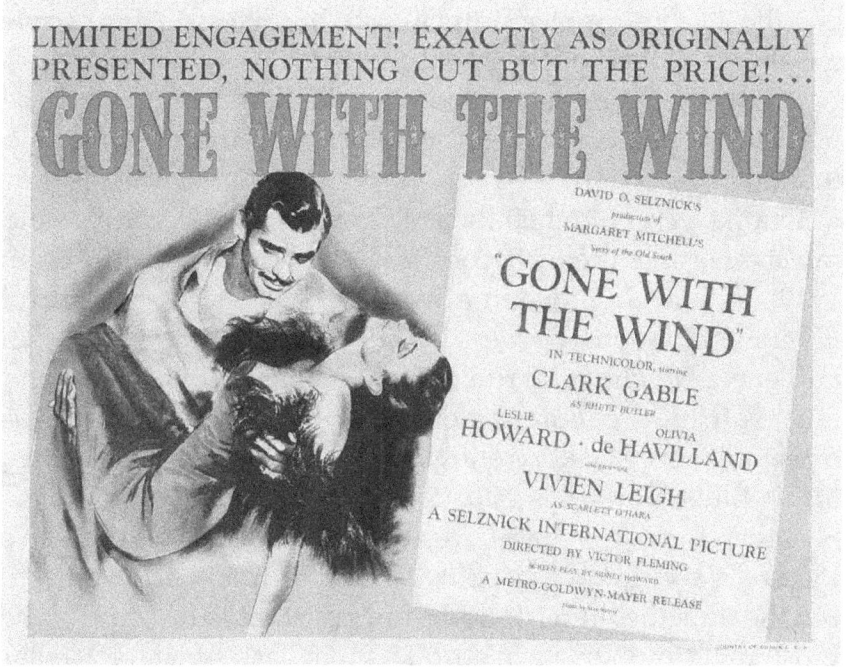

Gone With The Wind, Hollywood's big finish for its finest year (1939, in case you couldn't guess) was perhaps the most anticipated and controversial picture of its time. The hunt for heroine Scarlett O'Hara was publicized to the hilt, with producer David O. Selznick testing stars, starlets, and unknowns for the part, until finally giving the role to beautiful and feisty Vivian Leigh. The desperate public demand for Clark Gable as the only man who could be Rhett Butler led to Selznick's having to turn over to M-G-M the distribution and ultimate ownership of the picture, but it was worth it. The incredibly popular novel, however, was essentially a fluke, a story written by Margaret Mitchell that fell into a publisher's hand by chance, and which made the author so famous and wealthy she never published another novel in her lifetime. The film boosted the stock of pictures that blended romance and war and the problems that each brought the other. Most "war" pictures stressed the action, but few ignored the romantic possibilities. "GWTW" stressed not the Recent Unpleasantness but the lives of the people caught up by the exigencies of combat in one's own back yard. Later war pictures mixed both the military might and the personal drama but leaned toward the action, and so fall into that other *genre*.

Drama, yes, but when the entire cast is female, cattiness, to say the least, is the order of the day in *The Women* (M-G-M, 1939), an amazing idea in a world where Clark Gable, Errol Flynn, and Tyrone Power were box-office catnip to women audiences. Even the writers were women, Anita Loos and Jane Murfin. The only male in a position of authority was director George Cukor, renowned for his handling of women in his films. The trials and tribulations of one wife (Norma Shearer) form the basis for this, the ultimate "Woman's Picture" (also known as "three-hankie films" or "weepies"), but the tragedies and triumphs are punctuated by some of the most arch humor in pictures. In a cast of stars, stellar performances by Paulette Goddard, Joan Crawford, Rosalind Russell, queen of the lot Shearer, Mary Boland and Florence Nash made the screen sparkle with dewy drops of venom.

There was a dandy side-line in sports pictures, from comedies to biographies to straight dramas, with football, baseball, and prize-fighting being among the popular themes. Mickey Rooney took time off from Andy Hardy and musicals to make a few horse-racing stories. Joe E. Brown kidded ball players, Ronald Reagan played footballer George Gipp in *Knute Rockne All American* (WB, 1940) and pitcher Grover Cleveland Alexander in *The Winning Team* (WB, '52), and, in *Kid Nightingale* (Warner Bros., '39) John Payne was the fictitious Steve Nelson, whose ring tag was based on his talent and desire to sing. Most of these made-up sports heroes had to choose between the fame and money of the game, and the home-town girl, or the trust of children, or sometimes life itself, all of which caught the attention of men for the sport and women for the romance. *King of Hockey* (WB, '36) wove tragedy into its sport, and *Pigskin Parade* (Twentieth Century-Fox, '36) and *Horse Feathers* (Paramount, '32) featured football sequences for comedy, while *Death on the Diamond* (M-G-M, '34) added a murder mystery to baseball.

The lead role in Metro's *Maisie* (1939), from a story by Wilson Collison, was intended for Jean Harlow, but her untimely death resulted in the part going to pretty and competent Ann Sothern, and the picture being scaled back to a programmer. When the film was well received, a series was the obvious response, but unprepared to follow up the adventures of tough cookie Maisie Revier, the studio retooled their earlier *Red Dust* as *Congo Maisie* (M-G-M, '40) to give the writing staff time to develop further projects for the character. Sothern was always a delight to watch, and gave the hard-boiled, soft-hearted girl a likeable quality that sustained her through ten pictures, ending in 1947. Robert Sterling, John Hodiak, and George Murphy supported Ann in her sometimes light-hearted, always heart-tugging, adventures.

"...Rosebud... ." Maybe the most famous single word in film history, the quote that sent William Alland on a fruitless hunt for the meaning of the word that might sum up the life of a man who was a crusader, a tyrant, a selfish little boy, a recluse, a maker of opinion, a shaper of history who lived to become history – Charles Foster Kane. In a clever series of flashbacks, easy to follow even though chronologically jumbled, the reporter interviews the people from the past of *Citizen Kane* (RKO Radio, 1941), portrayed by a fine cast of players mostly from the Mercury Theatre including Joseph Cotton, Everett Sloane, George Coulouris, Agnes Moorehead, Ruth Warwick, and Ray Collins. Based (somewhat) on the life of William Randolph Hearst, with bits and pieces of other magnates and a lot of imagination, in a screenplay coauthored by Herman J. Mankiewicz, and with some of the most striking cinematography in pictures (by Gregg Toland), "Kane" was a *tour de force* of cinematic technique by a young man who wasn't all that keen on making movies in the first place: the man who co-wrote, directed, produced, and acted (but declined star billing) in this favorite film: Orson Welles. Welles went on to a checkered career, always entertaining, but also often at odds with studio bosses.

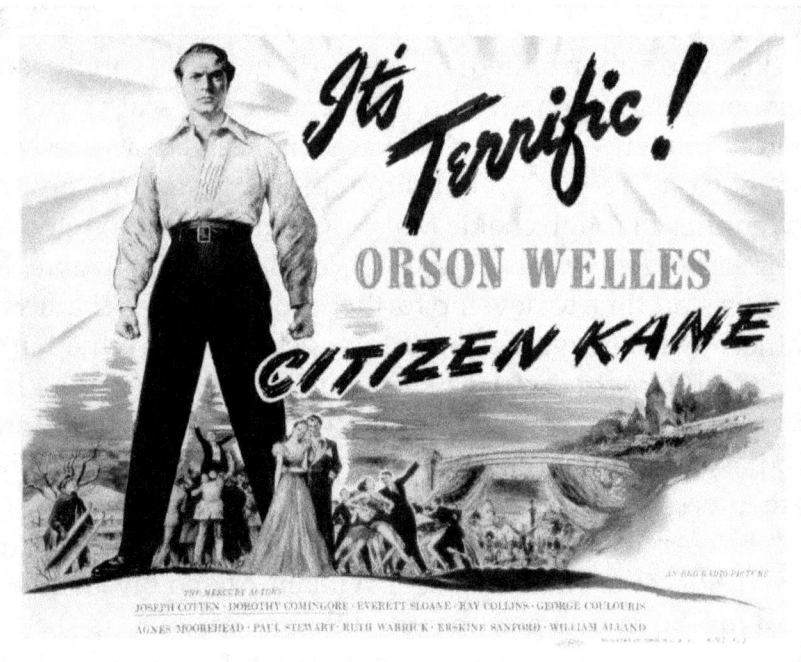

Alan Ladd had been a dependable, likeable young fellow in various small roles (*The Green Hornet* [Universal, 1939], *The Black Cat* [Universal, '41], and *The Reluctant Dragon* [RKO Radio, '41]) for a few years when he got the role of taciturn killer Raven in Paramount's 1942 *This Gun For Hire* (based on a work by Graham Greene), and a star was, to coin a phrase, born. As Raven, Ladd conveyed a complex, repellent, and yet somehow sympathetic character, emotionless and ruthless on the job, but kind and gentle to kids and kitties... until he crosses paths with adorable, vulnerable Ellen Graham (Veronica Lake), who gums up the works. Robert Preston as Ellen's boyfriend detective Michael Crane, and Laird Cregar as the contractor Willard Gates provided excellent support, but it was the interaction of Ladd and Lake that sold the story, a beginning to an outstanding star career for Ladd, and a harbinger of *films noirs* to come. *Lucky Jordan* in '42 and *The Blue Dahlia* in '46 (both from Paramount) followed Ladd in this tradition, though Ladd moved on to other *genres*, Westerns and Adventure, while Paramount continued to excel in the field with pictures like *Double Indemnity* ('44).

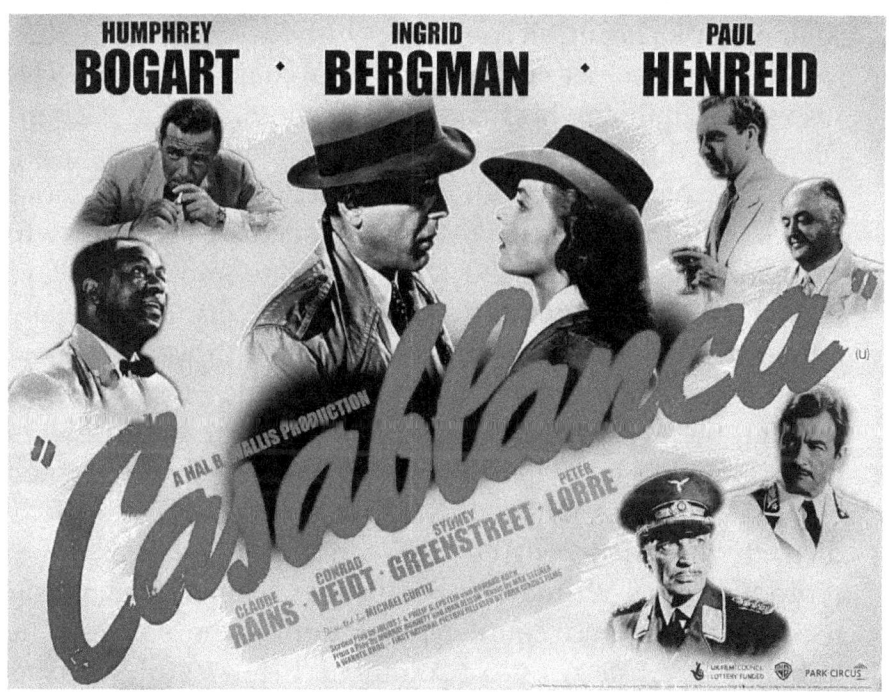

"If she can stand it, I can. Play it," says Rick Blaine, famously mis-quoted for decades, in *Casablanca* (WB, 1942), a contender for the best picture of all time. Based on an unproduced play, and desperately scripted day by day while shooting proceeded, the film overcame its unlikely beginnings to end up a perfect combination of drama, adventure, comedy, music, and suspense. The story hardly needs to be recounted, but in brief, expatriate Richard Blaine, his heart broken by the apparent desertion of his love, has "retired" from life to Casablanca in the early years of the War, only to have his lost love – and her husband – show up at his joint, the most popular watering hole in the desert oasis. Watching Rick wrestle with his heart and his conscience is watching a triumph of characterization – it's almost an insult to call it mere acting. And it took a great performance to stand out amid a cast including Sidney Greenstreet, Peter Lorre, Conrad Veidt, Paul Henreid, Ingrid Bergman, and Claude Rains. For many fans, seeing the picture marked the beginning of a beautiful friendship with Rick, Ilsa, and Louis.

"The Whistler" was only a peripheral character in the 1944-1948 series that bore his name; and the nominal star, Richard Dix, was a different person in each film (except the closing entry in which he did not appear). Like their radio-series source, the films told a new story of suspense each time, with someone bound up in the toils of doom, and not always escaping them, in events witnessed and very occasionally influenced by the Whistler, whose catch-phrase, "I know many things, for I walk by night", guides the audience through the events as they unfold. Individual pictures were based on works by writers like Cornell Woolrich and scripted by Eric Taylor, with superior results. The Whistler's distinctive whistle, carefully scored to be difficult to reproduce, was written by bandleader Wilbur Hatch, and used as theme and counter-point during the stories. The initial picture, *The Whistler* (Columbia, 1944), featured Dix as a man who puts out a contract on his own life, only to change his mind and discover his killer isn't about to quit.

Over at RKO Radio, Val Lewton carved out a comfortable niche for himself in the "horror" field. But while the Front Office wanted "Universal style" pictures, what they got were subtle, moody, artfully crafted – yet still commercial – pictures like *Cat People* (1942), a sexy take on lycanthropy, and its sequel *The Curse of the Cat People* ('44), an examination of the divine spirit that survives the animal nature of Man, and *I Walked With a Zombie* ('43), no less than *Jane Eyre* in the Caribbean. For Lewton, Robert Wise directed *The Body Snatcher* (1945), a close adaptation of the Robert Louis Stevenson tale of fright, of a 19th century Edinburgh doctor (Henry Daniell) who, constrained by religious-backed laws and superstition, must use resurrectionists – body snatchers – to acquire cadavers for teaching anatomy students. As the head grave-robber Boris Karloff gives a fine performance, and scenes with Bela Lugosi (in their last picture together) are frighteningly effective. Lewton's *Isle of the Dead* ('45) *Bedlam* ('46), and *Mademoiselle Fifi* ('44) are also effective, well designed pictures.

Out Of The Past (RKO Radio, 1947) exemplified the coming post-War trend away from "horror" and B detectives to a new, gritty, seamy, shadowy kind of realistic picture that would be called *"film noir"*. Most were mysteries, but the format was equally suited to dramas. When a gas-station owner is corralled into a web of murder and deceit, we learn that he was a private detective whose last job was such a mess that he walked away and created a new identity. But now he's back in again, and even though he knows it will end badly, he goes ahead with the deal. Jane Greer as Kathie Moffatt, ex-lover of Jeff Markham alias Jeff Bailey (Robert Mitchum), tries to play him, but he knows she's up to no good. Daniel Mainwaring pseudonymously scripted from his novel *Build My Gallows High* and Jacques Tourneur (a graduate of the Val Lewton unit) directed for producer Warren Duff, with Kirk Douglas, Rhonda Fleming, Steve Brodie, and Virginia Huston in the cast. This type of film continued strongly through the '50s, influencing troubled-teen pictures and even Westerns and science-fiction pictures.

A tale of naked ambition with dialogue that all but sparkles, *All About Eve* (20th Century-Fox, 1950) tells of Eve Harrington (Anne Baxter) who in her drive for success

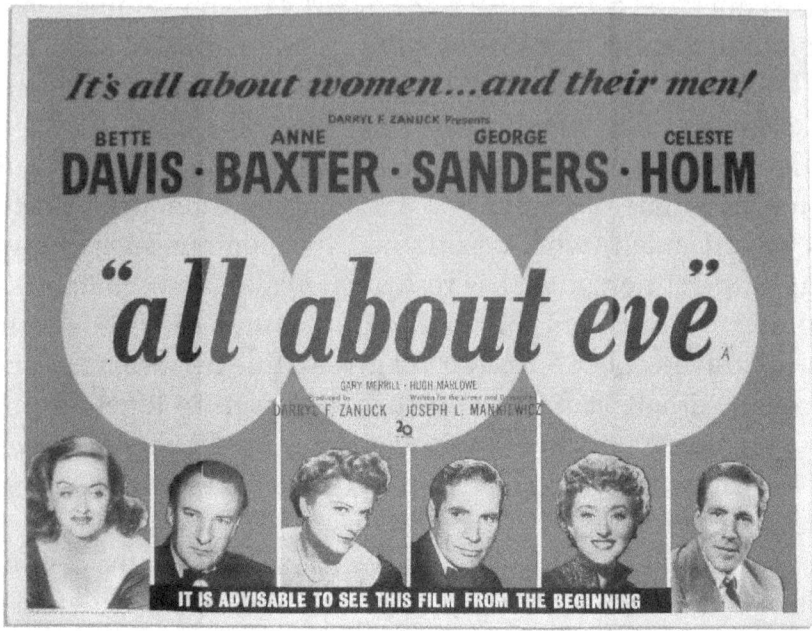

insinuates herself into the life of aging theatre star Margo Channing (Bette Davis, who has said she based her characterization on Tallulah Bankhead), and slowly takes over the older woman's life. Writer/director Joseph L. Mankiewicz crafted this cynical look at Broadway with a deft touch, drawing outstanding performances from Marilyn Monroe and George Sanders and the rest of the cast, and garnered a clutch of Oscars, including Best Picture, Best Director, and Best Screenplay, while Sanders earned a Best Supporting Actor prize for his typically arch (and yet not over the top) performance. Backstage stories, often the province of musicals, nonetheless provided a scenic backdrop for dramas, in such titles as *A Double Life* (U-I, '47) and Chaplin's *Limelight* (UA, '52), the murder mystery *Lady of Burlesque* (UA, '43), and of course a host of comedies.

James Dean shines as a troubled teenager, smart and honest but neither wise nor experienced, who learns that his

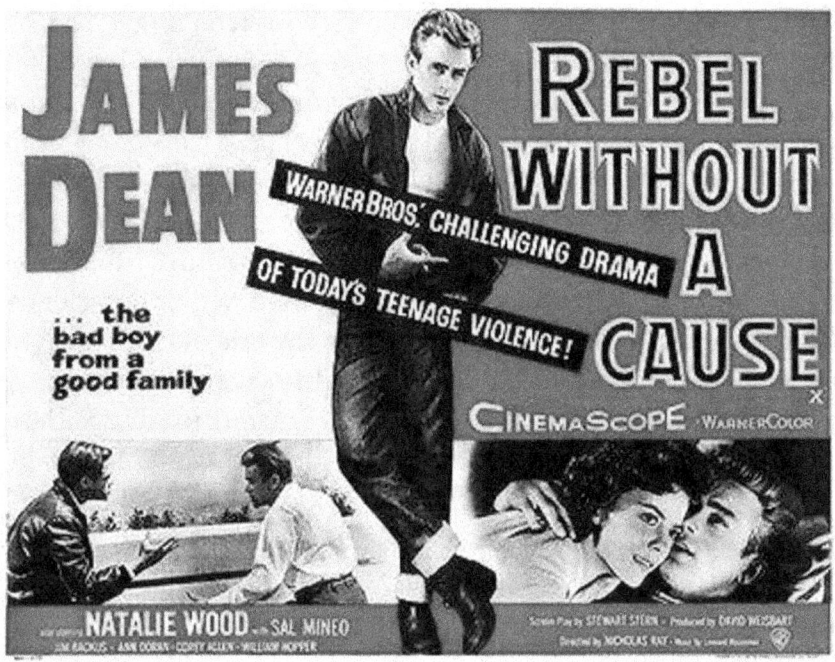

troubles aren't unique as he tries to find his way in the lost generation of the '50s in Nicholas Ray's *Rebel Without a Cause* (WB, 1955). Parents who don't understand that they're smothering their children, the lure of hot rods and hot co-eds, society that seems determined to marginalize them: all these troubles of teen-agers became a major theme of the decade, and rock 'n' roll music was often linked to their frustrations and depredations, as in the M-G-M picture *The Blackboard Jungle* ('55). In "Rebel", Natalie Wood was gamely making the often awkward – sometimes insurmountable – transition from child star to ingénue, while James Dean's performances in a handful of pictures made him a shooting star who blazed across the silver screen before his tragic and untimely death in a car crash. Programmers like *High School Confidential!* (MGM, '58) followed the trend with varying degrees of success, while exploitation pictures that "four-walled" (that is, were played in limited, local engagements) that tapped teenage angst had begun as early as *Reefer Madness* (States

Rights, '36) and others. For a later view of teen angst, see *The Breakfast Club* (Universal, '85).

A perfect example of a "horror" film that is really a drama is the French film by Georges Franju, *Les yeux sans visage* (Lux Film, 1960; *The Horror Chamber of Dr. Faustus* [Lopert Pictures Corporation, '62] in US). The title translates to "Eyes Without a Face", which better describes the picture than the exploitative American title (double billed with the science-fiction shocker *The Manster*), as it tells the tale of a doctor who surgically "steals" faces from beautiful young women to transplant on his daughter, horribly scarred in an accident. Though the doc keeps on trying, the transplants fail to take; between procedures the girl (Edith Scob) wears a blank mask – literally eyes without a face. Haunting, lyric, puzzling but powerful, the film is a stunning example of pictures made outside Hollywood. Franju's other pictures, including *Judex* (Svensk Filmindustri, '63; Continental Distributing ['66] in US) and *Nuits rouges* (Planfilm, '74; *Shadowman* [New Line Cinema, '75] in US), show his unmistakable style.

Even beyond our target era, historical events continue to hold a fascination for film-makers and audiences alike. The 1839 incident dramatized as *Amistad* (DreamWorks, 1997) involved a mutiny by slaves (kidnapped Africans later claimed to be of Cuban origin by the slavers) aboard a ship stopped by the United States Revenue Cutter service (forerunner of the Coast Guard), and the legal problems that resulted from the seizure of the men. Were they cargo, which meant they'd become the property of the Naval officers, or stolen goods, legally the property of Spanish crown? Could they be so coldly condemned, or should they be granted the right to plead their case? Djimon Hounsou starred as Cinque, one of the Africans, who awaits his fate while lawyer Matthew McConaughey makes his case. Featured in the cast were Nigel Hawthorne (as Martin Van Buren) and Anthony Hopkins (as John Quincy Adams). Directed and co-produced by Steven Spielberg, the film's frank dialogue (by writer

David Franzoni) and deft handling of the subject matter, material which could have sparked outrage from black Americans, was engrossing and found favor with audiences. In real life, the men were deemed victims and freed.

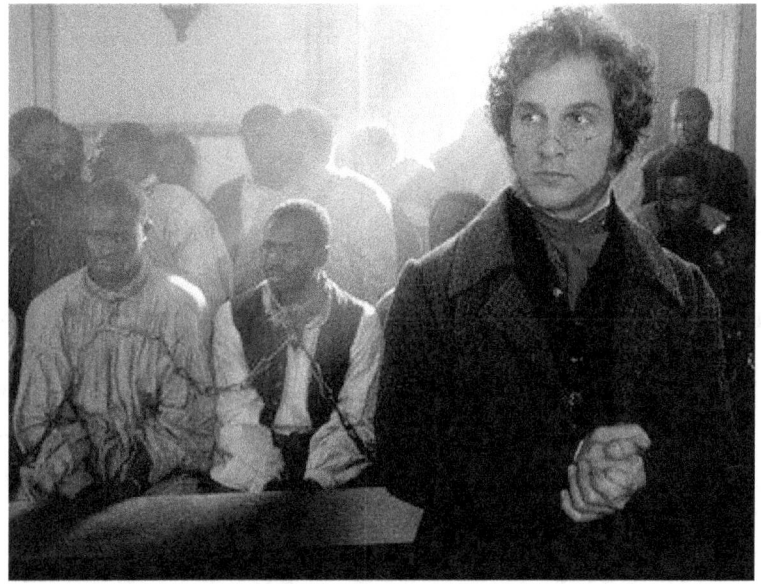

The trial scene from *Amistad*.

As you see, Drama is a broad and well mined category for the cinema. Only slightly removed from Drama, signaled by a greater emphasis on suspense, is...

CHAPTER TWO: MYSTERY

DETECTIVES COME IN many guises: police, private individuals, even criminals in need of proving their innocence (at least in a particular instance), and trace their literary roots to Edgar Poe, whose C. Auguste Dupin was followed by Sherlock Holmes, the most famous of the consulting detectives. Mysteries and the investigators who solved them were popular in early films, though the advent of synchronized dialogue made their puzzles and solutions all the more entertaining. Charlie Chan, Philo Vance, and Nick and Nora Charles (in the "Thin Man" series) amazed and charmed viewers. Audiences loved trying to outsmart the detectives, and didn't mind the obvious red herrings provided by type-casting. It was all great fun, being mystified. Private eyes quickly became a mainstay of second features. With their "familiarity breeds content" attitude, they embraced detectives, who could return to the screen as often as five times a year. Chan and Holmes (who moved effortlessly into the Bs), Simon Templar, Boston Blackie, Michael Shayne, the Falcon, and others attracted audiences with their continuing exploits. After the advent of the Second World War, the B detectives were eased out by the hard-bitten *films noirs*, A pictures featuring Humphrey Bogart, Dick Powell, and other big-name stars. But the final series investigator didn't even start until 1955, and was played by, of all people, long-time Western great William Elliott.

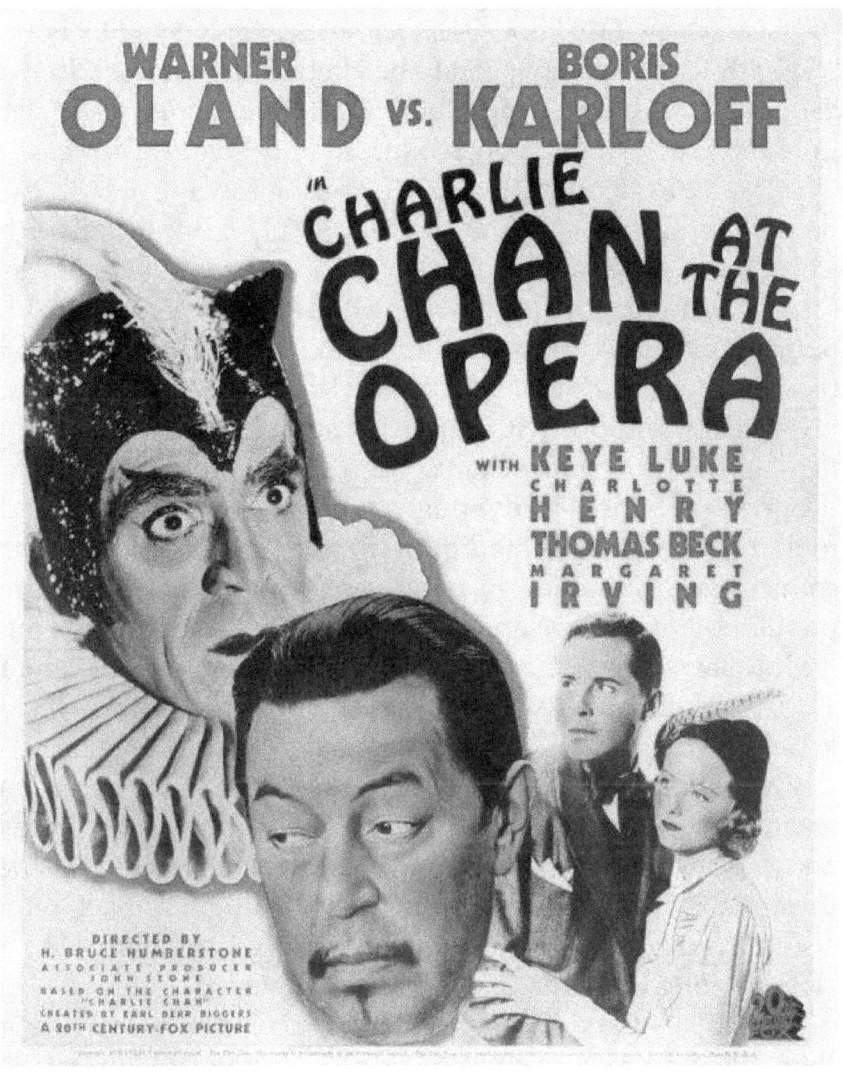

Charlie Chan, one of fiction's most famous detectives, actually gained his most fame on film. In a series that lasted some 20 years, the Hawaiian sleuth (of Chinese heritage) solved 45 mysteries and was portrayed by several actors from 1929 to 1949. Swedish actor Warner Oland, who'd been a splendid Fu Manchu, assumed the role in *Charlie Chan Carries On* (Fox Film, 1931), and continued until shortly before his death in 1937. Among his most interesting cases are *Charlie Chan in London* (Fox Film, '34), *Charlie Chan in Egypt* (Fox Film, '35) with Rita Cansino (soon to be Hayworth); *Charlie Chan at the Circus* (20th Century-Fox, '36); *Charlie Chan at the Opera* (20th Century-Fox, '36) with Boris Karloff; and *Charlie Chan at the Olympics* (20th Century-Fox, '37) featuring footage of both the Berlin Olympic Games and the zeppelin *Hindenberg*; all with Keye Luke as Chan's number-one son, Lee. When illness forced Oland to retire (so ill was he that he soon passed away), Sidney Toler took over, continuing at 20th Century-Fox with pictures like *Charlie Chan at Treasure Island* (20th Century-Fox, '39) a real stand-out with Cesar Romero; and *Charlie Chan at the Wax Museum* (20th Century-Fox, '40). When the studio dropped the series, Toler bought control of the character and took it to low-budget studio Monogram Pictures, where the comic black chauffeur Birmingham Brown (played by the popular Mantan Moreland) was added. The series petered out with Roland Winters as Chan in 1949, though a subsequent TV series, animated cartoon series, and occasion features have kept the character alive on screen.

Philo Vance, the urbane raconteur and amateur detective created by SS Van Dine, had a long series of print adventures and was the star of many pictures, beginning with 1929's *The Canary Murder Case* (Paramount), with William Powell, who also played Vance in *The Kennel Murder Case*, (WB, 1933), a slow-moving but engrossing mystery in which Vance tries to prove that a locked-room suicide was actually murder. Basil Rathbone had a shot as Vance, as did Warren William in *The Dragon Murder Case* ('34) and *The Gracie Allen Murder Case* (Paramount, '39), the latter written especially for the scatter-brained comedienne (and later written as a novel by Van Dine, a big fan of Miss Allen). When Alan Curtis played him in *Philo Vance's Secret Mission* (Eagle-Lion, 1947), Vance bowed out as a B-detective.

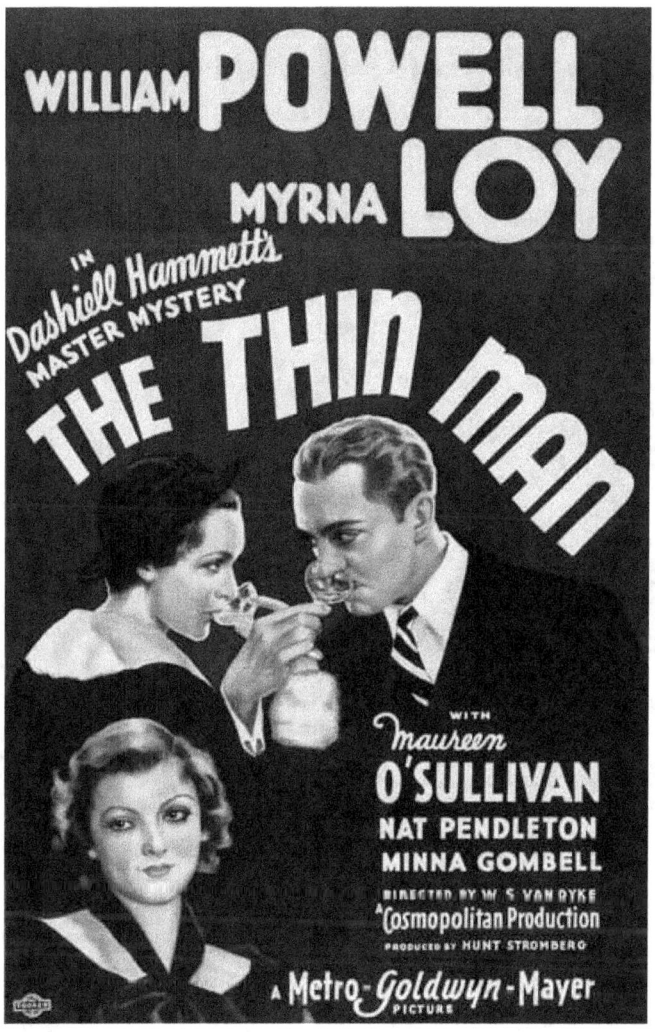

Dashiell Hammett's suave and slightly inebriated sleuth Nick Charles had already retired upon his marriage to lovable Nora when he was brought in to solve the case of *The Thin Man*. When M-G-M brought the story to the screen in 1934, with Myrna Loy and William Powell as the Charleses, it spawned a series of six top-drawer mysteries, one every two to three years (the stars were too valuable to be tied to a single series), unfortunately identifying Nick as the "Thin Man", though the character was someone else in the novel. Metro kept the "Thin Man" moniker in all the subsequent titles, from *After the Thin Man* ('36) to *Song of the Thin Man* ('47). Though the following five pictures weren't up to the first, they all still rank among the best of detective films.

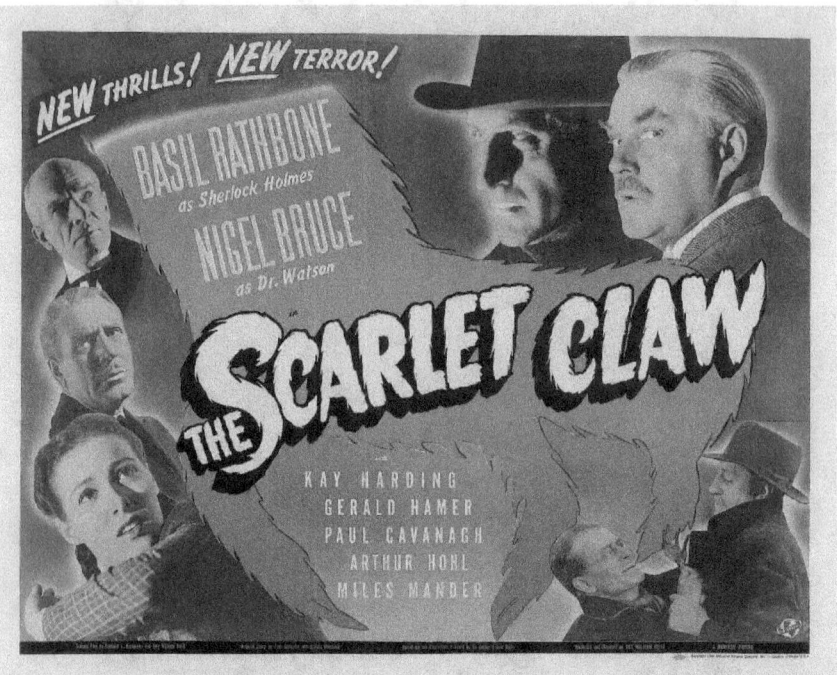

Most famous, though among the least canonical, Sherlock Holmes and Doctor Watson team, Basil Rathbone and Nigel Bruce made 14 feature films between 1939 and 1946, some of which are superb, the least of which are interesting. Earlier Holmes pictures had featured performers like John Barrymore and British actor Arthur Wontner, but it was Rathbone who truly shined: 20th Century-Fox's period-pieces *The Hound of the Baskervilles* and *The Adventures of Sherlock Holmes* (both 1939) are excellent, the second featuring George Zucco as master villain Professor Moriarty. When Universal took over the series in 1942, they posited "If Holmes were alive today..." and made a contemporary version, with good stories and characterizations, beginning with *Sherlock Holmes*

and the Voice of Terror and *Sherlock Holmes and the Secret Weapon* (both '42) awash in Second World War action and mystery. A diminishing accent on the time period in the later entries like *The Scarlet Claw* and *The Pearl of Death* (both '44) provided top-notch thrills as well. Later incarnations of Holmes have had varying degrees of success, with one of the most interesting being *A Study in Terror* (Compton Film Distributors, '65; [Columbia Pictures, '66] in US) where Holmes (John Neville) tackles the case of Jack the Ripper.

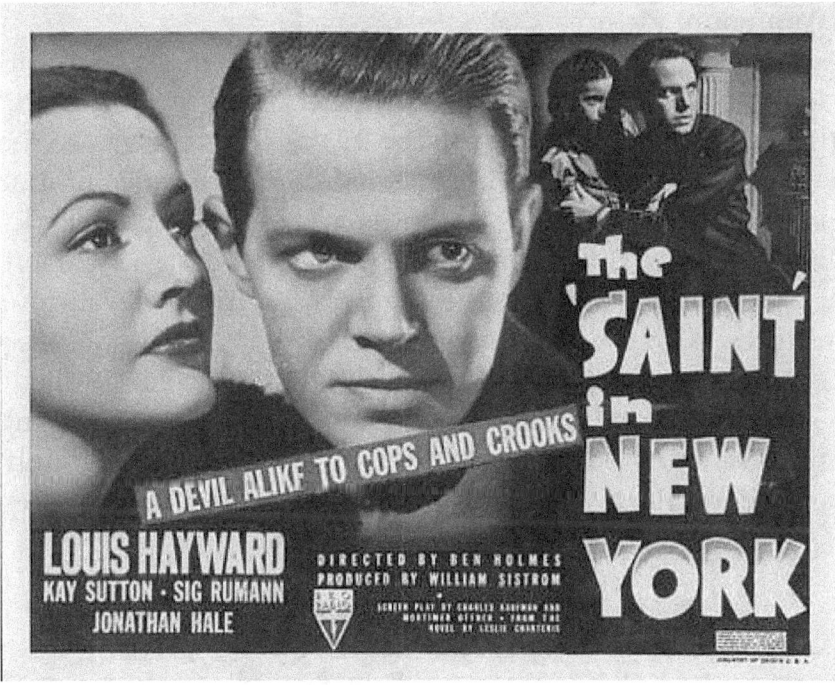

Leslie Charteris' modern Robin Hood of Crime had already had many adventures before averting international disaster and gaining a pardon for all past crimes by the time he became the adventurer of the movies. His first, *The Saint in New York* (RKO Radio, 1938) cast Louis Hayward as Simon Templar, doing an excellent job in a script closely adapted from a Charteris novel picked to appeal to American audiences. Later, George Sanders played a more subtle and less robust version of the character in titles like *The Saint Strikes Back* (RKO Radio, '39) and *The Saint's Double Trouble* (RKO Radio, '40), but Sanders, chafing under the B-picture yoke, demanded his release after five pictures. Later "Saint" installments continued through *The Saint's Return* (Exclusive Films, '53; *The Saint's Girl Friday* [RKO Radio, '54] in US) in which Hayward resumed the role. After that, Templar moved to television, where Roger Moore assumed the mantle and made the Saint a household name. More recently, Val Kilmer played an updated version of Templar in *The Saint* (Paramount Pictures, '97).

Counterparts to the Hardy Boys, the famous teen girl sleuth, Nancy Drew, in novels written by "Carolyn Keene" (the house name used mostly by Walter Kanig) came to the Warner Brothers screen in 1938 and 1939 in a series of four programmers, beginning with *Nancy Drew – Detective*. Perky Bonita Granville was Nancy and John Litel her dad Carson, with Frankie Thomas as her hapless boyfriend, in all four pictures. All the gritty realism Warners had handy was used as mere background for these light-hearted thrillers. Granville continued in pictures, later marrying industrialist/producer Jack Wrather; Nancy languished until television brought her back in the "The Hardy Boys/Nancy Drew Mysteries" (ABC-TV, 1977–1979).

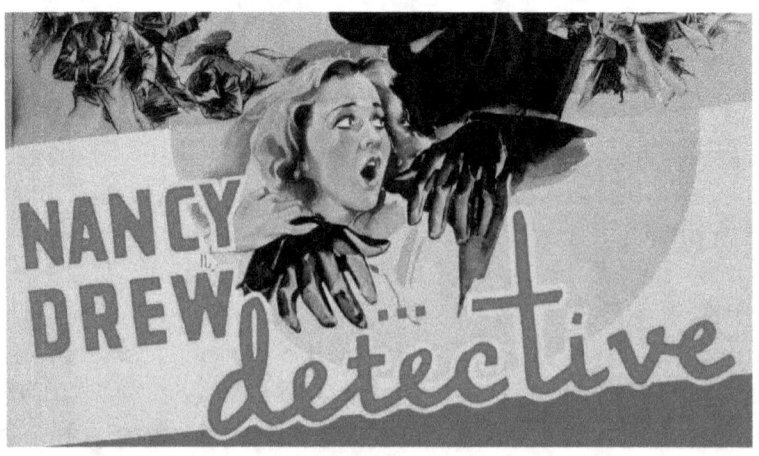

Little Monogram entered the Oriental sleuth game with James Lee Wong, a detective created by Hugh Wiley and published in *Collier's* Magazine. In an era when a Swede and a midwesterner could play Chan, Wong was played for star identification by Boris Karloff – who did a creditable job in five of six films between 1938's *Mr. Wong, Detective* and 1940's *Doomed to Die*. With narrowed eyes and no special make-up, Karloff portrayed the character with dignity and that singular low-key performance that kept the audience watching, even when the mystery wasn't all that impenetrable. Keye Luke then appeared as the youthful Wong in a belated "origin" story, 1941's *Phantom of Chinatown*, but the series abruptly ended without further incarnations.

Author Louis Vance created gentleman thief Michael Lanyard, known as "the Lone Wolf", thus introducing a new phrase into the language. Many actors had played the part in various mute and early-talker pictures when Warren William, a popular player who had also been Perry Mason and Philo Vance, was given the opportunity to play Lanyard in *The Lone Wolf Spy Hunt* (Columbia, 1939) and subsequent films in the series, including *The Lone Wolf Strikes* ('40). His droll, amused reactions to danger and disaster made audiences smile and his accomplices shudder. Though Lanyards changed, Jameson, his dogsbody, was usually played by the delightful Eric Blore, who stayed when Gerald Mohr took over for *The Notorious Lone Wolf* ('46) and two of three subsequent pictures.

Nick Carter was nearly the grand old man of print detectives, having first appeared in 1886, but when M-G-M tried him out in 1939, little more than the name survived. In the first, aptly titled *Nick Carter, Master Detective*, Walter Pidgeon made his first of the three films, but it was his unwanted sidekick, Bartholomew the bee man (Donald Meek), who really sold the series, with his bumbling (well, he was a *bee* man, after all) and periodic rescues of the hero. Carter and Bartholomew made only two more pictures, *Phantom Raiders* and *Sky Murder* (both '40), but they were both great fun, and it was a shame more didn't follow. Carter returned to the screen over twenty years later in a pair of French productions, while his print version was refigured as "Killmaster" for a new paperback series.

Michael Shayne – the movies' most different detective – was a wise-cracking, responsibility-ducking, truth-redefining Irish-American based more or less on Brett Halliday's popular character. 20th Century-Fox, which had recently killed their burgeoning "Holmes" series, brought the property to the screen in 1940's *Michael Shayne, Private Detective* in the person of Lloyd Nolan for a series of seven pictures in four years. Nolan's Shayne lived up to his billing, and was essentially his own comedy relief, a nice change from the usual dumb sidekick. Another outstanding entry is *The Man Who Wouldn't Die* (20th Century-Fox, '42), which included science-fiction overtones. Hugh Beaumont, Ward of TV's "Leave it to Beaver", appeared in a later undistinguished short series in 1946 and '47.

Horatio Black of Boston, USA, had already been pardoned for known crimes when he jumped from print to film in *Meet Boston Blackie* (Columbia, 1941) in the person of Chester Morris. Morris' hobby – stage magic – enhanced the character, who never met a pair of handcuffs that could hold him, and he spent eight years and 14 films outwitting friendly enemy Inspector Farraday (Richard Lane), the one cop who never believed he'd reformed. Engaging stories, lively dialogue, and support from character actors like George E. Stone (who usually played Blackie's sidekick the Runt), Lloyd Corrigan, Cy Kendall, and Frank Sully made the whole series fun. It concluded in 1949 with *Boston Blackie's Chinese Venture*, shortly before the character jumped to television in the person of Kent Taylor in a continuation of the radio series, which had paralleled the films.

Dashiell Hammett's other great claim to fame was brought to the screen three times, once heavily Bowdlerized, but it was

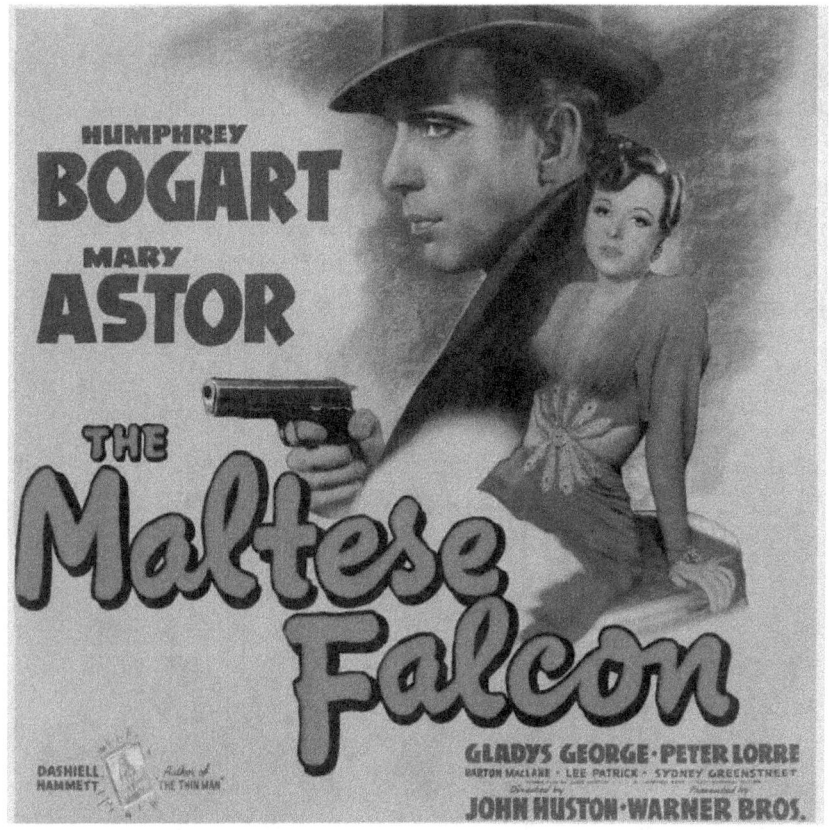

the third version that became one of the most memorable detective thrillers of the movies: *The Maltese Falcon* (WB, 1941). Samuel Spade, Joel Cairo, Brigid O'Shaunessy, and Casper Gutman the fat man (Humphrey Bogart, Peter Lorre, Mary Astor, and Sidney Greenstreet) squabble, cross, and double-cross each other to get control of the dingus that causes all the trouble. The photography, the music, even the set design, contribute to this compelling murder/caper mystery scripted and directed by John Huston. The previous version with the same title (from '31) starred Ricardo Cortez as a different but fascinating take on Spade, and an uncredited re-make, 1936's *Satan Met a Lady*, substituted Ted Shayne for Spade, a fat woman for the Fat Man, and the Horn of Roland for the black bird.

"The Falcon" was the creation of writer Michael Arlen, and when George Sanders had demanded release from the "Saint" series, RKO Radio simply cast him as this similar character, in *The Gay Falcon* ('41), an excellent expansion of the original short story, and started a new series. When Sanders wanted out of B harness again after the top-drawer *The Falcon Takes Over* ('42, based on Raymond Chandler's *Farewell, My Lovely*), the studio commissioned *The Falcon's Brother* ('42) and killed off Sanders' character in an heroic finale, allowing his real-life brother Tom Conway to take over the lead for a subsequent nine pictures, including *The Falcon and the Co-eds* ('43) and *The Falcon in Hollywood* ('44). An unrelated series from the late '40s starred John Calvert as Mike Waring, alias "the Falcon", a character from a radio series.

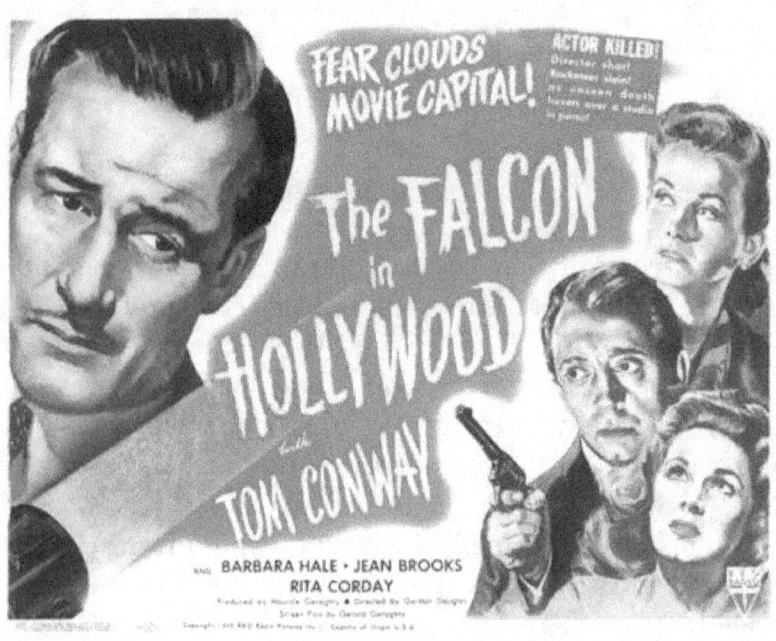

Columbia crossed drama with psychological mystery in the series that began with *The Crime Doctor* (1943), based on a radio series (which was almost certainly inspired by the more subtle character Dr. Dollar, also known as "the Crime Doctor" in a series of stories by EW Hornung, creator of Raffles, the amateur cracksman) but also adapting the screenplay from their own feature *The Man Who Lived Twice* ('36) that developed from a similar premise: A former criminal (long-time actor Warner Baxter in his own star vehicle) who's lost his memory in a car accident, finds a new calling while in rehabilitation and dedicates his life to psychiatry, in his new identity as Doctor Ordway. After solving the case of his own identity, he was led into mysterious adventures in films like 1947's *The Millerson Case* and the final installment, *The Crime Doctor's Diary* ('49). Though the stories usually involved murder, the accent was very much on the drama of psychological disturbances.

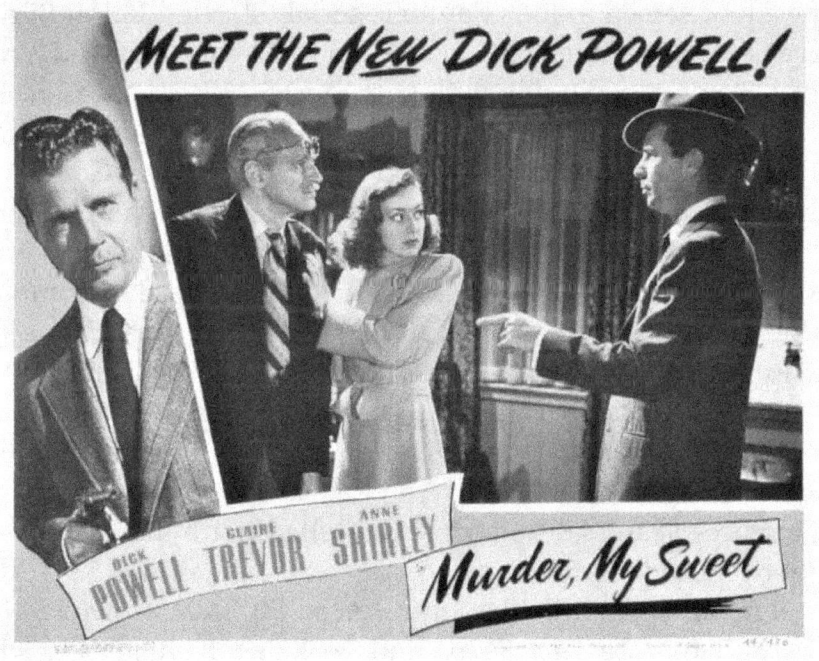

When Dick Powell starred as Philip Marlowe in RKO Radio's 1944 *Murder, My Sweet*, he not only gave viewers a crackling good performance but gave himself a new lease on professional life. The former song-and-dance man now became the tough guy of *films noirs,* beating up the Bad Guys – but mostly getting beaten up *by* the Bad Guys – in a top-notch adaptation of *Farewell, My Lovely* (a title nixed by the Front Office as too likely to be perceived as a romantic picture), with gritty streets, tough characters (cop Don Douglas and slick Otto Kruger), slinky dames (Claire Trevor and Anne Shirley), and a guy the size of the Statue of Liberty with fists like a freight train (Mike Mazurki as Moose Malloy). Powell continued in this vein, and later moved into production as one of the bosses of Four Star Television. The hard-hitting mystery had been filmed previously – as *The Falcon Takes Over* in 1942 with George Sanders.

Dick Tracy had first appeared in the newspaper funnies in Chester Gould's hard-edged strip in 1931, and had come to the silver screen in four Republic serials starring Ralph Byrd as a G-man version of the cop. When RKO Radio revived him for a B series, beginning with *Dick Tracy* in 1945, he was back to his police-department origins and maintained fidelity with the strip. After that and a second film with Morgan Conway, Byrd was brought back for the final two in 1947, ending with *Dick Tracy Meets Gruesome,* co-starring Boris Karloff as a petty crook with brains who stumbles into a secret worth a fortune: a side-effectless paralyzing gas. Strong stories, great cartoon-strip atmosphere (with characters with names like Dr. A. Tomic, I.M. Learned, and strip characters Tess Trueheart and Vitamin Flintheart [the last played as a knowing spoof of John Barrymore by Ian Keith]) marked this quartet as great audience-pleasers. The series was killed not by low interest but by studio politics.

Raymond Chandler had introduced Philip Marlowe in his first novel, *The Big Sleep,* and William Faulkner, Leigh Brackett, and Jules Furthman, and producer-director Howard Hawks, fashioned it into a complex vehicle for Humphrey Bogart in 1945, with Marlowe caught up in a baffling case involving the Sternwood sisters, steamy Lauren Bacall and over-sexed Martha Vickers. But when the notices for *To Have And Have Not* (in which Bogey and Bacall had set fire to the screen) came in, Jack Warner decided the new picture needed more scenes between the pair. To accommodate the new footage into an acceptable running time, other scenes were cut – including one that helped the viewer figure out what the Hell was going on – and the new version had its official release in 1946 (the earlier version had been screened to Overseas military audiences). It was and is still a hit. Bogey was enormously successful as the tough guy who had a soft spot in his heart for the dames – if they were tough enough to take him. Shot almost entirely indoors (even many exteriors), Hawks' direction never seems claustrophobic. The 1978 version (United Artists) with Robert Mitchum, transposed to Great Britain, was less a remake than a more faithful version of the novel.

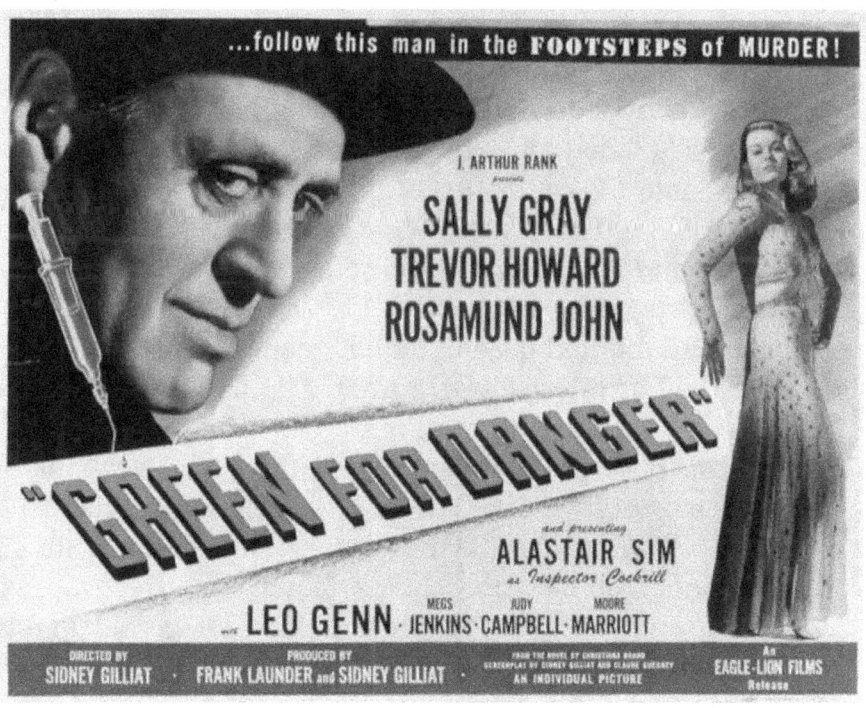

Alastair Sim made a dynamite detective as Inspector Cockrill in *Green for Danger* (General Film Distributors, 1946 [Eagle-Lion, '47] in US), plodding along, annoying staff and patients, bumbling through a murder case in a hospital during the Second World War, and generally being amusing and seemingly harmless to those keeping an eye on him. (Though many screen detectives would farm this field, TV's "Columbo" really nailed it for audiences.) From a novel by Christianna Brand, the film is such a delight that the lack of a subsequent series is a shame. Sim, a versatile and delightful screen personality, could and did play an amazing variety of characters from con-men to Ebenezer Scrooge. The film, like its source, played fair with the audience, handing them a major clew to the murder; one merely needed one bit of medical information.

When William Elliott took on the role of detective Andy Doyle in a series for Allied Artists (the former Monogram Pictures), he was returning to his roots (he'd been a dress extra in detective pictures before becoming "Wild Bill" Elliott, one of Hollywood's most popular cowboys), but B-series cowboys had faded away by 1954, having ridden off into the sunset or onto TV. In the first of the Allied Artists series, *Dial Red 0* (1955) he was "Andy Flynn", but when it was learned there was an LAPD cop by that name, his character became "Andy Doyle". The last of the cop series, *Footsteps In The Night*, in '57, marked the end of the B detective mysteries.

A best selling international author, Agatha Christie, creator of Miss Marple and Hercule Poirot, has attracted producers since 1928, providing movie-goers with several versions of her famous story (re-titled) *Ten Little Indians*, including *And Then There Were None* (20th Century-Fox, 1945) with an outstanding cast including Louis Hayward, June Duprez, Roland Young, C. Aubrey Smith, and Barry Fitzgerald. In this well constructed version, a collection of seemingly random people is lured to an island, where the mysterious and unseen "U.N. Owen" begins bumping them off, one-by-one, in line with a gruesome nursery-rhyme poem. At least two re-makes of this utilized the big-name "guest star" casting ploy to lure audiences. Christie's Miss Marple, the grand old lady of detection, received a series in the last days of the double feature, starring Margaret Rutherford, produced by M-G-M British, beginning with *Murder, She Said* ('61). Poirot had one outing in this period, as preposterously played by Tony Randall in *The Alphabet Murders* (M-G-M, '66). The film featured the last screen appearance of Austin Trevor, who had played Poirot in a trio of British mysteries in the early 1930s.

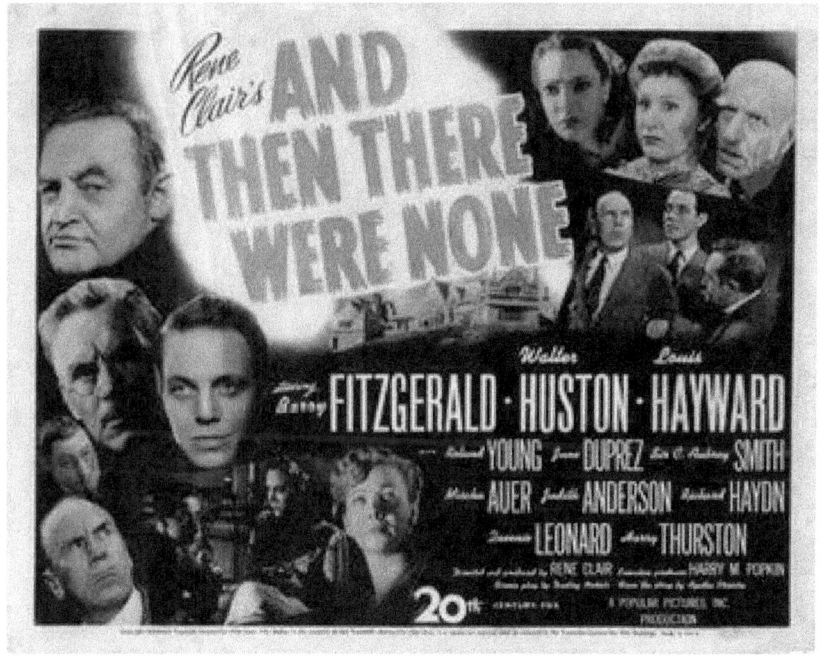

In more recent years, Poirot was finally allowed to appear as a serious (mostly) character for the International Big Screen in several big-budget all-star spectaculars, beginning with *Murder On The Orient Express* (Paramount, 1974) based upon *Murder on the Calais Coach,* one of Christie's most well known novels. The by-then traditional round-up of suspects was easy: all of the suspects were passengers on the same car on the famous train, and all portrayed by stars of the first rank, including Anthony Perkins, Sean Connery, Vanessa Redgrave, Ingrid Bergman, George Coulouris, Michael York, Jacqueline Bisset, Lauren Bacall, and Martin Balsam, with Albert Finney as the Belgian sleuth. Peter Ustinov followed for several features and TV-movies, and more recently Kenneth Branagh has assayed the role.

So mysteries started with drama and added that extra element of suspense, of the unknown, to the mix. And when you speak of the unknown, what's more unknown than...

CHAPTER THREE: SCIENCE FICTION

THOUGH "SCIENCE FICTION" is often relegated to the 1950s, with its overpowering wave of space and monster pictures, the big-budget thrillers and the poorest B exploitation drive-in fodder, the *genre* goes back to the very beginnings of film. Georges Méliès included in his series of imaginative motion-picture plays such adventures as *Le voyage dans la lune* (Star-Film, 1902; *A Trip To The Moon* [American Mutoscope & Biograph and Edison Manufacturing Company] in US). German cinema of the mute era included a number of science-based stories. In the US, however, for many years "science fiction" was just a sub-set of "horror", as films like *Frankenstein* and *Dr. Jekyll and Mr. Hyde* received the same marketing treatment as *Dracula*. Many films of the '30s and '40s hewed to scientific explanations for the basis of their stories, but there was little if any distinction between science and magic. Writer Kurt Siodmak, told to write "Wolf Man Meets Frankenstein", balked at mixing his Wolf Man – fantasy – with the Monster – science fiction – but wrote the screenplay anyway. Subsequent writers of the series displayed woefully inadequate knowledge of science, but they were the norm, not the exception, of screen-writers. Even the "obvious" science-fiction pictures of the '50s fell back on "and then a miracle occurred" to explain complicated ideas. Here are examples of an assortment of films that fit in this category, but, as you'll see, fantasy tends to crowd in at any opportunity.

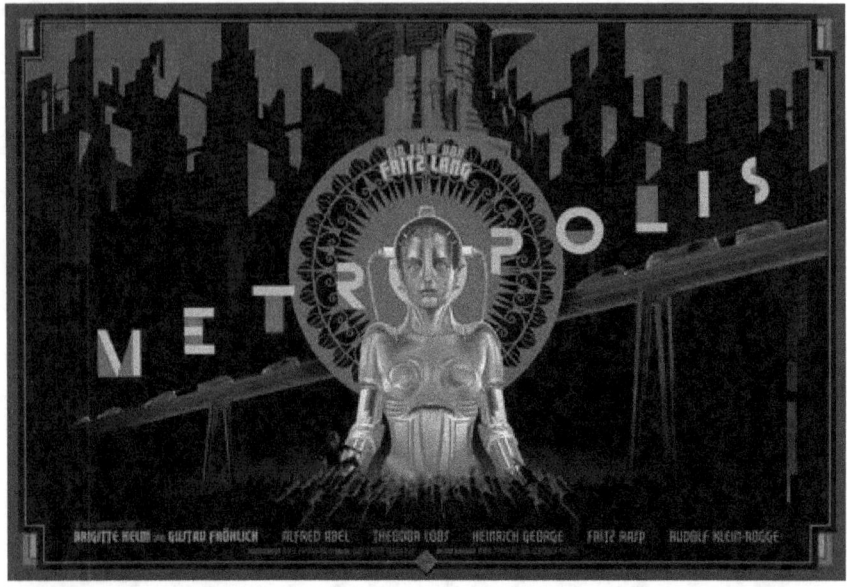

Metropolis (Ufa, 1927) can be looked upon as the root from which later science fiction grew. Though not the first, it was the film that made the greatest impression upon its audience – and built that audience beyond the confines of its native Weimar Republic to the entire world. The future civilization that has fractured into extreme examples of the "haves" and "have nots" – the wealthy who live in the towering skyscraper and the poor who live, basically, in the sewer – is a cautionary note that has been sublimated to the story of a beautiful girl used to promulgate a revolt among the workers to allow the wealthy to completely crush them. Brigitte Helm as Maria (and her robot/android double) is a mesmerizing presence throughout the film, and the scenes of the creation of the False Maria are captivating, still effective in these days of computer graphics. Long available in various shortened versions, a 2002

German restoration provides the best view of what audiences saw in the first release. Any comparisons to later nations and regimes may be left to the reader.

Though the focus of *Just Imagine* (Fox Film, 1930) was a musical satirical look at civilization in the unimaginably far future (1980!), its view of New York City showed the influence of *Metropolis* (*Q.V.*) on the art direction, with its vistas of towering cityscapes. The groundlings, however, do not live in sewers but in comparatively pleasant surroundings. Swedish comic El Brendel plays a man of the present who gets sick and goes to the hospital, only to end up in frozen sleep for 50 years, to wake and wonder at the changes in society, where many things are available at coin-operated machines (when he sees a couple getting a baby that way, he decries, "Giff me da Good Old Days" in his mock-Swedish accent that wasn't all that funny even then). But again, as was often the case, the wonders of the future are merely background: The real story is about a boy who, to prove he's a man to his girl's father, volunteers to make the first trip to Mars. Brendel goes along in the quest to aid True Love, but mostly so he can joke with the twin Martian races in this pastiche by the Broadway team of DeSylva, Henderson, and Brown. If nothing else, the film provided props and stock footage for "Flash Gordon" and "Buck Rogers" serials.

At Universal Pictures, when Carl Laemmle decided to follow *Dracula* (*Q.V. in fantasy*) with *Frankenstein* (Universal, 1931), he was touring well traveled science-fiction territory, though he thought of it as essentially the same type of fantastic fiction as the vampire tale. The stories of his childhood in east-central Europe were the stuff of vampires, the Golem, and witchcraft. So the science-fiction creation of the Monster was treated in the same fashion (in the original novel, the creature's origins are less scientific than alchemic; Mary Shelley was a product of her era). The story of a doctor who creates his own man had been filmed as early as 1910, but this version, starring Colin Clive and Mae Clarke, became an instant shock classic due to the performance of character-actor Boris Karloff, who shot to immediate stardom as the troubled, childlike, but homicidal monster under the direction of James Whale. The elongated,

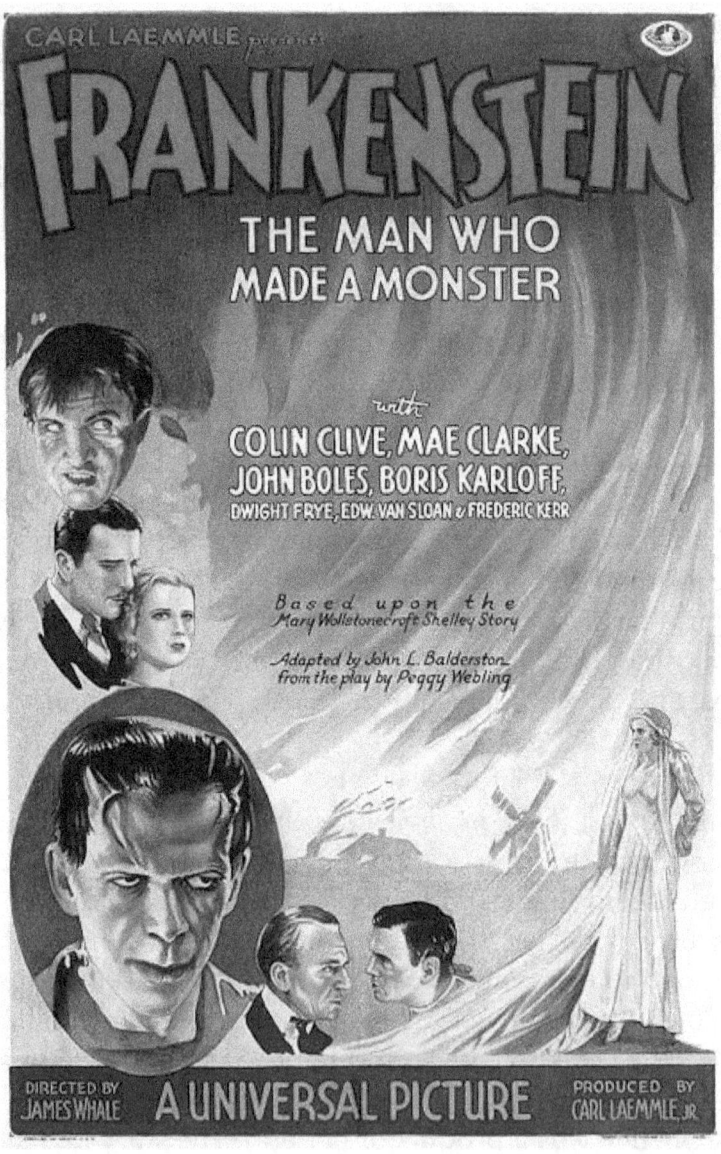

shadows, old sagging brick walls, bizarre electrical equipment all contributed to the "horror" look of the story, but the use of cadaver parts and lightning to spark life is deeply rooted in science. The Monster would go on to seven sequels, but only the first three can be considered "scientific": *Bride of Frankenstein* ('35), *Son of Frankenstein* ('39), and *The Ghost of Frankenstein* ('42); once the Monster met the Wolf Man, as Siodmak observed, science took a back seat.

Paramount, looking for some of that sweet thriller money, invested in a science-fiction story with as much built-in publicity value as *Frankenstein*, in their 1932 production of *Dr. Jekyll and Mr. Hyde*, starring the versatile Fredric March in the title roles. Using an effective but simple trick of lighting to achieve part of the transformation of the kindly, curious physician into the brutal, callous Hyde, director Rouben Mamoulian achieved a masterpiece of special effects to go along with March's characterization (which won an Academy Award). The story expands on the novella "The Strange Case of Dr. Jekyll and Mr. Hyde" by adding not one but two romances, but strays from the notion of good and bad into the civilized versus animalistic dichotomy. Unfairly overshadowed by the later Spencer Tracy version (M-G-M, '41), the film was kept from the public eye for many years. The story had been filmed before March, and would be filmed many times after (including as *The Two Faces of Dr. Jekyll* (Columbia,'60); *House of Fright* [A-I-P,'61] in the US), and parodied (*The Nutty Professor* (Paramount, '63) and others.

Universal all but cornered the market in thrillers, following their monster hits with a movie based loosely on HG Wells' *The Invisible Man* in a 1933 production. British actor Claude Rains, who would go on to character stardom in A pictures, made an impression on audiences without even showing his face as the dedicated scientist whose eagerness to succeed eventually destroys him. Outstanding special effects by John P. Fulton and an arch sense of humor to the screenplay bolstered this production. Belated sequels focused on relatives of the original invisible one: his brother used a somewhat improved serum to aid a friend falsely accused of murder in *The Invisible Man Returns* (Universal, 1940); another relative to aid the Allied cause in the Second World War (the prestige picture *Invisible Agent* [Universal, '42]). Other related pictures include the farce *The Invisible Woman* (Universal, '40) and *The Invisible Man's Revenge* (Universal, '44), while the superior comedy *...Meet The Invisible Man* (U-I, '51, starring Abbott and Costello) returned to the Griffin family, still trying to help the falsely accused.

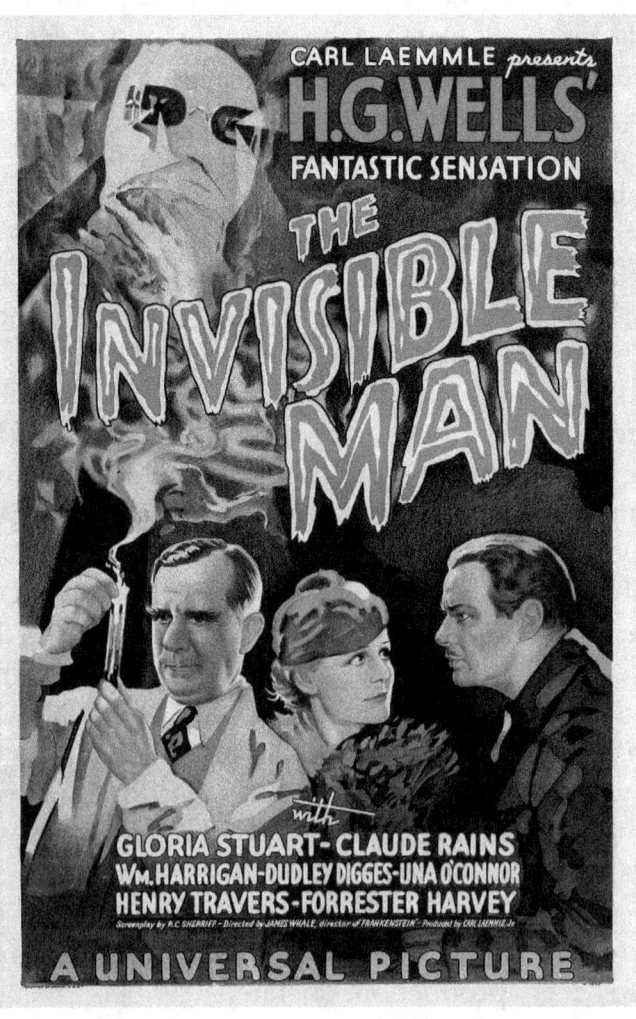

HG Wells was frequently called upon as the source for film. His *The Island of Dr. Moreau* became *The Island of Lost Souls* (Paramount, 1932), with Charles Laughton as the scientist trying to create superior beings through surgery, making men of lower animals. His triumph is a panther woman, and to prove she's truly human he arranges for a man to be brought to his remote island, in hopes she will seduce him, an idea to strain the Production Code had it succeeded. But this sort of thing rarely resulted in a happy ending for a man who seeks to become God. We'll hear more about Wells later.

Karloff – who needed a first name? – expanded on his *repertoire*, building a career on scientists, some mad, some zealous, some just unlucky. In *The Invisible Ray* (Universal, 1936), as Janos Ruhk, he finds a radio-active mineral in a meteorite but inadvertently poisons himself while experimenting with its dynamic power. Driven mad by the poison and the counter-agent that keeps him alive, he plots revenge on those closest to him, murdering them by delaying administration of the antidote long enough to acquire his glowing touch of death. Ruhk is a true movie mad-scientist, using his ray to restore sight to his kindly mother, and also having invented a way to read "the light rays from Andromeda" to view an event on Earth millions of years earlier. He'd play many such scientists, mad or just annoyed, in his future. Other variations on this theme include *Man Made Monster* (*Q.V.*) and *Hand of Death* (20th Century-Fox, '62)

Hiding in a remote retreat would be enough to unhinge anyone, and a zealous researcher like Dr. Thorkel (Albert Dekker), better known as *Dr. Cyclops* in the 1940 Paramount thriller, is no exception. After luring a group to his lab to verify his results, he finds them less guests and more intruders, and tries to rid himself of them and at the same time prove his experiments by shrinking them down to a size where opening a door becomes a team effort, as Janice Logan, Charles Halton, Frank Yaconelli, Thomas Coley, and Victor

Killian soon discover. A superior product from a studio not known for science fiction, it received the full Technicolor treatment.

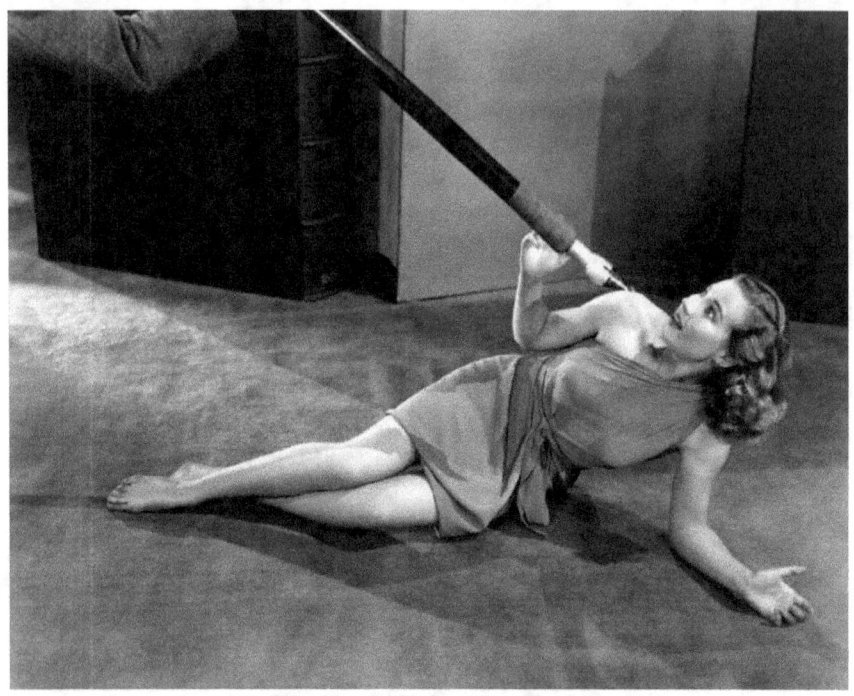

Publicity still for *Dr.Cyclops*.

Lon Chaney, Jr., (as he was then known), got his first "horror" role as Dynamo Dan McCormick, whose carnival electricity act had endowed him with immunity that brought him to the attention of scientists, one of whom used him in a dangerous experiment, creating of him a *Man Made Monster* whose electrical supercharge spelled death for anyone he touched in the 1941 Universal picture. This time, it was not through his own actions that he became a monster but from those of one of the great mad scientists of the screen, Lionel Atwill, who went on for five more years in this vein. Chaney, of course, went on to become the number-one monster portrayer of the War years, though usually in fantasy roles.

Surprised to see *The Mummy's Hand* (Universal, 1940) in

this category? Well, despite all the fantasy trappings (Egyptian gods, eternal life, curses), the saga of Kharis and his quest for his lost love Ananka depends from Tana fluid, that brew from an arcane leaf that gives life to the Mummy (three to keep his heart beating, nine to give him mobility); and Tana fluid is a chemical, just like Dr. Jekyll's formula. In this and the second in the series, *The Mummy's Tomb* ('42) keeping Kharis (who, by the way, isn't a mummy but a man buried alive in linen wrappings) alive with the Tana fluid is the only fantastic element. From the expedition that locates the tomb of the Princess Ananka to the revenge that follows a generation later in a small New England town, the saga of the Mummy stands solidly in science fiction. But in the *third* picture, the series moves, as you'll see, whole-heartedly into the adjacent category.

In the 1950s, science fiction really took off (so to speak) with Man's journeys to space. Though the serials had taken viewers to Saturn, Mars, and Mongo in the meantime, feature pictures didn't follow the lead of *Just Imagine* until 1950 – and then the fuel hit the rockets, big time. George Pal's *Destination Moon* (Eagle-Lion) won an Oscar for its Special Effects in telling the tale of four men claiming our satellite for the Good Guys (that is, the not-Communists). Excepting the science-fiction premise, the film was straight drama, detailing the real problems a simple Moon voyage could entail, with a heavy emphasis on accuracy as it was known at the time. So much publicity was generated about the film that a competitor (let's not say "rip-off" artist) produced and had a variation in theaters before "Moon" was finished. *Rocketship XM* (Lippert, '50), however, was a wild-and-woolly melodramatic quickie about an accidental trip to Mars made by three men and a woman, who discover the remnants of an advanced civilization on the red planet. Though "Moon" had and continues to have the better reputation, "XM" is a more entertaining picture; both should be seen.

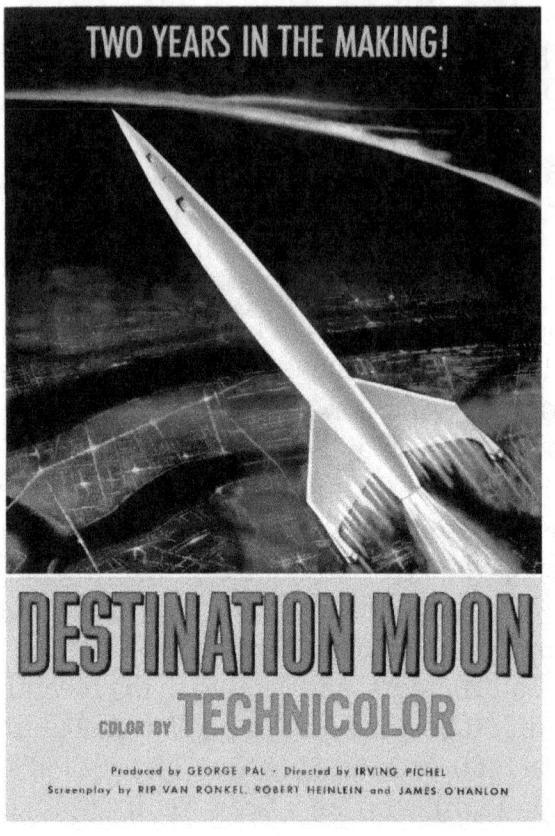

And it wasn't just our trips to outer space that lured audiences; there also came a number of voyages by other creatures *to* Earth! In *The Thing* From Another World (RKO Radio, 1951), a vegetable being from... Mars, perhaps?... having crashed in the Arctic, is thawed out by accident and terrorizes a lonely outpost of scientists and soldiers. The film, a great picture (well acted, photographed, and edited under the supervision of top film-maker Howard Hawks) but a poor adaptation (of John W. Campbell's "Who Goes There?", in which a shape-shifting alien can and does murder and assume the identity of anyone, creating high tension), the film explored the differences between cold reasoning and hot action. James Arness (assisted by Tom Steele and Billy Curtis)

played the strange visitor from another planet. A well done later version (*The Thing*, [Universal, '82]) hewed more closely to the original but lacked the punch of RKO Radio's version.

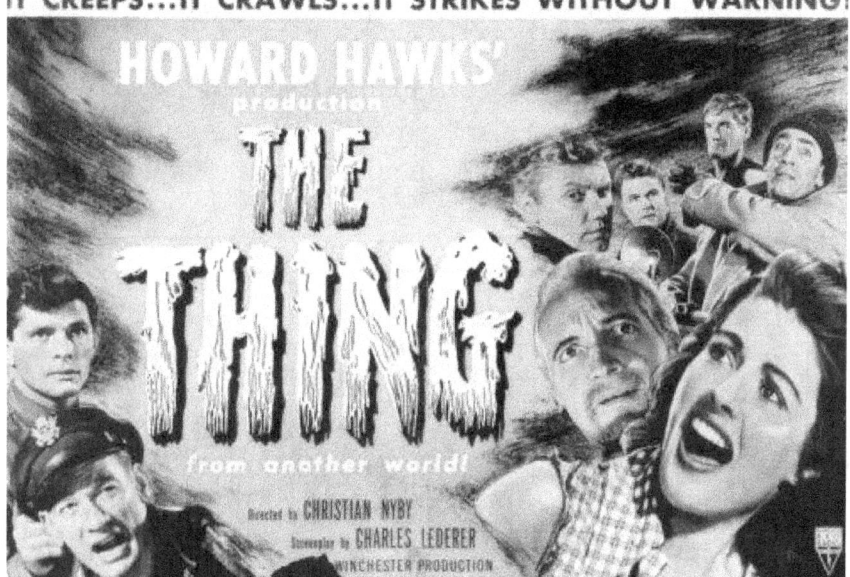

Scientists and soldiers examine flying saucer-like artifact found in the Artic in *The Thing*.

A more famous and decidedly benevolent visitor from another planet made his feature-film debut in *Superman And The Mole Men* (Lippert, 1951), though the Man of Steel had previously appeared in animated cartoons (from the Fleischer Paramount studio) and two serials (from Esskay Productions at Columbia). In this short feature, which served as a trial balloon for the subsequent TV series, George Reeves and Phyllis Coates starred as Clark Kent and Lois Lane, reporters for the Metropolis Daily *Planet*, who have come to a small town investigating trouble stemming from the world's deepest oil-well drill (trouble with oil drilling – some things never change). Dwarfish subterranean people climb up to our world, where, frightened by all the wonders of the surface but frightening to the surface people, they are mistaken for hostile invaders and attacked by the townspeople. Only Kent – in reality Superman – can save the day. But when the mole men retaliate with their ray gun (which looks remarkably like a vacuum cleaner), can even the Man of Steel prevail? Filmed quickly and inexpensively, it may be trying for some audiences today, but kids loved it in first release, and the response justified the production of six seasons of "Adventures of Superman". In '78, Warners brought us *Superman* (called "the Movie" in publicity) and its sequels and "re-boots".

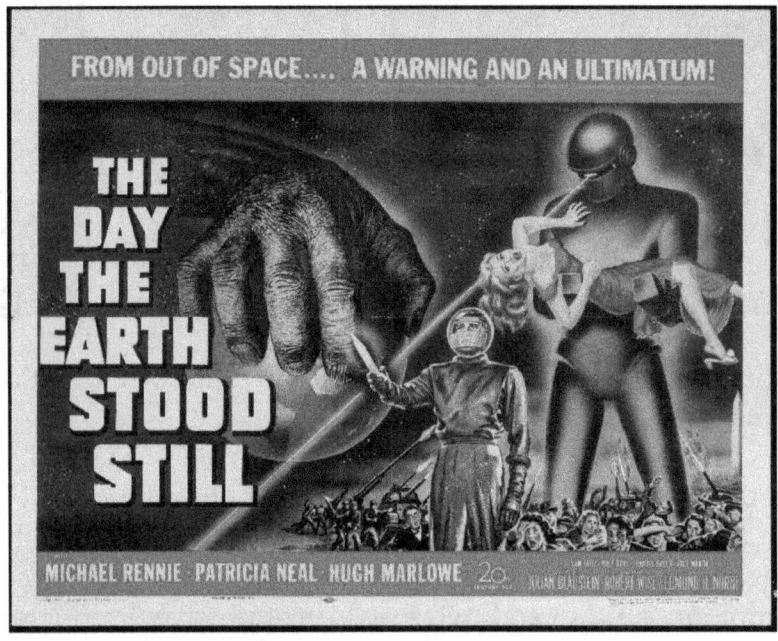

One of the outstanding science-fiction dramas of the period was *The Day the Earth Stood Still* (20th Century-Fox, 1951), a level-headed story about an alien (Klaatu, as played by Michael Rennie) who arrives on Earth offering to bring us into a galactic federation of peace – but only if we renounce our warlike behavior. Misunderstandings leave Klaatu wounded and fleeing into the city (Washington, DC), where he seeks to understand why Earth-people are so belligerent and why they fear him so. And he must reach an answer soon, for his companion, Gort, a robot, will presently activate and lay waste to this unworthy world. As a show of strength, Klaatu arranges for the cessation of all power – excepting, mercifully, hospitals and planes in flight – for an hour. The plan somewhat backfires, and it is up to one of Klaatu's Earth friends to try to save the day. A powerful – perhaps too powerful – message picture, it has stood the test of time, unlike its misguided remake (Twentieth Century Fox, 2008).

Film-makers Ivan Tors and Curt Siodmak created the OSI – the Office of Scientific Investigation – for *The Magnetic Monster* (UA, 1953). In the threadbare *film noir* style, later exemplified by TV's "Dragnet", the story unfolds when unaccountable magnetic disturbances lead to the discovery of "serenium", a new element created by a lone-wolf researcher. Highly radio-active, it also "grows" – extending magnetic force to draw in anything around it to increase its mass. Our heroes (including frequent SF hero Richard Carlson) realize that, unchecked, serenium could literally destroy the world! Their efforts to locate the element, and to neutralize it, are presented in straight-forward documentary style, with Carlson's ever-foreboding narration keeping viewers up on the plot. Tors and Siodmak envisioned a whole series of hard-science feature pictures, but the only big-screen follow-up was the stereoscopic *Gog* (UA, '54), in which an investigator looks into bizarre murders at a secret research station where a pair of non-humanoid-shaped robots (Gog and Magog, named for Biblical titans) are central to the not-very-mysterious doings. Here, the emphasis on explaining each scientific principle slowed down the action, and the way events were depicted detracted from rather than enhanced the mystery. But a good cast, including veteran character star Herbert Marshall, hero Richard Egan, and heroine Constance Dowling, and the two well crafted and somewhat eerie robots keep it interesting. Though further features never appeared, the OSI returned for a couple of episodes of Tors' "Science Fiction Theatre" TV series.

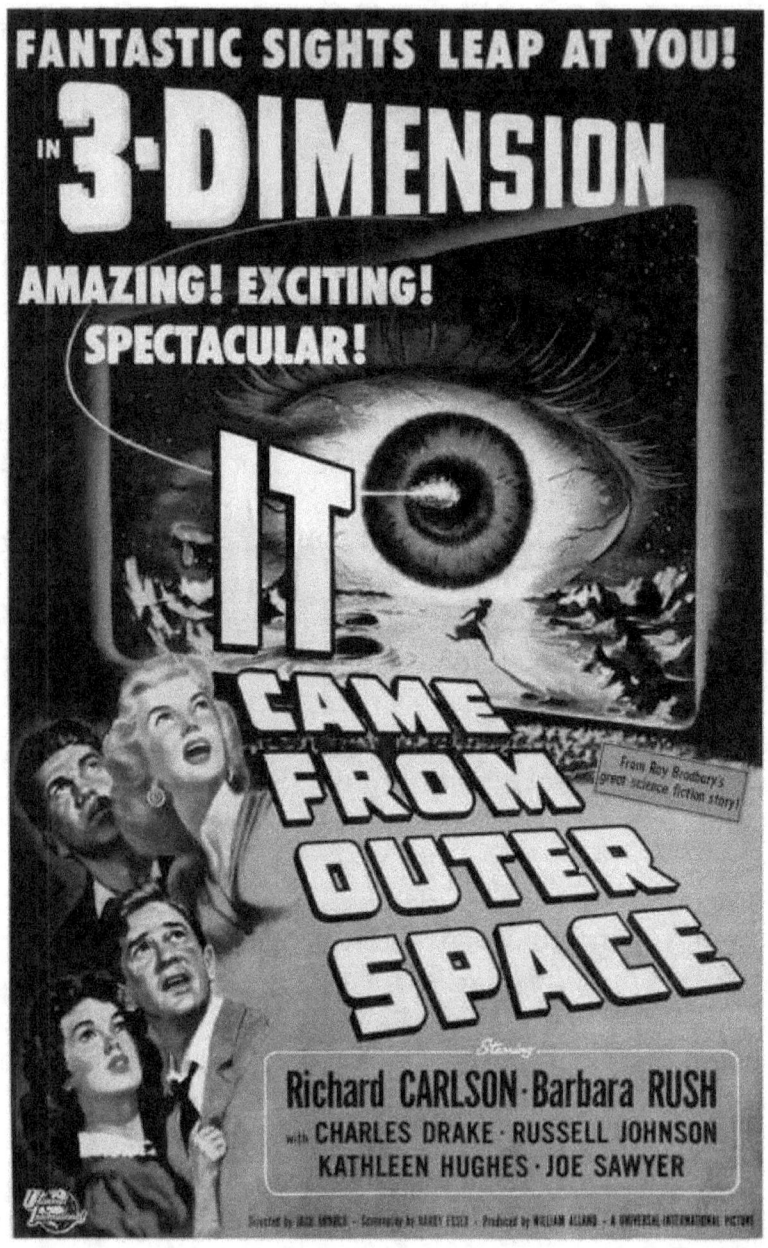

Though it was the exception rather than the rule, sometimes big-name science-fiction literature writers ventured into the film field. (Robert A. Heinlein's *Space Cadet* was the basis for the "Tom Corbett, Space Cadet" TV series, and his pilot for another series was re-edited into *Project Moonbase* [Lippert, 1953]). But one of the most well known writers outside the *genre* was Ray Bradbury, whose print work inspired *The Beast From 20,000 Fathoms* (*Q.V. in fantasy*). His best film was *It Came From Outer Space* (U-I, '53), the story of a crashed alien ship the inhabitants of which are merely trying to be left alone in their isolated desert redoubt while they repair their ship. Hideously ugly by Earth standards, and therefore scary and suspect, they are, as the story tries to say, just guys like us. Richard Carlson pretty much solidified his stalwart science-guy character in this, as he and heroine Barbara Rush try to keep level heads and stay between the aliens and the panicky townspeople. While most '50s "sci-fi" pictures were about destroying the monsters, this was about understanding.

Murky moors and quaint rural settings gave *Devil Girl From Mars* (British Lion, 1954) an eerie quality that mostly overcame the very inexpensive look of the picture. Forced to land at a distance from her target, London, Nyah the striking Martian woman (Patricia Laffan) makes do, cutting off the locals from outside help and using her giant robot Chani (which looks like an art-deco refrigerator), and prepares to take Earthmen back to her home to help re-populate the depleted civilization. Given the premise of a later film, *Mars Needs Women* (American-International TV, '67), that planet had a hard time balancing its population.

Universal Pictures, by now distributing through its parent company Universal International, got back into the thriller market by adapting their old monster stories to the new science-fiction craze. They even produced 1954's *Creature From The Black Lagoon* in 3-D (a stereoptical process mimicking depth), giving a startling look to the story of scientists (including '50s sci-fi stalwarts Richard Carlson and Richard Denning) who go exploring for Amazonian fossils and find more than they bargained for, and of the living fossil (Ben Chapman on land, Ricou Browning in the water) who conceives a passion for a beautiful girl (Julia Adams). The "gill man", an amazingly well crafted suit worn by the two performers, was such a success that all later fish-men either looked like him or went to ridiculous lengths to *not* look like him. Two sequels followed, making the gill-man the last of the great Universal monsters: *Revenge of the Creature* ('55) and *The Creature Walks Among Us* ('56); in the latter the gill-man undergoes surgery that basically robs him of his unique quality, ending the series. Other fish-man pictures include *The Monster of Piedras Blancas* (Filmservice Distributors Corporation, '59, an interesting counterpoint to the gill-man), *The She Creature* (A-I-P,'56), and *Destination Inner Space* (World Entertainment Corp., '66).

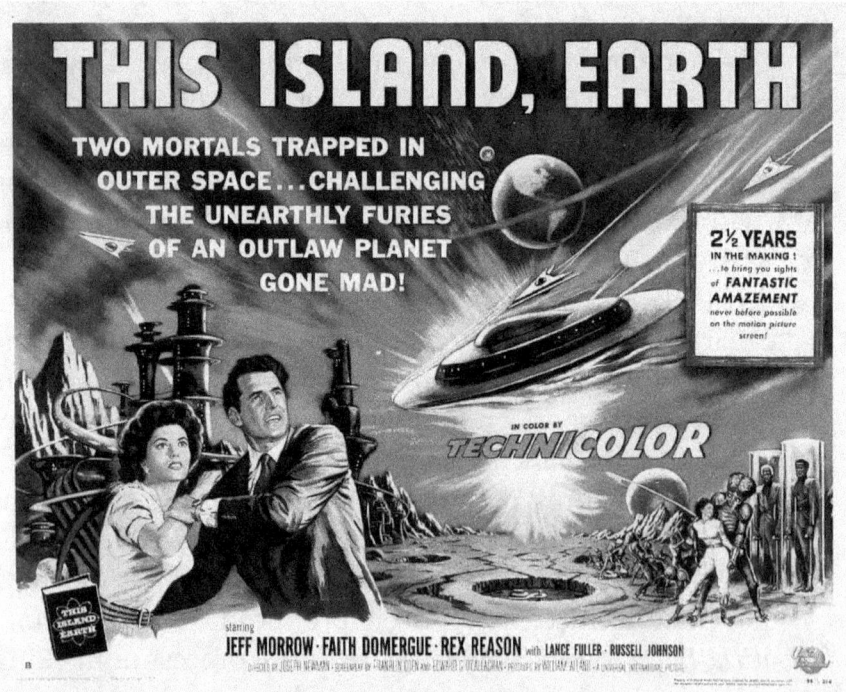

Beautifully rendered in startling Technicolor, *This Island Earth* (U-I, 1955) related the story of visitors from the besieged planet Metaluna, come to Earth to recruit – or compel – the geniuses of our science to save them from invaders. The first two-thirds or so was based on Raymond F. Jones' novel, but once Exeter (Jeff Morrow) removes his two scientist-friends (Rex Reason and Faith Domergue) from home to outer space, the screenplay deviated sharply. The film opens with a mystery, as a green ray saves our hero, Cal Meachum, from a plane crash, and then compounds it with an array of scientific gadgets the like of which Cal has never seen. Given the opportunity to learn more, he ends up being kidnapped to Metaluna, where their enemy has the aliens on the ropes. The somewhat unsatisfying conclusion is a far cry from Jones', where a "united nations" of outer space attempts to settle matters, and the fate of Earth among the stars hangs in the balance. Still, the film version is exciting and thought-provoking, and (at the behest of the Front Office) includes a "monster face", the impressive but unlikely insect-like Mutant. Other Universals tried the various sub-*genres*, like big-bug (*Tarantula* ['55]), lost civilization (*The Mole People* ['56]), prehistoric monster (*Monster on the Campus* ['58]), and youth-regeneration (*The Leech Woman* ['60]).

Columbia was in there pitching, with fantasy stories utilizing Ray Harryhausen's excellent table-top animation, but one of his pictures was "pure" science fiction: *Earth Vs. The Flying Saucers* (1956), in which spinning discs from a dying world bring would-be conquerors to our planet. Clever integration of real disaster footage with the ships, and the almost lifelike way in which Harryhausen depicts the craft, make the saucer scenes eerily effective. Many clever ideas are worked into the story, not all of them persuasively but still entertainingly. The climax, with scenes of destruction all over Washington, DC, is exciting and conclusive, and similar sequences in *Independence Day* (20th Century Fox '96) are clearly the grand-children of this invasion-from-outer-space thriller.

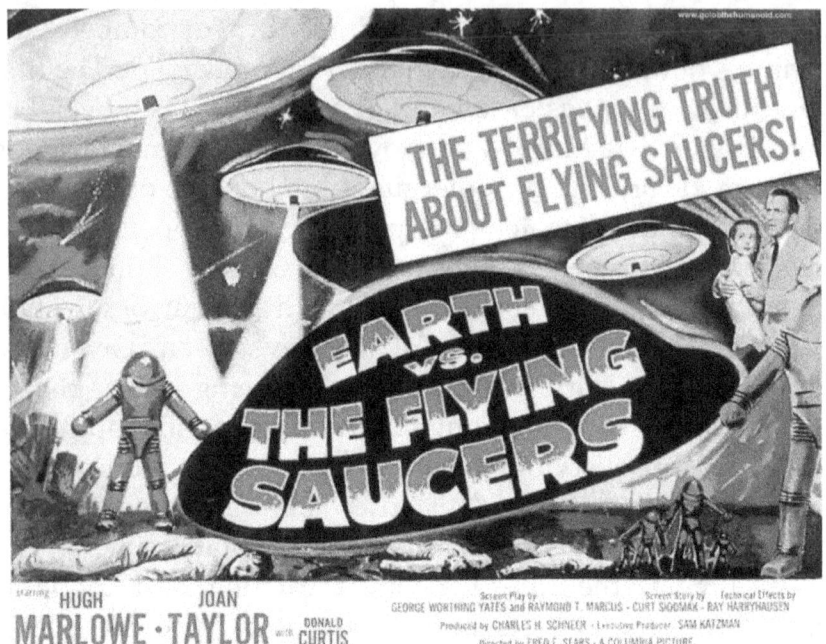

THE TERRIFYING TRUTH ABOUT FLYING SAUCERS!

EARTH vs. THE FLYING SAUCERS

Starring HUGH MARLOWE · JOAN TAYLOR with DONALD CURTIS

Screen Play by GEORGE WORTHING YATES and RAYMOND T. MARCUS · Screen Story by CURT SIODMAK · Technical Effects by RAY HARRYHAUSEN · Produced by CHARLES H. SCHNEER · Executive Producer SAM KATZMAN · Directed by FRED F. SEARS · A COLUMBIA PICTURE

What may be the quintessential '50s "sci-fi" movie is *Creature With The Atom Brain* – it has not just one but a bunch of creatures and they do have atomic-powered artificial brains. A cheapie from producer Sam Katzman, this 1956 Columbia release starred Richard Denning as a police scientist trying to solve the mystery of "atom-ray powered" corpses created, it proves, by a tame foreign doctor (Gregory Gay) in the pay of an exiled gangster plotting revenge on those who booted him out of the U.S. The finale, with a dozen or so creatures attacking the cops all at once, is a corker.

Perhaps the best of the "space opera" pictures was from the most prestigious studio. Metro-Goldwyn-Mayer, which boasted "more stars than there are in heaven", produced this 1956 adventure, in which United Planets cruiser C-57-D arrives on a rescue mission to Altair IV, the *Forbidden Planet*,

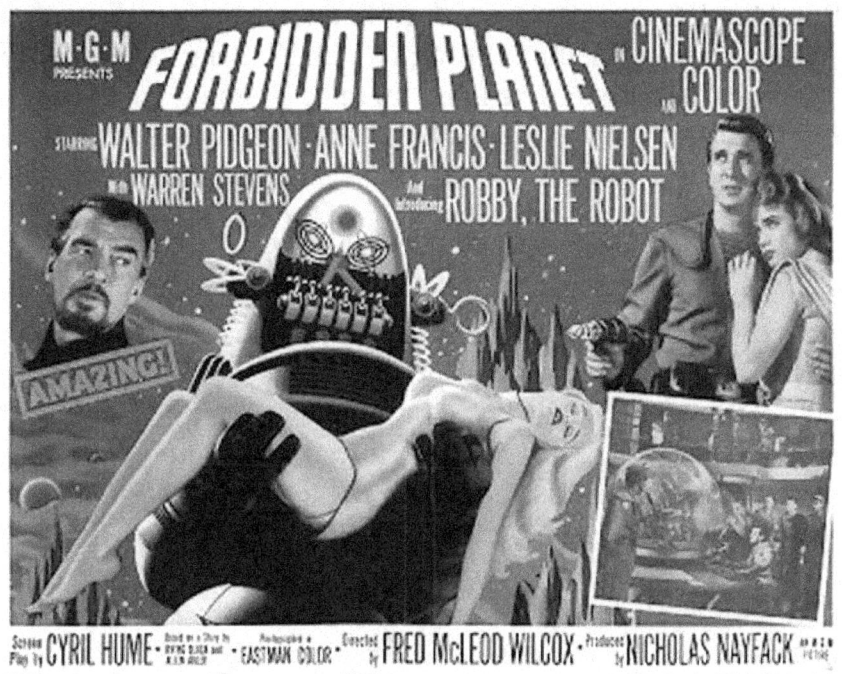

only to discover the previous ship's personnel all dead but one: Morbius (Walter Pidgeon), who has lived in peace with his daughter Altaira (Anne Francis), and who is greatly disinterested in being rescued. Morbius warns Captain J.J. Adams (Leslie Neilson, long before he turned to comedy) that "forces" on the planet will rise up and destroy the interlopers, and by gosh, they do, as an unseen power lays waste to spacemen and their equipment. The supporting character Robby, the Robot; a strong script, adapted in part from the Shakespeare play *The Tempest*; top-notch set design; and eye-popping special effects (including animation provided by the Walt Disney studio) make this an outstanding picture in the tradition that buoyed up the original "Star Trek" series in the next decade.

Backward time travel violates the laws of physics as we know them, so for now we'll call such films science-fantasy and let them fall on that side of the line in the next chapter. But Allied Artists' *World Without End* (1956) *is* science fiction – the heroes, catapulted through a "time barrier" – end up in the future, where they remain; there's no "going back". Once they're there, they settle into a battle between the usual "norms" and "mutants" (atomic radiation, naturally, the culprit), but also court intrigue as their new hosts have widely divergent ideas about these intruders. Very well done, with a double helping of ideas explored, enough to set it apart from its obvious inspiration, *The Time Machine* (though there was a lawsuit about it). And one more thing makes it interesting: one of the stars is Rod Taylor – who'd star in the official adaptation of the Wells classic just four years later!

Two films in this period would make an interesting double feature: *The Monolith Monsters* (U-I, 1957) and *The Night the World Exploded* (Columbia, '57). In the former, a meteorite-borne mineral threatens to over-run the Earth, as, when wet, it draws the element silicon from anything around it – including people. But the bigger picture is that the mineral grows to towering heights, until the spires collapse under their own weight, and then the fragments begin to grow. In the latter, another modest (was there any other kind) thriller from producer Sam Katzman, unexpected Earth tremors threaten society, leading investigating scientists to discover a mineral, dubbed "Kirkite" (for its discoverer, who is killed making the discovery) that, exposed to air, increases in size until it explodes. Such disruptions wreck the land, even causing volcanoes to erupt. Interestingly, *both* pictures utilize the same stock footage of a dam being blown up (from *Born to Be Wild* ['38], a Republic melodrama) to resolve the problem (though in traditional '50s style, what might happen *next* time is ignored).

A sensationalistic title conceals a surprisingly erudite film, Paramount's 1958 *I Married A Monster From Outer Space*, that tells the story of inhabitants of a small town kidnapped and

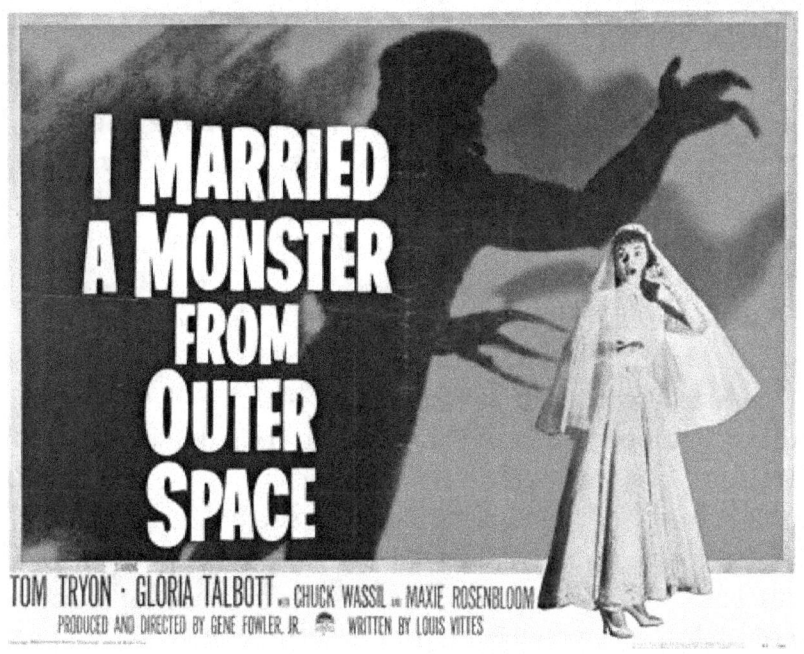

I MARRIED A MONSTER FROM OUTER SPACE

TOM TRYON · GLORIA TALBOTT with CHUCK WASSIL and MAXIE ROSENBLOOM
PRODUCED AND DIRECTED BY GENE FOWLER, JR. · WRITTEN BY LOUIS VITTES

used as templates for invaders (who transmit the physical characteristics of their captives to the aliens in the field) in hopes that they can mate with Earth women. Sound familiar? Yes, but the approach this time is on the human drama of a woman (Gloria Talbott) who knows there's *something* wrong with her bridegroom, but has no idea what it could be or how dangerous it could be for her – or all of Earth! The disguise of the husband (Tom Tryon) is disturbed by electrical discharges during a storm, but fortunately for the bride, she never sees his true appearance until the very end of the picture, as the Earth-people and their heroic canine pets do battle with the monsters.

At first as invisible as the "planetary force" in *Forbidden Planet*, the monsters of *Fiend Without A Face* (M-G-M, 1958) – detached thoughts given form by a scientist's experiment gone overboard – wreak havoc near a Canadian air base, leaving behind corpses with the brains sucked out! The very power of thought become manifest, the creatures become palpable in the last two reels as brain-and-spinal cord creatures in this British entry. Marshall Thompson, hero of several science-fiction films, must try to stop the "fiends", by the tried-and-true but ridiculous method of blowing up a nuclear control-panel to shut down the reactor powering them. Will he succeed in time to save pretty heroine Kim Parker? What do *you* think?

Earlier entitled "Invasion of Mars", *The Angry Red Planet* (A-I-P, 1960) found four stereotypical Earth explorers (stalwart hero Gerald Mohr, elderly scientist Les Tremayne, ethnic engineer Jack Kruschen, and inevitable babe Nora Hayden) arriving on Mars to find it a bizarre reddish environment with monsters and a society uninterested in contact with their solar neighbors. Most appealing of the Martian animals is the bat-rat-spider-crab, an unlikely evolutionary development but fun to watch as it skitters across the landscape. When it is fended off by being blinded, audiences could only hope that the poor critter's eyesight would be restored when its frozen eyeballs thawed. The production, by Norman Maurer (better known as a latter-day "Three Stooges" producer) and Ib Melchior (an actual science-fiction writer), was poorly received, at least in part to the use of "Cinemagic", a special effect in which black looks washed out and everything else looks bright red, for the Martian exteriors. But its saving grace is that it is told in flashback from Hayden's point-of-view, and her understanding of what happened could be considered... poor.

An accidentally created portal into the future casts *The Time Travelers* (A-I-P, 1964) into an era where "normal" humans live in cave-cities and hope to build a rocket to escape a devastated Earth and its mutant inhabitants. Working on their "time viewer", a team (Preston Foster, Merry Anders, Philip Carey and Steve Franken) discover it is permeable and step through it into a barren landscape which proves to be (gasp) the future! Trapped there, they work on a way back but

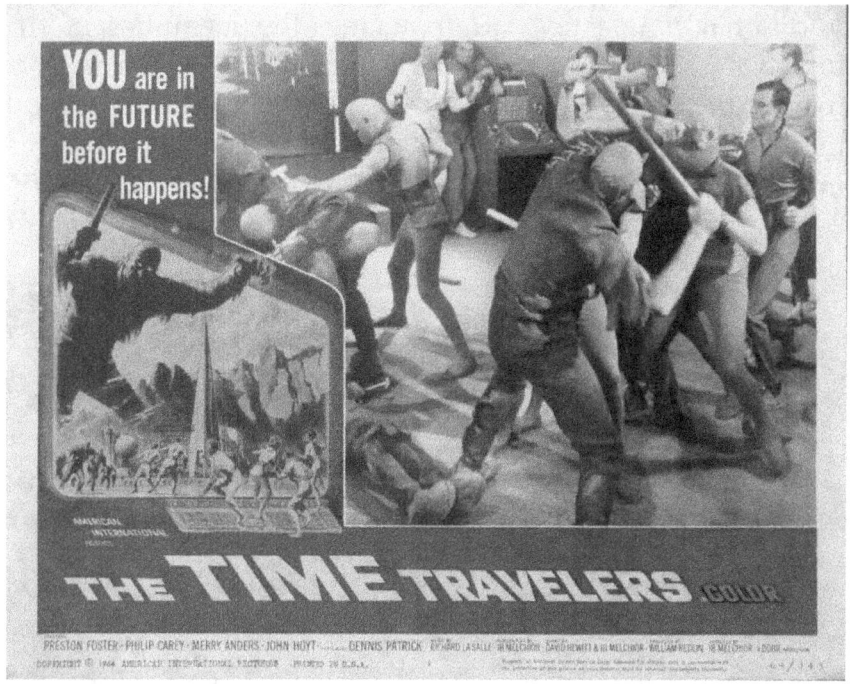

also help the future people in their bid to leave Earth for another planet. A guest appearance by monster-magazine editor Forrest J Ackerman enlivened the proceedings, which, after solidly being science fiction, edged into the realm of fantasy when the travelers built a new portal to return to their own time – and almost made it.

Since then, Science Fiction took a turn, more often comingling with Fantasy, and when not, taking a decidedly downbeat view of the future. At first glimpse, the 1982 Warner Brothers release, *Blade Runner*, based on Philip K. Dick's "Do Androids Dream of Electric Sheep?", seems like more gloom and doom, but by the end of the film we see it is only the metropolitan areas that are a mess, crowded, smoggy, awash in advertising. Again, a cop is the hero, on the trail of a "replicant", an artificial human who leaves a trail of death in his wake as he seeks to delay his own pre-programmed inevitable demise. Harrison Ford (the cop) and

Sean Young (who may be a replicant herself) play out a traditional movie love affair against the inequities of the future in a stylish and compelling narrative. Since its original release, the film has been re-cut, restored, and altered several times, making it all things to all people, but muddling its impact. After many years, a sequel, *Blade Runner 2049* (WB, 2017), appeared, to a mixed reception.

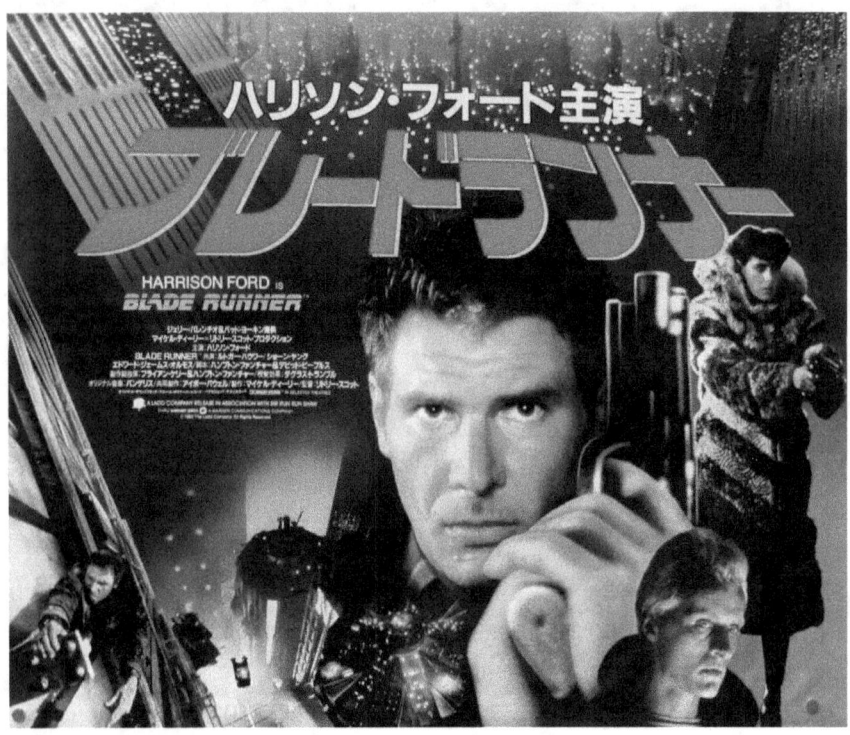

As you've seen, even some of these science-fiction stories slipped a bit into the realm of fantasy, particularly when it came to Martians. And a couple of series jump the line completely, so it's an easy step from science fiction to…

CHAPTER FOUR: FANTASY

THEY WERE LUMPED in with "horror" films, but only the ones about Dracula, zombies, genies, witches, Cat People, and other creatures of magic all fall solidly into fantasy. So too, though there will be argument about this, do the giant dinosaurs that survive to bedevil modern man. These fantastic characters trace their cinematic origins to the mute cinema, to experimental and brief adaptations of Poe and Shelley. Universal's monsters would receive the most attention, certainly, with the later Hammer Films' versions a close second, but all of the studios dipped into the field: 20th Century-Fox, Columbia, even mighty M-G-M took their shots, and the poverty-row producers like Monogram and Producers Releasing Corporation gave audiences a (low-budget) alternative in the '40s. While "horror" was the by-word in the '30s and '40s, and "science fiction" the catch-phrase of the '50s, there was really little difference in the approach. Studio writers didn't much care about distinctions between the two *genres*, and so mixed elements of either with the other. The stars of fantasy overlapped those of the gothic-style science-fiction titles: Karloff, Lugosi, Lionel Atwill, George Zucco, all effective as menaces or red herrings, and the kids and grown-ups alike loved 'em all. And it wasn't just monsters – there were Arabian Nights fantasies, talking animals, even a dancing worm. After the "sci-fi" style faded out after 1962, the "horror" film diverted off into "slasher" pictures (many of which have no fantasy elements and are an extreme form of drama), and fantasy has become the driving force for blockbusters like the "Star Wars" and "super-hero" pictures (fantasies using the form of science fiction), and the "Harry Potter", "Narnia", and "Twilight" series.

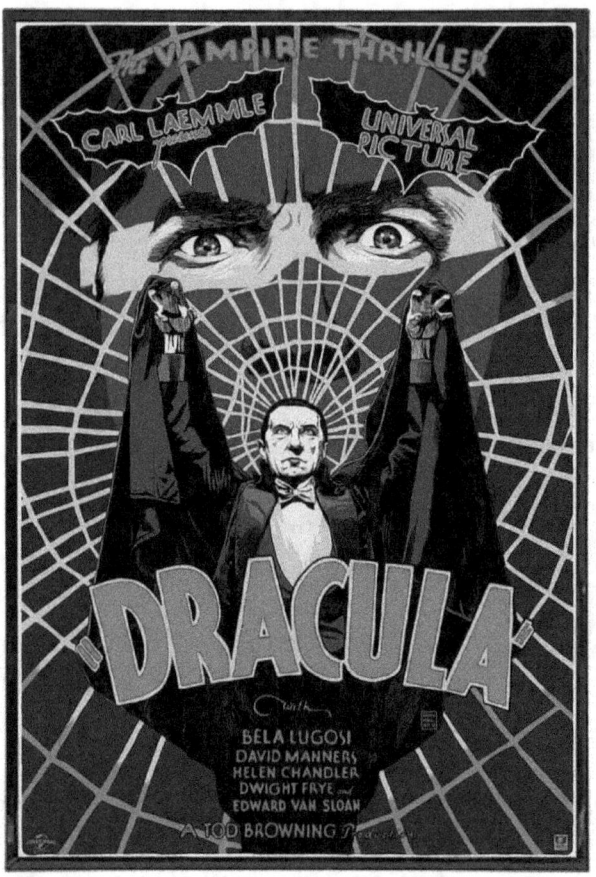

Dracula was a proven hit on Broadway when Universal Pictures bought it for the screen. But they passed on the otherwise unknown star of the play, Bela Lugosi, in favor of the number-one "horror" star, Lon Chaney. Chaney's untimely death led to Lugosi retrieving his role in the theatrically staged 1931 Tod Browning production. After a well photographed opening filled with mystery and suspense, a musty castle filled with spider webs and vampire women, the story resorts to a close adaptation of the stage story, as Dracula seeks his victims in the English neighborhood of Dr. Seward's sanitarium, until the knowledgeable Professor Van Helsing (Edward Van Sloan) is summoned. A simultaneously photographed Spanish-language version was much more cinematic but lacked the star power of Lugosi. When Lugosi turned down the role in Universal's *Frankenstein* (1931), he virtually sealed his fate as a featured player instead of star, though he did sometimes rise to the top, as in the serial *The Return of Chandu* (Fox Film, '34) and in the '43 Columbia Pictures release, *The Return of the Vampire*, where, as Armand Tesla, he is caught and destroyed during the World War, only to be resurrected by a *Nazi* bombing raid 20 years later to revenge himself on the people who doomed him to the darkness. Lugosi would play the Count on film only once more, in *Meet Frankenstein* (*Q.V in Comedy.*), but the two films would cement him as Dracula in the public's eye.

Universal scored again with *The Mummy* (1932), with Karloff as an ancient Egyptian courtier, buried alive for the sin of trying to bring his dead-princess love back to life, and himself restored to life in the 20th century, where, adopting modern dress and a new identity, he seeks the reincarnation of his beloved princess Anhk-es-en-amon – who just happens to be living right there in Cairo as Helen Grosvenor (Zita Johann). But she has a life and a boyfriend, and doesn't want to relive the past, and when her friends come to her aid, they discover "Ardeth Bey" is a wielder of the Black Arts, who will stop at nothing to regain his princess. Later "Mummy" pictures left this one alone and created new mummies to chronicle. Universal remade *The Mummy* in 1999 more in name than events, but there have been many others to carry on the Old Traditions, like Kharis (*Q.V. below*).

Fredric March, it seems now, could play anything:

Columbus, Dr. Jekyll and Mr. Hyde, Twain, LaFitte, and even that shade whom all men fear in *Death Takes A Holiday* (Paramount, 1934). When Death leaves his post, the world goes wild as accident victims, suicides, even the aged survive. But the film concentrates on the "vacation", as Death, adopting the human guise of Prince Sirki, seeks to learn what life is all about and to discover why he is so feared. But he finds more than he bargains for, when the beautiful, ethereal Grazia (Evelyn Veneble) falls in love with him – and he with her! Can Death claim this mortal girl, taking her from all that Life has to offer? It is a choice he must make, balancing his love against his selfishness. The plot was revisited in *Meet Joe Black* (Universal, '98). A similar take on the idea of Death off the job is *On Borrowed Time* (M-G-M, '39), where an aged, ailing grandfather (Lionel Barrymore) tricks Death (Sir Cedric Hardwicke) into a trap, preventing his own – and everyone else's – death.

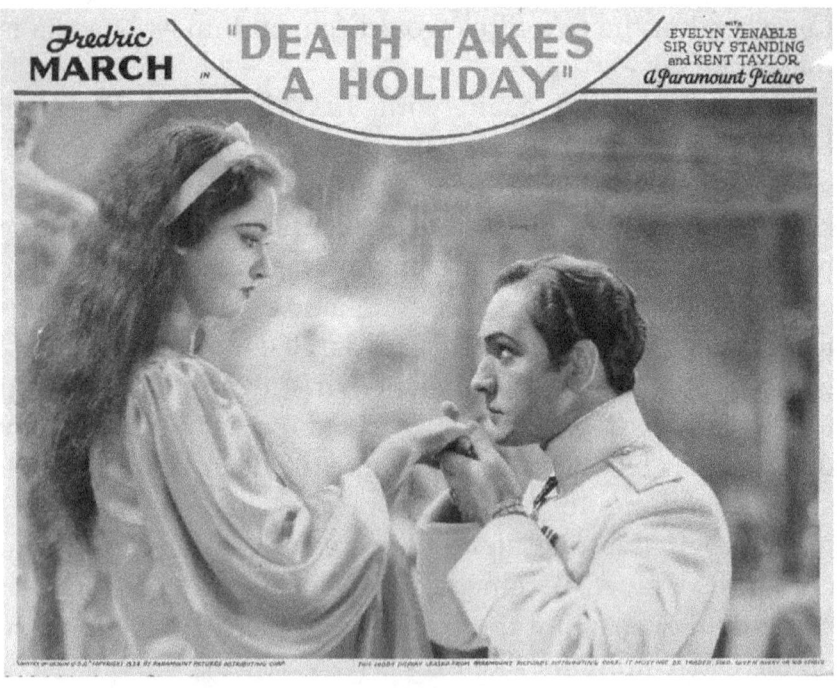

You'll run into Stan Laurel and Oliver Hardy several times in these pages (*Q.V. in Comedy and in Short Subjects*), but their most delightful outing was the 1934 Metro release, *Babes In Toyland*. Stanny Dee and Ollie Dum are employees in Santa's Workshop, but take time out to become involved in trying to help beautiful Bo-Peep (Charlotte Henry) escape the toils of the evil and lascivious Barnaby (Henry Kleinback [soon to become Henry Brandon], in a wonderfully over-the-top portrayal). They succeed, but Barnaby, banished, returns with an army of bogeymen to wreck the town and capture Bo-Peep. Luckily, the boys have misread instructions and built one hundred six-foot toy soldiers instead of six hundred one-foot toy soldiers. But can even this "March of the Wooden Soldiers" (the film's re-release and TV title) win the day? Other Laurel and Hardy features and shorts often played with minor fantasy elements, but this is their masterpiece. A Disney re-make, with Gene Sheldon and Henry Calvin (both from Disney's popular "Zorro" TV series as the Stanny and Ollie characters), appeared from Buena Vista in 1961.

Thorne Smith had a corner in stories of the fantastic and the funny, with ghosts, living statues, and gods and titans, and perhaps the most famous was *Topper* (M-G-M, 1937), the story of a staid banker whose life is turned topsy-turvy by the ghosts of two clients. Fun-loving George and Marion Kerby (Cary Grant and Constance Bennett), teasingly aid their former banker Cosmo Topper (Roland Young), trying to free him from the shackles of a domineering wife and hum-drum life, causing him frustration and embarrassment along the way. Billie Burke as Mrs. Topper, Alan Mowbray, and Arthur Lake (Dagwood to "Blondie") brighten the film, a highlight of the career of producer Hal Roach, whose connection with comedy (Laurel and Hardy, "Our Gang", and so much more) was a beacon to film-makers and movie-goers alike. Topper's saga continued in *Topper Takes a Trip* (UA, '38), based on the Smith sequel, and *Topper Returns* (UA, '41), an all-new comedy, designed for the then-current audience, in which

Topper assists the ghost of a wrongly murdered girl (Joan Blondell) in preventing the killing of the intended victim. Eddie "Rochester" Anderson appears as his usual character, having left Jack Benny's employ. In the '50s, a popular television program re-told Topper's adventures.

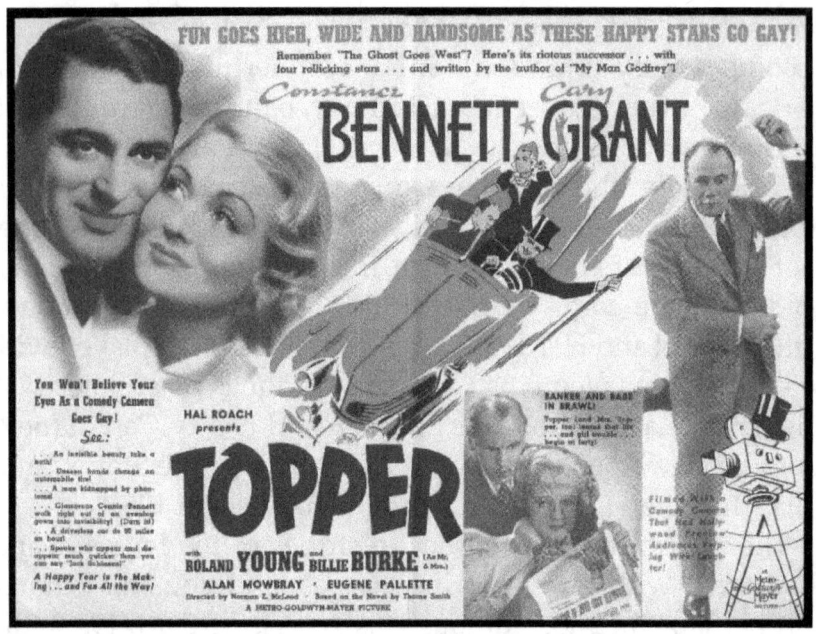

No one but Walt Disney knew that his plan for a feature-length animated fantasy would be a hit. But Walt went ahead with his project, and he and his new distributor, RKO Radio, would profit greatly from the release of his *Snow White and the Seven Dwarfs* in 1937 to world-wide accolades. The story, with the seven miners helping the young princess when her wicked stepmother tries to eliminate her, had been told before and would be told again, many times (including a misfired ice-skating fantasy version, *Snow White and the Three Stooges* [20th Century-Fox, '61]) but Disney's version is the one people cherish, though it isn't a very representative version of the original fairy tale. Max Fleischer, Disney's chief competition in the field, responded with *Gulliver's Travels* (Paramount,

'39), but, while entertaining in its own way, it showed that Disney was the boss of this arena.

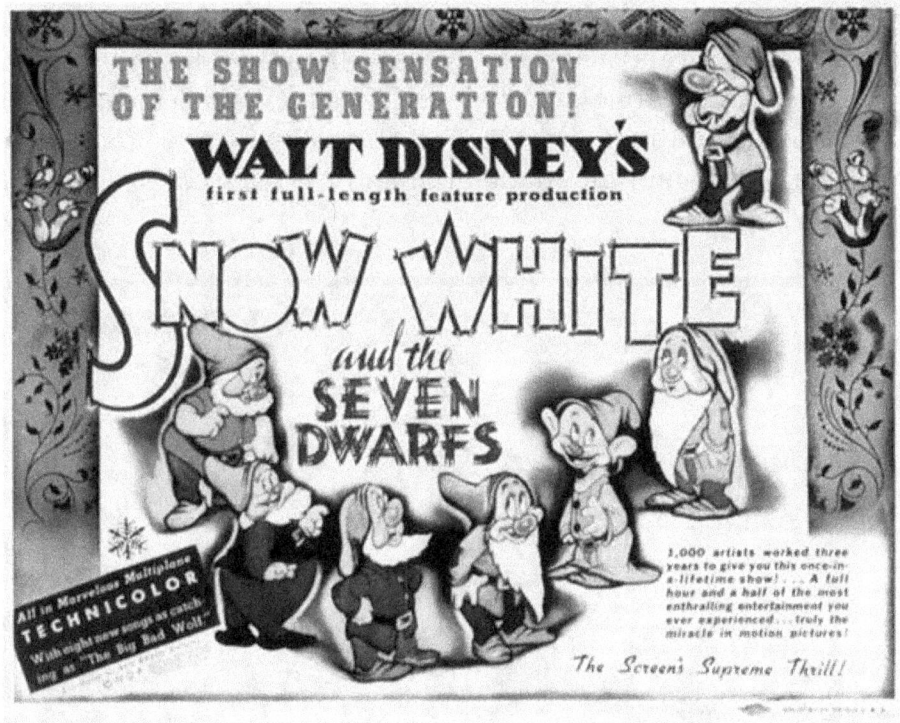

Charles Dickens wrote his story of miserly Ebenezer Scrooge in December of 1843 as entertainment and as a cautionary tale, but it was the charm of the story that attracted film-makers many times over the years. Lionel Barrymore became so associated with the role on an annual radio broadcast that, when M-G-M decided to film *A Christmas Carol* in 1938 and Barrymore's injuries precluded his playing the part, Lionel himself appeared in the picture's trailer – the "preview of a coming attraction" – to place upon his replacement Reginald Owen the seal of approval. However, deprived of its top box-office star, Metro scaled back the production, shortening the running time and deleting a few scenes. Though the final version was still first rate, with fine performances and excellent period settings, it just wasn't as big a hit as expected. It would be overshadowed by the British Renown Pictures Corporation 1951 release of *Scrooge* starring Alistair Sim and a host of stars as the fantastic characters, with superior stylishness. Other versions of the story include two animated outings, "Mr. Magoo's Christmas Carol" (NBC-TV, '62; a very faithful adaptation) and *Mickey's Christmas Carol* (BV, '83).

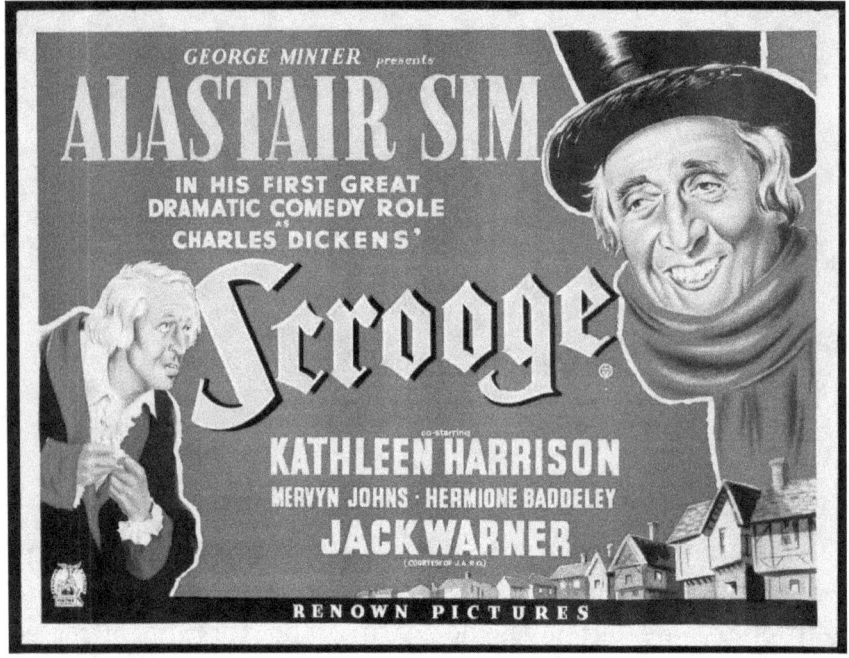

The Arabian Nights were long a source of film wonder, even before *The Thief Of Bagdad* (UA, 1940), was brought to the screen by Alexander Korda, a remake of the also wonderful version starring Big Doug Fairbanks (UA, '26). Marvelous to behold, the remake tells of Prince Achmed (John Justin) and his unlikely ally Abu the thief (Sabu) in their attempts to save the kingdom, defeat the evil vizier (a wonderful characterization by Conrad Veidt), and rescue the inevitable beautiful princess (June Duprez). The wonders of the flying mechanical horse, the robot woman assassin, the giant spider, and especially the Genie (Rex Ingram) delight the eye and thrill the imagination. In this vein, you'll also find yet *another* remake, *Il ladro di Bagdad* (Titanus '61; *The Thief Of Baghdad* [M-G-M] in US) with Steve Reeves, and the animated *1001 Arabian Nights* (Columbia, '59) with Mister Magoo (a truly entertaining version), and even the three "Popeye" featurettes (*Q.V. in Short Subjects*).

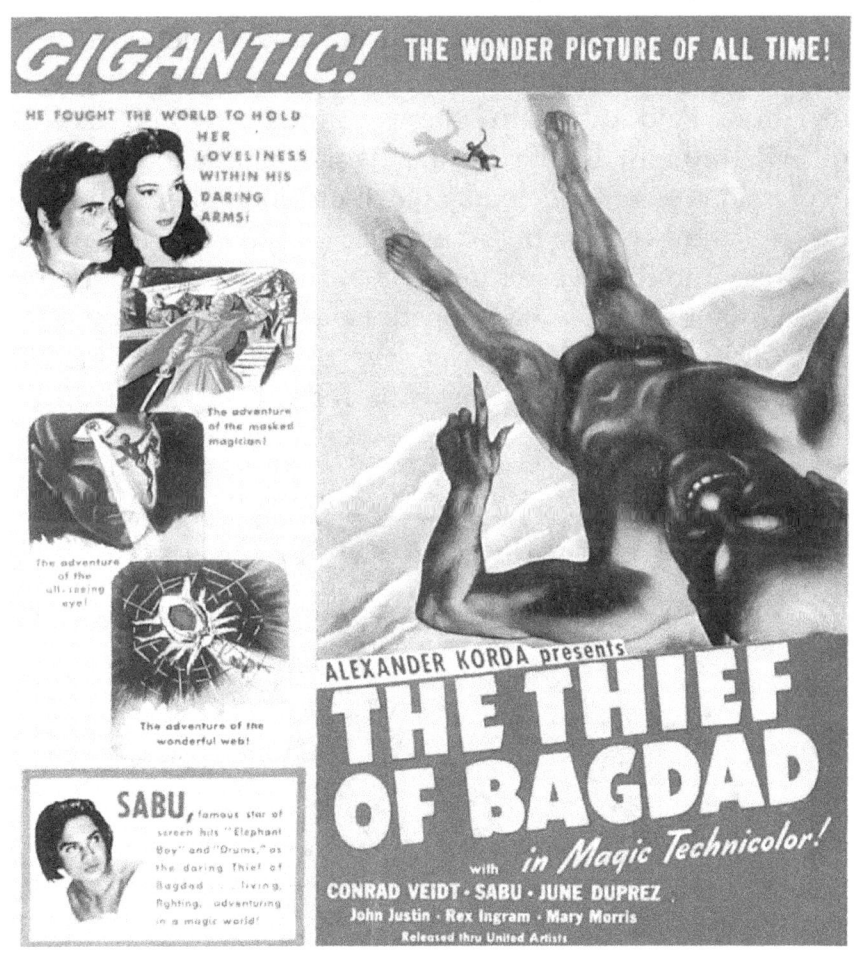

Walt Disney believed that animation and music were

inextricably linked and that each could synergize the other. His masterwork in this field came to the screen in the 1940 RKO Radio release, *Fantasia*, wherein fauns, angels, demons, hippos, gods, dinosaurs, even Mickey Mouse and the film soundtrack danced to the accompaniment of Stokowski's conducting of classical themes. In "The Rite of Spring" the story of evolution is told, from unicellular life to the last days of the dinosaur; "Dance of the Hours" brings us ballerina elephants and hippos and dancing crocodiles; Beethoven's Sixth Symphony conjures up the frolics of the ancient Greek gods; Mickey Mouse (a guaranteed ticket-seller) becomes "The Sorcerer's Apprentice", and Modest Mussorgsky's "Night on Bald Mountain" shows us the power and majesty of evil (brought to life by the demon Chernobog, whose expressions were modeled by Bela Lugosi) that fade with the dawn and the coming of "Ave Maria". It brought great music squarely into the lives of millions of movie-goers, though it wasn't the hit Disney had hoped. Later attempts, *Make Mine Music* (RKO Radio, '46), *Melody Time* (RKO Radio, '48) and *The Three Caballeros* (*Q.V.*), better captured the audiences of the '40s.

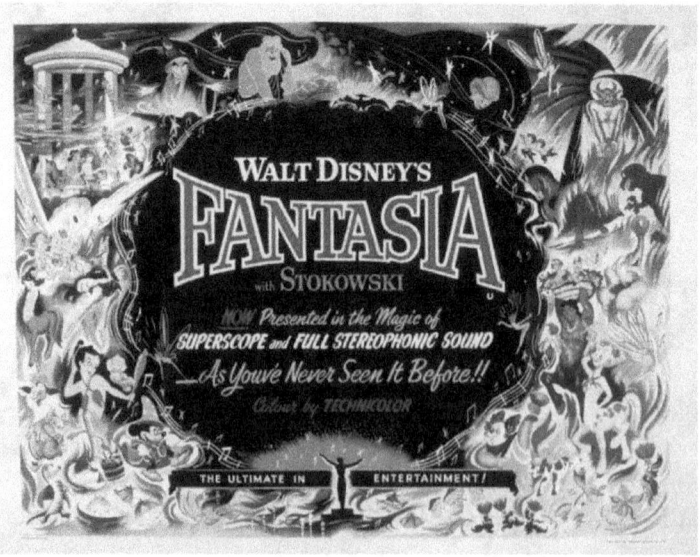

A successful Broadway show, *Heaven Can Wait*, was renamed *Here Comes Mr. Jordan* for Columbia release in 1941 (see below). A tender-hearted heavenly "messenger" (Edward Everett Horton) snaps up the soul of a prize-fighter (Joe Pendleton, played by Robert Montgomery) just before his plane crashes. But as he learns from his boss, Mister Jordan (Claude Rains), the fighter wasn't scheduled to die! Jordan tries to rectify things by installing the fighter's soul in the body of a just-murdered millionaire, but Joe tries to use his new body to win the championship title he'd missed out on, by hiring his old manager, Max Corkle (Jimmy Gleason). Meanwhile, the scheming wife and lawyer who'd murdered the millionaire are trying to find a way to bump off moneybags – this time for keeps! Add in a pretty dame (Evelyn Keyes), and you've got a clever, heart-warming, and highly entertaining piece of fantasy. The '78 Paramount remake, reverting to the original title, starred Warren Beatty, with James Mason as Mr. Jordon. The original title was used in 1943's *Heaven Can Wait*, a 20th Century-Fox picture directed by Ernst Lubitsch, in which Henry Van Cleve (Don Ameche) relates to the Devil (Laird Cregar) the story of his life, expecting his misdeeds will condemn him to Hell. A delightful, witty romp with the whimsical touch for which Lubitsch was known.

Universal Pictures had mined the "horror" field through the '30s until the excesses of *The Raven* (*Q.V. in Drama*) had killed their golden goose. But, after a triumphant re-issue of their two landmark "horror" classics, a new administration regained the field and in 1941 scheduled a film starring their new "King of Horror", the son of the man with a thousand faces, who was billed as "Lon Chaney, Jr." as a special entitled *Destiny*, featuring an all-star cast, in the mode of their previous *Son of Frankenstein*. But as often happened, the film was scaled back, and given the more bankable title *The Wolf Man*. Bitten by a werewolf, young Lawrence Talbot becomes a werewolf himself, doomed to eternal life and cursed to kill the one he loves – which is bad news for his new girlfriend (Evelyn Ankers). Chaney, as hard as he tried, was not too believable as the son of an English Lord, especially in the company of Claude Rains as that Lord, Warren William, Patric Knowles, and Bela Lugosi and Dame Maria Ouspenskaya as the gypsies, but kid audiences were crazy about him, leading to the inevitable sequels as he crossed paths with the other Universal monsters in *Frankenstein Meets the Wolf Man* ('43), *House of Frankenstein* ('44), and *House of Dracula* ('45), in which he was finally "cured" of the curse... Except that the cure seemed to have worn off, because the Wolf Man was back in *Meet Frankenstein* (*Q.V. in Comedy*).

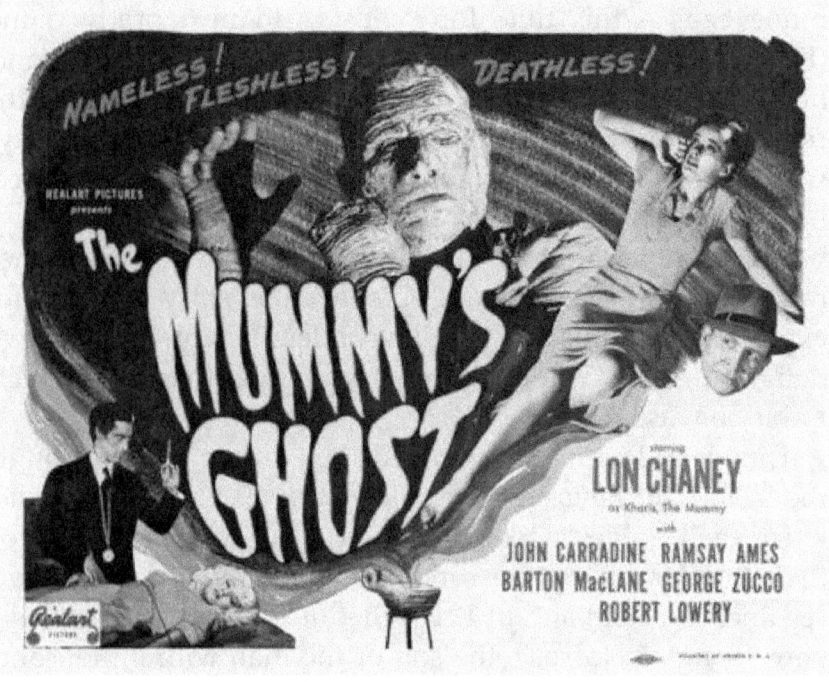

As the "Frankenstein" series jumped from science fiction to fantasy with the inclusion of the Wolf Man (and later Dracula), the "Kharis" series slipped over the same way, as reincarnation entered the picture. In *The Mummy's Ghost* (Universal, 1944), we learn that Kharis' lost love has returned to life in the body of young Amina Monsouri (Ramsay Ames), for, as hieroglyphics on Ananka's tomb warn, her spirit was freed the moment her coffin was removed from its resting place 30 years earlier ("Ghost" seems to take place shortly after "Tomb", which was 30 years after "Hand", the first picture). Now, Kharis must locate the girl so that she may be returned to Egypt. But when the priest assigned to aid Kharis sees the beautiful girl, he is possessed by lust for her, which is unfortunate, Kharis being the jealous type. Surprisingly, in this picture the Mummy gets the girl, carrying her off into the swamp as she reverts (for no clear reason) to a mummified state. Only a year later (but a generation of story-time), Kharis and Ananka would resurface near a little Cajun village on the other side of the swamp (and not, as often claimed, in far-off Louisiana) in *The Mummy's Curse* ('45), the last of the series. Hammer's picture *The Mummy* ('59) is not a remake of the Karloff film but of the first three Kharis pictures. Later similar films include *Curse of the Faceless Man* (UA, '58) and Hammer's follow-ups *The Curse of the Mummy's Tomb* (Columbia, '64) and *The Mummy's Shroud* (Twentieth Century-Fox, '67).

When a composer (Ray Milland) and his sister (Ruth Hussey) find and move into a charming old house on the seacoast, they soon discover that what seemed like a bargain comes with a sinister side; for the mansion is haunted by a spirit who is definitely *The Uninvited* (Paramount, 1944). Eerie happenings, a séance, possession, and an aura of impending doom make this among the scariest ghost stories ever to come out of Hollywood. Based on a popular mystery romance by Dorothy MacArdle, it features spooky settings and simple but effective special effects. For another scary ghost story, see *The Haunting* (M-G-M, '63). For more romantic tales, try *The Ghost and Mrs. Muir* (20th Century-Fox, '47) and *Blithe Spirit* (General Film Distributors, '45; UA in US).

In Columbia's 1944 *Once Upon a Time*, we meet young "Pinky" Thompson (Ted Donaldson) with a remarkable pet:

a caterpillar that dances to the tune, "Yes, Sir, That's My Baby". Hoping his pet, Curly, could become a star, he seeks out Broadway producer Jerry Flynn (Cary Grant), who sees a gold mine in the creature and avariciously cuts the boy out of the picture. Feeling betrayed, the boy runs away, but later, when Curly turns up missing, Jerry learns a lesson about life and tries to win back the boy's trust by leading the hunt while giving up his own dreams of wealth. A charming, mild fantasy about the relationships of children and adults and how each generation fails to understand the other.

Disney was always pushing the limits of what movies could do, and his early fascination with combining live-action and animation, as seen in his "Alice in Cartoonland" shorts, reached its zenith in a picture geared to bolster Pan-American brotherhood during the Second World War. In *The Three Caballeros* (RKO Radio, 1945 [produced 1943]), Donald Duck and his friends José Carioca and Panchito sang and danced with Aurora Miranda, Dora Luz, and other Latin American stars in a cinematic delight as they treat Donald to a holiday in Mexico and Brasil, with comedy, music, and amazing fantasy episodes. Disney's earlier featurette, "Saludos Amigos" (RKO Radio, '43) explored much the same territory, though without the significant live action/animation interaction. A later film to feature animated characters and live people side-by-side is, of course, *Who Framed Roger Rabbit* (BV, '88), another masterpiece of the form.

By the mid-'40s, the conventions of the Arabian Nights were so well known that a spoof of the *genre* could be a hit. Columbia's 1945 *A Thousand And One Nights* starred Evelyn Keyes as a genie who, love-struck for beggar-turned-prince Cornel Wilde, is naturally reluctant to help him secure the love of *his* life, the Princess Armina (Adele Jergens), but must because that's how genies work. Her attempts to foil his plans result in his losing her and returning to pauperhood, endangering his life. Phil Silvers, later TV's "Sergeant Bilko", is our hero's jive-talking sidekick "born a thousand years ahead of his time", who reluctantly follows our hero into danger. A beautiful Technicolor fantasy, it even featured an appearance by Rex Ingram, more or less reprising his genie character from *The Thief of Bagdad*.

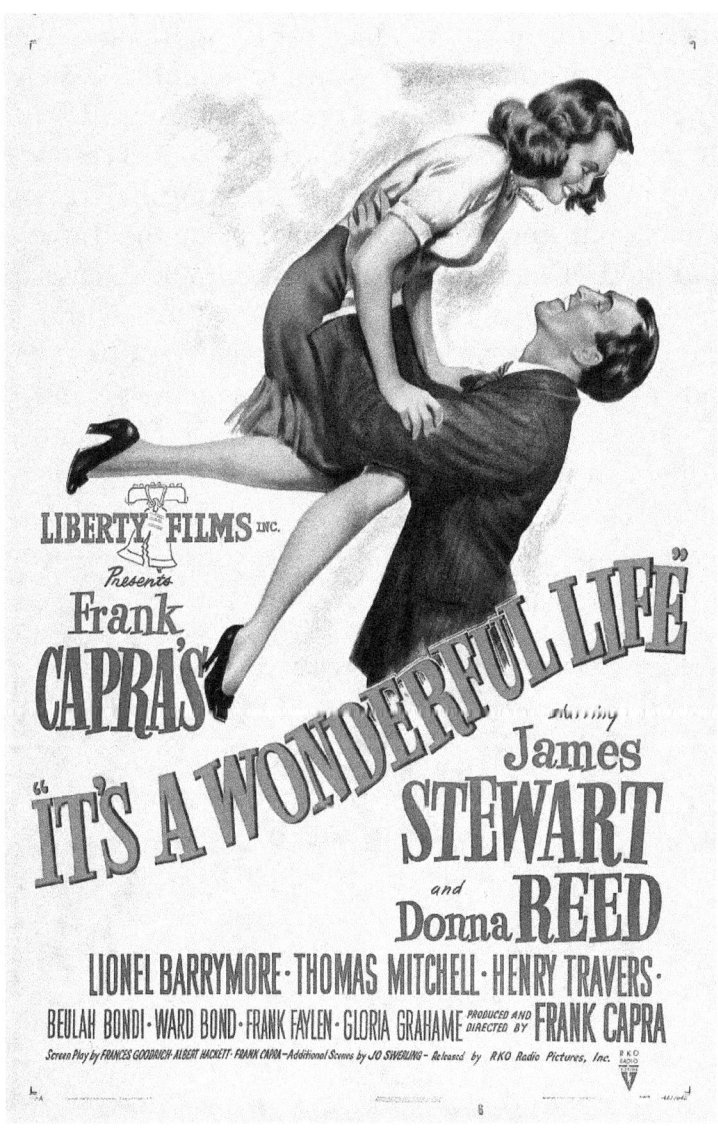

Probably the most endearing fantasy film of all is the Frank Capra picture, *It's a Wonderful Life* (RKO Radio, 1946), in which George Bailey (James Stewart) discovers what life would be like for those around him if he'd never been born – the hard way. When he finds his life (which he had once envisioned as involving world travel, adventure, and excitement but turned out to consist of staying home, being the rock to which others cling for support, and what he perceives as drudgery) has come to naught, leaving him facing ruin and disgrace, he contemplates suicide. But the timely intervention of Clarence Oddbody, angel second class, allows him to see that his life had meaning by erasing him from it. No one knows him, the town villain he'd worked so hard to hold at bay now runs the miserable excuse for his home town, and the people he loves are lost without him. Watching George beg for his life back, and the utter joy when he finds Zuzu's petals in his pocket (watch the picture; you'll understand) is an amazing scene. Capra was a master of corny old American values in pictures like *It Happened One Night* (*Q.V. in comedy*).

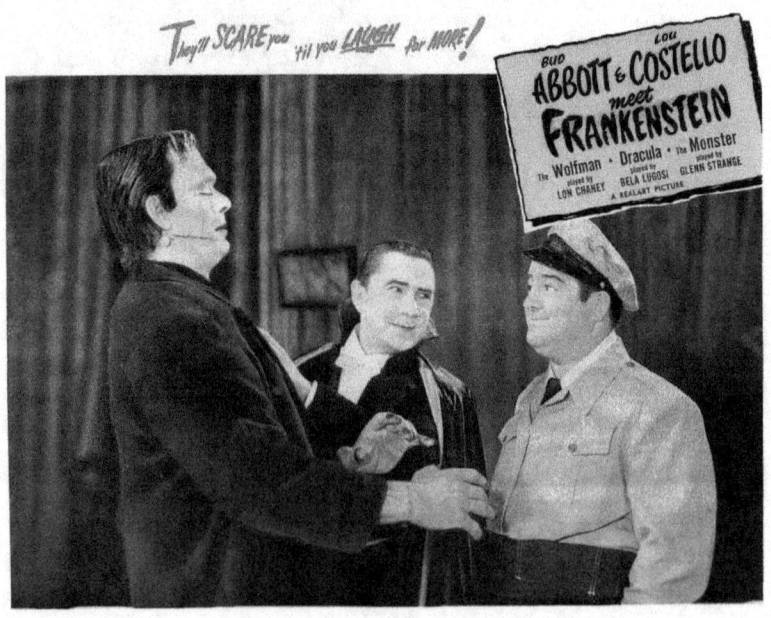

The team of Bud Abbott and Lou Costello (*Q.V. in comedy*) were the kings of funnymen in the 1940s, but their studio had become somewhat tired of them after the War. Seeking a new avenue for the boys, Universal assigned them to a picture ultimately titled *Meet Frankenstein* (U-I, 1948), which has proved to be one of their best and most enduring pictures. Part of its success is that the "monsters" are played straight. Except for a few bits of business between Wilbur Grey (Lou) and the Frankenstein Monster (Glenn Strange), all the funny stuff is left to the boys. When Dracula (Bela Lugosi) arrives in Florida, he joins Dr. Sandra Mornay (Lenore Aubert), who has lined up a perfect prospect for the Count's plan – to replace the Monster's brain with a new one, one so dumb, so pliable, that it will never rebel against Dracula's will – that is, Wilbur's brain. On Dracula's trail comes Lawrence Talbot (Lon Chaney), trying to foil the plan. Of course Wilbur's pal, Chick Young (Bud) figures Talbot's just crazy, but soon has reason to believe the man who says he turns into a wolf every night of the full moon ("You and eighty million other guys," cracks Wilbur). The very strong story-line, a serious "monster adventure", just has a couple of comics who get caught up in the action, making this picture a gem for "monster" fans *and* A&C fans.

A belief among olden-time mariners was the mermaid, the half-woman, half-fish that had its origins in the sirens of Greek mythology. By the 20th century, mermaids in movies were usually more benevolent than the man-killers of Old, often mischievous and curious about Men. So it was with *Miranda* (General Film Distributors, 1949) about a mermaid played by Glynis Johns who captures a man and only allows him his freedom on the condition that he take her to show her what life on dry land is like. The film has a very British understated charm to it, and generated *Mad About Men*, a belated sequel released by the same distributor in '54, in which Miranda again comes ashore, trading places with her look-alike cousin. Both films benefitted from the support of

111

popular character actress Margaret Rutherford. A Hollywood try at the same idea, *Mr. Peabody and the Mermaid* (U-I, '48) suffers from a harsh dose of intruding reality. For comparison, see the charming Disney version of the Hans Christian Anderson tale, *The Little Mermaid* (BV, '89).

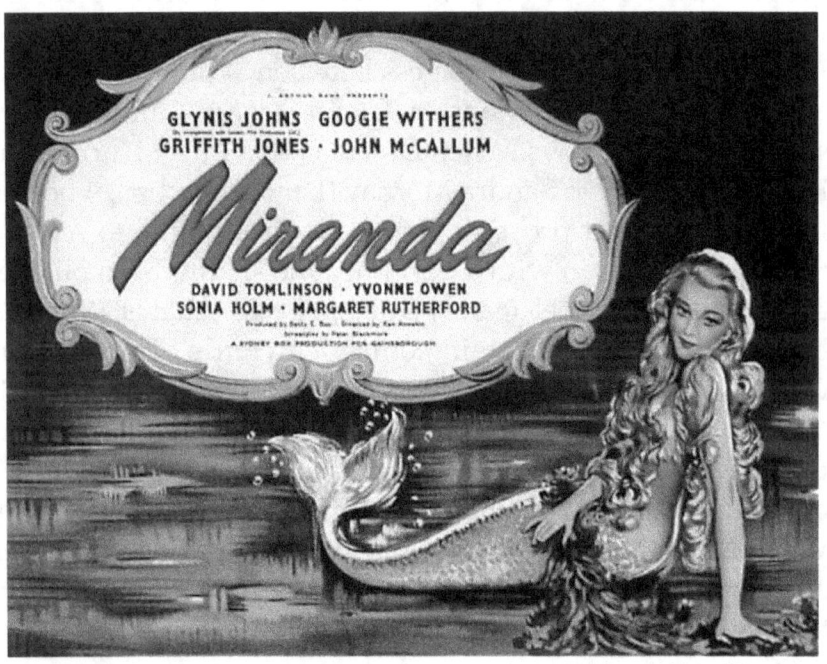

The re-release of the classic *King Kong* (*Q.V. in Adventure*) triggered a new wave of giant animals in the science fiction of the 1950s, but the dinosaurs depicted were too often too big (violating the square/cube law) or too evolutionarily challenged to be science, so they must be science-fantasy. Among the best was the 1953 Warners picture *The Beast From 20,000 Fathoms*, in which a "rhedosaurus" (animated by Ray Harryhausen), freed from an Arctic ice formation where it had been in suspended animation, migrates to the submarine canyons at New York City, along the way wreaking havoc, including demolishing a lighthouse (in a scene reminiscent of the Ray Bradbury story, "The Foghorn"; for the details of this, see *Keep Watching the Skies* by Bill Warren, McFarland). In its wake came numerous dinosaur pictures, including *Dinosaurus* (Universal, '60) and *One Million Years B.C.* (Warner-Pathé, '66; [Twentieth Century-Fox, '67 in US]).

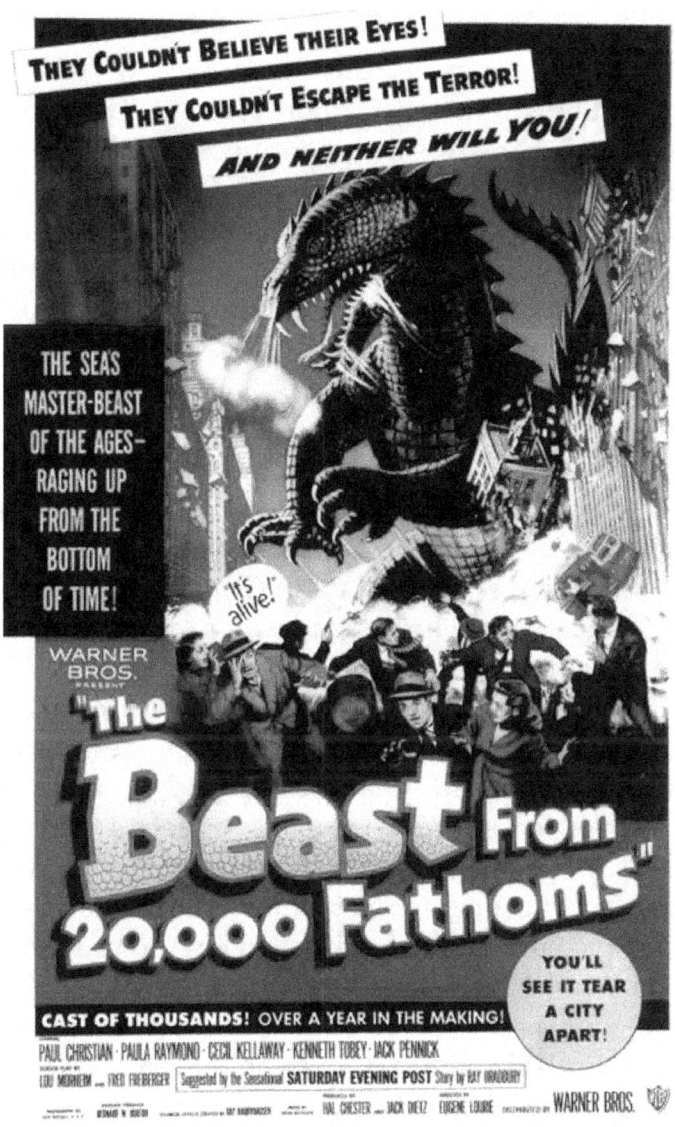

Beginning the dinosaur "offshoot" of "big bug" pictures was by far the best, *Them!* (WB, 1954), with James Whitmore and James Arness, and scientists Joan Weldon and Edmund Gwenn, on the trail of ants. But ants the size of freight cars! Their evolution stepped up by atomic radiation over generations, the ants have reached a size where their very existence threatens Mankind. Presented as a mystery (the nature of "them" is a puzzle solved slowly), the picture presents a serious, well considered idea of what might happen and how humanity would respond. That ants could not grow to such a size – their enormous weight would snap their legs long before they could grow that much – is a fact left out of the narrative, but the reality of the creatures, not animated models or photographically enlarged but full-sized armatures right there on the set with the actors, is too amazing to not accept. Among later films of this type, *Tarantula* (U-I, '55), and *The Black Scorpion* (WB, '57) are each interesting, though less startling, films.

The ultimate "dinosaur" of pictures is really more of a dragon, what with his radioactive-flame breath and all. An allegorical treatment of the destructive power of the nuclear age, atomic doom is personified in *Gojira* (Toho, 1954) as the monster causes the Hiroshima-level ruin of Tokyo. With footage of Raymond Burr replacing a Japanese actor, the film reached America in '56 as *Godzilla* King of the Monsters! (RKO Radio), and was such a hit that the monster, destroyed at the end of the picture, had to be "resurrected" in the form of a close relative for sequels – lots of sequels – and spin-off pictures with monsters like Rodan and Mothra. Toho continued making giant-monster movies from the '50s, slowly changing the city destroyers into saviors of Mankind, even comedians. After a brief shut-down from 1975 to 1984, Toho returned with new monster films, including their popular characters Godzilla and Mothra (who'd been a hero from the beginning).

Ray Harryhausen's animated science-fantasy movies had been hits on the double-feature circuit, and in 1958 he got the

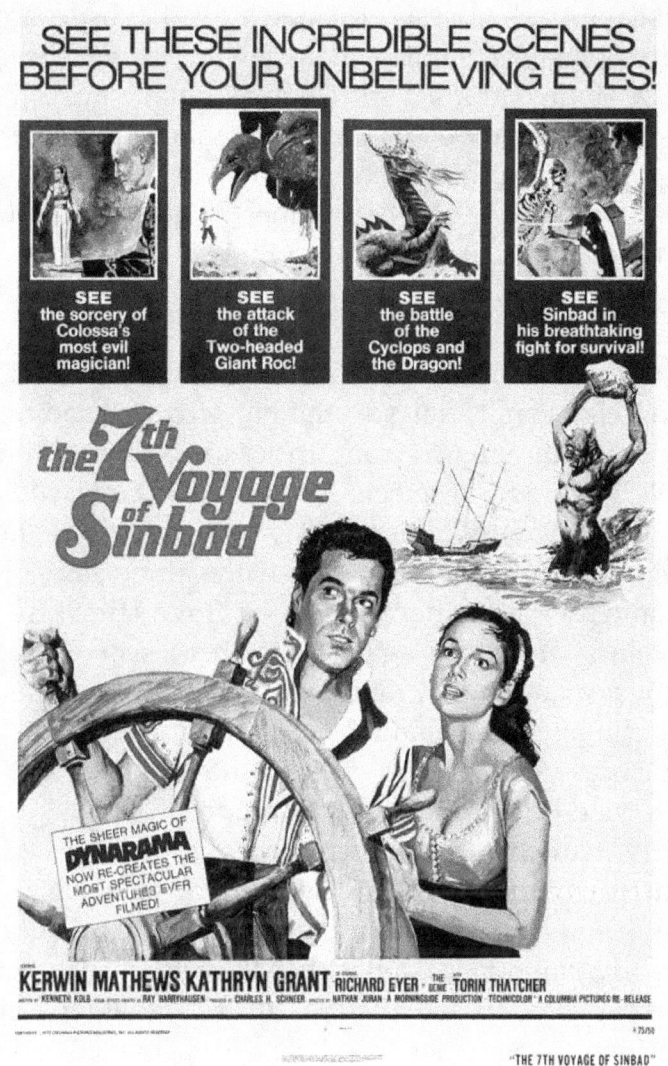

"THE 7TH VOYAGE OF SINBAD"

chance to make Columbia's fabulous adventure, *The 7th Voyage Of Sinbad*, with a diminished princess (Kathryn Grant), a dragon, cyclopes, and a dynamic sword-fighting skeleton, all perpetrated by fiendish wizard Sokura (played by the marvelous Torin Thatcher). Actor Kerwin Matthews proved a fine Sinbad, able to pantomime the complicated set-ups onto which animated characters, like the skeleton, were later added. Filmed primarily on location in Europe, the picture has a scope and majesty to match its fantastic scenario. Matthews played a similar character in *Jack the Giant Killer* (UA, '62), again battling Torin Thatcher, made by technicians who'd had the nerve to visit Harryhausen to study his techniques. Though a sneaky trick to play on the animator, the resulting film was a winner with kid audiences. Harryhausen himself returned to Sinbad years later, in *The Golden Voyage of Sinbad* (Columbia, '74) and *Sinbad and the Eye of the Tiger* (Columbia, '77).

Walt Disney made a fortune and entertained millions by adapting classic fairy tales to the big screen, smoothing out and stripping the subtext from stories like "Snow White" and *Cinderella*. His wide-screen Technicolor fantasy *Sleeping Beauty* (BV, 1959) trimmed 100 years out of the tale but included delightful characters like the three fairies, Flora, Fauna, and Merryweather, and added "love's first kiss" to the story, telling the story against the themes of Pyotr Ilyich Tchaikovsky, with new animation techniques and a rip-roaring climax, with valiant Prince Philip riding to the rescue of his princess, engaging in single combat the evil Malificent, who's turned herself into a giant dragon.

The best of the time-travel stories is *The Time Machine*, brought to charming life by George Pal in a 1960 M-G-M picture. It tells, in flashback, the story of Victorian scientist George (dynamic Rod Taylor, hardly a textbook Victorian) and his voyage to the distant future, where he finds a civilization in desperate need of old-fashioned guts. The peaceful Eloi live on the surface in eternal sunshine, but are a stagnant remnant of Man, and are essentially cattle to the subterranean Morlocks, who still have technology but have devolved to cannibalism. George tries to rouse the Eloi to oppose the Morlocks, but finds they pretty much don't care. But when the Morlocks capture a girl (Yvette Mimieux) of whom George is fond, he takes matters into his own hands. Trimming down the novel and adding a few crude touches didn't hurt the box office of this opulent adaptation, one of

Pal's last features. A different take on the future is found in *Things to Come* (UA, '36), based on Wells' 1933 novel *The Shape of Things to Come*, with war, privation, and eventually plenty coming to Mankind.

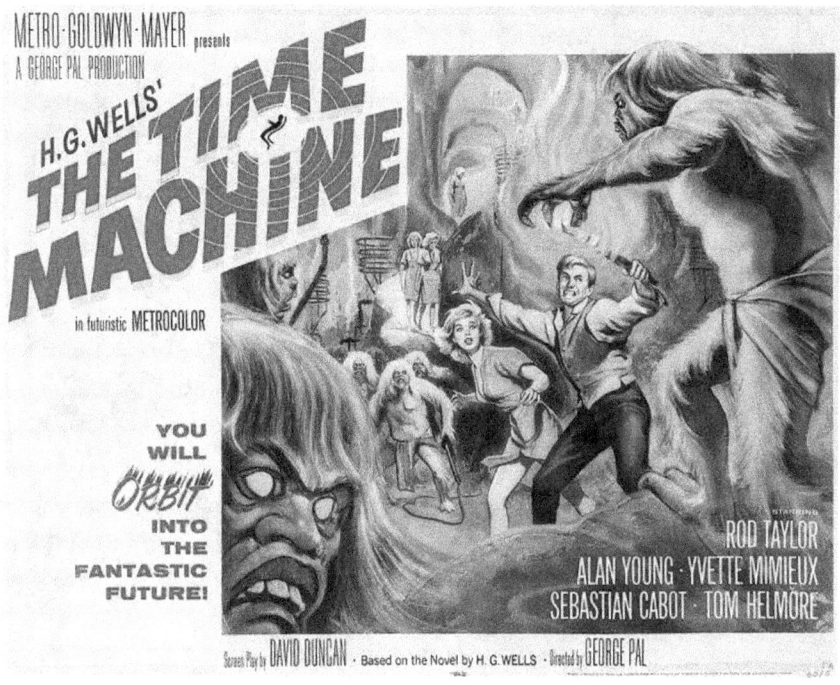

Another in the "giant monster" sweepstakes (with a man in suit instead of an animated model) was the King Brothers production, *Gorgo* (M-G-M, 1961), with a new twist: mother love. When Gorgo is brought from the Irish Sea to London, his captors are unaware that the dragony beast is a baby! Soon his mother comes crashing across town to retrieve her child, wrecking local landmarks (which Gorgo's captors had thoughtfully passed on their triumphant drive through the city). Mankind is helpless against the biggest mother of them all, who retrieves her child and survives to be starred in a series of comic-book sequels from Charlton Publications. Directed by Eugène Lourié, who had already helmed two previous dinosaur pictures (*The Beast from 20,000 Fathoms*

(*Q.V.*) and *Behemoth the Sea Monster* (Eros Films, '59; *The Giant Behemoth* [AA, '59] in the US), *Gorgo* is a worthy completion to his parlay.

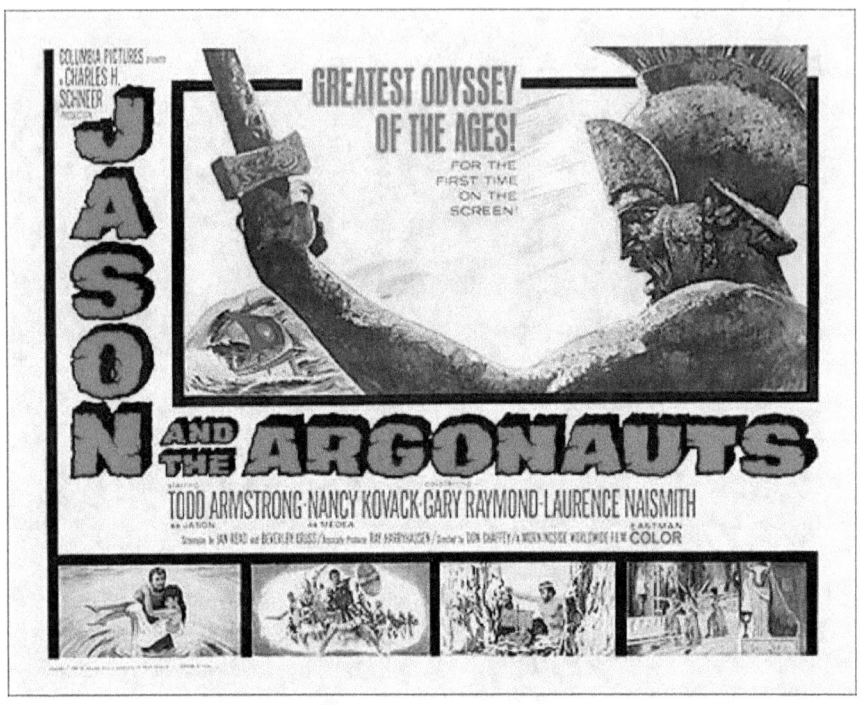

Jason and the Argonauts (Columbia, 1963) is another great adventure into the realm of fantasy. Todd Armstrong as Jason outfits his ship, the *Argo*, and, with a crew including the mighty Hercules, sails to fabled Colchis to obtain the Golden Fleece and win back his kingdom from his usurping uncle. On the trip, the Argonauts encounter Talos, a living giant statue of bronze, the Hydra with its multiple heads, and the children of the Hydra's teeth, living skeletons! All these wonders were accomplished on the screen through the painstaking genius of Ray Harryhausen, using the stop-motion technique he dubbed "Dynamation", as he had in *The 7th Voyage of Sinbad* (*Q.V.*) and others. Unfortunately, the story stops abruptly, without Jason regaining his throne; a planned sequel was canceled even before the film was released.

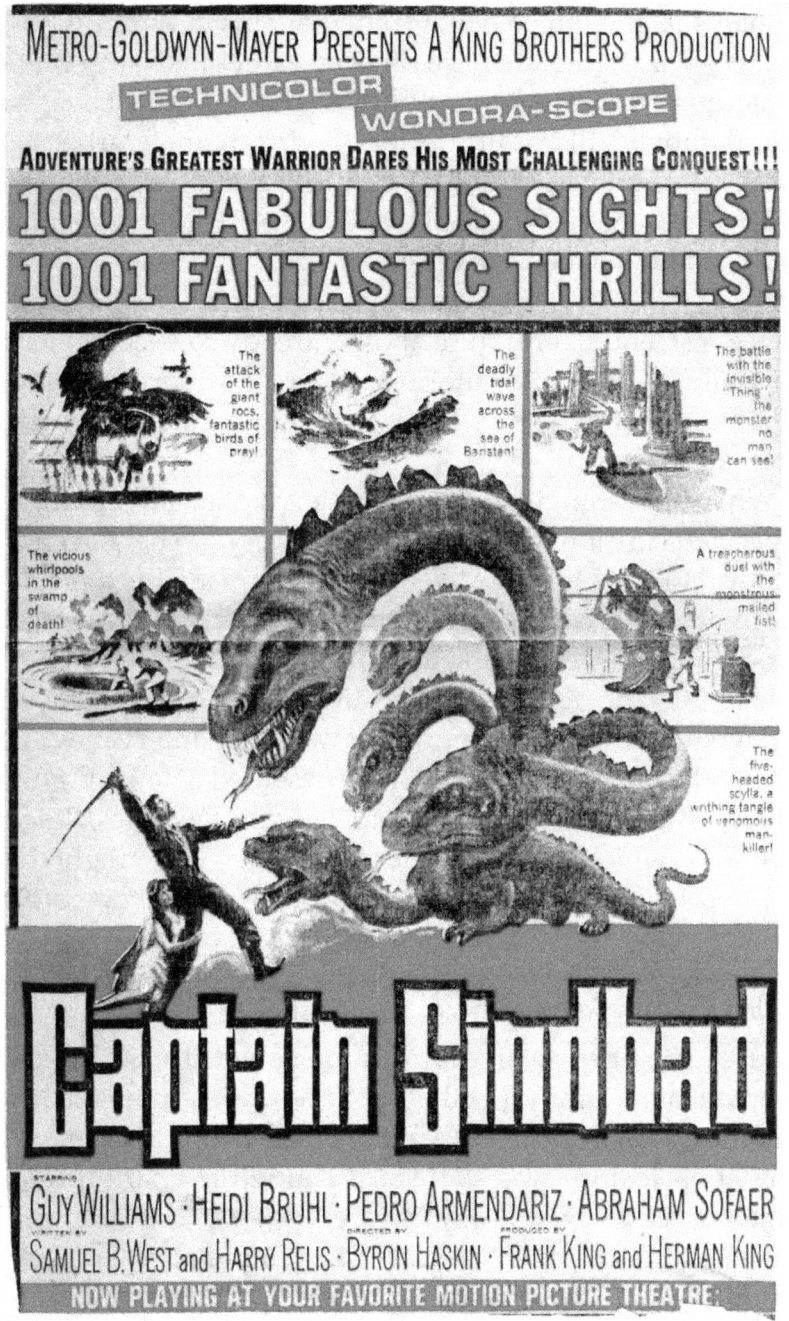

The King Brothers followed *Gorgo* with an Arabian-Nights style adventure, *Captain Sindbad* (M-G-M, 1963) with Guy Williams as the fabled sailor, pitted against a tyrant with his own pet wizard. Mechanical devices, rather than stop-motion armatures, portrayed the menaces, but the result was still entertaining. Villain El Kerim (Pedro Armendariz), who keeps his heart in a crystal case in a high cupola in the midst of an unreachable no-man's-land, is unstoppable – unless Sindbad and his men can brave the perils and reach the heart. Even as they try, El Kerim has the inevitable beautiful princess (Heidi Bruhl) in his power, ready to execute her for her failure to appreciate his glory. Supporting players Abraham Sofaer and Henry Brandon headed up an international cast.

What if Washington Irving had heard of an adventure that suggested to him his classic short story, "The Legend of Sleepy Hollow"? That's the premise of Tim Burton's 1999 Paramount release, *Sleepy Hollow*, where the headless Hessian horseman enacts the curse that keeps him from eternal rest, murdering and terrorizing the little New York town until pedagogue Ichabod Crane (Johnny Depp) intervenes. Told with style and substance, the film presented a new view of an old story, and paved the way for a later TV series, "Sleepy Hollow", which told of different events that might have inspired Irving, and brought the familiar characters into the present.

A novel by EB White provided the basis for a picture, *Stuart Little* (Columbia, '99) about a somewhat anthropomorphic mouse who tries to live in a human world even to being adopted by a family (in the book, he was a mouse born of human parents). This live-action and computer-generated animation feature was successful enough to spark a sequel, which was as good as its predecessor, continuing the charming but not overly sweet saga. Hugh Laurie and Geena Davis played the "parents", while animated Stuart was characterized by Michael J. Fox.

The DC Universe and Marvel Comics Universe pictures, too numerous to discuss in detail (and covered elsewhere in any event) derived from earlier films like *Superman and the Mole Men* (*Q.V. in Science Fiction*) and the serial versions of Superman and Batman, and from TV versions of the Fantastic Four, Spider-Man, and the Hulk. But the current films, including *Wonder Woman* (WB, 2017) and *Aquaman* (WB., '18) from DC, and the interwoven series that began with *Iron Man* (Paramount, '08) and has developed into *Avengers* Infinity War (Walt Disney, '18) and beyond have brought to "super-heroes" the same sort of public acclaim that "Star Wars" brought to science fantasy. (For more on "Star Wars", look elsewhere – pretty much *any* elsewhere.)

Fantasy continues to be among the most popular of film *genres*, with today's "Space Opera" and "Super-hero" sagas breaking new records with each successive release. But there's another *genre* which calls heavily on fantasy for many of its most impressive titles. Rarely in real life does a person spontaneously burst into a song-and-dance routine, but it happens all the time in...

CHAPTER FIVE: MUSICALS

WHEN JOLIE SAID, "You ain't heard nothin' yet," he wasn't kidding. That ad lib signaled the end of Pictures as people had known them for thirty years, and paved the way for the Musical. Musicals come in a wide range of story-telling, from the opera (where everything is sung), light opera (where most of the story is told in song), "traditional" musicals (where the songs enhance the plot), to revues (where the singing and dancing are the entire point of the film). Warner Brothers, whose Vitaphone had brought Al Jolson's voice to the masses, concentrated on backstage stories leavened with the studio's trademark gritty realism; Fox discovered little Shirley Temple and fashioned song-laden star vehicles for her. RKO Radio found the teaming of Fred Astaire and Ginger Rogers box-office gold, and M-G-M gave us revues bolstered by their galaxy of stars. The Four Marx Brothers brought their stage successes to screen via Paramount, and later developed original musical comedies for Metro, the studio that excelled in staging and production values, and which eventually produced the ultimate movie musical, *Singin' In The Rain*. Nightclub and radio performers like Benny Goodman and Kay Kyser were brought to the big screen in biographies and comedies. Hollywood's song-writers and Broadway's tunesmiths continue to this day to supply an unending supply of bright, happy stories with singing and dancing, basic American entertainment.

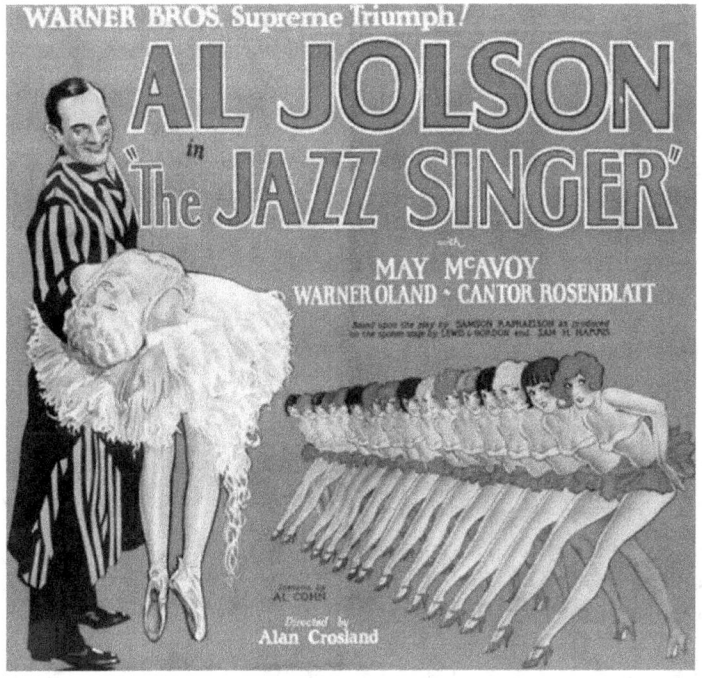

The Warner Brothers had been experimenting with talking pictures in a series of musical short subjects, and with sound effects and music in the feature-length *Don Juan*, in which the clash of swordplay astounded the audiences, when they released 1927's *The Jazz Singer*, offering the huge Broadway star Al Jolson in a melodrama with musical sequences through the Vitaphone system, where sound is provided on synchronized discs. The film was otherwise mute, with inter-titles and spoken titles carrying the action forward, except for Jolie's ad lib, "You ain't heard nothin' yet", which became the first dialogue heard in a major motion picture. But the people hadn't come to hear people talk; it was the songs and Jolie's personality that sold the picture. In its wake came the "talkers", and by 1930, films without spoken dialogue were as dead as the do-do (unless you were Chaplin). Jolson became the first star of the singing talkers, in pictures like

Mammy (WB, '30) and, later, *Rose of Washington Square* (Twentieth Century-Fox, '39).

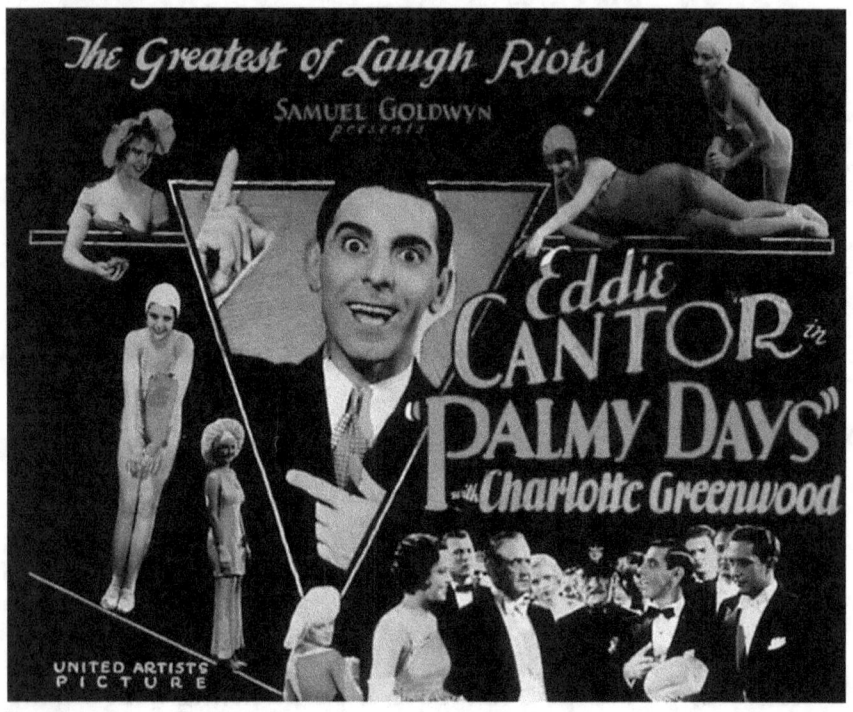

By 1931, Vitaphone was gone, replaced by Photophone, with the soundtrack included on the film strip, and Samuel Goldwyn was bringing to the screen the "other" big stage star of the period, Eddie Cantor, in musicals like *Palmy Days* (a United Artists release). Backed by a gaggle of Goldwyn Girls, the screen's answer to the famed Ziegfeld Follies Girls, Joe Simpson (Cantor), the stooge of a phony swami, Yolando (Charles Middleton), somehow ends up as the efficiency expert at a bakery. With plenty of opportunities for "Banjo Eyes" Cantor to sing and cavort, it was one of several similar vehicles for the star, including *Roman Scandals* (UA, '33) and UA's 1936 release of *Strike Me Pink*, which caught up Ethel Merman and Parkyakarkus with gangsters in an amusement park, but which had been tailored by author Clarence

Budington Kelland for Harold Lloyd (!).

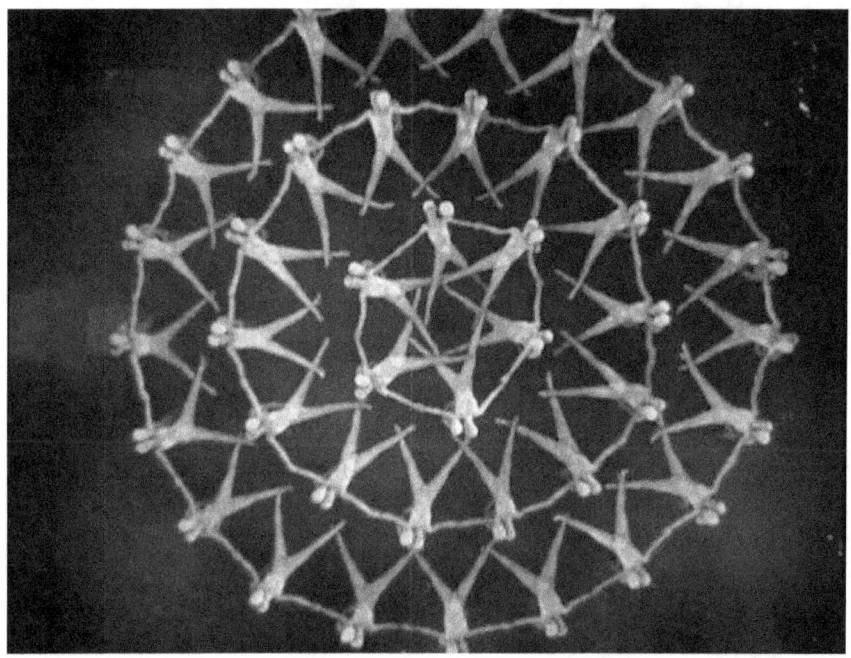

Busby Berkeley choreographed some astonishing geometric patterns in his musical numbers, but he always focused on individuals in the midst of the designs (though it was puzzling how many of his numbers, beautiful as seen from directly above, were supposed to be taking place on a stage; wonder what the theater audience in the film, from their point-of-view, thought was going on?). Warner Brothers' 1933 *Footlight Parade*, after an hour and some of plot about a Broadway producer making a comeback by staging musical prologues to accompany talking pictures, concludes with three dynamite numbers back-to-back-to-back: "Honeymoon Hotel" and "By a Waterfall" with Dick Powell and Ruby Keeler, and "Shanghai Lil" with James Cagney (the producer, pinch-hitting for a drunk juvenile), and Keeler. Add Joan Blondell as the long-suffering girl Friday who loves the producer, and comedy from Frank McHugh, plus a stunning array of chorines, and you've got the typical backstage musical. Warners would produce a number of these, including *42nd Street* ('33) and *Dames* ('34) and their "Golddiggers" series, but they weren't the only studio. Consider *Kiss Me Kate* (M-G-M, '48), *A Chorus Line* (Columbia, '85) and the *very* backstage musical, *The Phantom of the Opera* (WB, 2004).

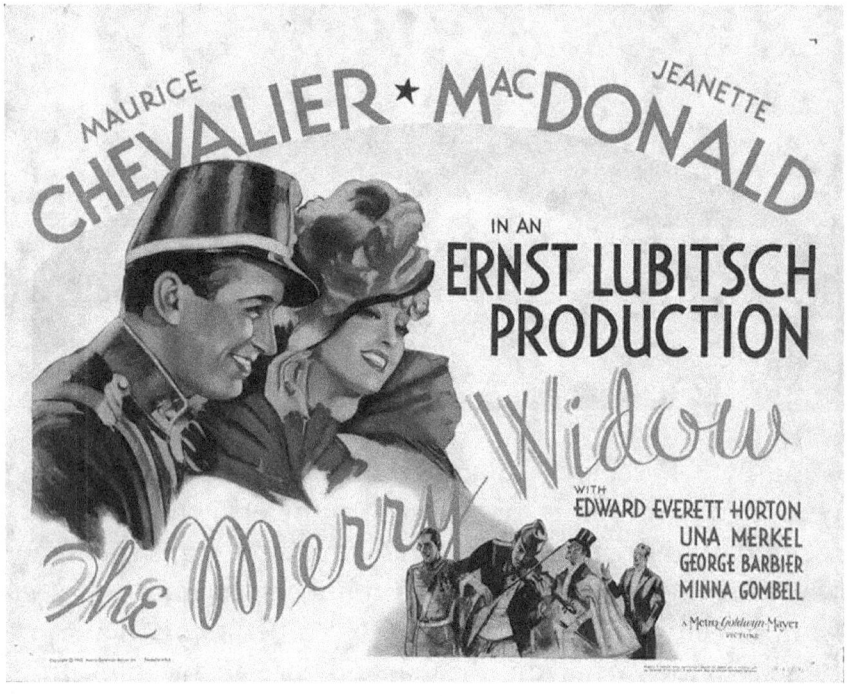

Ernst Lubitsch had a golden touch with women's pictures, and a deft hand at slick, classy looking musicals, including several with singing stars Maurice Chevalier and Jeanette MacDonald, though the trio had their off-screen disagreements. Their final team effort, *The Merry Widow* (M-G-M, 1934) is a grand love story, with all the complications required of a romantic comedy, with gentle humor (and a few great guffaws). When the widowed Sonia (MacDonald) tires of solitude, she packs up and leaves her home, the Ruritanian kingdom of Marshovia, for Paris, and the country goes into a panic: she's the wealthiest tax-payer and if she leaves, the country will be bankrupt. The king sends the nation's number one lothario, Count Danilo (Chevalier) to woo her back. But she's playing a game of her own, and when Danilo's true purpose in making love to her is revealed, she rejects him. The complication? He's really fallen in love with her, and now his failure will result in his execution! Comedy masters Edward Everett Horton, Donald Meek, Una Merkle, Sterling Hollaway, George Barbier, and a host of beauties enhance this charming musical. A French-language version, filmed simultaneously with a replacement supporting cast, propelled the film to world-wide success, though its domestic revenues showed a slump in interest for this quaint type of film. Boyer would soon return to France, while MacDonald would be teamed with Nelson Eddy for a number of similar but less charming pictures.

Fox's greatest asset was the amazingly poised and professional child, Shirley Temple, whose films were highly popular at the time (and, thanks to their outstanding supporting casts, still of interest today). Her song-and-dance couplings are among the most charming in film, with partners like Jack Haley, Buddy Ebsen, and, in *The Little Colonel* (Fox Film, 1935), the incomparable Bill "Bojangles" Robinson. Robinson later said that the idea for his "stair dance" came to him in a dream. Though later one of the most used clips of famous dances, the scene was originally cut from prints shown in the Old South. Throughout the '30s, little Shirley's pictures were box-office gold (like *Bright Eyes* [Fox Film, '34] and *Wee Willie Winkie* [20th Century-Fox, '37]), but in the '40s she'd outgrown her girlish charm, and though she continued in pictures throughout her teen years, it wasn't until she was an adult that she made a comeback on TV. Her last public face was as the US Ambassadress to the United Nations.

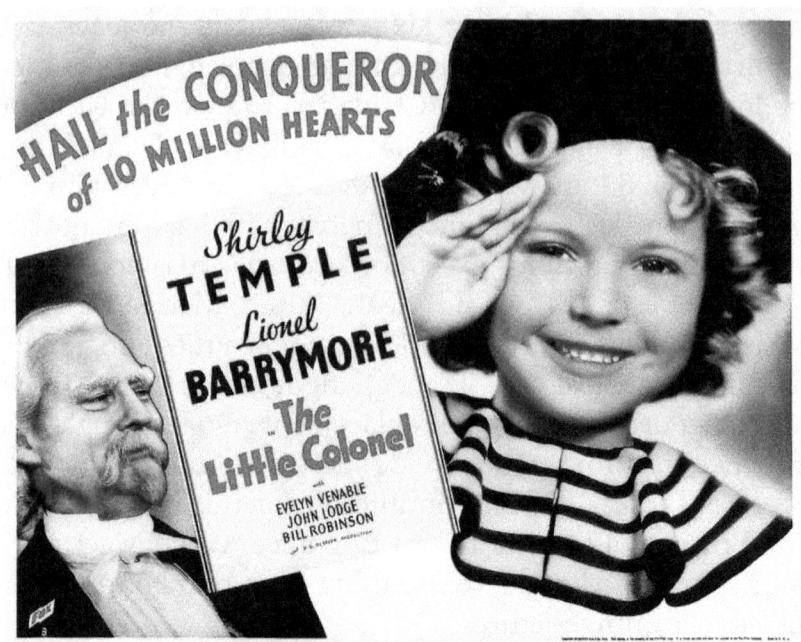

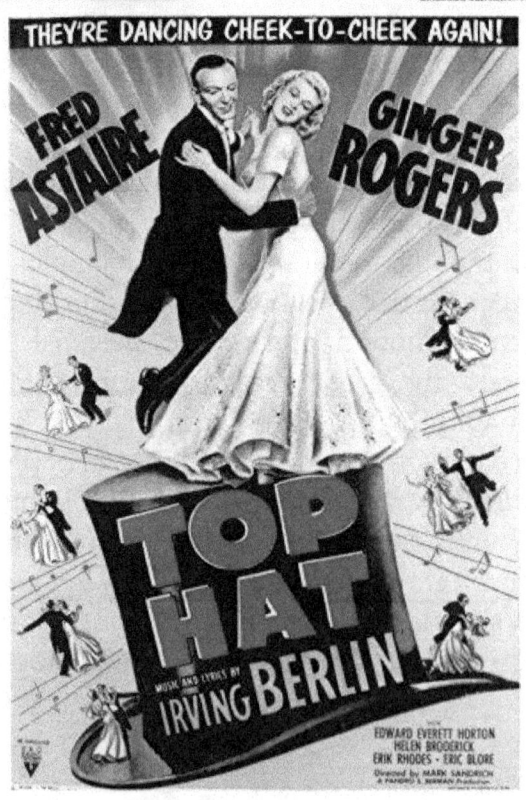

RKO Radio teamed Fred Astaire and Ginger Rogers as an "extra" couple to add interest in 1933's *Flying Down to Rio*, but the studio saw a good thing there, and elevated them to a front-line team, eventually co-starring them in nine pictures. All were fun, with *Swing Time* (RKO Radio, 1936) featuring numbers like "Pick Yourself Up" (in a "learn to dance" studio) and "A Fine Romance". Fred was always debonair, Ginger always beautiful; sometimes at odds with each other in the first reel, they always somehow ended up together by the fade-out. Among their other features, *Top Hat* ('35), and *Carefree* ('38) are particularly fine. The films were good enough that M-G-M lured Astaire away in the '40s, and eventually reunited him with Rogers one more time, in 1949's *The Barkleys of Broadway*.

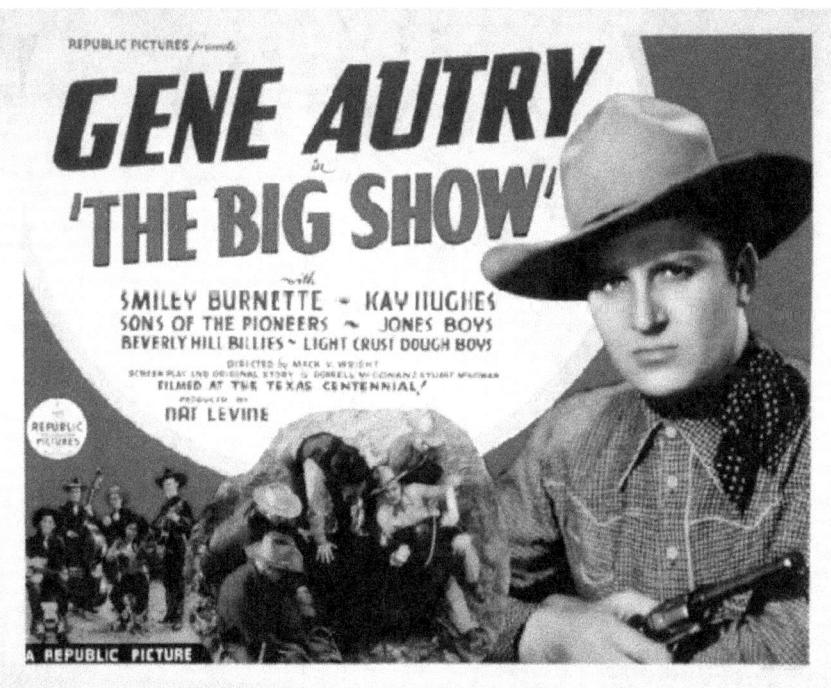

Not all musicals were sophisticated, high society affairs. In the mid-'30s, a new musical star burst on the scene: Gene Autry, whose down-home charm and powerful voice made up for his lack of histrionic skills. In one of his first pictures, *The Big Show* (Republic, 1936), he played a dual role, as snooty movie-star Tom Ford and his likeable stunt-double Gene, who ends up pinch-hitting for Ford at the Texas State Fair and turns out to be such a hit that he replaces Ford as the star of a new series of musical westerns (a parallel to real life, where Gene took over for fading, tempestuous star Ken Maynard). For over 15 years (with a break for service in the Army Air Corps during the Second World War), Gene was a box-office champ, and parlayed his fame into his own production company, eventually owning television stations and the Los Angeles Angels baseball team. Other Autry musical westerns of note include *The Old Barn Dance* (Republic, '38) and *Riders in the Sky* (Columbia, '49).

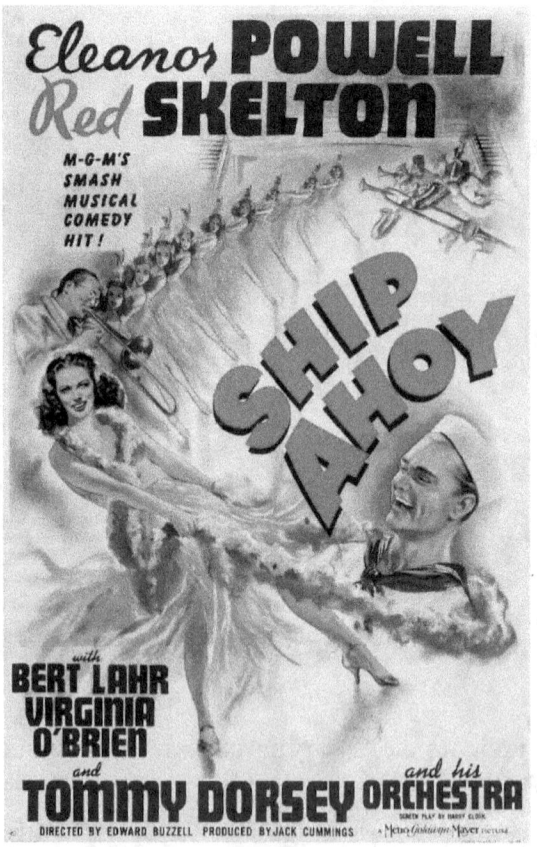

Alice Faye was Fox's grown-up musical star, and under Darryl Zanuck after the merger became a multi-purpose actress, in musicals, comedies, dramas light and heavy, and biopics. 20th Century-Fox's leading man, Tyrone Power, was likewise put in everything from light comedy to swashbucklers. *Alexander's Ragtime Band* (20th Century-Fox, 1938) was a sort of fake biographical film, with Ty as Roger Grant, who because of a mistake ends up with the professional name "Alexander", Faye as the band's girl singer, and Don Ameche as a songwriter who apparently wrote all of Irving Berlin's tunes. The ups and downs of musicians, with their rivalries and love-spats, play out against one swell song after another. Typical of biographic musicals, it played fast and loose with history, as also seen in *The Fabulous Dorseys* (*Q.V.*).

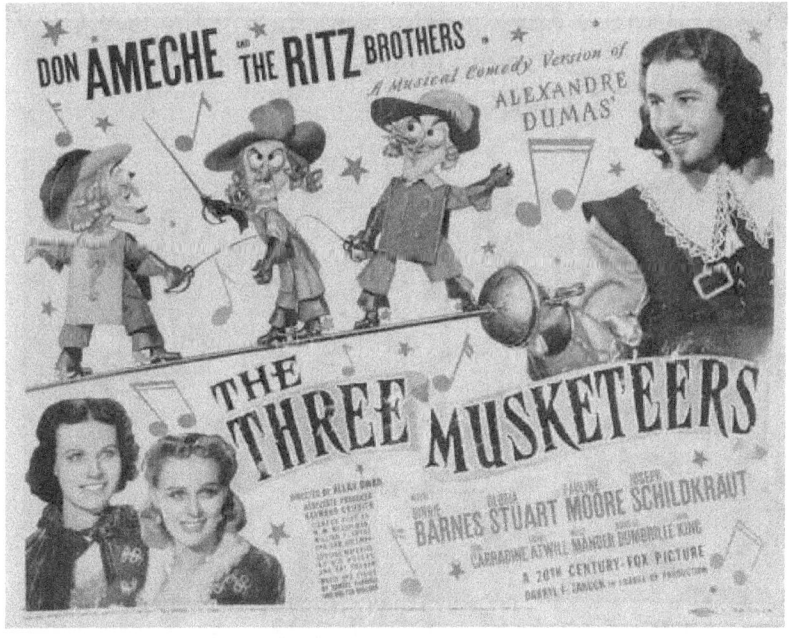

The Main Title reads A Musical Comedy Version of *The Three Musketeers*, and that's what this 1939 20th Century-Fox picture is. Don Ameche is a singing D'Artagnan, and the story begins just like the book, until the musketeers (Douglass Dumbrille, John King, and Russell Hicks) stop off on the way to their duel with the upstart Gascon and get drunk at an inn. That's when three lackeys (the Ritz Brothers, the studio's comedy-team stars) decided to dress up in their uniforms, only to find out that impersonating a musketeer is an offense punishable by death! So they just keep up the pose, and the rest of the story goes along familiar lines (though one wonders what becomes of the real musketeers, who are never seen again). Harry, Jim, and Al take up as D'Artagnan's somewhat reluctant aides, even at one point posing as jesters to distract the guards while the Queen's jewels are recovered from the henchmen of M'Lady DeWinter (Binnie Barnes). The Ritzes and Ameche have plenty of opportunities for song along the way. Two other versions of the story were produced in the "Golden Age", from Radio Pictures in '35 and M-G-M in '48, and many other versions, including the 20th Century Fox 1974 extravaganza but none of them was a musical – even the Metro one starring Gene Kelly!

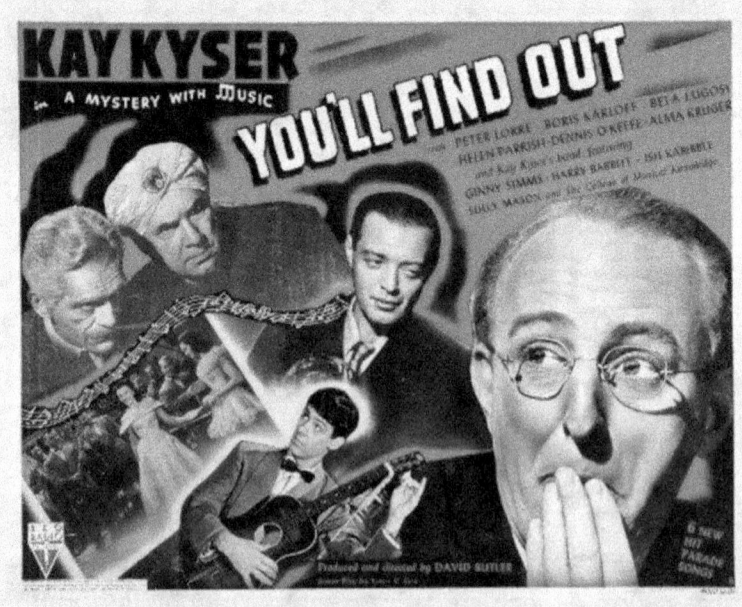

Professor Kay Kyser and his "Kollege of Musical Knowledge" was a popular radio program that mixed comedy with songs. The affable Kay and goofy sidekick Ish Kabibble handled the laughs; Harry Babbitt, Sully Mason, and Ginny Simms the lyrics. When RKO Radio brought the band to the big screen in 1939 for the first of five pictures, they named it *That's Right – You're Wrong* after a catch-phrase from Kay's show. It featured comedy and songs in the radio-show sequences, making it sort of a step-child of the backstage musical. The follow-ups included *You'll Find Out* ('40; with Karloff, Lugosi, and Peter Lorre) and *Around the World* ('43). Kay and Company moved on to Metro for the 1943 *Swing Fever* and finally to Columbia for 1944's *Carolina Blues*.

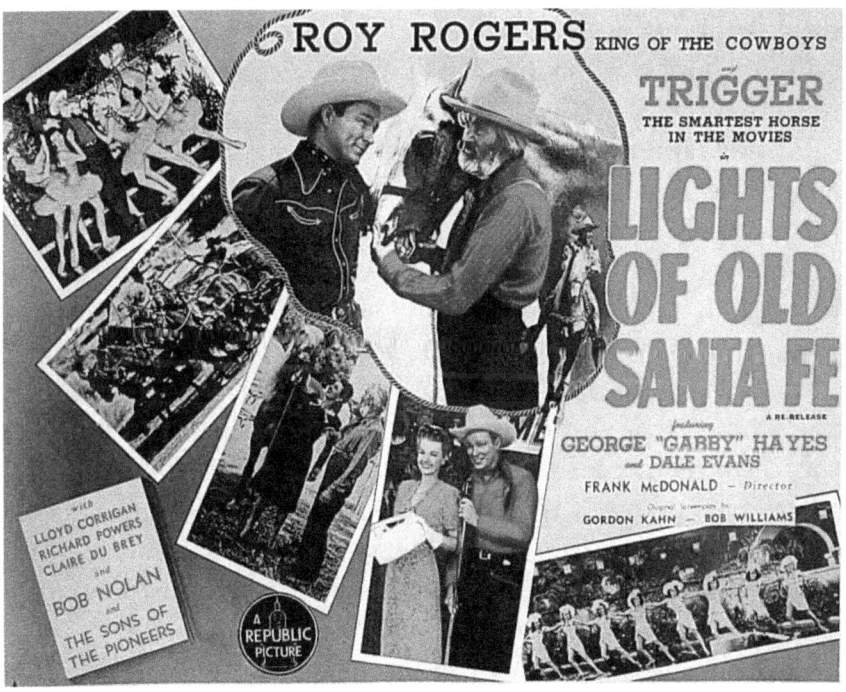

Lights Of Old Santa Fe was one of Republic Pictures' "Specials", a standard Roy Rogers B picture with extra production values and two more reels. Roy had begun with the Sons of the Pioneers group, but had been elevated to stardom by Republic Pictures' boss Herbert J. Yates as "insurance" against his star Gene Autry, but soon tied his friend for top spot among cowboy heroes. In the 1944 release, Roy has to save Dale Evans, his frequent co-star and real-life wife, from unscrupulous suitor Richard Powers (who had previously been Radio Pictures' cowboy star Tom Keene), while finding time to sing with the Sons of the Pioneers. Most of his films ran about an hour, with top ridin', ropin', and romancin', plus comedy supplied by the enormously popular George "Gabby" Hayes, who'd partner with pretty much every important Western star and eventually got his own TV series. Roy was usually "Roy Rogers", though for a while he was various historical characters. Other Rogers vehicles include *Days of Jesse James* ('39), *Don't Fence Me In* ('45), and the all-star outing *Trail of Robin Hood* ('50). Roy also co-starred with Bob Hope in the musical-comedy Western, *Son of Paleface* (Paramount, '52).

Besides the many bandleaders and singers who appeared as themselves in pictures, there were numerous "biography" films, stories in which well known actors portrayed other well known public figures, like Steve Allen in *The Benny Goodman Story* (U-I, 1956) or Danny Kaye as Red Nichols in *The Five Pennies* (Paramount, '59). In *The Fabulous Dorseys* (United Artists, '47), Tommy and Jimmy appeared as themselves, even though the story was mostly fabrication developed from the disagreement that broke up their band. Each brother formed his own group, and both enjoyed tremendous success in the following years. That they were not *too* unhappy with each other is indicated by their agreeing to appear together in this picture.

In a rare instance, a non-musical had a musical sequel, a 1947 Columbia picture. When the Muse Terpsichore (Rita Hayworth) learns of a Broadway musical that ridicules her sisters and their contributions to art, she persuades Mr. Jordan (Roland Culver) to send her *Down To Earth* with heavenly messenger 7013 (Edward Everett Horton) to enlist the aid of theatrical promoter Max Corkle (James Gleason). At first planning to sabotage the musical, she gains a part in the play (she *is* the goddess of dance, after all), but falls in love with the writer/producer Danny Miller (Larry Parks), and abandons her plan. But then she realizes – she's immortal and he isn't! How can their love survive? Well, good old Mr. Jordan has a plan, too. Gleason and Horton had played the same parts in "Jordan" in '41; Culver's part had been originated by Claude Rains. *Xanadu* (Universal, '80) is a virtual uncredited remake, with Gene Kelly in his last starring dancing role.

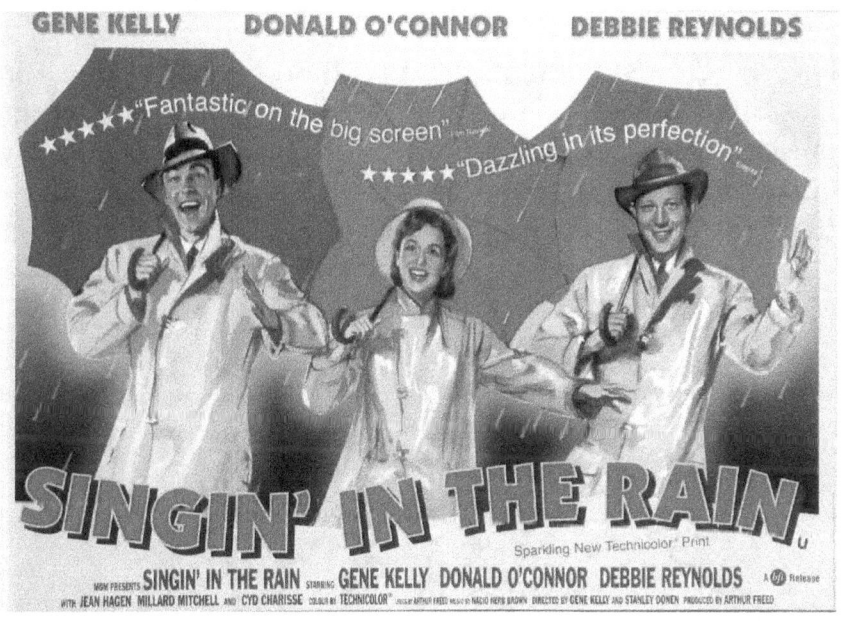

Really, it's science fiction, but it's also the most wonderful musical ever. The wonder of *Singin' In The Rain* (M-G-M, 1952) is that it was concocted by writers Adolph Green and Betty Comden under the most adverse conditions, stringing together a collection of old songs by Arthur Freed, song-writer and producer who supervised the picture, for Stanley Donen and Gene Kelly to direct. In this story of the coming of sound to pictures, all the clichés and truths about Old

Hollywood were trotted out to do their tricks: the harried director, the silent star with the horrible voice (Jean Hagen in an absolutely swell performance), the lightweight star who proves to be a real talent, and the girl from nowhere who becomes a big star (Debbie Reynolds as Kathy Selden). Forced by the coming trend to make their big romantic stars, Don Lockwood and Lina Lamont, into singing stars, the heads of Monumental Pictures fear they are doomed by the scratchy, repugnant voice of Lina Lamont, but after the disastrous premiere of their first talker, sidekick Cosmo Brown (Donald O'Connor) has a great idea – they'll dub Kathy's voice over Lina's (to accomplish which they use technology 20 years in advance of their time). All does not go well, but if pictures have taught us anything, it's that things work out well in musicals. Even though perfectly placed for a backstage musical, all of the numbers involved people spontaneously bursting into songs and dances, like Don (Gene Kelly) rhapsodizing his new-found love by "Singin' in the Rain", or when Don, Cosmo, and Kathy suddenly improvise "Good Morning" while solving their problem.

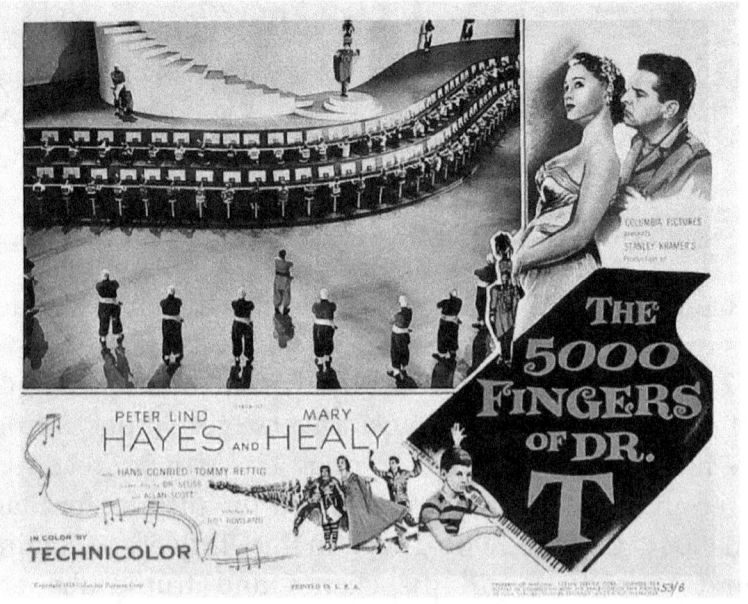

The 5,000 Fingers Of Dr. T (Columbia, 1953) is a concoction of astonishing proportions, with notable contributions to the script, set design, and music by Theodore Geisel – Dr. Seuss. Young Bart Collins, forced to practice piano when he'd rather be out having boyish fun, falls asleep and dreams that he's at Dr. Terwilliker's "Happy Finger" Institute – a concentration camp with a piano designed to be played by 500 boys all at once. Free-form architecture, stairs to nowhere, a dungeon reserved for non-piano players only, and Siamese-twin guards conjoined at their long beards are all contributions to the musical nightmare. Yes, dreams aren't really fantasy; one experiences all sorts of impossible things in dreams... *but* when Bart wakes up, he discovers that he and Zablodowski the plumber (Peter Lind Hayes), who became sort of blood-brothers in the dream, now each has a band-aid on his thumb! Top-billed husband and wife Hayes and Mary Healy, Broadway personalities, were perceived as the box-office draw, but it was young Tommy Rettig and Hans Conried who were the "real" stars, as when Conried, as Dr. T, prepares for opening day in his "do-mi-do" duds, source of a delightfully Suessian song, with nonsense lyrics that seem to make sense. Trying to think of other similar pictures of this sort is a fool's mission. This is a singular film experience, but one other picture has a similar outlook:

Red Garters (Paramount, 1954) is another bizarre fantasy musical, set in the Old West's Limbo County, where buildings are backless façades, with only enough structure to make them identifiable as a saloon, a hotel, a stable. Clever comedy sends up Western conventions as one gunslinger hunts for the man who killed his brother, whom he therefore – according to "the Law of the West" (please remove yore hats, pardners) – must kill in response (and, one guesses, hope *he* doesn't have a brother, or else this could go on until the West is pretty empty). Jack Carson, his usual blustering self, is backed up by Gene Barry, Buddy Ebsen, Patricia Crowley, and especially beautiful songstress and co-star Rosemary Clooney, who handles much of the singing and dancing, backed by a chorus of beauties.

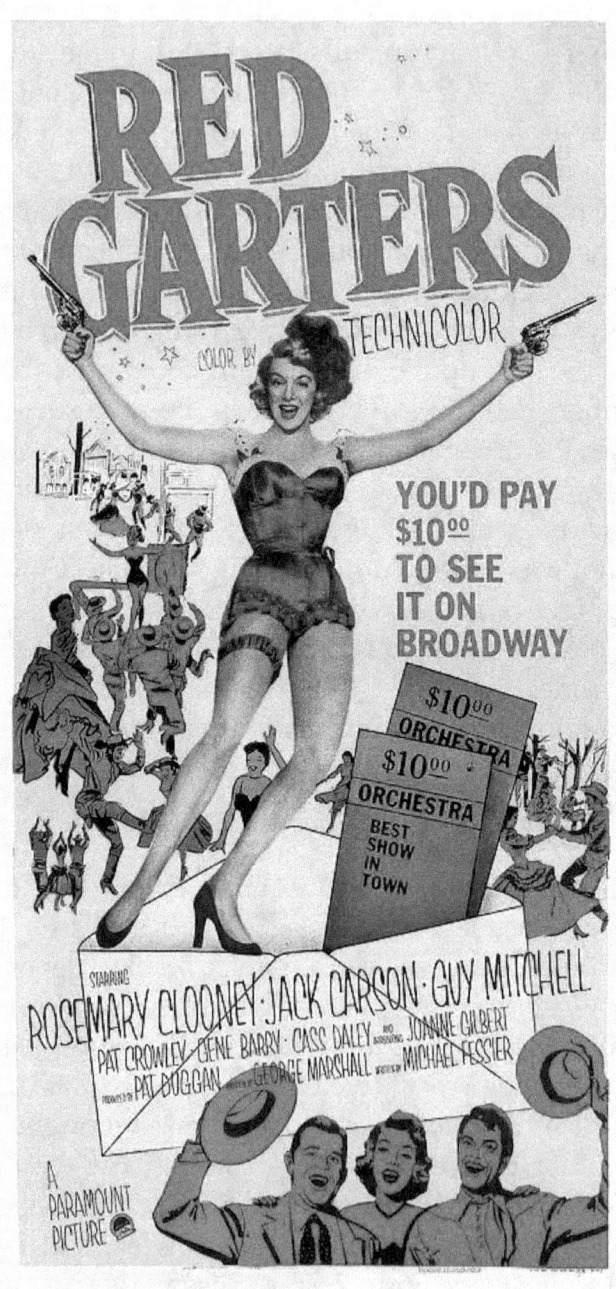

The noel *The Year the Yankees Lost the Pennant* by Douglass Wallop became the basis for a hit Broadway musical, which in turn became a delightful movie, as a fanatic baseball follower, fed up with his team losing all the time, says he'd sell his soul to the Devil to get them to win the league championship. Which is where the diabolical Mr. Applegate (Ray Walston) comes in, restoring the man's youth and giving *him* a chance to be the agency to defeat them *Damn Yankees* in the 1958 Warner Brothers release. Of course, Applegate is the original dirty double-crosser, so as the pennant race looks won, he sends a temptress (Gwen Verdon) to "Shoeless Joe" (Tab Hunter) to sway him in his purpose in the erotic number "Whatever Lola Wants". Walston gets his own song, 'Those Were the Good Old Days", and his otherworldy performance led to his eventual casting as the title character in TV's "My Favorite Martian".

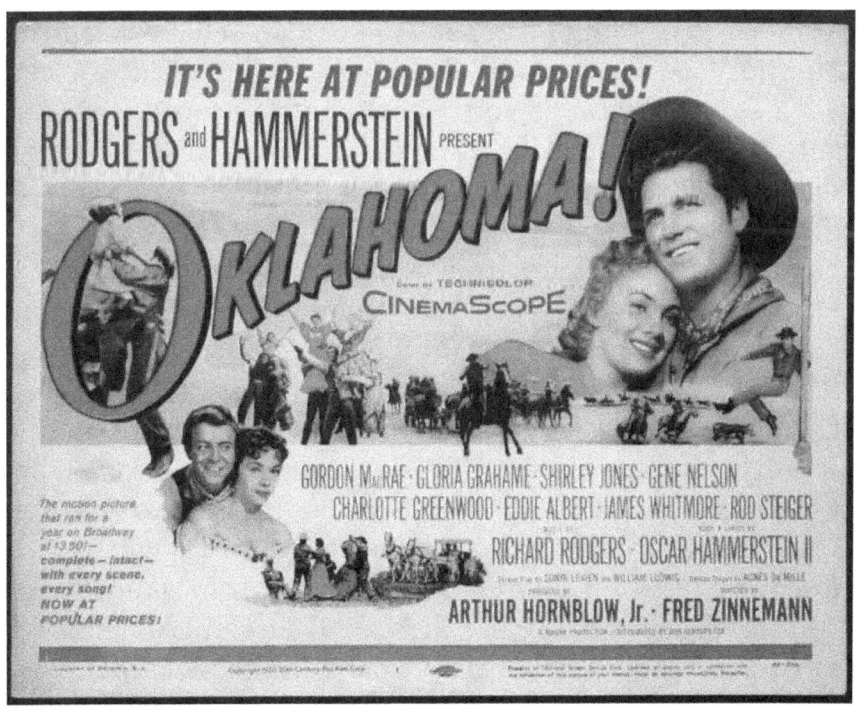

It's two – two – two movies in one. Literally, as *Oklahoma!* (RKO Radio and Magna Theatre Corporation, 1955) was filmed twice at the same time, in the incompatible widescreen systems CinemaScope and Todd-AO (and each version released by a different distributor [in the order above]). Each scene was shot once with each camera aperture, and though the dialogue, blocking, songs, and camera set-ups were identical, each version was edited by a separate team, and cutaways, inserts, and timing vary between the two, making them different works of art, almost like a film and its re-make. It was the second time the work had made a landmark impression; the original theatrical show, in 1943, revolutionized Broadway musicals. On film, Laurey (Shirley Jones) has a tempestuous romance with Curly (Gordon McRae), which, unusual for a musical, does not end well. Charlotte Greenwood, Gloria Grahame, Barbara Lawrence, Eddie Albert, and Rod Steiger contributed top-notch support to these great films, with songs like "Oh, What a Beautiful Mornin'" and "Surrey with the Fringe on Top".

One of America's favorite newspaper cartoon strips had already been a B picture (in 1940) and an animated-cartoon series before it became a Broadway musical bringing to life all the crazy characters of Dogpatch, USA, in *Li'l Abner* (which became a feature film from Paramount Pictures in 1959): Lucifer Ornamental and Pansy Yokum (Joe E. Marks and Billie Hayes), Marryin' Sam (Stubby Kaye), Daisy Mae Scragg (Leslie Parrish), and Li'l Abner himself (Peter Palmer). When Dogpatch is selected as the most worthless spot in the country, all are excited, until they learn that it means there will be an "A-tom bomb" test there. Sadly about to abandon their home, the Dogpatchers get a reprieve when it is discovered that the town is the only source of Yokumberries – source of a powerful elixir that can make a Li'l Abner out of an ordinary man. Millionaire General Bullmoose schemes to get the tonic for his own profit, and uses the annual "Sadie

Hawkins Day" race to trap Abner into the clutches of his henchwoman Appassionata Von Climax (!). Most of the favorite cartoon-strip characters are here, with delightful songs like "Jubilation T. Cornpone" and "I's Past My Prime" helping drive the plot. Like *Singin' In The Rain*, *Li'l Abner* is one of the "secret" science-fiction hits of the '50s.

A by-God spellbinder, that's the man known as Professor Harold Hill (Harold Hill, Harold Hill [Robert Preston]) also known as *The Music Man* in the 1962 Warner Bros. feature that brought to film the Meredith Willson stage musical. A little piece of pseudo-nostalgia (it's not the way things were, it's the way we *wish* they'd been) shot on the Warner back lot, with its charming picture of small-town America, complete with snoopy neighbors, pompous local big-wigs, and gullible yokels (who nonetheless get to the ultimate con-man, whose real name is Greg something). There's also the repressed librarian, Marion Paroo (Shirley Jones), whose libido is stirred by the handsome stranger when he starts a full-scale musical number in her library, and goes along with his gaff when she sees the change it has wrought in her sad little brother (Ronny Howard). Everyone shines in this extra-long treat, with songs like "Trouble" and "Shipoopi" and the superb "76 Trombones" to please the ear and tickle the funny-bone.

Elvis Presley was a hip-swingin', hot-mama-lovin' certified hit with the kids as a singer, and he and his manager, Colonel Tom Parker, knew that he'd need good pictures if he was going to be a movie star, too. So they sought properties that allowed for not just singing but comedy, or drama, or adventure as well, and peopled them with great character actors. He began with *Love Me Tender* for Twentieth Century-Fox in 1956, and worked through pictures like *Paradise, Hawaiian Style* (Paramount,'66) and *Double Trouble* (M-G-M, '67), but the most popular and one of his best was *Viva Las Vegas* (M-G-M, '64), in which local Las Vegas girl Rusty Martin (the hottest female star of musical fare, Ann-Margret) diverts the at-first unwanted (as it goes in this sort of picture) attention of Elvis as happy-go-lucky race-car driver Lucky Jackson (no relation to your author, I assume). Songs like "The Lady Loves Me" and "My Rival" are worked into the narrative, while numbers like "Appreciation" and the title tune are on-stage in the best "backstage musical" tradition, while the climactic auto race puts a terrific finish on the show.

Early in the career of director Richard Lester, he tied in with the '60s' answer to Elvis, the famous Beatles, John, Paul, George, and Ringo (you don't need their surnames, do you?) in the pseudo-*cinema verité* A Hard Day's Night, (UA, 1964) following the boys on their tour as celebrities, with plenty of music but also time for understated comedy. For *Help!* (UA, '65) he and the boys went wild, with the story of an Eastern cult, a sacrificial ring, a mad scientist (well, it's the national health, you see...), Scotland Yard, Jamaican police, and bravery. When a sacrificial maiden promised to heathen god Kaili sends her special ring to Ringo, the drummer is marked as the next victim, and the cultists, led by Leo McKern, trail the boys from England to Switzerland (where they meet an errant Channel swimmer and do another musical number) to Jamaica, where Ringo is captured and readied for sacrifice. Is Ringo doomed? Can the boys save him? Certainly the local police, led by a Scotland Yard Superintendent (Patrick Cargill) won't.

Larger-than-life talent Zero Mostel starred on Broadway and film as the lyingest, cheatingest, *sloppiest* slave in all of Rome ("Oh... Pseudolus.") in *A Funny Thing Happened On The Way To The Forum*, another Richard Lester-directed romp, released by United Artists in 1966 with a great cast: Phil Silvers, Buster Keaton, Michael Hordern, John Crawford and Annette Andre as the young lovers, Jack Gilford, and a Pertwee named John (who recognizes the slave just from the adjectives, and whose brother Michael co-wrote the screenplay). The plot develops from the slave's desire for his freedom, but complications arise when his young master falls in love with a virgin promised to a vainglorious Roman soldier who won't take "no" for an answer. Add in a dotty old neighbor seeking his lost children, a father who wants nothing more than to lose his shrewish wife, and you have a comedy that promises something for everyone, with funny, memorable songs ("Everybody Ought to Have a Maid", "Miles Gloriosus", "Comedy Tonight") and a slam-bang chase finale.

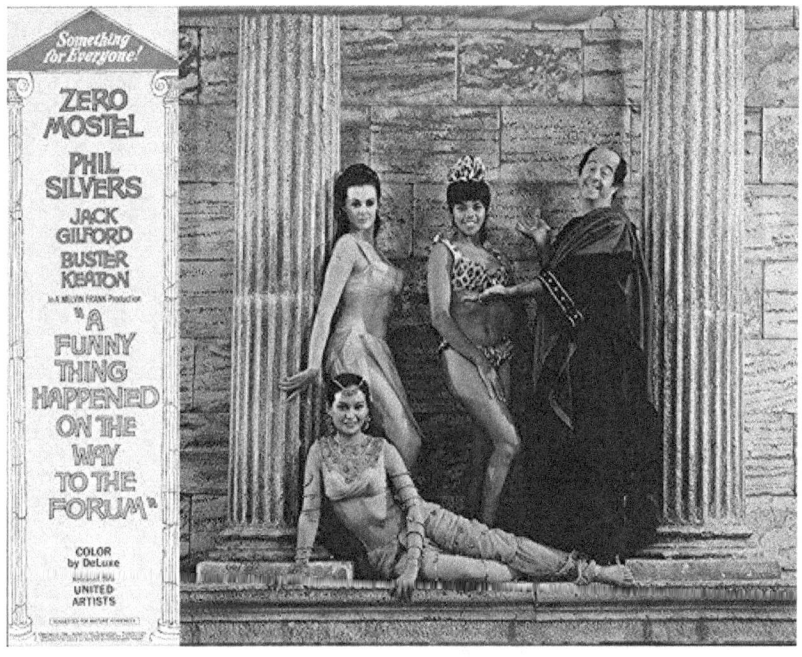

Over a decade later, in which musical pictures had fallen from favor (excepting adaptations from the Stage) came an original that showed that not all musicals are comic (remember *The Jazz Singer*?), but even a Musical Tragedy can have its funny side. Choreographer and film-maker Bob Fosse told his life story (with a seriously sad projection of his future) in *All That Jazz* (20th Century-Fox, 1979), with Roy Scheider standing in for Fosse as Joe Gideon, obsessed with creating the perfect film, pounding down uppers to wake, downers to sleep, and alcohol to relax, driving himself to the brink of death once, and recovering only to begin pushing himself over the edge once again. His death fantasies conjure women from his past, as well as Angelique (Jessica Lange as Death herself) from his future, and chorus girls – always chorus girls, seen in his mind's-eye view of the hospital doing a number around his bed. Gideon's entire life is summed up in his ritual morning call, "It's showtime!"

Many of these pictures featured comedy, and there were comedies that featured a bit of music in the mix, so what's more natural than to slide across that highly permeable dividing line into...

CHAPTER SIX: COMEDY

THE COMEDY FILM has been a major force in cinema since the earliest days, with star vehicles for Buster Keaton, Charlie Chaplin, and others attracting huge audiences. During the B-picture era, studios relied on comics not only for relief in horror and adventure films and diversions in musicals, but as the centerpieces of their own shorts and features, which kept audiences laughing through Depression and War and the Baby Boom. In vehicles and series, actors like Leon Errol and Arthur Lake became household names whose next picture would be awaited eagerly. Hal Roach brought down the house with Laurel and Hardy and "Our Gang". Paramount, with its string of music-laden comedies starring Bob Hope or Eddie Bracken, kept 'em laughing. Republic contributed bucolic fun with Judy Canova and the Weaver Brothers and Elviry. Family Comedies, some inspired by the more serious "Hardy Family" pictures at M-G-M, were a staple at every studio. Columbia's "Blondie" series, based on the world-famous newspaper feature by Chic Young, with 28 installments over 13 years, is one of the most successful franchises in film history. Series comedy easily made the transition to television, and big-screen laughs still rock movie houses, though often with more "adult" humor than the classics.

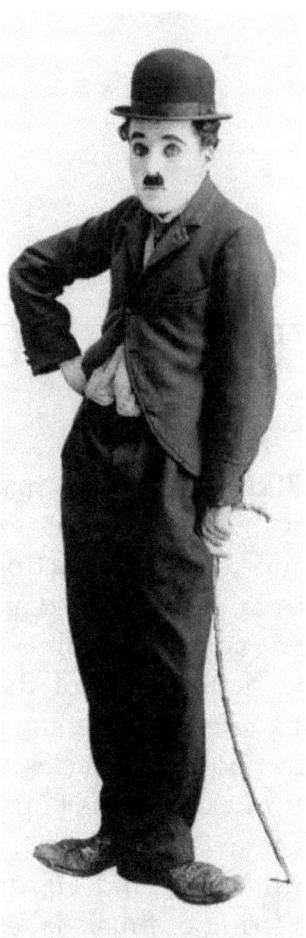

Early comedy was the province of many funnymen, but the standouts were three of the best: Charles Chaplin, whose "Little Tramp" character shuffled and slid through feature-length comedies like *The Gold Rush* (UA, 1925), and *Modern Times* (UA, '36), a parable about man trapped in the cogs of the machine age; until his final appearance in Chaplin's first All-talking Picture, *The Great Dictator* (UA, '40), in which he dared to ridicule Hitler even before the U.S. entered the War. Harold Lloyd, never without his trademark spectacles (which he had only to remove to be anonymous in public) and his daredevil feats in pictures such as *A Sailor-Made Man*

(Associated Exhibitors, 1921) and *Safety Last!* (Pathé Exchange, '23), famous as the picture in which Lloyd scales a tall building, at one point dangling from a clock-face. The Great Stone Face belonged to Buster Keaton, whose acrobatic timing and genius at dreaming up situations brought us *Sherlock Jr.* (Metro Pictures Corporation, 1924), in which he enters a film being screened, and *Steamboat Bill, Jr.* (UA, '28), as well as his Civil-War masterpiece, *The General* (*Q.V. in War*). His last great comedy, *The Cameraman* was made for M-G-M after his producer, Joseph Schenk, sold out in 1928; after that Metro's interference with his films resulted in a decline, though Buster continued to make films until *A Funny Thing Happened On The Way To The Forum* (*Q.V. in Musicals*). There was also this accidentally created comedy team, but you'll find them below.

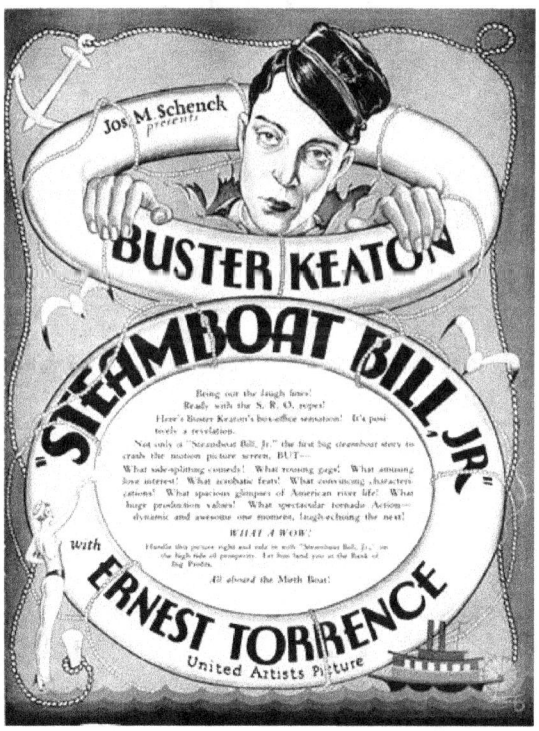

The marvelous Four Marx Brothers (Chico, Zeppo,

Groucho, and Harpo) had worked their way to the pinnacle of live theatre before their Broadway musical show *The Cocoanuts* (Paramount, 1929) was brought to the silver screen.

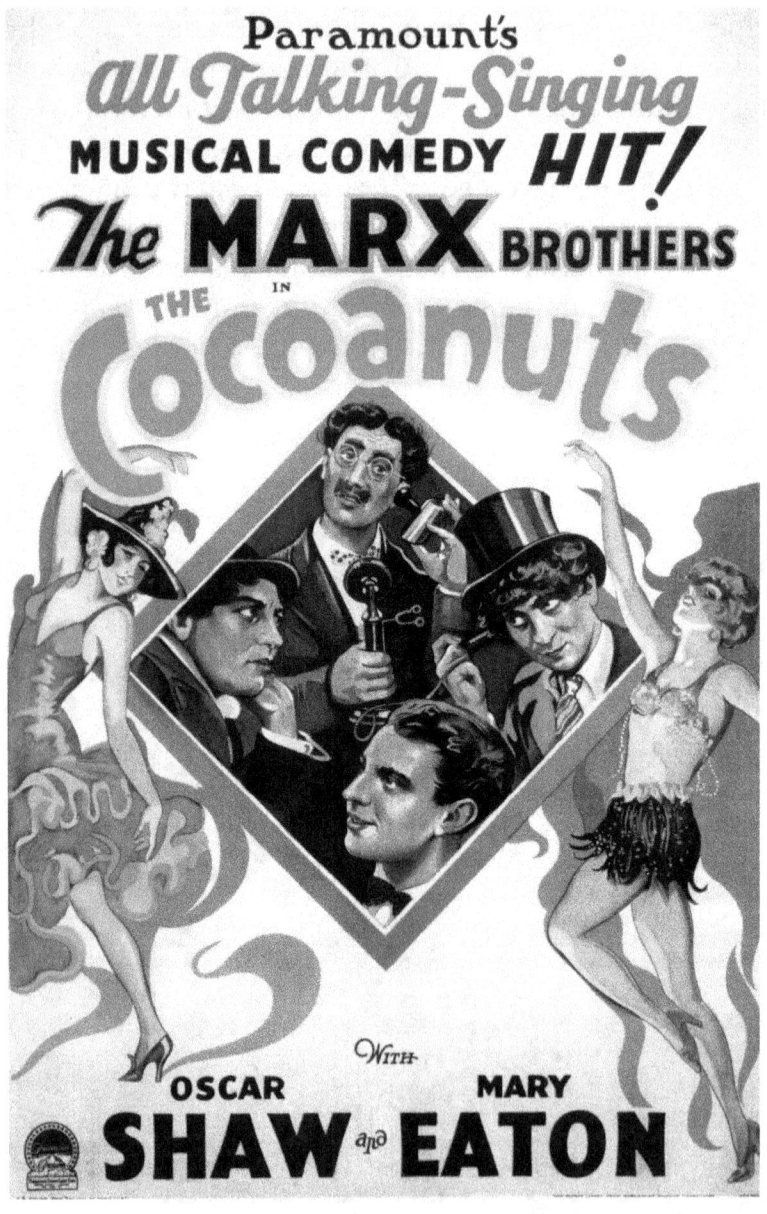

Shot on Long Island (because the brothers were still on

Broadway), the film is very "stage-y", with locked-down cameras and few close-ups, but it highlighted the witty *repartée* for which Groucho was already becoming famous, and musical interludes by Chico and Harpo. Zeppo rarely shined, being the least wacky of the boys, but still did his part as straight-man. By '33, with a picture a year under their belts, their arch, incisive, and madcap humor had been neatly melded to film technique in their 1934 political-satire triumph, *Duck Soup*. Soon they'd be lured to Metro, where Irving Thalberg would shepherd them (without Zeppo, who retired from the act) to perfection in *A Night At The Opera* in '35. But after Thalberg's untimely death, studio head Louis B. Mayer would be less conscientious in his care for the boys, and though their next picture, *A Day At The Races* ('37) was almost as great, later efforts would decline, with great bits (like "Lydia, the Tattooed Lady" in *At The Circus* ['39]) popping out of otherwise ordinary pictures.

Comedy came in many guises, and sometimes the royalty of drama would prove to be as funny as their comic colleagues. In the first film to win five Oscars (Best Picture, Actor, Actress, Director, and Screenplay), Robert Riskin's script and Frank Capra's direction brought to the screen Claudette Colbert and (on punitive loan-out from Metro) Clark Gable in *It Happened One Night* (Columbia, 1934). When Colbert, an heiress, takes it on the lam when her father tries to annul her marriage to a fortune hunter, she meets, while escaping on a bus, reporter Gable who blackmails her into letting him help her re-unite with her husband, sure there'll be a great story in it. But things don't work out the way either of them plans. A clever script includes such highlights as Colbert showing Gable how to hitch-hike (by showing some leg at the roadside) and the pair platonically sharing a cabin by hanging a blanket called "the Wall of Jericho" down the middle of the room. The power of "the movies" on society was proved when, in the wake of the revelation that Gable wore no undershirt, sales of the garment plummeted nationwide! As previously mentioned, Capra's Columbia comedies, little slices of Americana joshingly called "Capra-corn", (like *Mr. Smith Goes to Washington* ['39] and *You Can't Take It With You* ['38]) were always welcome at the box-office, and did much for the reputation of Harry Cohn's studio.

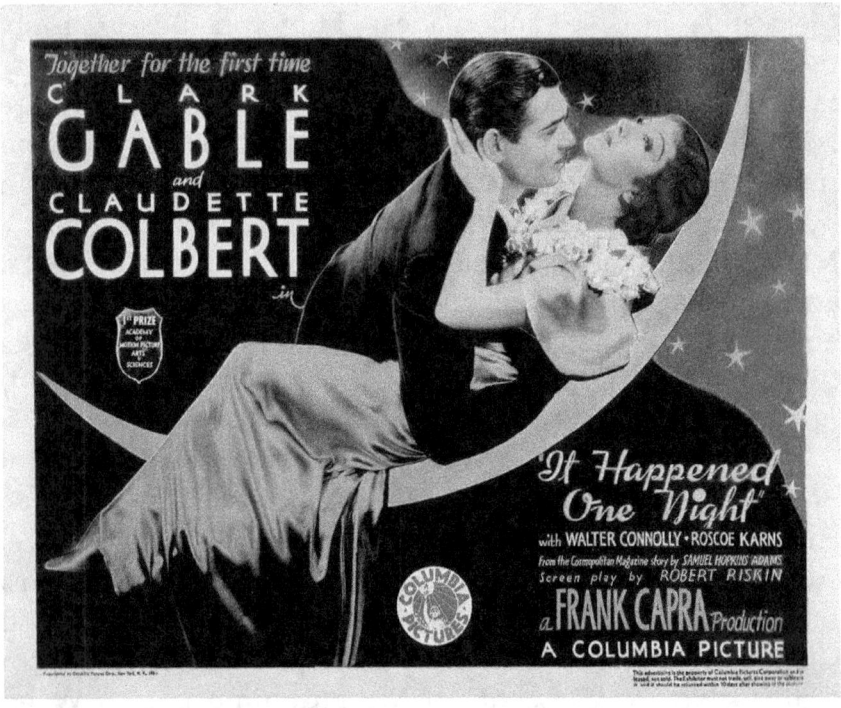

Stan Laurel and Oliver Hardy, already among the best of the short-subject stars by 1930, were boosted up into feature pictures by their producer Hal Roach and the concerns that shorts were going out of style. Many of their early features, like *Babes in Toyland* (*Q.V. in Fantasy*) were great fun, and they were equally successful in their more straightforward comedies like *Bonnie Scotland* (M-G-M, 1935), in which Stan and Ollie inadvertently (that's them, all right) join a Scottish regiment sent out to the frontier in India, or their superb *Sons of The Desert* (M-G-M, '33), where they try to prevent their wives from learning that they'd been to a lodge convention.

All too often in their features and shorts, one or both had shrewish wives to placate. After a break-up with Roach, the team re-united at 20th Century-Fox, where, in the '40s, they were overwhelmed by the high-energy comedy of Abbott and Costello. The story of their last days with Roach and their last hurrah on tour in the United Kingdom in 1953 is related in *Stan & Ollie* (Sony Pictures Classics, 2018).

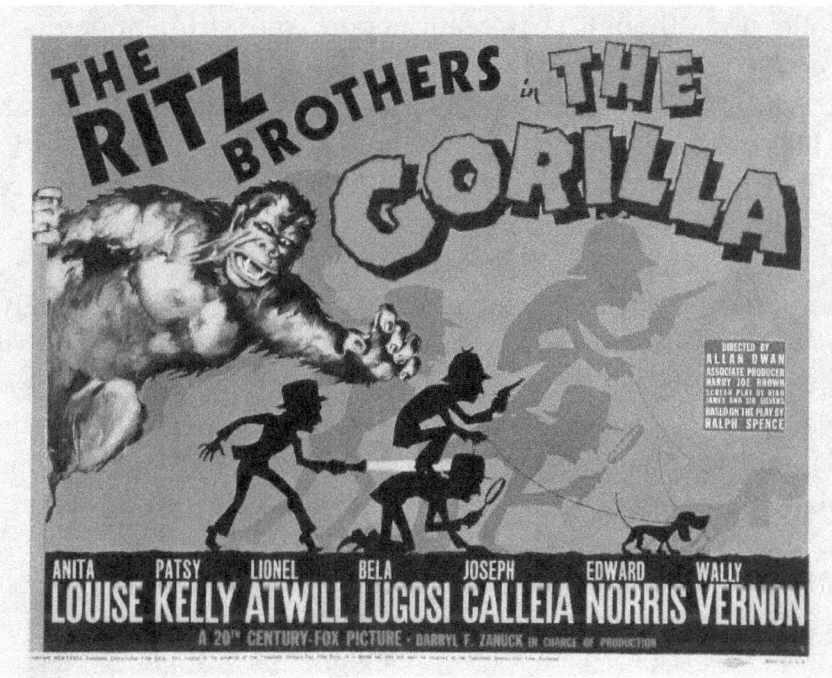

Another brother act that jumped from Broadway, Al, Harry, and Jimmy Ritz appeared in a string of variable comedies, including their comic version of "The Three Musketeers" (*Q.V. in Musicals*). As detectives Harrigan, Mulligan, and Garrity, they tried with all their (half)wits to solve the mystery of *The Gorilla* (20th Century-Fox, 1939). Hired by Lionel Atwill, who fears he may become the victim of a criminal known as "the Gorilla", the boys find themselves facing an actual gorilla, and haunted-house gags and mayhem ensue. At the rate of about one a year, the Ritzes turned out pictures like *One in a Million* (20th Century-Fox, '36) and *Argentine Nights* (Universal, '40).

America's favorite newspaper cartoon strip came to the screen in 1938 in Columbia Pictures' *Blondie*, first of the long running series starring Penny Singleton, (formerly brunette Dorothy McNulty), Arthur Lake as knot-headed but ever-hopeful Dagwood, Baby Dumpling (the billing for child actor Larry Simms), and Spooks as Daisy, the family dog. Faithfully following, though expanding upon, the strip, any given picture would have Dag getting in trouble at work, the construction company run by Julius Cæsar Dithers (Jonathan Hale, who was concurrently playing Inspector Fernack in "The Saint" series), and then, through a combination of Blondie's brain and sheer dumb luck, coming out on top. In the first picture, though he's unable to meet officially with an important prospective client, he happens to all unknowingly befriend the very fellow. As the series progressed, a fourth member of the family was introduced (Cookie, their new daughter, in *Blondie's Blessed Event* ['42], in which Baby Dumpling finally persuades his parents to call him by his name, Alexander), and, when Hale asked for more money, Dithers was replaced by George M. Radcliffe (Jerome Cowan) in *Blondie's Big Moment* ('47). Though useful as a proving ground for new talent, the series was discontinued at the end of the 1942-'43 season, but public demand brought it back in 1945, and it maintained its popularity through the rest of the decade, quietly closing with *Beware of Blondie* in 1950.

Lupe Velez and Leon Errol formed a dynamite partnership as Carmelita and Uncle Matt in RKO Radio's 1939 comedy, *The Girl From Mexico*, and it proved so popular that the studio created a series for the two, beginning with that year's *Mexican Spitfire* (from Velez's well known nickname around Hollywood), virtually a remake of the previous season's

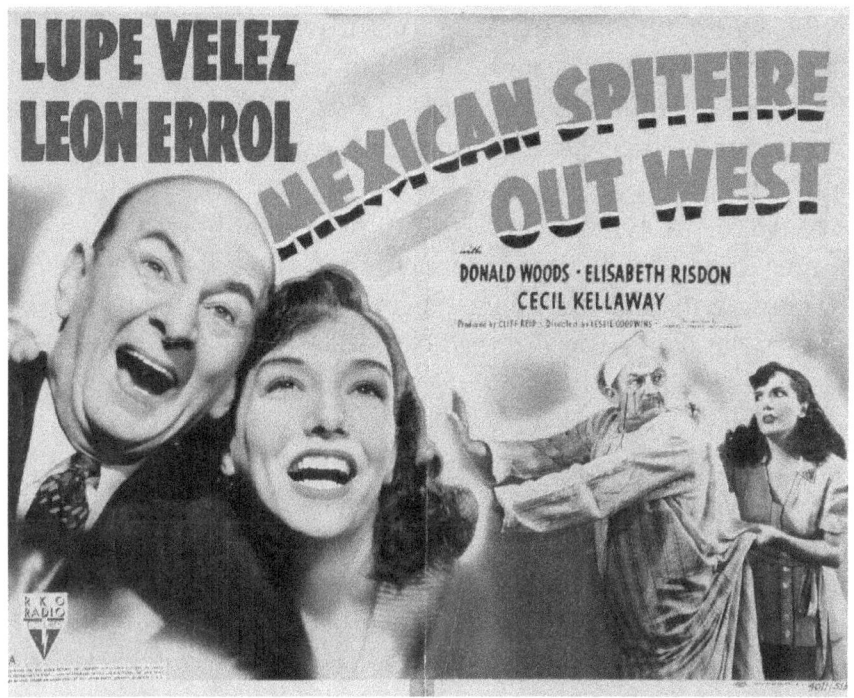

picture, but with the addition of extra characterizations for Errol, who played uncle Matthew Lindsey and his approximate lookalike Lord Epping, and Matt-as-Epping (with the aid of what Carmelita called his "billy-goat's face"). For the rest of the series, Carmelita's advertising-exec husband would be trying to please client Lord Epping, while she "helped", often getting Uncle Matt to impersonate Epping. A running sub-plot involved Matt's wife, who disapproved of Carmelita, touting her nephew onto another woman, which led, in *Mexican Spitfire Out West* ('40), to Carmelita trucking out to Reno in search of the wily divorce papers! Of course, each entry had a bout of endless confusion about Uncle Matt switching places with Lord Epping (who was so benighted he often couldn't tell which one he was). The series was a brief hit, running for seven installments through *Mexican Spitfire's Blessed Event* in 1943.

W.C. Fields was an irascible genius of the put-upon but

153

wily school, in picture after picture from Paramount. Ill-tempered, constantly annoyed, but always a laugh-getter. Films like *Million Dollar Legs* (1932), where he plays the President of the wacky country Klopstokia (home of goats and nuts), trying to save his country by competing in the 1932 Los Angeles Olympic Games, and *It's A Gift* ('34) in which Bill hopes to own an orange ranch in California, despite his nagging wife and problems at every side, still provoke laughs today. After *The Big Broadcast of 1938* ('38), Fields moved to Universal, where he made a quartet of his most idiosyncratic pictures. He teamed with fellow Paramount expatriate Mae West in 1939's *My Little Chickadee*, where as Cuthbert Twilly, a man who never met a whiskey he didn't like, he becomes the dupe of one Flower Belle Lee, who uses him to gain – of all things – respectability. The towering egos of the two stars made things difficult on the set, but Fields, a gentleman underneath it all, allowed West her way. *The Bank Dick* ('40), is a whirlwind of comedy subtle and broad, with nary a sensical character in sight. Bill's last starring role, as himself in *Never Give a Sucker an Even Break* ('41) is a tour-de-force, with Fields trying to sell a script for his next picture to the studio. The story, involving a beautiful damsel and her harridan mother (the formidable Margaret Dumont) atop a lofty and unreasonably tall butte, a plane with an open-air observation deck, and a wayward gorilla, all but drives producer Franklin Pangborn to distraction. The film wrapped around this scenario, with a specious view of studio life, a wild car-and-fire truck chase, and a scene in a soda shop (it was supposed to be a saloon, but the censor cut it out – Bill even tells us so) is so over-the-top it never fails to delight. Fields made only a few more films, mostly in cameo roles or specialty numbers, before his demise in 1946.

"Olsen and Johnson are coming!" was the cry that went up at Universal Pictures in 1943's *Crazy House*. Their huge Broadway success, *Hellzapoppin'*, had been turned into a feature in 1941, though the off-the-cuff, bizarre, throw-in-everything-including-the- kitchen-sink stage show had to be

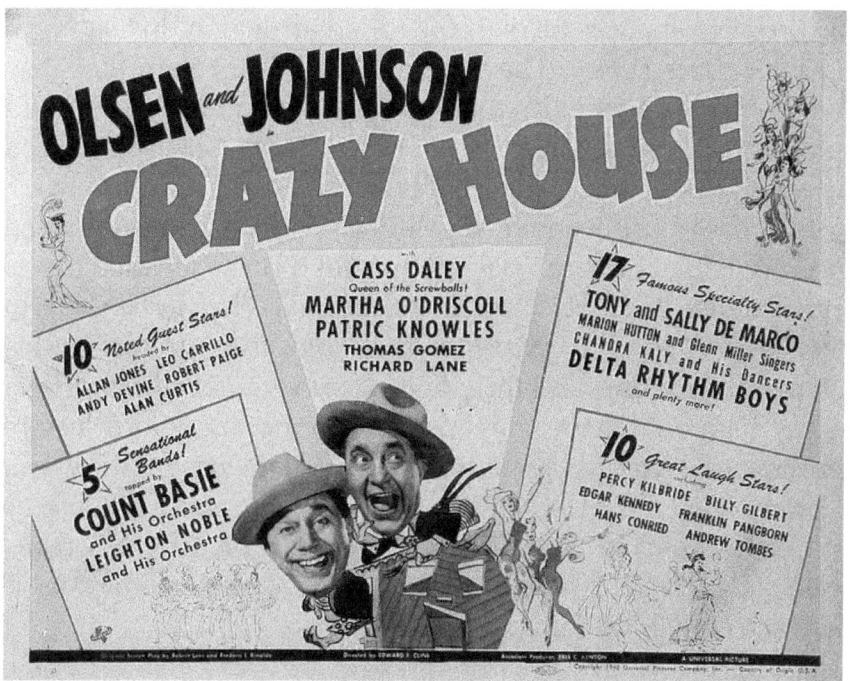

toned down for the screen (well, it didn't have to be, but putting in a plot and a romance gave O&J more material to crack wise about), the picture version still had enough gags for two regular comedies. Ole Olsen and Chic Johnson returned to Universal in triumph, ready to make their next picture, only to find themselves booted out after the entire studio panicked at their approach. Cameos by Johnny Mack Brown, Leo Carrillo, Evelyn Ankers, and even Basil Rathbone and Nigel Bruce as Holmes and Watson, brightened the first reel of this comedy, after which they settled down to make their *own* picture. Spoofing Hollywood the way they'd spoofed Broadway made for a fun picture, but not the wacky Olsen and Johnson people had come to expect from their live antics. A few other pictures followed (they'd made a couple in the '30s, as well), including their equally wacky *Ghost Catchers* (Universal, '43).

Universal's *real* top comedy stars, Bud Abbott and Lou Costello, had stepped from the top rank of live theater and radio performances to a sort of "added attraction" in *One Night in the Tropics* (1940). They proved such a hot item that they were soon starring in their own vehicles, featuring their polished burlesque routines. *Buck Privates* ('41) introduced them as stars, and a handful of service comedies followed, interspersed with comic mysteries. Their contract allowed one "outside" picture a year, which for a while meant a Metro picture like *Bud Abbott and Lou Costello in Hollywood* ('45). In 1945's *The Naughty Nineties*, they did their unforgettable "Baseball" routine, and flirted with fantasy in *The Time of Their Lives* ('46; in which they performed not as team) before embracing it in *Meet Frankenstein* (*Q.V. in Fantasy*), *Abbott and Costello Meet Dr. Jekyll and Mr. Hyde* ('53), *Jack and the Beanstalk* (Warner Bros., '52) and their last Universal picture, *Abbott and Costello Meet the Mummy* ('55), but by that time they were about to break up the act.

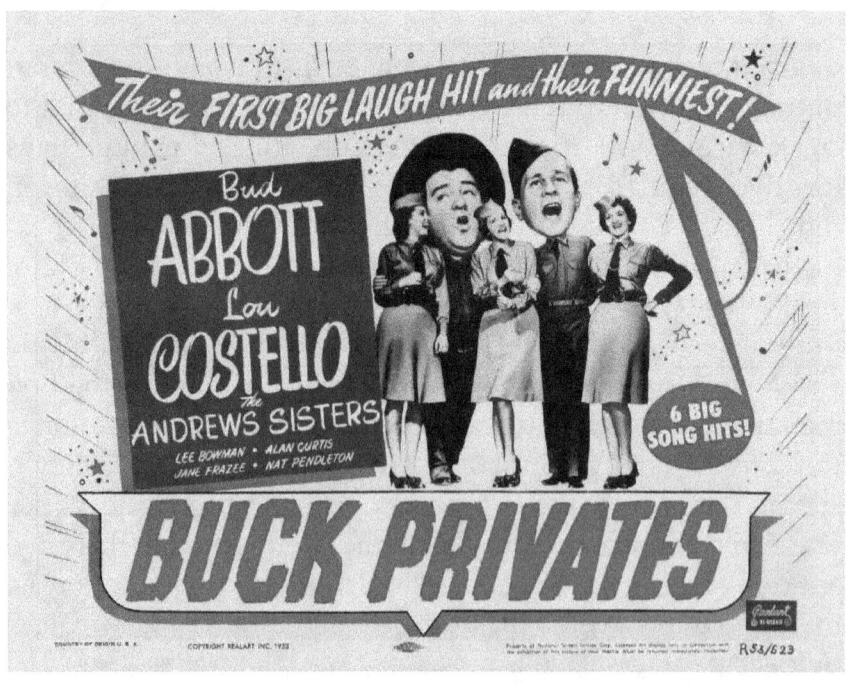

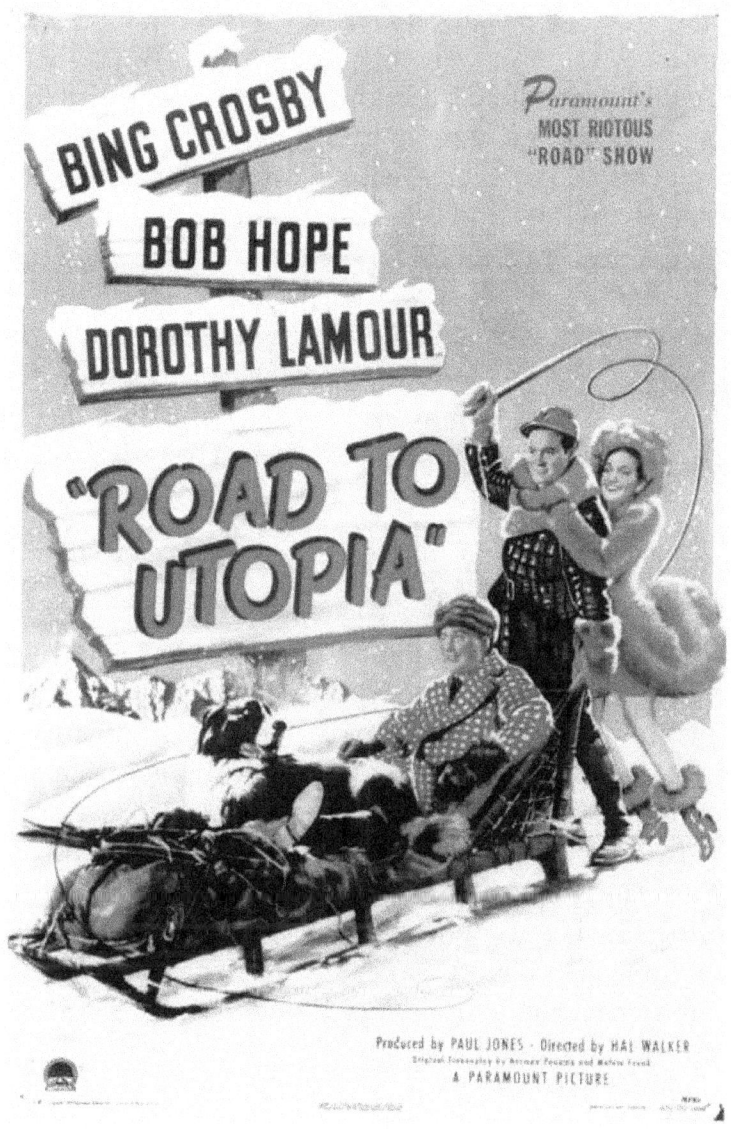

"Anybody here seen Sperry and McGurk without their beards?" 'Cause they look a lot like Bing Crosby and Bob Hope, in the fourth of their "Road" pictures, *Road To Utopia* (1945). Told in flashback, with dubious help from comic Robert Benchley, the tale spins out as Bing and Bob go looking for gold in Alaska, but run afoul of (and impersonate) two rough characters, and meet Dorothy Lamour, a talking bear, Santa Claus, and an overly affectionate dog. Typically for the films, characters talk to the audience, reality intrudes (briefly) on the proceedings, and there's a sting at the end of the picture. The "Road" vehicles had begun with '40's *Road to Singapore*, with Bing and Bob last-minute replacements for the intended stars, Fred MacMurray and Jack Oakie (for a script which had originally been written as *Beach of Dreams* for Burns and Allen), but it was a serendipitous switch. Many think the third picture, *Road to Morocco* ('42) is best, but the middle three ("Morocco", "Utopia", and '47's *Road to Rio*) are all top laugh-getters. The "Road" pictures were always eagerly anticipated by audiences, and greatly enhanced the solo careers of their stars. The last one, *The Road to Hong Kong* (UA, '62), with spies, rocket launches, and a memory drug, is a bit of a stretch but still funny.

RKO Radio tried to promote their own version of Bud and Lou in the persons of contract players Wally Brown and Alan Carney, in the short lived "Rookies" series (two pictures) and several otherwise unassociated pictures, in all of which they played Jerry Miles and Mike Streger. In *Zombies On Broadway* (1945), Miles and Streger had to handle both Sheldon Leonard and Bela Lugosi in the plot, when the former forces them to go to the Caribbean, where they meet the latter conducting unorthodox (as usual) experiments. The characters also appeared in *Genius At Work* ('46) with Lugosi *and* Lionel Atwill, and *Girl Rush* ('44).

America's foremost violinist, Jack Benny, was an early star of the talkers. His picture career never took off the way his phenomenal radio series did, but every once in a while he'd make a great picture. So don't believe Jack – *The Horn Blows At Midnight* (WB, 1945) is a delightful comedy, in which Jack dreams he's an angel sent to sound "Taps" for humanity by blowing his horn at... well, you get the idea. When he fails to do so, because he's lost his trumpet, angel Elizabeth (Alexis Smith) comes down to aid her friend Athanael (Jack), but finds him with temptress Fran (Dolores Moran), whom fallen angels Osidro (Allyn Joslyn) and Doremus (John Alexander) have bribed to make sure Athanael doesn't sound that Last Trump, as it would be the end of their cushy lives on Earth (and where fallen angels go isn't a nice place). The knockout climax, with Athanael caught in a giant mobile coffee billboard, is pretty amazing.

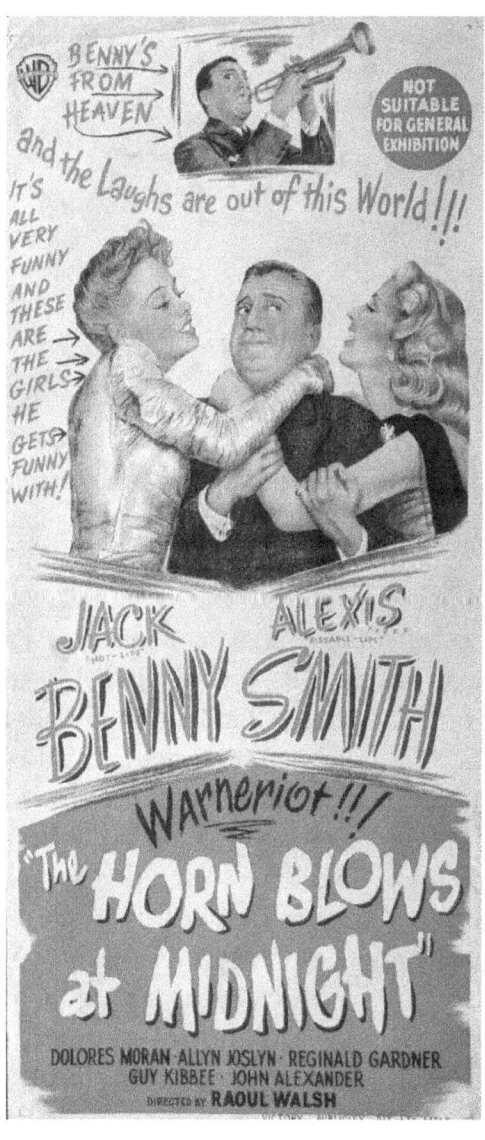

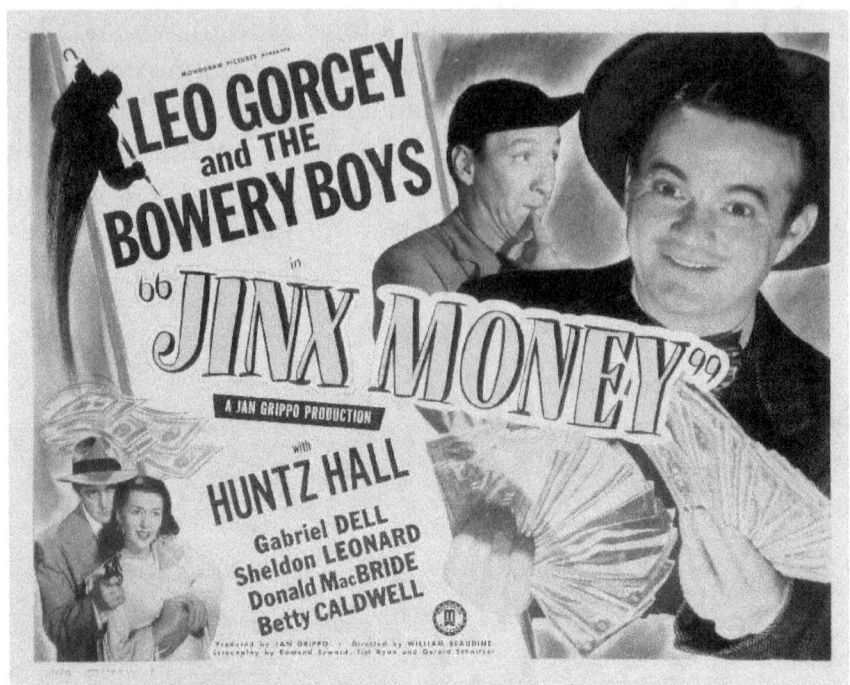

The Bowery Boys series was created and developed by Leo Gorcey, Huntz Hall, and producer Jan Grippo, and began with *Live Wires* (Monogram, 1946). The two actors (who had come to Hollywood for the film version of Sidney Kingsley's *Dead End*) had been starring in the "East Side Kids" series for Sam Katzman, but Gorcey had quit over a refused salary-increase request (though Katzman probably didn't care: he was already on his way to Columbia by then). This gave Gorcey a chance to mold new characters in the same style as before, but the new series had one other profound change: the "East Side" films were comedy-dramas, with serious stories infused with humor. The "Boys" would be straight comedy, with only feinting passes at serious subjects. The films, though painfully cheap, were popular with young audiences, who were rolling in the aisles at the bizarre malapropisms of "Slip" Mahoney (Gorcey) and the mind-numbing stupidity of "Sach" Jones (Hall) which was usually rewarded with a whack across the head from Slip's fedora. With numerous entries each year, the series carried on through 1958, though Gorcey had left the series in 1956 upon the death of his father Bernard, who had played Louis Dumbrowsky, proprietor of the "Sweet Shoppe", the Boys' hangout in the films. If one enjoys this low-brow comedy style, the best entries are, as usual, the early ones, such as *Jinx Money* ('48) and *Master Minds* ('49); the latter is particularly amusing when character actor Glenn Strange portrays Sach after a mind-switch. The last few episodes, without Gorcey, are mostly just contract-fillers, though the next to last, *Up In Smoke* (AA, '57), is a nice send-up on Faust, with Sach making a deal with the Devil.

Warner Brothers tried to make their own Bing and Bob out of Dennis Morgan and Jack Carson, two players who'd done dramas, comedies, and musicals separately and together. They'd scored hits with *Two Guys from Milwaukee* (1946) and its '48 follow-up *Two Guys from Texas*, and so promised a new Carson/Morgan picture for the '49-'50 season. But as the time came, and they hadn't a new picture ready, the studio whipped up a back-lot comedy (like a back-stage musical) entitled *It's A Great Feeling* ('49), assembled at break-neck speed. In this spoof of Hollywood as it existed in the minds of the audience, Jack, as himself, is frustrated because nobody will agree to direct him because he's such an inveterate ham. But for financial reasons he *needs* to make his next picture, *Mademoiselle Fifi*, and decides to direct it himself. But that means he needs a star, and with his reputation, not even his best friend Dennis will work with him. Jack uses ingénue Doris Day (as Judy Adams, not as herself) to trick him into taking the part. Jack's approach to film-making is less than successful – in fact his screen test of Judy drives producer Arthur Trent (Bill Goodwin) into a nervous breakdown. Many guest stars and wacky characterizations made a lot of fun for film fans.

John Ford directed John Wayne and Maureen O'Hara in 1952's *The Quiet Man*, a wonderful story of romance and the clash of Auld Customs with the modern world, one of the Duke's two versions of *The Taming of the Shrew* (the other was *McLintock!* [UA,'63]). Filmed on location on the Emerald Isle, with a cast of Irishters from the Hollywood community, it's proved to be one of the endearing classics and a feather in the cap for distributor Republic Pictures. When Sean Thornton (the Duke) returns to his homeland, he meets and sets to marry beautiful Irish rose Mary Kate Danaher (O'Hara), but hasn't counted on the enmity of her rough-and-tumble blowhard brother (Victor McLaglen) or her own Irish stubbornness. Though the Duke was better known for Westerns and War pictures, he – like the other two stars – made a good showing in comedy when given the occasion. (Incidentally, the later *McLintock!* was directed by Andrew McLaglen, son of their "Quiet Man" co-star.)

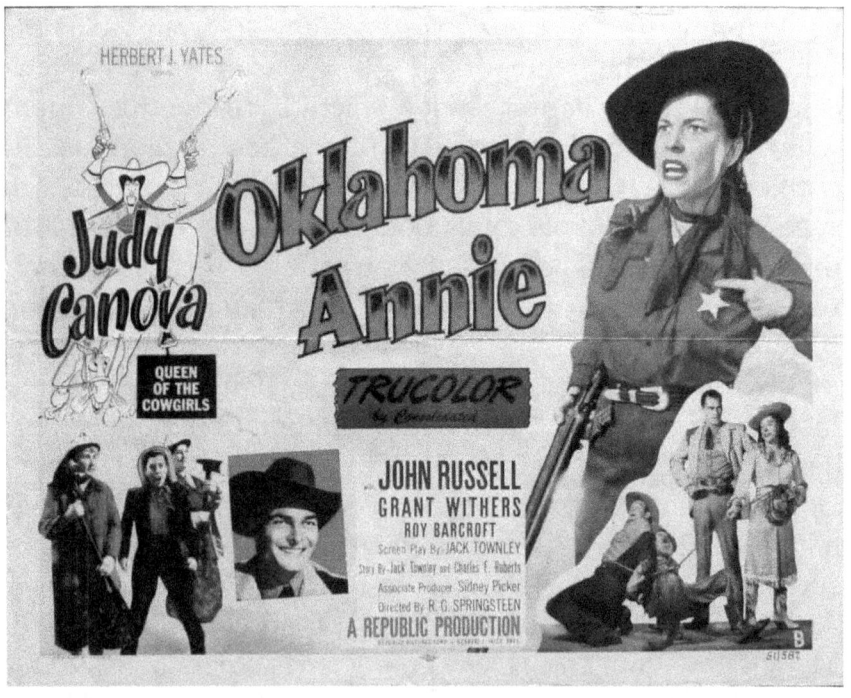

Judy Canova was a big star on the cornpone circuit, and her string of comedies for Republic, often supported by rural comic Andy Clyde, were big hits in the midwest and south. Traditional cowboy themes buoyed the star's engaging performances in films like *Chatterbox* (Republic, 1943) with Joe E. Brown as a cowboy star who isn't all he appears, and *Oklahoma Annie* ('52). They even had a nodding acquaintance with science fiction in *Carolina Cannonball* ('55), in which the rural trolley line Judy runs gets a boost from a misplaced atomic missile.

Since then, comedy has continued to reign at the box office, with wacky installments like *Airplane!* (Paramount, 1980), stories built up from TV programs (*The Blues Brothers* [Universal, '80] from NBC-TV's "Saturday Night Live" being the best), big-budget spoofs like "*Top Secret!*" (Paramount, '84) and *The Naked Gun* (Paramount, '88) and its sequels. But tops in the field was Mel Brooks, a dynamic force from television, whose hits like *Blazing Saddles* (WB, '74) and *Young Frankenstein* (Twentieth Century Fox, '74) forged a category of film comedy that had audiences rolling in the aisles.

Comedies could go for the knockabout yocks, or the clever-retort chuckles, or even the "what was that supposed to mean?" puzzled laugh, anything that seemed funny. And when the studios began releasing comedy features in the nineteen twenties, they'd already had years of experience, in films that packed jokes, as well as drama, mystery, and education in...

CHAPTER SEVEN: SHORT SUBJECTS

ONCE, ALL MOVIES were Short Subjects – for over 15 years a half-hour was considered about as long as a person could put up with watching the galloping tintypes at a sitting. But film-makers strove for more time to tell their stories, and by 1912 "feature length" pictures were born. But that was hardly the end for one- or two-reelers, and – now known familiarly as "shorts" – they added to the programs of long-form movies. Comedies had been extremely popular, as audiences all over the world needed no language skills to appreciate sight gags, and newsreels provided insight into world events in the same way as TV news programs do today (though of course at a week or so removed). Animated cartoons were a staple that was enhanced by the coming of sound, and every studio reached out to sign an animation house to distribute. The best of the mute comedies added clever dialogue and surprising sound effects to the merriment. Stage and radio comics became stars of their own series, and funnymen of the features gained extra exposure in two-reel stories. Informative shorts like the Pete Smith Specialties, the "Crime Does Not Pay" series, and James A. Fitzpatrick's "TravelTalks" opened entire worlds of sights and speculation to people who had never traveled more than fifty miles from the place they were born. Hal Roach's "Our Gang" and Columbia's "Three Stooges" brought laughter through the 1930s all the way to the '50s, when the short-subject format moved with ease to television, where the farces and situation comedies thrive to this day.

COMEDIES

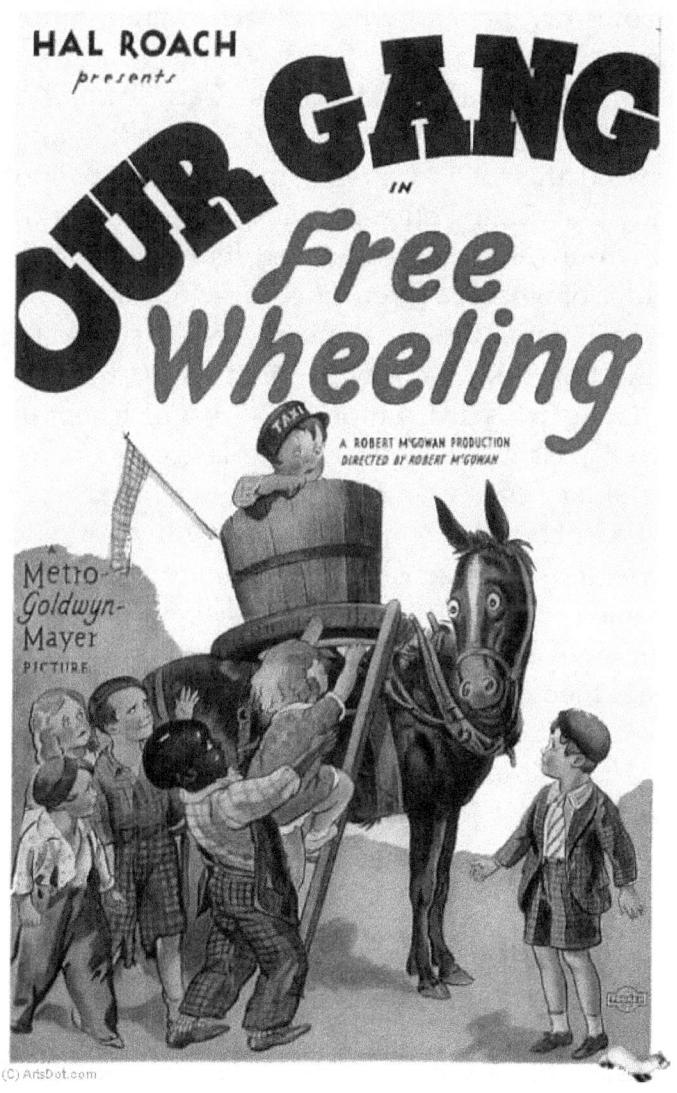

Hal Roach's Rascals were already a traditional short-subject series when sound enhanced "Our Gang" (the title of the first short featuring Hal Roach's Rascals) in "Small Talk", (M-G-M, 1929) the first talker in the long-running (221 installments) series. Youngsters who were now old pros left the series to younger, fresher faces, like young Jackie Cooper, who was so good that his stay with the Gang propelled him to features almost immediately, and Spanky McFarland, hardly out of diapers when Roach made him a star, introducing him in "Spanky" ('32). As the years progressed, *new* new faces, like Darla Hood and Carl "Alfalfa" Switzer joined the group, which then rather stagnated, holding those kids beyond their best years. Comedies like "Mike Fright" ('34) and "Our Gang Follies of 1938" were big hits with kids and grown-ups, for the Gang acted like kids, not like some adult's idea of what kids were like. Director Robert McGowan and writer Hiram "Beany" Walker kept the stories fresh and funny. As Roach stepped away from shorts to features, he sold the Gang to his distributor, M-G-M, which kept the series going well past its glory years. The last couple of seasons, with an older Spanky and the annoying Mickey (Gubitosi, later to be Robert Blake) and "Froggy" (Billy Laughlin) tried to teach lessons in citizenship and tolerance, to the detriment of the comedy aspects.

Comic stars made numerous shorts between their feature-film assignments: ANDY CLYDE, as the young old man, had a long string of comedy shorts, and enlivened many feature pictures, like Paramount's 1932 *Million Dollar Legs* (*Q.V. in Comedy*), where he played a super-speedster. He later spent several years as "California Jack Carlson" in William Boyd's popular "Hopalong Cassidy" series, and eventually brought a version of his "old man" character to TV's "The Real McCoys". LEON ERROL was a top short-subject star for RKO Radio, shooting scores of two-reelers between frequent feature-film appearances, many of which were made for his home studio, especially the "Mexican Spitfire" series (*Q.V. in Comedy*). He also co-starred against the Great Fields in *Never Give a Sucker an Even Break* (*Q.V. in Comedy*), and played comedy relief in otherwise serious pictures. ROBERT BENCHLEY was a staid, seemingly ordinary sort of fellow, but his fussy habits, his absent-mindedness, and hit-and-miss erudition made his "lecture" comedies a hit with audiences at Loew's theatres. His visit to the Disney Studios for *The Reluctant Dragon* (RKO Radio, '41) enlightened and entertained viewers, though his "helpful" remarks intercut into *Road to Utopia* (*Q.V. in Comedy*) may have been more puzzling than useful. EL BRENDEL's claim to fame in those days was his comic-opera "Swede" character ("Yumpin' Yiminy!") and while his feature-film appearances dwindled as audiences tired of the character (as seen in *Just Imagine* [*Q.V. in Science Fiction*], his shorts, like "Mr. Lemon of Orange" (Fox Film, '31) and "Okay, José" (Warner Bros., '35) continued to appear throughout the 'thirties.

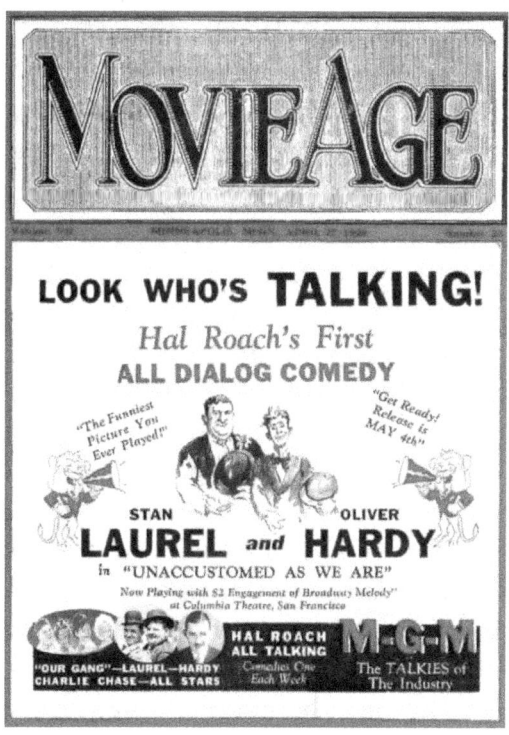

STAN and OLLIE hardly need any introduction, especially in the Academy-Award winning "The Music Box" (MGM, 1932). Stan Laurel was already a star of short subjects like "Hoot Mon!" (Pathé, '19) and "Dr. Pickle and Mr. Pride" (Selznick Distributing Corporation, '25), when producer Hal Roach teamed him up with the rotund and easily exasperated Oliver Hardy. The pair made dozens of shorts under Stan's supervision, including little gems like "Big Business" and "Unaccustomed As We Are" (both M-G-M, '29) before moving up to features. They had been kings of pantomime comedy, and sound and voice only enhanced their popularity in shorts and later feature pictures, with Stan's whiny apologies and Ollie's harrumphs to accompany his well known tie-twiddle. Throughout the '20s and '30s, they were the kings of the comic screen, and though their style was overtaken by the raucous Abbott-and-Costello antics in the '40s, their legacy as the Masters has endured.

When a short starring THE THREE STOOGES is entitled "Disorder in the Court" you can imagine the sort of outrageous moments in that 1936 release. Larry Fine, Moe Howard, and Curly Howard had parted ways with Ted Healy, who had been the guy whose stooges they had been, and became stars at Columbia Pictures, staying (with post-Curly replacements Shemp Howard and Joe Besser) until the studio closed its short-subject department in 1959. Their first two-reelers, including "Woman Haters", a musical novelty, and "Three Little Pigskins" (both '34) are among the funniest, with actual jokes interlaced with the slapstick, but the loss of Curly, everyone's favorite (he had a stroke from which he never recovered) and his replacement with Moe's other brother Shemp started a decline in quality, though some of the "Shemps", like 1953's 3-D "Spooks", have their moments. Shemp's passing in 1955 led to the casting of solo comic Joe Besser as the third stooge, though his shorts are, through no fault of his own, among the poorest. Even in these declining years there were a couple of gems, like 1957's "Space Ship Sappy", where the boys go to the planet "Sunev", an indeed-backward Venus. When their contract expired, Columbia, run by other hands than old boss Harry Cohn, declined to renew and closed their short-subject unit. But the Stooges weren't finished yet – *Q.V. in comedy*, as we say.

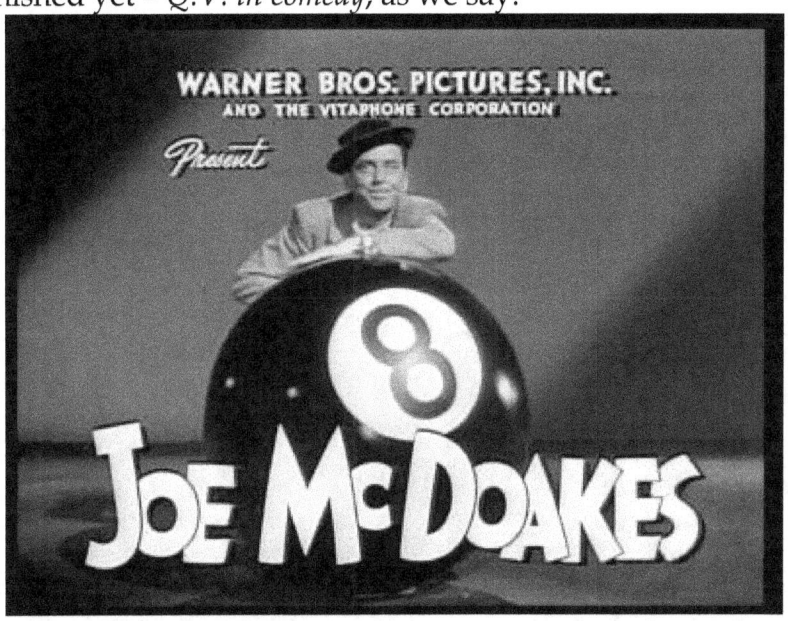

Late in the game, Warner Bros. began the Joe McDoakes "Behind the Eight Ball" series, starring George O'Hanlon and sometimes Phyllis Coates as his wife, which began as an imitation of the Pete Smith Specialties (*Q.V. below*), with episodes like "So You Want to Keep Your Hair" (1946) but evolved into sitcoms like "So You Want to Build a House" ('48), with occasional forays into bizarre parodies like "So You want to Be a Detective" ('48), in which Joe becomes "Philip Snarlowe" with narrator Art Gilmore as his sidekick, and "So You Want to Be in Pictures" ('47), where Joe, who wants, well, you get it, obtains a role at Warner Bros. studios, where, while proving he'll never be a danger to any paperbag's structural integrity, also crosses paths with actor George O'Hanlon – who dismisses the suggestion that he and Joe bear any resemblance to each other! The series was shepherded by Richard L. Bare, who later did similar chores for TV's "Green Acres".

INFORMATIONAL

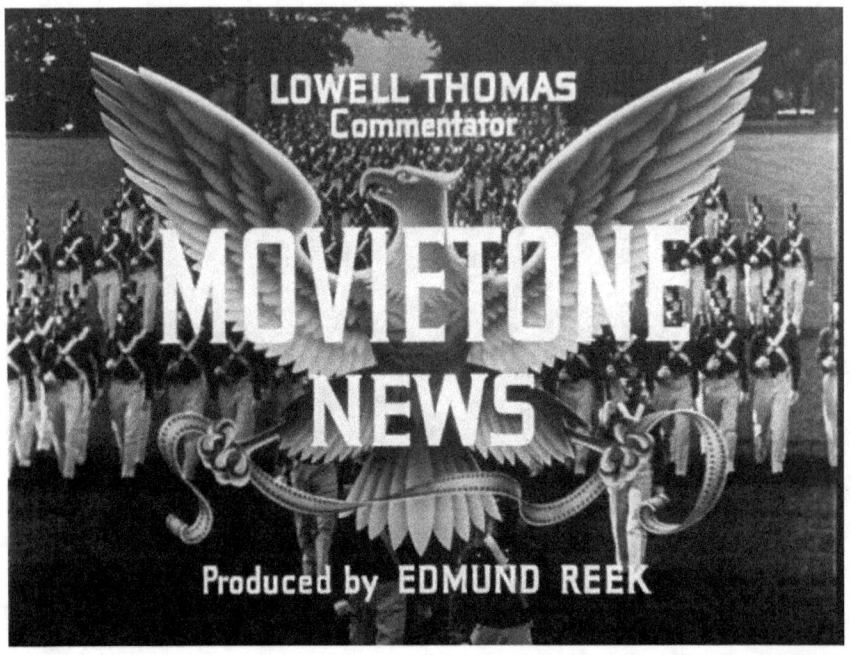

Newsreels were a staple of the weekly visit to your neighborhood "Gem" or "Odeon", showing what the newspapers and radio could only describe. Fox Film brought the events of the world to your local Bijou with "MovieTone News", with news, sports, travel, and human-interest features. Other studios brought out Paramount News ("The eyes and ears of the world"), "The March of Time", Pathe (with its crowing cock logo), and others over the years. Universal Newsreel, which brought not only news but "behind the scenes" clips from upcoming Universal pictures, even told the story of Orson Welles' 1938 Hallowe'en "War of the Worlds" broadcast and its effect on audiences who'd tuned in part-way through and foolishly believed it reported a real invasion (tabloiding it up and making more of it than had actually happened). Few of these still exist in their original form, but many were cannibalized for "Events of the Day" shorts with highlights from the best of a particular year. Of course, the format was the template for the network-television news programs that replaced the newsreel.

M-G-M ran a number of informational/dramatization two-reelers throughout the '30s and '40s: Metro's crime reporter brought us words of wisdom and lessons that proved that "Crime Does Not Pay", with stories of racketeers, con men, baby-traffickers, and other desperate desperadoes, and incidentally provided a proving ground for upcoming talent like young Marsha Hunt, Barry Nelson, and Tom Neal. The series could sometimes depict more hard-hitting crime action than the features, as shorts were subject to less scrutiny by the Breen Office (the Hollywood censors of the period). The "Specialties", usually narrated by a Smith named Pete and often starring hapless hero Dave O'Brien (who had parallel careers as western and serial hero, and as stunt man) getting the bejeezus beat out of him, were humorous looks at many aspects of life, from trying to get the best flavor gumball from a penny machine to keeping one's toupee in place under pressure. Pete Smith also had a sideline in historical "Gems", including several relating the prophecies of Michel de Nostradamus to current events (apparently he had a lot to say about Hitler). The Popular Science series, produced by Jerry Fairbanks and released by Paramount Pictures, chronicled the progress of science, industry and popular culture during its 15-season run. James A. Fitzpatrick, "the Voice of the Globe", took us to faraway ports of call as well as local landmarks in his "Traveltalks", with visits to Ireland, India, the Danube, and a particularly heart-breaking installment, "Paris on Parade", depicting the 1938 exposition in Paris, just before the second World War. During the war, the series retreated to U.S. and Canadian locations to keep the series rolling while international travel was all but impossible. Many episodes would end with narrator Fitzpatrick saying, "...And so, as the sun sinks slowly in the west, we bid goodbye to beautiful [insert name of place]." In the days when world travel was rare, they were glimpses of the exotic to the movie-goer.

DRAMATIC/HISTORICAL

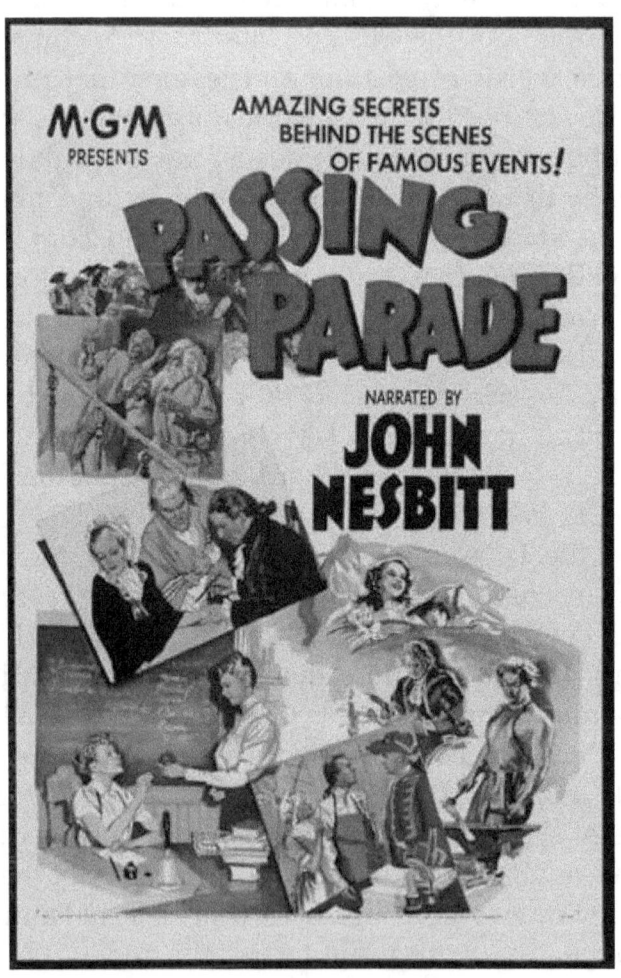

Many of the studios produced short subjects to tell of historical events, from Nathan Hale's stand to Custer's Last Stand. Warner Bros. in particular mined their vast feature-film trove to provide stock footage for historical and western two-reelers, in which lesser actors were filmed in new inserts to match stars of a decade earlier. (Robert Shayne, for example, matched up to footage from *The Lash* [1930], in "Gun to Gun" ['44]), one of many of these profitable shorts. Among M-G-M's similar product was "The Flag" A Story Inspired by the Tradition of Betsy Ross ('27) starring Enid Bennett as Betsy and Francis X. Bushman as General George Washington in a fanciful story weaving in the problems of a patriotic wife with a British husband. Hundreds of such shorts were produced, exhibited in theatres, and eventually shown in classrooms all across the nation. John Nesbitt produced and narrated "The Passing Parade", a panorama of historical events famous and mundane, from lesser known moments of history to simple backward glances at home and hearth, from subjects like Alfred Nobel and Eli Whitney to the Bowery and even "Our Old Car", tracing one family's motor vehicles from horseless carriage to teen-ager's hot rod, in the M-G-M series.

ANIMATED CARTOONS

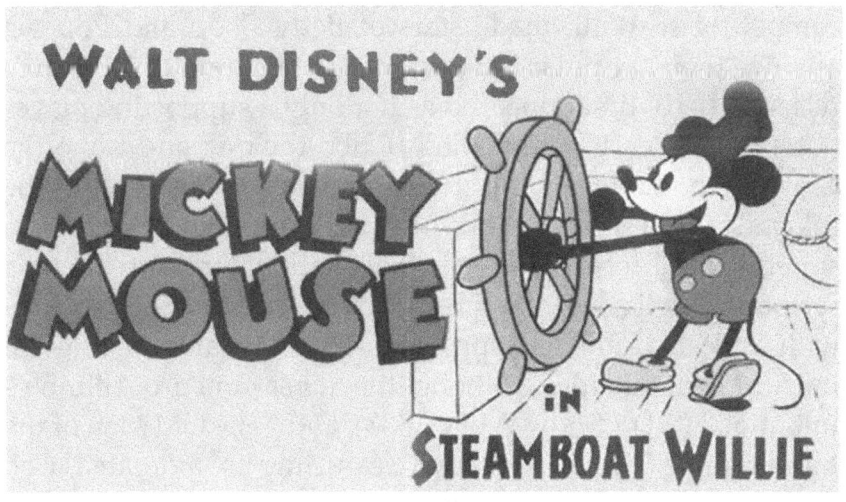

Walt Disney held back the first few Mickey Mouse

animated cartoons to re-tool them for sound, so that Mick would be the first "all-talking" cartoon character, from his debut in "Steamboat Willie" (1928). The Mouse would go on to scores of animated cartoons, along with his friends and co-workers Goofy, Minnie Mouse, Pluto, and especially Donald Duck, who began his career with "The Wise Little Hen" (UA, '34) but flourished in later years to rival the Mouse in popularity. Disney had begun with characters like Oswald the Lucky Rabbit (*Q.V. below*) and "Alice", a live-action girl in animated surroundings, but once on his own became the yard-stick against whom other studios were graded. Disney's artists were masters at the cross-over, now highly regarded in features, and when Mickey, Donald, and the Goof teamed up for pictures like "Clock Cleaners" and "Lonesome Ghosts" (both RKO Radio, '37), audiences couldn't get enough. Disney also indulged in a bit of sugar-coated education, in series like Jiminy Cricket's "I'm No Fool" and one-shots like "Toot Whistle Plunk and Boom" (RKO Radio, '53). And from the start with a little mouse, Walt Disney built an empire for children of all ages.

The Fleischer Studios, a family concern and a fan-favorite competitor to Walt, made stars of Betty Boop and Popeye, among their popular characters. In Paramount Pictures releases, Betty first appeared as not only a supporting player but a dog, in cartoons starring Bimbo the dog and Koko the Clown, who had been the studio stars in the '20s "Out of the Inkwell" series, and Max the producer and Dave the supervising director built her into a national treasure. Betty's cartoons had the sexy flapper involved in bizarre adventures with talking animals, spirits, and even famous real-life musical personalities. Among the most fun are "Bimbo's Initiation" ('31), "Snow White" ('33), and "The Old Man of the Mountain" ('33), the last two featuring an animated Cab Calloway. Popeye the Sailor first appeared with Betty, but immediately became the star of his own series, which adapted the sailorman's girl, Olive, and the bad guy who'd been in the strip at the time, Bluto, into the long-running romantic/fistic triangle, in shorts like "Choose Your 'Weppins'" (1935) and "The Anvil Chorus Girl" ('44), and three double-length featurettes in which the sailorman collided with the Arabian Nights ("Popeye the Sailor Meets Sindbad the Sailor" ['36], "Popeye the Sailor Meets Ali Baba's Forty Thieves" ['37], and "Aladdin and His Wonderful Lamp" ['39].)

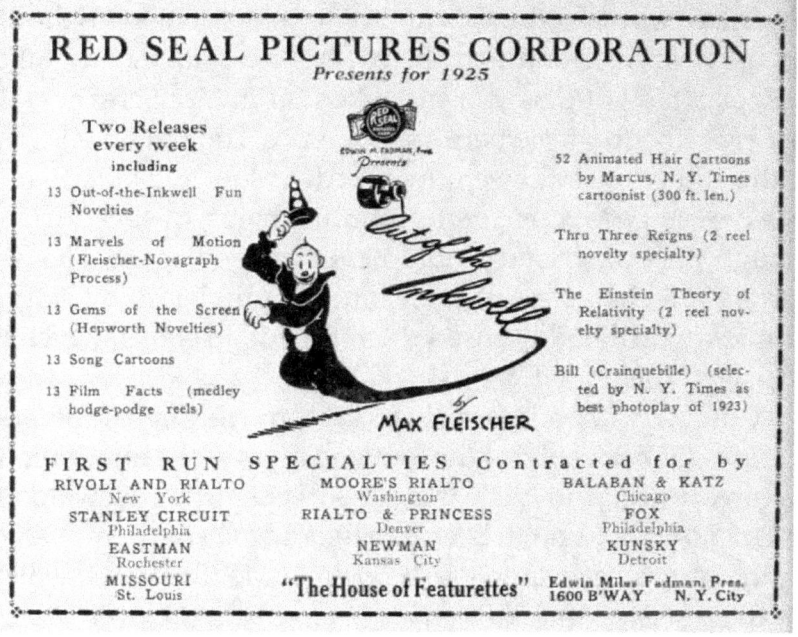

What had started out during the 1930s as a gritty New York cartoon shop changed when the studio moved to Florida and got aspirations to challenge Disney (at the urging of their distributor, Paramount), and their other series, like the "Stone Age" cartoons, lacked the bite of the early shorts. In their closing days, the Fleischers brought the Man of Steel to the screen in a series beginning with "Superman" ('41) and continuing in well drawn and designed action shorts. When Paramount leveraged the Fleischers out of their own company and re-named it, the new producers initially kept up the quality but turned out a declining series of shorts for over a decade. Famous Studios relied increasingly on dumb jokes and childish situations for their cartoons, with Popeye shorts more schematic, as were their new characters, like Baby Huey (a giant duck), Herman and Katnip (Tom and Jerry clones), Buzzy the Crow, and Little Audrey (a replacement for Little Lulu, a character to which the Fleischers' license had expired). But after Popeye, their most popular character was Casper, the Friendly Ghost, who continued to delight audiences through the '50s and onto television, even though almost every cartoon had the exact same plot as any other. Casper often got a new friend, like Lou in "Ice Scream" ('57) or Ferdy the fox in "There's Good Boos Tonight" a '48 short with a rather unsettling ending: Ferdy is shot and killed – only to have his ghost appears to continue being Casper's friend, though the new friend would never be seen again. The new Paramount characters were eventually purchased by Harvey Comics, which had licensed them for comic books, which re-packaged them for TV.

Walter Lantz released his cartoons through Universal Pictures (and was one of the few survivors of the International Pictures purge), in his early days focusing on Oswald the Lucky Rabbit (who'd been created by Disney) and Andy Panda. A perfect example is "Spooks", a 1930 release inspired by the re-issue of *The Phantom of the Opera* (*Q.V. in Drama*). Other Lantz characters included Chilly Willy the penguin and Wally Walrus, but the breakout star for the studio came as the result of a vacation trip by the Lantzes: When, on a camping trip (so the story goes) Lantz and his wife Grace were annoyed by a pesky woodpecker on their cabin roof, which gave Walter the idea for a wacky character who, voiced by the wife, would become Woody Woodpecker. Originally a wacky trouble maker, in cartoons like "Knock Knock" ('40), he would evolve into a more Everyman type, as in "Under the Counter Spy" (U-I, '54), continuing to release through the '50s before moving to television.

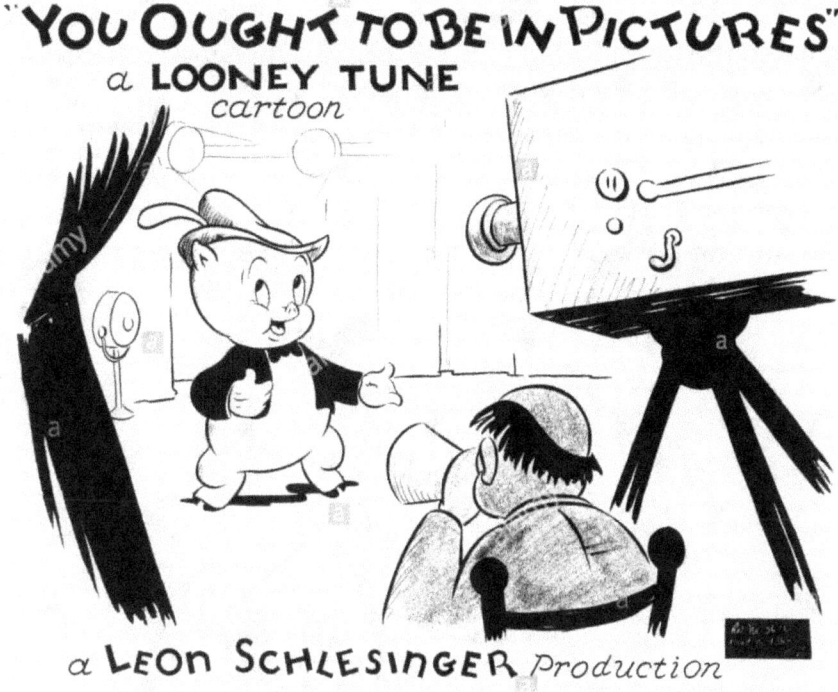

"YOU OUGHT TO BE IN PICTURES"
a **LOONEY TUNE**
cartoon

a **LEON SCHLESINGER** Production

Early Leon Schlesinger Cartoons for Warner Bros. were full of song-plugs and Hollywood caricatures. Titles like "Mr. and Mrs. Is the Name" (1935) featured a mermaid, her boyfriend, and a mean octopus, but did use the title song. In "Hollywood Steps Out" ('41), they spoofed William Powell, Spencer Tracy, young Doug Fairbanks, Errol Flynn, Wallace Beery, and others. In '33, series characters like Bosko (an unfortunate stereotype) and Buddy (a boring hero) were replaced by Porky Pig, Egghead, and eventually many more famous characters, under the capable hands of Robert Clampett (for example, "Wabbit Twouble" ['41] credited to "Wobert Cwampett") and Isadore Freleng, and Fred "Tex" Avery. By the time their distributor, Warner Bros., assumed command in '44, those newer characters were the top grossers. The two biggest stars were Bugs Bunny and Daffy Duck, each popular on his own but even better teamed up in shorts like "Rabbit Fire" ('51) or "Ali Baba Bunny" ('57) both directed by Chuck

177

Jones, one of most popular animation creators. Jones also created the Road Runner and Wile E. Coyote, in another series that was popular despite its one-joke premise. One cartoon taking a cue from Fleischer's "Out of the Inkwell" series was 1940's "You Ought to Be in Pictures", in which Daffy persuades Porky Pig to try his luck in live-action features, prompting Porky to jump off the drawing board and venture into the great world. You may be familiar with the premise if you've seen *Who Framed Roger Rabbit* (BV, '88).

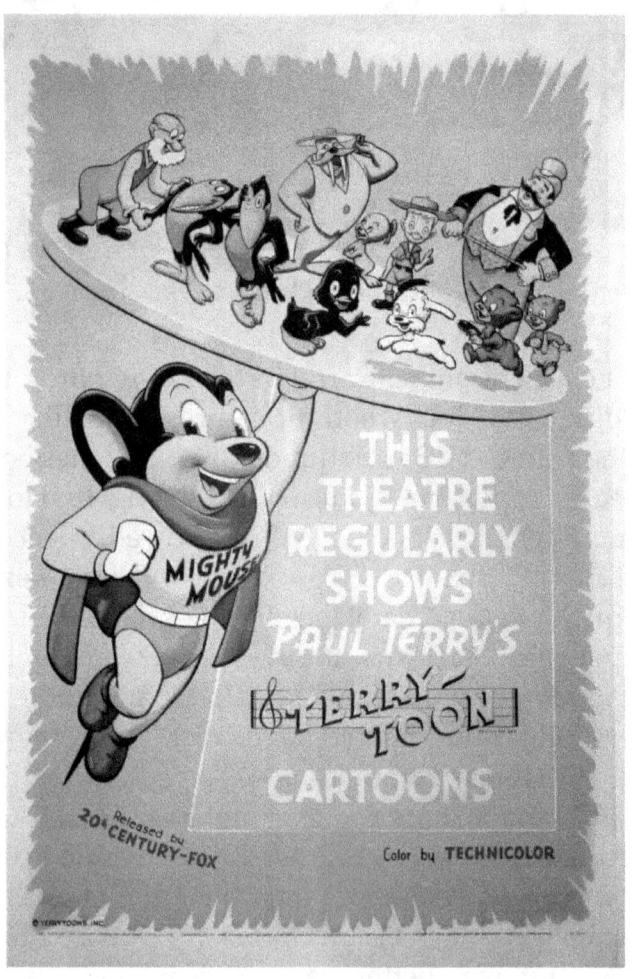

Paul Terry was another producer who'd started in the

mute-cinema days, with characters like Farmer Al Falfa and Kiko the Kangaroo, and his studio's later work, released by 20th Century-Fox was often caught up in following the leads of Disney and Lantz, with characters like Dinky Duck, Gandy Goose, and Sourpuss, though he had a couple of stars. Heckle and Jeckle, the talking magpies, often hit the mark, said mark being the funny-bone, in shorts like "The Power of Thought" (1948), where the magpies realize they're cartoon characters and can do *anything*. The most popular character, though, began as a bald-faced rip-off of the Man of Steel, "Super-Mouse", but after a chat with National Comics' lawyers, became Mighty Mouse and continued in a long-running series that dabbled in melodrama – a recurring villain, Oil-can Harry, was a parody of silent-serial fiends – and even operetta, as seen in "Krakatoa" (20th Century-Fox, '45) and a host of others. Terry entered into partnership with CBS to create "Tom Terrific" for TV, and both the magpies and the mouse got their own Saturday-morning shows.

M-G-M had its deal with a cartoon factory, Harmon-Ising (which had previously produced for Warners), making pleasant but undistinguished shorts ("Abdul the Bul-bul Ameer" [1941] is a wackily notable exception), but signed Fred Quimby to produce their animated cartoons. Quimby brought us Tom and Jerry, Little Cheeser, and others, but it was former Schlesinger animator Tex Avery , who'd walked from Warners after an artistic dispute, who brought inspired lunacy to the studio, in a series of outrageous comedy cartoons, featuring Droopy, Screwy Squirrel, and the lady known as "Red", the creation of top-notch animator Preston Blair. Avery's cartoons were noted for their bizarre story-lines and violent confrontations. Any animated cartoon with his name on is a guaranteed laugh-getter, but a few prime examples are "Screwball Squirrel" ('44), "Little 'Tinker" ('48), and "Little Rural Riding Hood" ('49), the final appearance of "Red".

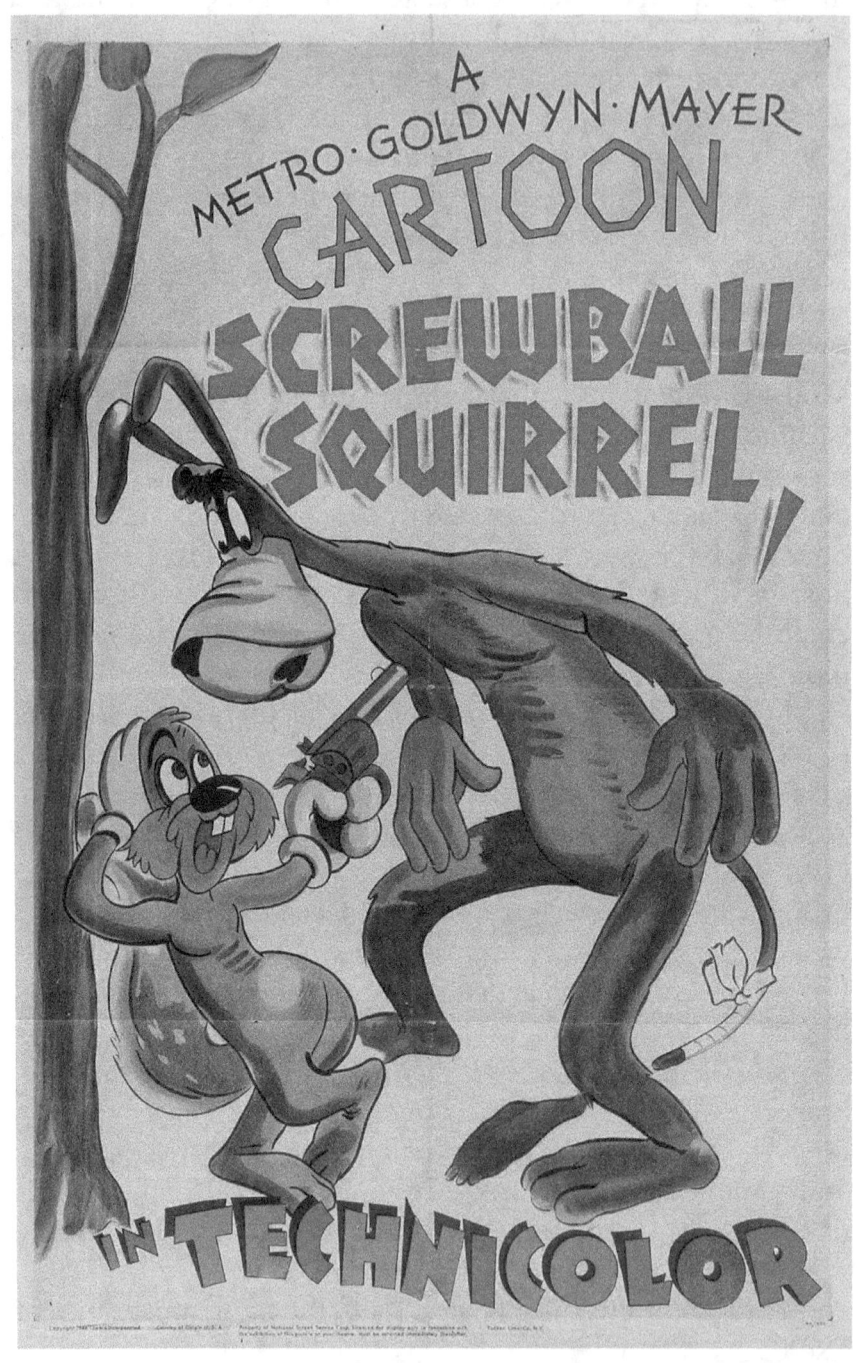

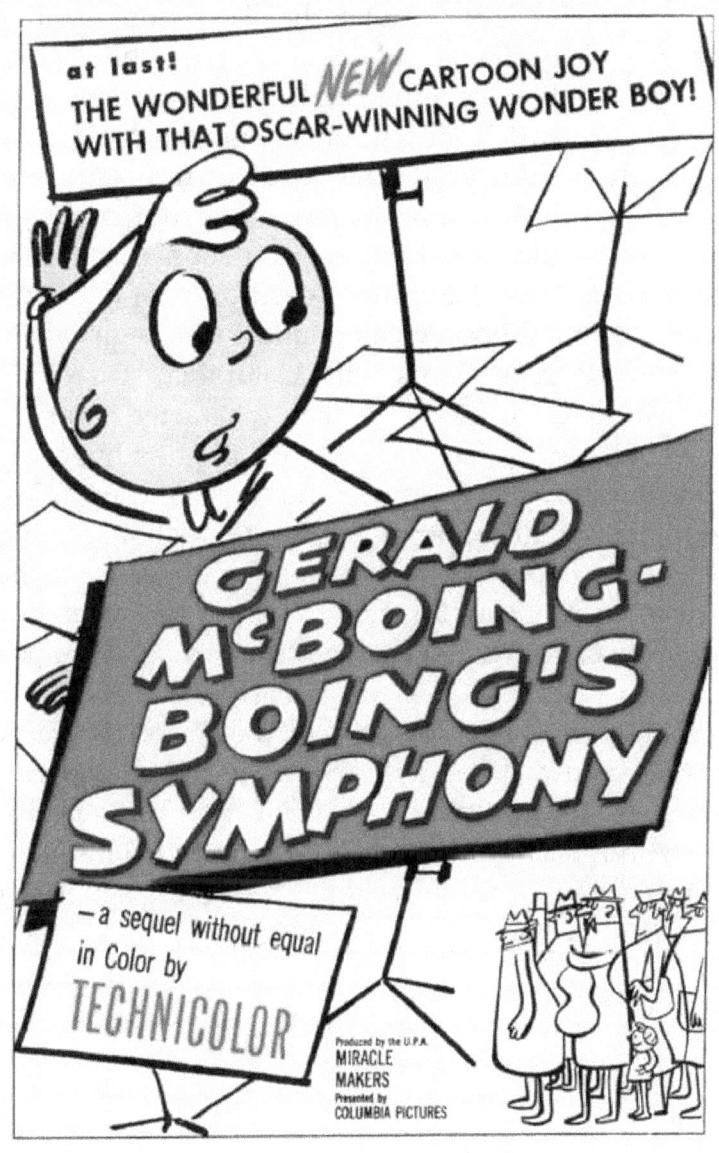

United Productions of America was a late-comer to theatrical animation, with spare art and limited animation but hatfuls of clever new ideas. Their long-running character, Mister Magoo, a crotchety, nearsighted, lovable old coot, first appeared in the 1949 short "Ragtime Bear". UPA made a name for itself in the late 1940's and early 1950's, due mainly to its modern visual style, a radical departure from the classic style of Disney animation. Beginning as Industrial Films and Poster Service, UPA started out doing commercially sponsored films. As the studio grew, the name of the company was changed. Stephen Bosustow, by then sole proprietor, signed a contract with Columbia Pictures, and soon was producing shorts utilizing the Columbia owned "Fox and the Crow" characters (who'd been created under the ægis of Screen Gems, UPA's predecessors with Columbia). Director John Hubley wanted to do a human character, and talked Columbia into accepting Magoo, who became a huge success, eventually starring in a feature and a prime-time TV series. Their other popular character was Gerald McBoing-boing, the kid who didn't speak in words but in sound-effects, though the story possibilities for such a character were limited. Magoo went on to TV and feature-film stardom in the '50s and '60s.

One other major contributor to the "Short Subjects" or Extra Added Attractions, as they were usually billboarded on theater marquees, was a class of film that bridged the gap between shorts and features, a collection of films that told long stories two or three reels per week; the action-packed thrillers known as the...

CHAPTER EIGHT: CHAPTER PLAYS

REPUBLIC PICTURES CALLED them "cliffhangers", but to the kids they were "serials" or more often just "chapters", and to the Industry they were "Chapter Plays" and they date back to 1912's *What Happened to Mary* (composed of individual episodes, each complete in itself) and '14's *The Adventures of Kathlyn* (the first serial made up of chapters with cliffhangers, where the action was interrupted at a crucial moment), and were popular entertainment from then on. *The Perils of Pauline* (also '14) was the most famous of the pre-talking era, followed and enjoyed by kids and adults alike, but by 1930 the form was almost exclusively aimed at the youth market, and in the '30s serials began to be adapted from radio series and newspaper cartoon strips, media themselves aimed at kids. The chapter play had begun to fade by mid-decade, but when Henry MacRae produced *Flash Gordon* for Universal in '36, the serial was virtually reborn, and the formation of Republic Pictures at that same time assured the serial a home where production values were paramount. Harry Cohn at Columbia completed the three-horse parlay of major serial-distributing studios, and when Sam Katzman produced the last theatrical serial, the 1956 *Blazing the Overland Trail*, for them, it wasn't really the end of the form:

183

the serial merely moved to television, where it has thrived ever since. But the originals, the chapter plays of 1930 to 1956, continue to hold a special place in film history.

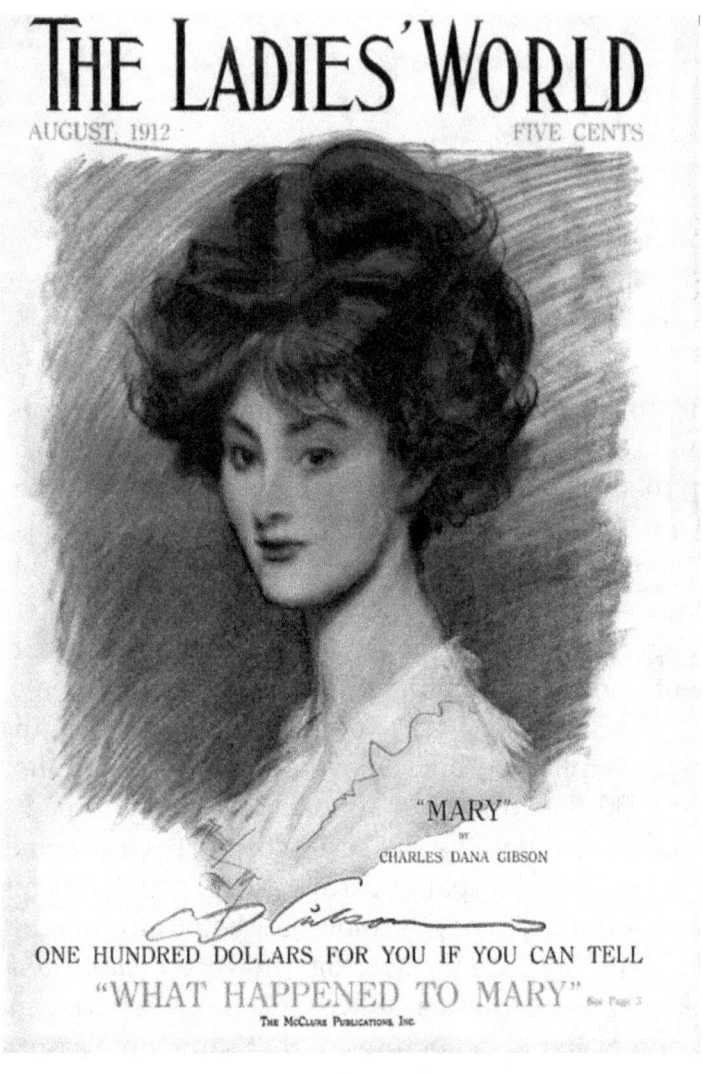

THE LADIES' WORLD

AUGUST, 1912 · FIVE CENTS

"MARY"
BY
CHARLES DANA GIBSON

ONE HUNDRED DOLLARS FOR YOU IF YOU CAN TELL
"WHAT HAPPENED TO MARY" See Page 3
THE McCLURE PUBLICATIONS, INC.

Readers and viewers had the chance to find out *What Happened To Mary* when this very first motion-picture serial, an Edison production distributed by General Film Company, began its monthly episodes in July 1912. The single reel (about 12 minute) installments mirrored a text version appearing concurrently in "The Ladies' World" magazine, a McClure publication, which involved audience participation by sponsoring a "what will happen" contest. Star Mary Fuller was already a veteran of five years, and appeared in over 200 films, including a "Mary" sequel, 1913's *Who Will Mary Marry?* before retiring in 1917.

The second significant US serial, Selig Polyscope's *The Adventures Of Kathlyn* (1913-14), was the first cliffhanger, with more action than "Mary", the exciting use of animals from the Selig Zoo, and with action lapping into the following chapter. Issued twice monthly, its genesis was in an attempt by the Chicago "Tribune" (which concurrently published the story in its pages) to boost circulation. Star Kathlyn Williams was Kathlyn Hare, and character actor Lafe McKee, who was already part way through a career that lasted from 1908 to 1935, starred, and the film started a tradition – the cliffhanger – that would endure beyond the demise of the serial itself.

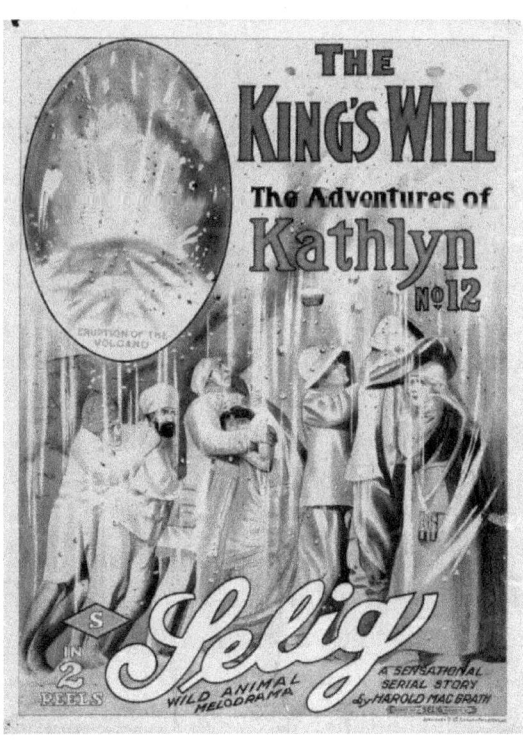

Pearl White's name became synonymous with the "old-time" serial due both to her prolific output and the 1947 Paramount biopic starring Betty Hutton and bearing the same title as her most famous chapter play, *The Perils Of Pauline* (General Film Company, '14). Though reverting to the closed-story format, it may have created the *term* "cliffhanger" with its frequent use of the New Jersey Palisades as a background. Like its predecessors, the serial's inception was in newspapers, this time William Randolph Hearst's syndicate. The 20 episodes were popular enough to warrant a follow-up, White's *The Exploits of Elaine*, which generated its own sequels and established Pearl as a serial heroine. In a climactic moment so iconic that it became the source of dozens of parodies from Daffy Duck to Dudley Do-right, Pauline was in one episode tied to the tracks by villain Raymond Owen (Paul Panzer, whose career as a character actor lasted until the early 1950s). In 2008, the serial was selected by the Library of Congress as being "culturally, historically, or æsthetically significant".

In 1930, after several partial talkers that had met with mixed reviews, producer Henry MacRae persuaded Uncle Carl Laemmle to allow him to make the new Universal serial, *The Indians Are Coming*, an all-talking picture. The production was halted for several days to re-tool and then to re-shoot portions of the picture. Seeing popular cowboy star Colonel Tim McCoy and getting the chance to hear galloping horses, whooping Indians, and blasting gunshots helped sell the picture and brought thousands of kids into neighborhood movie-houses. Chapter re-capitulations, previously title cards, were this time spoken by an old prospector-type, hanging out on a porch and delivering the foreword in a folksy manner. MacRae was a dynamic producer who loved airplanes, kid heroes, and the serial, and was the man who gave the now-neglected artform its respectability in the "golden age".

Universal's *The Vanishing Shadow* (1934) featured the first real robot in serials (a previous metal man, Robot Q in *The Master Mystery* [Octagon Films, '18-'19], had proved to be a human in disguise), as well as a host of super-scientific devices: an invisibility belt and not just one but *two* death rays – and they were the tools of the *good guys*. Onslow Stevens, later a regarded character-actor, was Our Hero, and in a typical Henry MacRae twist, heroine Ada Ince is the daughter of the bad guy, Walter Miller. Later serials with robots included *The Phantom Empire* (Mascot, '35) with Gene Autry and *Mysterious Doctor Satan* (Republic, '40).

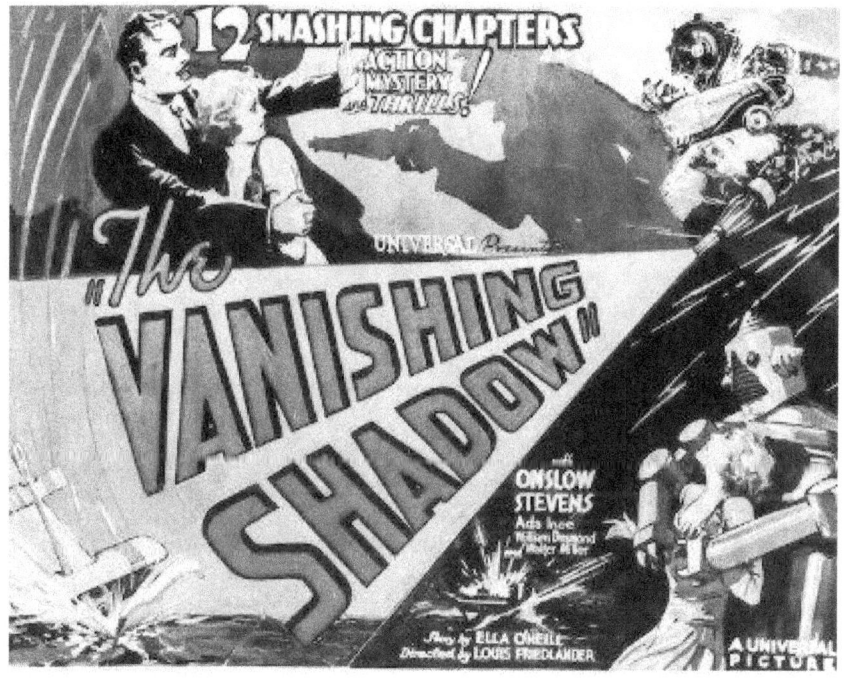

Nat Levine's Mascot Pictures had been established specifically to produce serials, and though they were cheap, Mascot was one of the leaders in the pre-talking days. They stayed on through the '30s, with Rin-tin-tin and cowboys, but one of their best was *Burn-'Em-Up Barnes* (1934), a rambling tale of a race-car driver and his boy side-kick in Los Angeles. Action star Jack Mulhall was Barnes, with young Frankie

Darro, who was also a stuntman, playing his pal. Extensive on-location shooting around Hollywood also makes this a great snapshot of the town in the beginnings of its glory days.

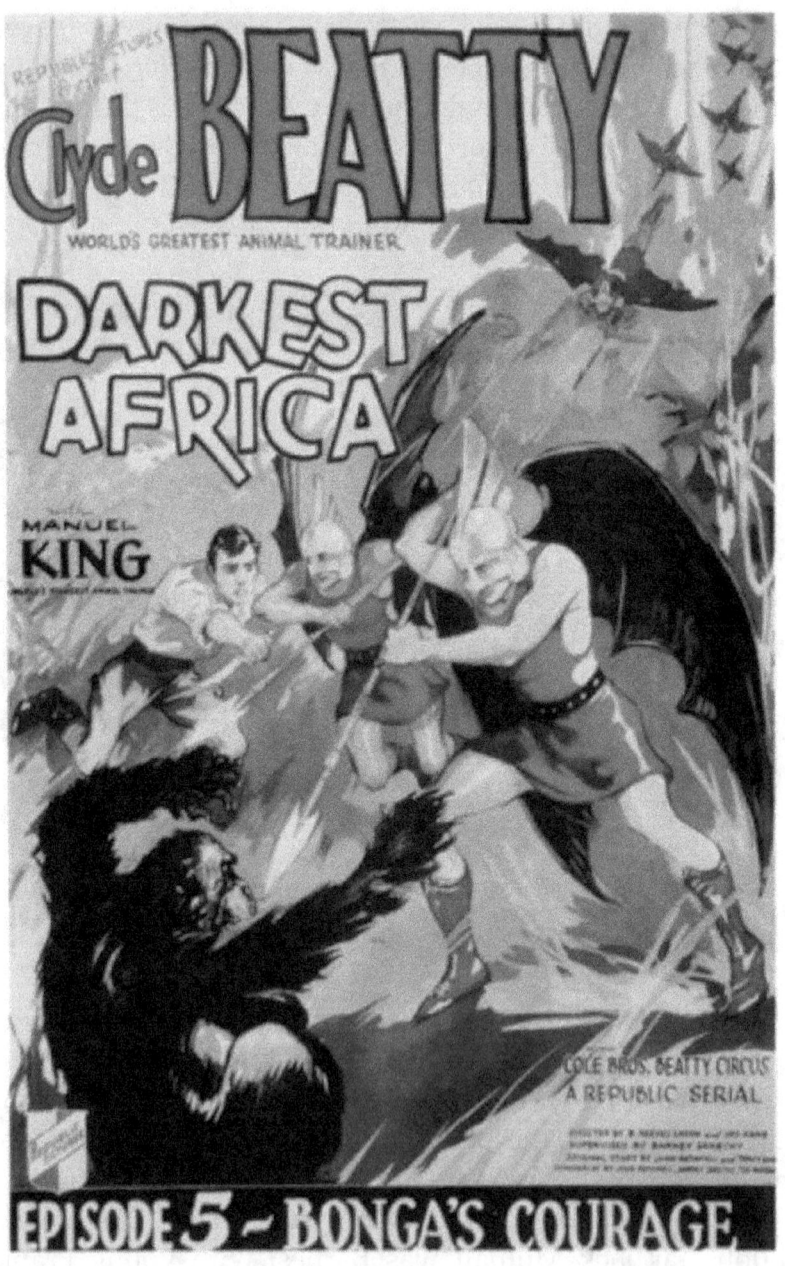

In late 1935, Herbert J. Yates of Consolidated Film Laboratories leveraged Mascot, Liberty, and Monogram studios and several independent companies to create Republic Pictures Corporation, and upgraded the production values to among the best in the industry, with full musical scoring, top lab work, and even quality film stock, to make the finished product rival the best in town. Their first serial, *Darkest Africa* (1936) had been begun by Mascot but became a spectacular under the new management, as real-life big-game hunter Clyde Beatty discovered a lost city, a beautiful princess, and flying Bat-men, portrayed by oversized dummies flown on wires by John Coyle and Howard and Theodore Lydecker, kings of special effects. Comparing this with Beatty's first serial, Mascot's *The Lost Jungle* ('34) shows what a difference the upgrade could make to a picture.

The serial was all but moribund when two things revitalized it. One was the creation of Republic Pictures; the other the production of *Flash Gordon* by Henry MacRae, king of serials and among the most important producers in Hollywood. The 1936 Universal serial played not only neighborhood theatres but big-city movie palaces, where kids and adults alike thrilled to the outer-space adventures of Larry <Buster> Crabbe as Flash, Jean Rogers as pretty Dale Arden, and fiendish Charles Middleton as Ming the Merciless. A picaresque tale, the serial follows the Earth-people as they journey among the many kingdoms on the planet Mongo, seeking allies in the battle against Emperor Ming. Startlingly faithful to the Sunday newspaper strip by Alex Raymond, the film cost twice as much as a "regular" serial (for which MacRae was chastised by the incoming new owners, though his position was restored after the serial made some four times as much as serials usually did at the time), with ray-guns, rocket-ships (one of which had appeared in *Just Imagine* (*Q.V. in Science Fiction*), and a rather adult sub-plot, courtesy of writer Ella O'Neill, with Ming lusting after Dale, and Ming's daughter on the make for Flash. Sequels

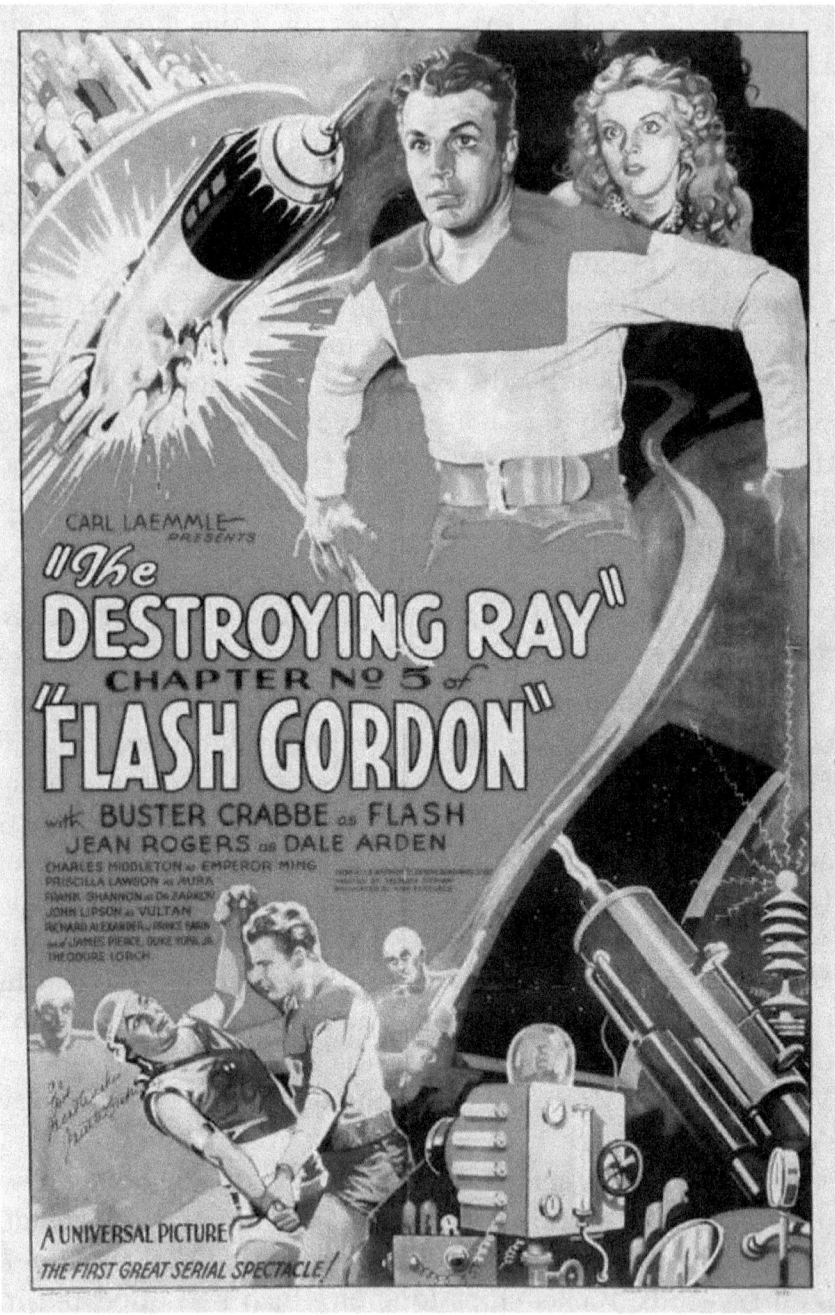

were guaranteed, with *Flash Gordon's Trip to Mars* in '38 and *Flash Gordon Conquers the Universe* in '40. The third serial boasts fantastic plots and beautiful costumes, courtesy of Universal's extensive list of period pictures and the Western Costumes collection. Buster was the king of serial heroes, making nine, his others being *Tarzan the Fearless* (Principal, '35), *Red Barry*, (Universal, '38), *Buck Rogers* (Universal, '39), *The Sea Hound* Dare Devil Adventures of Captain Silver (Columbia, '47), *Pirates of the High Seas* (Columbia, '50; almost a remake of *The Sea Hound*), and *King of the Congo* (The Mighty THUNDA) (Columbia, '51-'52).

Only a few independent producers remained in the serial market after the coming of sound. One of last was Sam Katzman's Victory Pictures, which brought out the 1936 chapter play *Shadow Of Chinatown*, starring one of the screen's great villains, Bela Lugosi, as Victor Poten, a Eurasian filled with hate for both sides of his heritage. When Poten uses a popular book as a template for his depredations, its author, Martin Andrews (Herman Brix, later known as Bruce Bennett) falls under suspicion. Reliable henchman Charlie King, ingénue Joan Barclay, and beautiful Luana Walters as an Oriental temptress, add to the interest in this leisurely paced but interesting picture. Katzman's career was long lasting, as he later moved from Monogram to Columbia and eventually became producer of A pictures in the '60s.

Republic, only a year old in 1937, brought us *Dick Tracy*, based on the popular newspaper strip (*Q.V. also in Mystery*), but Tracy was now a G-Man, which gave more latitude for adventures but also because studio head Herbert Yates sought real-life fed Melvin Purvis for the role (though it fell to Ralph Byrd, who portrayed Tracy admirably). In this very *noir*-ish story, Tracy battles the Spider Ring (led by a miscreant called "the Lame One") in an assortment of exploits. Unknown to Tracy is that the Lame One has captured Tracy's own brother, and by surgery, made him an amnesiac and a criminal, and altering his appearance, making for extra thrills for the audience. High-flying action, courtesy of the Lame One's plane, the "Wing", and daredevil action compensated for long stretches of talk and comedy in the picture, and it was popular enough to warrant sequels: Tracy came back in *Dick Tracy Returns* ('38, with villain Charles Middleton), *Dick Tracy's G-Men* ('39), and *Dick Tracy Vs. Crime, Inc.* ('41), in which he battles an invisible villain. Tracy, of course, returned in four RKO Radio Pictures, animated cartoons, and a big-budget Buena Vista feature in 1990.

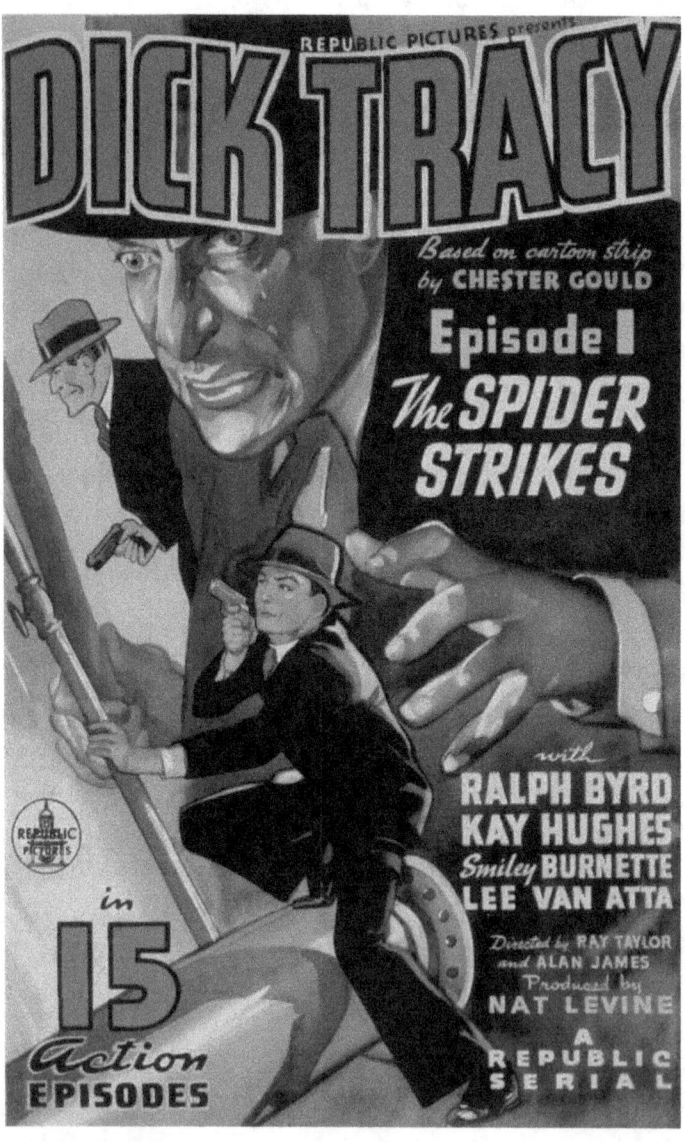

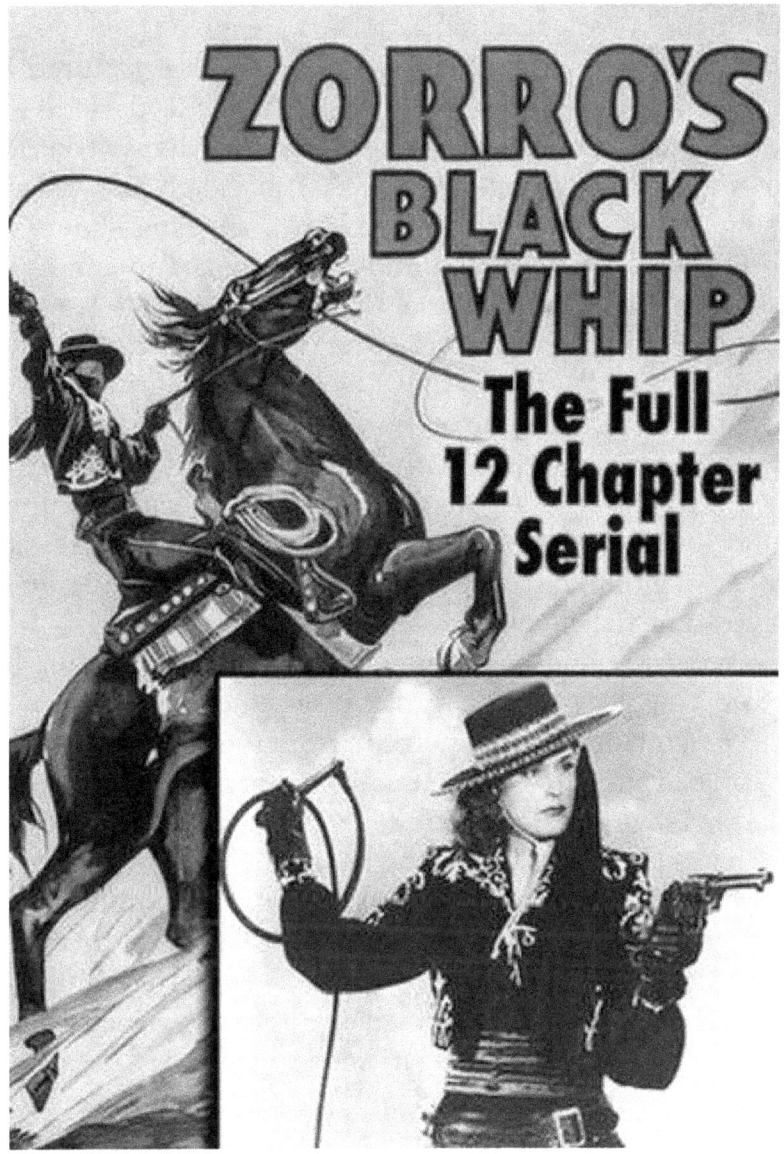

Yates knew that characters from other media were a guaranteed draw, and so spent extra money lining up new characters after the success of "Tracy", and started with that masked rider of Old California, Johnston McCulley's "Zorro", first in a Magnacolor feature, *The Bold Caballero* (1936) and a modern-dress serial, *Zorro Rides Again* ('37-'38). Later cliffhangers involved other latter-day relatives (*Son of Zorro* ['46-'47] and *Ghost of Zorro* ['49]), but the best featured the original, *Zorro's Fighting Legion* ('39), with Reed Hadley as Diego Vega and his masked other identity. Extensive outdoor shooting, a well wrought plotline (with villain Don del Oro posing as a god of the Yaqui Indians), amazing stuntwork, and a vital, pulse-pounding underscore make this among the best of the chapter plays. Other Republic Zorro-like characters figured in *Don Daredevil Rides Again* ('51) with Ken Curtis, and *The Man with the Steel Whip* ('54) with Richard (Sergeant Preston) Simmons in one of the studio's last cliffhangers. But the most surprising was *Zorro's Black Whip* ('44) with Linda Stirling as the masked hero who wore her dead brother's leather outfit and whipped the Bad Guys into submission. (Not to mention that later in the story, her boyfriend puts on her costume to ride to the rescue.)

Toward the end of the nineteen thirties, the serials, like feature films, experienced a golden age, and many of the most well remembered cliffhangers are from the period 1938-1940. One that transcended its straitened budget with a striking master villain was Republic's 1938 *The Fighting Devil Dogs*, in which the Lightning used super-scientific devices such as his aircraft the Wing and weapons the awesome thunderbolt ærial torpedo and lightning-bolt pistol in a campaign of conquest. He soared above his enemies in the Wing (a prop left over from *Dick Tracy*), clad in his snappy black outfit, complete with a helmet that has been suggested as inspiration for that of Darth Vader in *Star Wars* (20th Century-Fox, '77) with a ruthlessness seldom matched by villains in any medium. The Lightning was portrayed by character-actor Lester Dorr (who was not the actor revealed as the villain's other identity) with the voice of Edwin Stanley (a typical way serials concealed the villain's real identity), opposed by Lee Powell and Herman Brix as heroic U.S. Marines in ten exciting out of twelve chapters (two chapters were used as "recapitulation" installments, where the characters sat around discussing the plot to date while the audience saw repeat footage). *The Torpedo of Doom* (NTA, '66) the condensed feature version of the serial, improves the picture by editing out the dragging re-cap sequences.

Harry Cohn got Columbia Pictures into the serial business by contracting to release the independent chapter plays of the Weiss Brothers in 1937, and then absorbing the company into his studio, resulting in an upswing in quality. One of the studio's best is the 1938 *The Spider's Web*, based on a popular pulp-magazine character. Warren Hull starred as criminologist Richard Wentworth and his alter-egos underworld character Blinky McQuade and the masked Spider (though his rather conventional cape, cowl, and fedora were a far cry from the bizarre vampire-like characterization of the pulps). For fifteen chapters, the Spider battled the forces of the Octopus, an *outré* character clad in a white robe, who never left his sanctum sanctorum, to prevent the villain from seizing control of the "key industries of the nation". All of the now well-worn clichés were trotted out, including the Spider's identity almost being discovered. 1941 saw *The Spider Returns*, but, though the Spider and his faithful servant Ram Singh (Kenneth Duncan) returned, the picture was aimed at a more juvenile audience, with villain the Gargoyle guilty mainly of over-acting. Columbia's serials were for a time farmed out to producer Larry Darmour, and on his death production was resumed in-studio, bringing several interesting serials in the period 1942-1945, using the leftover sets and costumes from feature pictures. 1944's *The Desert Hawk*, starring Gilbert Roland, is an example of the variety of settings Columbia could use.

The Lydecker brothers created explosions, floods, crashes, flying men, and miniature cars and boats for features and cliffhangers at Republic, all impressive and among the best, even today. For 1939's *Daredevils Of The Red Circle* they convincingly flooded an underwater tunnel for the climax of chapter one. In the story, escaped convict Harry Crowell –

better known by his prison number, 39013 – wrecks the enterprises of his former partner and incurs the enmity of three athletic carnival performers, played by Charles Quigley, Herman Brix, and David Sharpe. 39013 was played by both Charles Middleton and, when masked, Miles Mander. Exciting thrills met the daredevils each week, while 39013's prisoner, Granville (Manders again) languishes in a cell with a death-trap ready to kill him if the villain should ever fail to return in time to re-set the device.

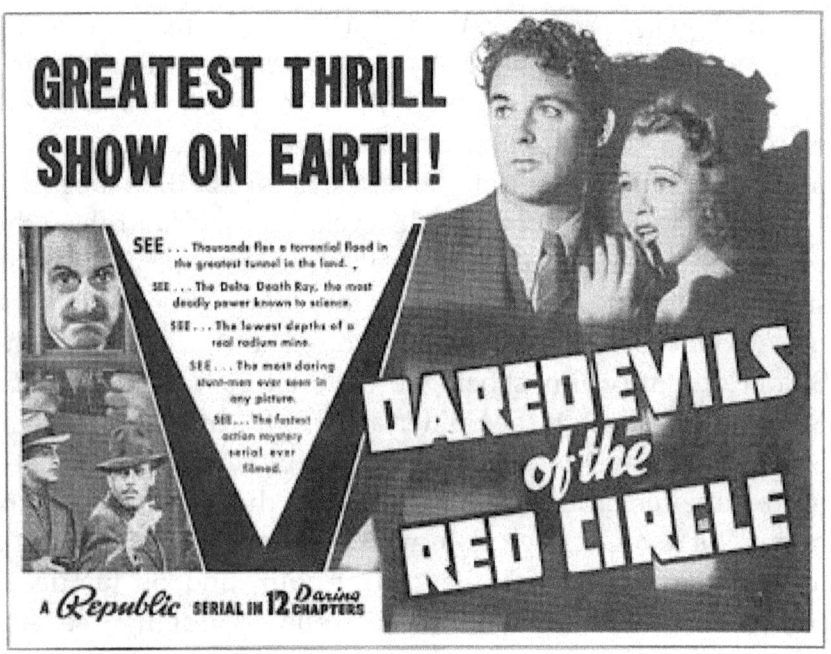

Perhaps the best of all serials was Republic's 1940 offering, *Drums Of Fu Manchu*. Using the title of the most recent Sax Rohmer novel about the Oriental master fiend and incidents from several books, it told the story of the plan of the "Illustrious One" to rule Asia through the acquisition of the scepter of Genghis Khan. On his trail, assistant hero Allan Parker (Robert Kellard) took on the fighting from the doctor's traditional foes, Sir Denis Nayland Smith and Flinders Petrie

(William Royle and Olaf Hytten). The picture played rather more fairly than usual with the cliffhanger resolutions (which would in some serials involve changing what had happened last time) and featured one of Hollywood's top character actors, Henry Brandon, as Dr. Fu Manchu. The action moved from America to Asia, as the Doctor followed a trail of clews to locate the lost tomb of the Great Khan, leading to a spectacular climax when Fu Manchu *does* acquire the scepter. A particularly effective cliffhanger has Nayland Smith a captive, about to go under the knife to become a victim of the surgery that transforms a man into a robot with no will of his own. Could that be the end of Smith? Well, it *is* the chapter 14 cliffhanger, so... .

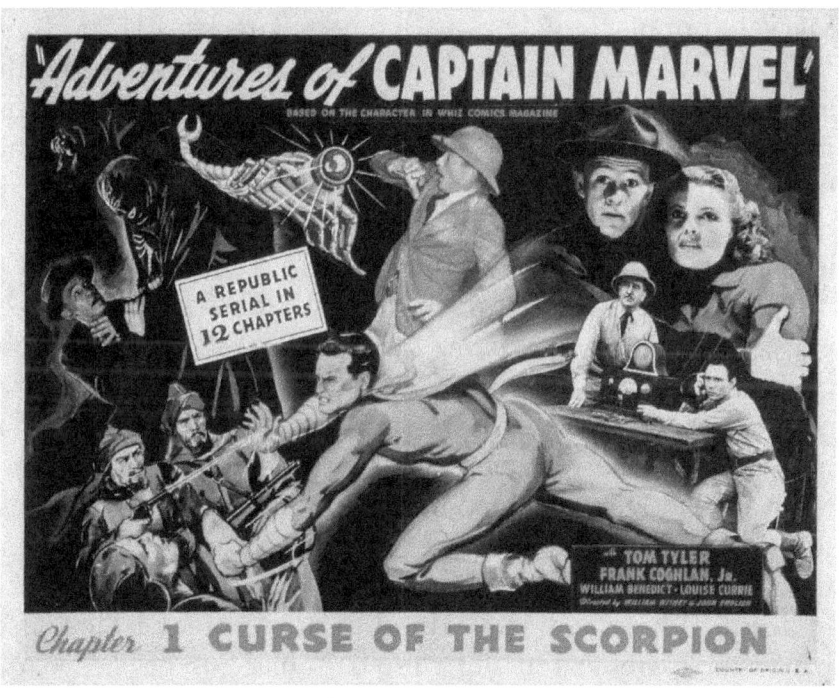

Republic continued its place of pride among studios with its 1941 production of *Adventures Of Captain Marvel*, the very first serial based upon the new medium of the comic book. Fawcett's hero was a second choice after Superman (they had begun a script, but found National Comics too demanding regarding the character's usage), but he proved to be a huge hit with kids all across the nation. To battle the World's Mightiest Mortal, writers created the Scorpion, a masked fiend voiced by Gerald Mohr, who attempts to acquire all the pieces of an alchemical atomsmasher discovered in a tomb complex in Siam. When the pieces are divided among the expedition members, the Scorpion hunts down each member and acquires his piece – and kills the possessor. Thrilling stunt work by David Sharpe, who when he leaped into the air made you believe he was flying, and a well crafted dummy figure made Captain Marvel a hit with kids and even impressed the grown-ups. Youthful Frank Coghlan, Jr., played Billy Batson, who, by calling the magic word "*SHAZAM!*" became Captain Marvel (popular cowboy actor and character player Tom Tyler), and Louise Currie, Billy Benedict, and Harry Worth top-lined the cast. The character vanished in 1953 when publisher Fawcett abandoned a long copyright-infringement battle with National Comics, but was later revived and recently re-named "Shazam" as the "Captain Marvel" name is being used by Marvel Comics.

When Universal brought *Gang Busters* to the screen in 1942, it was in a more *outré* story than the realistic radio drama created and produced by Phillips H. Lord. The police are confronted by the clever Professor Mortis, who holds his gang in thrall by bringing them back from the dead and keeping them alive only by repeated treatments. Hero Kent Taylor has to endure losing his job as a cop (a frequent problem for Universal policemen), and, in order to join the gang being put to death and revived, in his quest to stop Professor Mortis. It may seem extreme, but Our Hero has an ace up his sleeve (or at least he hopes so). Veteran character player Ralph Morgan (brother of Metro's Frank) plays Mortis in a very understated, calm manner, making him seem all the more dangerous, though he rarely leaves his hide-out beneath the city's subway system.

The Second World War hit the serials pretty hard for three seasons (until the Office of War Information requested the studios soft-pedal War themes). Republic's *Spy Smasher* was in production when Pearl Harbor was bombed, and the script was speedily re-tooled to no longer be coy about the identity of The Enemy. Its January 1942 release made it the first War picture to call a *Nazi* a *Nazi*. The studio followed with *King of the Mounties* ('42, with a *Nazi*, a Japanese, and an Italian villain trio), and a pair starring Rod Cameron as agent Rex Bennett: *G-Men Vs. The Black Dragon* ('42-'43, with Japanese fifth-column work in Los Angeles), and *Secret Service In Darkest Africa* ('43 [retitled *Manhunt in the African Jungles*], with Nazis in Casablanca). All four were loaded with explosive action. Columbia released *The Secret Code* ('42), *Batman* and *The Phantom* (both '43), while Universal brought out pictures from *Adventures of Smilin' Jack* ('42, based on a comic strip) to *Adventures of the Flying Cadets* ('43). Their *Raiders of Ghost City* ('44) was a War picture in disguise, with Prussian spies meddling in Civil War intrigue.

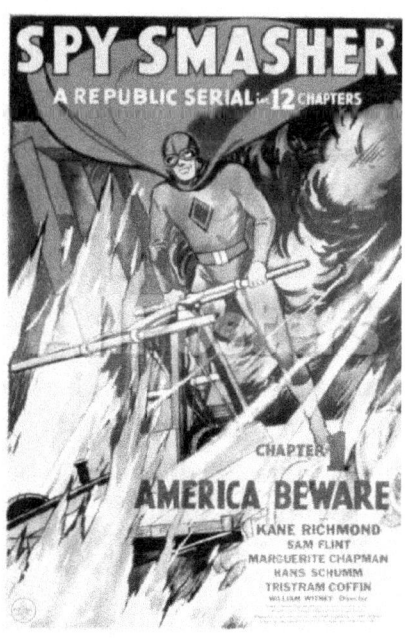

In 1944, producer Sam Katzman, who'd been making B horror and "East Side Kids" pictures as Banner Productions for Monogram, approached Columbia Pictures with a promise to deliver releasable serials at bargain rates. His offer accepted, he began his new venture, Esskay Productions, with a test picture, *Brenda Starr, Reporter* (1944-45), based on the popular syndicated newspaper strip by Dale Messick. It was released before *The Monster and the Ape* ('45), the last serial of the previous regime. Popular and pretty Joan Woodbury starred as Brenda, with serial hero Kane Richmond (who'd starred in several serials, including *Spy Smasher*) for extra box-office value. It was the beginning of a profitable arrangement between Katzman and studio head Harry Cohn that lasted some 15 years.

When Universal was merged with International Pictures, the new hierarchy decreed an end to B pictures, serials, and other low-budget projects, a move that proved disastrous. In the previous two years, the industrious Morgan B. Cox had assumed the reins of the serial unit, producing a variety of entertaining pictures. *The Scarlet Horseman* (1946) gave us a masked hero (with as his secret identity a wheelchair-bound gunsmith [Paul Guilfoyle]), a dynamic sidekick (so stock footage could be introduced), and a comedy-Mexican pal, versus a mysterious figure known as "Matosca", who seeks sanctuary for the local Indians in the Llanos Estacados, the "Staked Plains" of northwest Texas. But things aren't what they seem in this complex tale, as alliances shift, villains fight among themselves, Matosca is revealed long before the last chapter, and the Horseman and company set up for a sequel (which never came). Only a few months later, at the end of production on *The Mysterious Mr. M* ('46), a clever suspense tale starring Pamela Blake, Dennis Moore, Richard Martin, and Byron Foulger, the new owners, International Pictures, would without warning close down the serial unit. It was a foolish move for the new Universal-International, which had no theater chain to guarantee situations for their films

(Universal had used serials to promote long-term relationships with independent theatres).

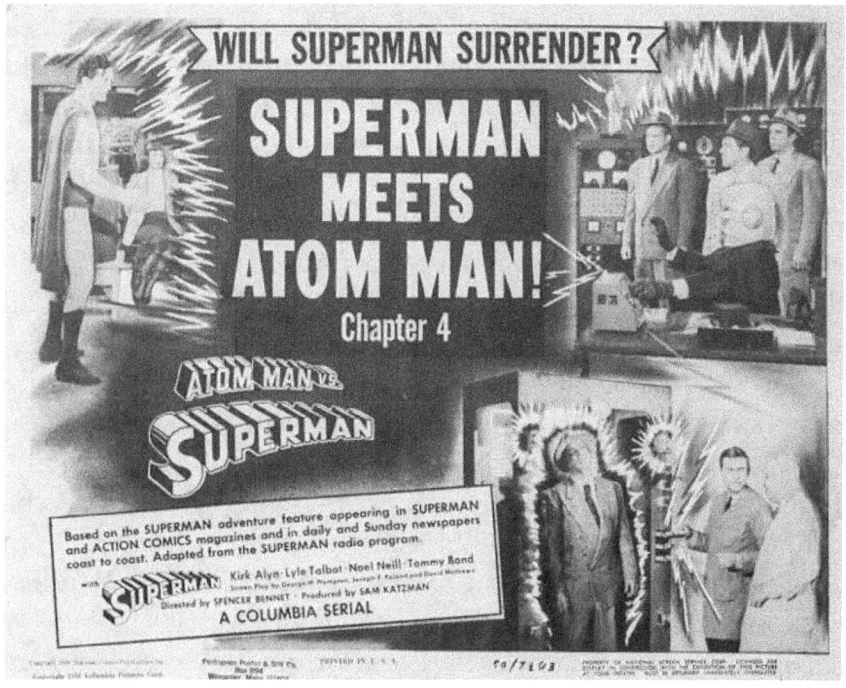

The Man of Steel finally came to the cliffhanger screen in Columbia's 1948 *Superman*, which, like *Flash Gordon*, played big-town cinemas, and was popular enough to warrant a sequel, '50's *Atom Man Vs. Superman*. In the first serial, balletic actor and serial hero Kirk Alyn portrayed Clark Kent, whom we follow from his small-town roots to Metropolis, where he joins the staff of the Daily *Planet* newspaper, meeting editor Perry White (Pierre Watkin), reporter Lois Lane (Noel Neill), and cub/camera boy Jimmy Olsen (Tommy Bond). It is only in chapter three that we get to the plot, as the beautiful and evil "Spider Lady" (Carol Forman) launches a scheme to get control of the "Relativity Reducer Ray" which, despite its highfalutin name is just a disintegrator. In the follow-up, the principals return and are joined by Superman's arch-enemy of the comics, Luthor (Lyle Talbot, in an excellent performance) and the "Atom Man", a mysterious figure in a bizarre sparkly helmet. In both serials, Superman was credited as playing himself, with the flying scenes done mostly through cartoon animation. Less than a year later, a Man of Steel more familiar to modern audiences would appear in *Superman and the Mole Men* (*Q.V. in Science Fiction*), among other more recent versions. Other National Comics serials included *Batman* ('43), and *Batman and Robin* ('49; a rather poor outing, though it featured an interesting villain, the Wizard), *Hop Harrigan* America's Ace of the Airways ('46), *The Vigilante* Fighting Hero of the West ('47), and *Congo Bill* ('48).

Serials had been based upon radio programs, pulp magazines, newspaper strips and comic books, even novels. Only one was based upon what was then the arch-enemy, television: Sam Katzman's *Captain Video* Master of the Stratosphere (Columbia, 1951-52). Cheap and crude – in keeping with its source – it featured space travel, outlandish weapons, and robots (recycled from Gene Autry's serial, *The Phantom Empire* [Mascot, '35]) and originally created for an unused sequence in Metro's *Dancing Lady* ['33]). Judd Holdren and Larry Stewart starred, with frequent heavy Gene Roth as the villainous Vultura. To help show it wasn't just the TV show, extraplanetary sequences were tinted in red or green by the CineColor studio. Holden briefly cornered the market in space heroism, returning for the surprisingly entertaining *The Lost Planet* Conqueror of Space (Columbia, '53), but also participating in a bold experiment over at Republic.

Attempting to create a TV series, Republic found assorted studio-union regulations insurmountable obstacles, and re-edited a three-part pilot and added nine more episodes to create a serial without cliffhangers, *Commando Cody* Sky Marshal of the Universe (1953), twelve wild and woolly episodes with the masked sky marshal (Holdren, re-booting the hero of Republic's '52 *Radar Men From the Moon*) battling the efforts of a self-styled Ruler (Gregory Gay) to conquer the planets of our solar system. Cody and his assistants Joan Gilbert (Aline Towne, queen of '50s serial heroines) and William Schallert (Ted Richards) or, later, Dick Preston (Richard Crane) visited solar and extrasolar planets, finally tracking the Ruler to Mercury in a two-installment finale. Loads of stock footage (including most shots of Cody's flying suit, first used in *King of the Rocket Men* ('49) ensured excitement in each episode.

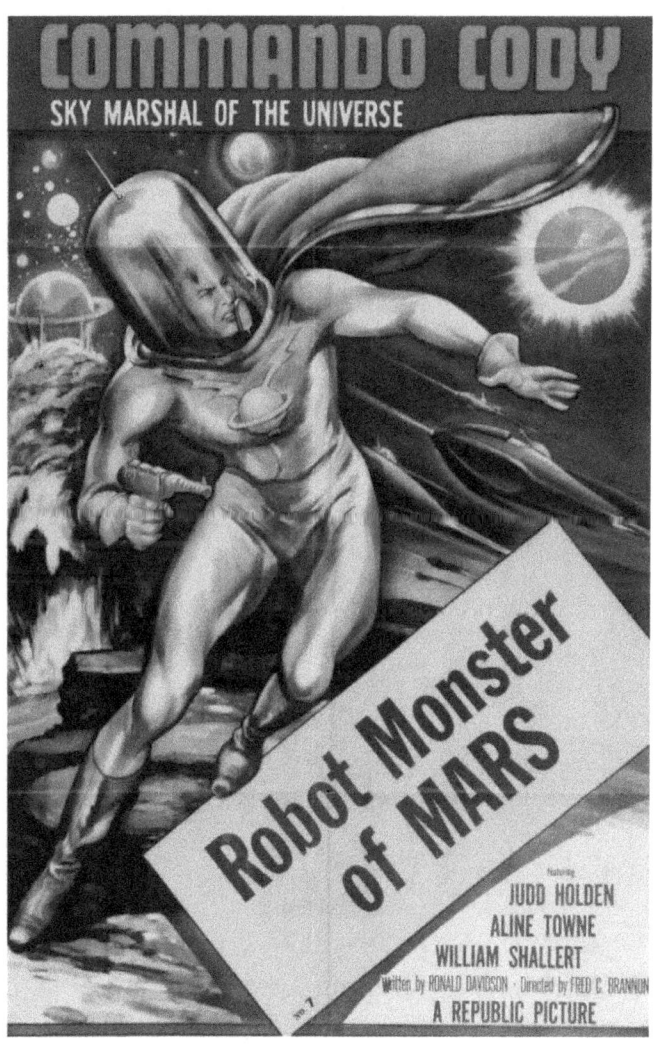

Republic Pictures, suffering from inflation, age, and television, called it a day with 1955's *King Of The Carnival*, a mystery serial about hero Bert King (of the carnival, see? [Harry Lauter]) and helper June Edwards (Fran Bennett) tackling counterfeiters operating under the cover of a circus. Very little action, and only a feint at a mystery villain (he usually just stayed off-camera, but did wear a clown suit at least once) made for a sad last chapter play. Even the Main Title Theme is sort of forlorn.

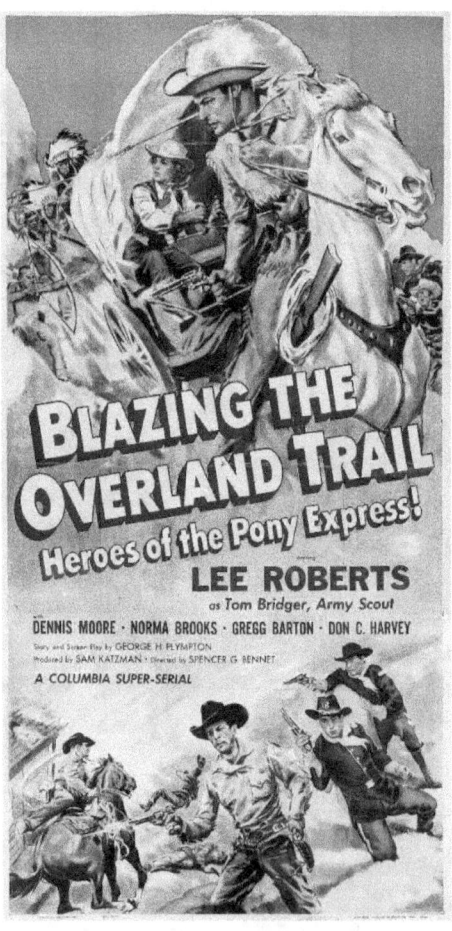

Sam Katzman, still plugging away for Columbia, likewise called it quits after *The Adventures of Captain Africa* Amazing

Jungle Avenger! a few months after Republic, but requests for more serials from thousands of theater managers changed his mind. He would crank out two more serials over the next twelve months, finishing with the final theatrical serial produced in the United States, *Blazing the Overland Trail* (1956), which starred Dennis Moore, who had also starred in Universal's last serial a decade earlier. Katzman's decision to assemble two more chapter plays showed little enthusiasm from a man who was straining at respectability: so loaded with stock footage were they that they could barely be called "new" pictures. When Sam closed down after "Blazing", nobody complained.

A large fraction of the serials were devoted to one particular *genre*, and many of the stars and character performers of the cliffhangers worked in those features, as well. In fact, at Republic, an actor could spend three weeks on a serial, and, without missing a beat, show up for work the following Monday in the latest of the studio's many...

CHAPTER NINE: WESTERNS

COWBOYS AND INDIANS, the opening of the West, Manifest Destiny. All of these were recent history when the movies became popular entertainment, and as U.S. films went out to other countries, their viewers were as thrilled by the lure of adventure as had been the dudes who had stayed back East while their cousins had opened the Frontier. Westerns had been a staple during the pre-talking era, and the shorter running times of the "matinee" westerns intended for Saturday-morning kiddie-shows made it easy for them to become true B pictures. Early stars were rodeo champs or war heroes like Hoot Gibson and Buck Jones. With sound (the first all-talking outdoor picture was Fox's 1929 *In Old Arizona*, a Cisco Kid tale) audiences could not just see the West, but hear the lowing of the cattle, the clash of hoofbeats, even the rustling of the wind in the trees, and a new sound: the singing of the lonesome cowpoke. Kids thrilled to Buck and Tom Mix, to Johnny Mack Brown, John Wayne, and later to Gene Autry and Wild Bill Elliott. So prolific and popular were the oaters that they got a separate "Top 10" box-office list. As the '30s progressed, cowboys divided neatly into singing and non-singing, and modern and historical categories, and continued through the B-picture era, many becoming early hit TV shows. Since the '60s, Westerns have faded, though foreign audiences continue to love the *genre*, and, once every few years or so, Hollywood offers up a new blockbuster like *Silverado* ('83) or *Tombstone* ('93).

Among the early stars of the *genre* were performers like Harry Carey (a tough, no-nonsense hero who was also immensely popular, with audiences and studio people alike. After his starring days were over, he became a reliable character actor in films like *Mr. Smith Goes to Washington* [Columbia, 1939]); Tom Mix (who starred for many years in mute Westerns, beginning with *In the Days of the Thundering Herd* [Selig, '14] and continuing into the talking-picture era, where he finished his screen career with a serial, *The Miracle Rider* [Mascot, '34]); Ken Maynard (who starred in "oaters" from *The Man Who Won* [Fox Film, '23] to *Harmony Trail* [Meridian Pictures, '44]); Bob Steele (actually Robert North Bradbury, Jr., son of a top action director but who made it on his own talents. Hero of several series, he sometimes played a villain, was one of the "Three Mesquiteers" for Republic Pictures, and side-slipped easily into crime pictures like *The Big Sleep* [Warner Bros., 1945-'46], where he played a hired gunman); Colonel Tim McCoy (real-life military hero who stepped into film with his no nonsense characterization of the upright Good Guy); Tom Tyler (who continued as a cowboy hero even after becoming a character actor and western villain); and a favorite with kids and adults, who moved with ease among Westerns, Dramas, and Comedies, Charles "Buck" Jones (who made features and serials until his untimely death in 1942, when he expired from smoke-inhalation suffered while rescuing people from the Boston Cocoanut Grove fire).

But the biggest name to come from those early days – and who continued for five decades – was John Wayne, who had labored in the B fields for years when he graduated to front-line status with the John Ford production *Stagecoach* (UA, 1939). Though Claire Trevor got top billing, it was the Duke's portrayal of the Ringo Kid that caught America's fancy, and Wayne continued as a star for the rest of his life; here are some highlights. Wayne stayed at the top, in Westerns, War pictures, and Dramas, and worked with the top directors.

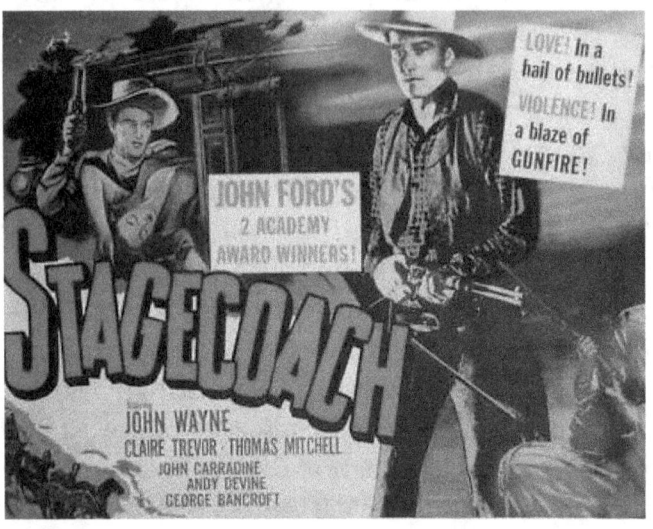

Howard Hawks produced and directed one of the greatest of Westerns – one of the greatest of American adventures – *Red River* (UA, '48), with themes of personal loyalty, honor, and justice interwoven into the story of a proud cattleman. John Ford had been making outstanding Westerns for 30 years when he starred John Wayne in *The Searchers* for Warner Bros. release in '56. The hard determination of the Duke in his quest to recover his niece from her Red Indian captors showcased the director's famed landscapes from Monument Valley to Hollywood's Bronson Canyon. *El Dorado* (Paramount, '66) starred John Wayne (as Cole Thornton) and Robert Mitchum (as JP Harrah) in another of Howard Hawks' passes at the "jailhouse siege" storyline, just as good as before, and different enough to hold the interest. The script, by science-fiction writer Leigh Brackett, was studded with fine action and humor. By the time of *The Shootist* (Paramount, '76) the Western was at a low ebb, and the Duke was on his way out, and knew it, when he agreed to star in this last film as JB Books, a gunfighter, aged and ill and unable to keep up with the changing times in the last days of the frontier, who tries to show a young admirer the error of idolizing a shootist. Lauren Bacall and James Stewart joined him, and up-and-coming star Ron Howard was the boy who learned a hard lesson. After this last poignant role, the movie star who went from Glendale High School to the top of his profession rode off into the sunset.

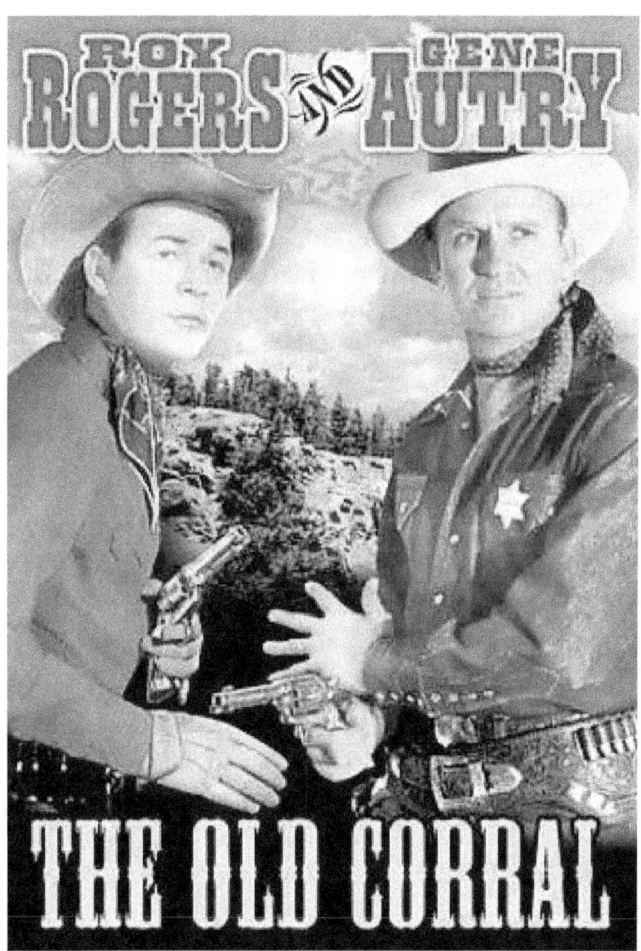

Rogers and Autry on DVD cover, over-emphasizing Roy's part in the film.

The two biggest names in the singing-cowboy racket were Roy Rogers and Gene Autry. Gene, an unlikely hero, had become a star when he replaced obstreperous Ken Maynard at Mascot. Roy, originally hired as an "insurance" player to curb Gene's success at Republic, stepped into the number-one spot when Gene volunteered for service in the Army Air Corps in the Second World War. But, far from rivals, the two were good friends and mutual supporters. Their pictures topped the Western box-office figures as long as those numbers were kept, and their pictures were always well received. In rural parts of the country, a Roy or Gene picture could easily get billing over even an M-G-M masterpiece. Between them they set the style for a balance of action, song, and comedy. Gene had Smiley Burnette, his real-life partner, a great comic and a writer of songs both serious and funny, and later Pat Buttram; Roy had George "Gabby" Hayes, the grizzled old curmudgeon of the West, and later Pat Brady from the "Sons of the Pioneers" musical group that had often supported Roy in song. (*Q.V. each in Musicals*).

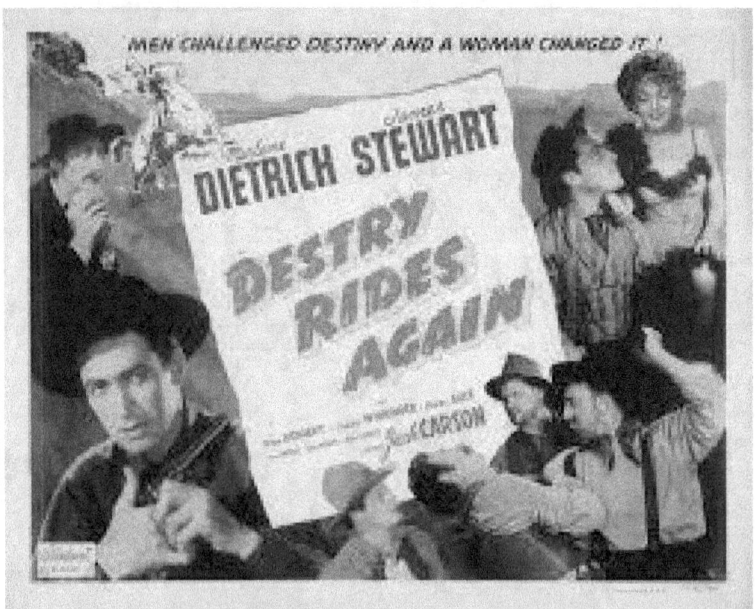

Though one hardly thinks of him as a Western star, James Stewart made some of the best, from the classic action film with a great sense of humor, *Destry Rides Again* (Universal, 1939), with Marlene Dietrich, Brian Donlevy, and Samuel S. Hinds, in which a peaceable young fellow shows up to tame a raucous frontier town, to *Winchester '73* (U-I, '50), where an older, grittier Stewart heads out on the trail of the prized rifle, stolen by an unscrupulous owlhoot (Dan Duryea) who happens to be his brother, to *The Man Who Shot Liberty Valance* (Paramount, '62), John Ford's take on how truth and legend diverge, in which Jimmy co-starred with John Wayne, where Jimmy is the dude victimized by the gun-slinging varmint Valance and Wayne the guardian angel Stewart doesn't want but needs.

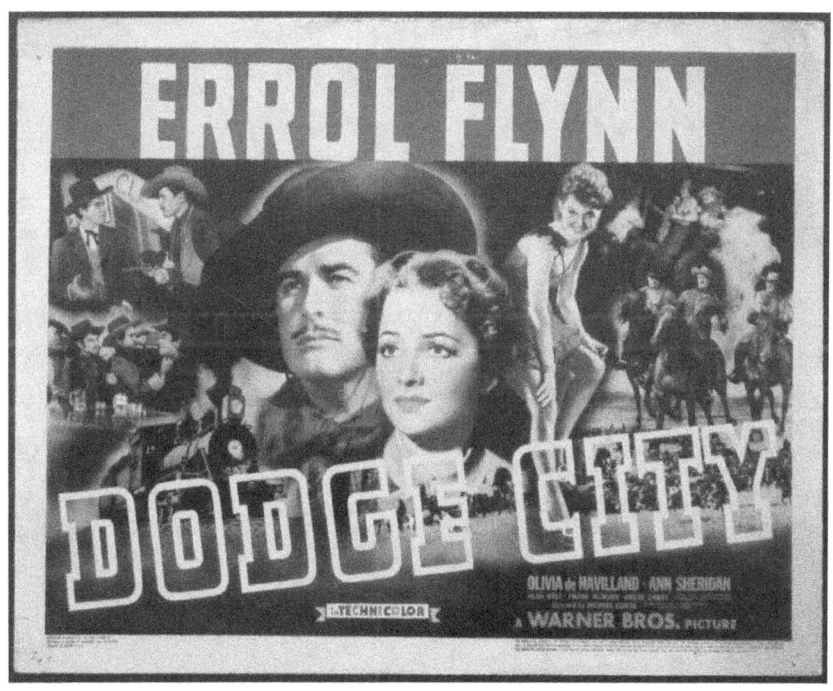

A surprisingly popular player in Westerns was swashbuckler Errol Flynn, whose *Dodge City* (WB, 1939), with Flynn and sidekicks versus Bruce Cabot, the town boss, and henchman Victory Jory, who are keeping the town as rough and wild as possible for their profit, spawned an assortment of follow-ups. In *Virginia City* (WB, '40), Flynn escapes from a vile Confederate prison and heads out West to prevent Southerner Randolph Scott from seizing a shipment of silver for the Confederacy. With plenty of action, and a sequence which prefigures a similar scene in *Casablanca* (*Q.V. in Drama*) with Yankees and Confederates trying to out-sing each other in a saloon. The picture also featured Guinn "Big Boy" Williams and Alan Hale (Senior) as Flynn's sidekicks, and – still in the days when the studio was trying to decide what to do with him – Humphrey Bogart as a Mexican *bandido*. Flynn would pop up in Westerns from time to time, through *Silver River* (WB, '48).

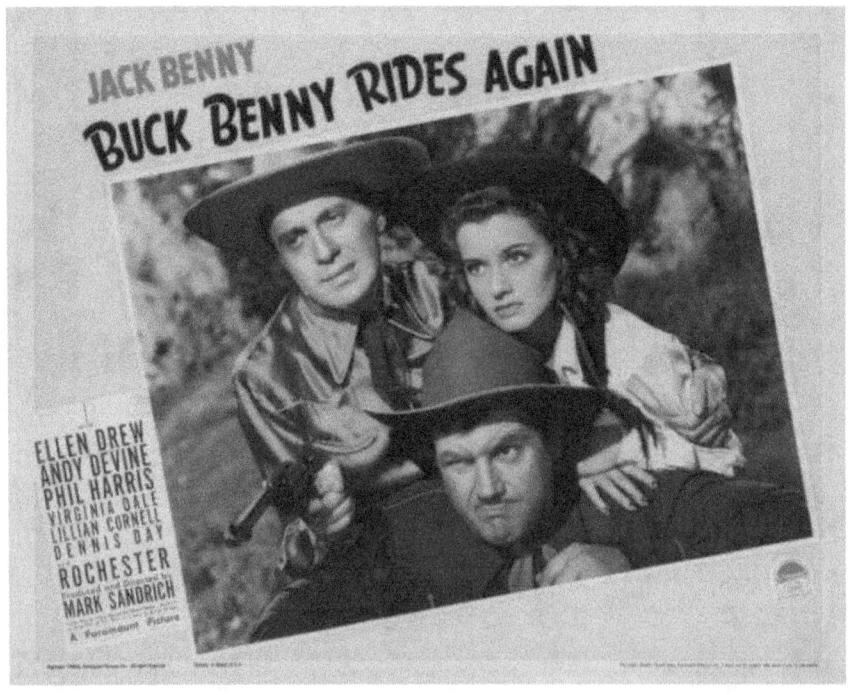

Westerns were a great source of comedy, as America's foremost violinist Jack Benny proved in *Buck Benny Rides Again*, a 1940 Paramount Picture in which Jack, to impress cowgirl Ellen Drew, tries to prove he's a rootin', tootin', bad-guy shootin' buckaroo with the help of Rochester, Andy Devine, and Phil Harris – and Carmichael the bear. Music and cowboy action filled the screen. Other Western comedies included *Ride 'Em, Cowboy* (Universal, '41) with Abbott and Costello, *Way Out West* (M-G-M, '37) with Laurel and Hardy, and *Son of Paleface* (Paramount, '52) with Bob Hope and Roy Rogers.

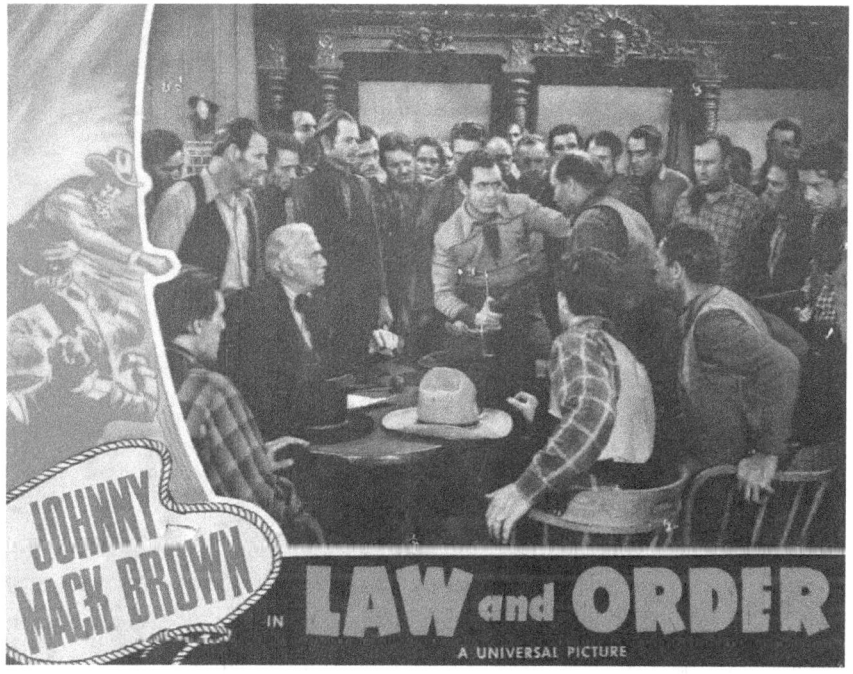

Johnny Mack Brown, a former football great who had starred as *Billy the Kid* in 1930, moved comfortably into B westerns and serials, and had a long career with many seasons at Universal, where he made pictures like *Law and Order* ('40) and *Silver Bullet* ('42). In the latter, he starred as "Silver Jim" Donovan, seeking the man who had shot him in the back with a silver bullet! How the film got made at a time when the Lone Ranger was the most popular cowboy hero is a mystery that endures to this day. All of JMB's Universal pictures, some co-starring Tex Ritter, are atypical in that Brown doesn't play himself but a different guy each time, and are among the best B westerns to reach the screen. Beginning with the 1943-'44 season, Johnny moved to Monogram Pictures, making pictures like *The Fighting Ranger* ('48) until retiring in the mid-'fifties.

Buster Crabbe was already a kid favorite as Flash Gordon when Producers Releasing Corporation began billing him as "King of the Wild West" in a series that had begun as "Billy the Kid" (with Bob Steele) but under protests from parents' groups had dropped the owlhoot's name, changing the hero to Billy "Carson". All these are of a type; PRC was not known for its high-quality product. But all are entertaining and easy to take. In 1941's *His Brother's Ghost*, for example, he appeared with his comic sidekick, Al "Fuzzy" St. John. Fuzzy was among the most popular "comedy relief" sidekicks, who could joke around but be credible in comic-action during the fisticuffs. When Buster left over producer Neufeld's parsimony, up-and-coming Lash LaRue took his spot, as the Cheyenne Kid, beginning with *Law of the Lash* (PRC, '47) and Fuzzy had a new top-kick.

Gordon Nance, a dress extra at Warners, was transformed into William Elliott thanks to Harry Cohn, and soon became "Wild Bill" when he played his historical namesake in the serial *The Great Adventures of Wild Bill Hickok* (Columbia, 1938). After starring at Columbia, in additional serials and several seasons of features, he was hired away by Republic with the promise of a role he coveted. When the studio began a "Red Ryder" series with *Tucson Raiders* in 1944, Elliott's casting had been mandated in the contract with creator Fred Harmon, and it was a part that fit Wild Bill like the leather chaps he wore. He was joined by George "Gabby" Hayes and by Bobby (later Robert) Blake as Little Beaver, and though Gabby moved on after the first two pictures, Blake stayed for the entire run, even when Elliott was replaced by Allan Lane. Wild Bill had moved on to A-Picture stardom, in complex,

214

good bad-man roles in specials like *Plainsman and the Lady* (Republic, '46). Later, he stepped down to Allied Artists for some less expensive but good cowboy pictures, finishing up as the last of the B-series detectives (*Q.V. in Mystery*).

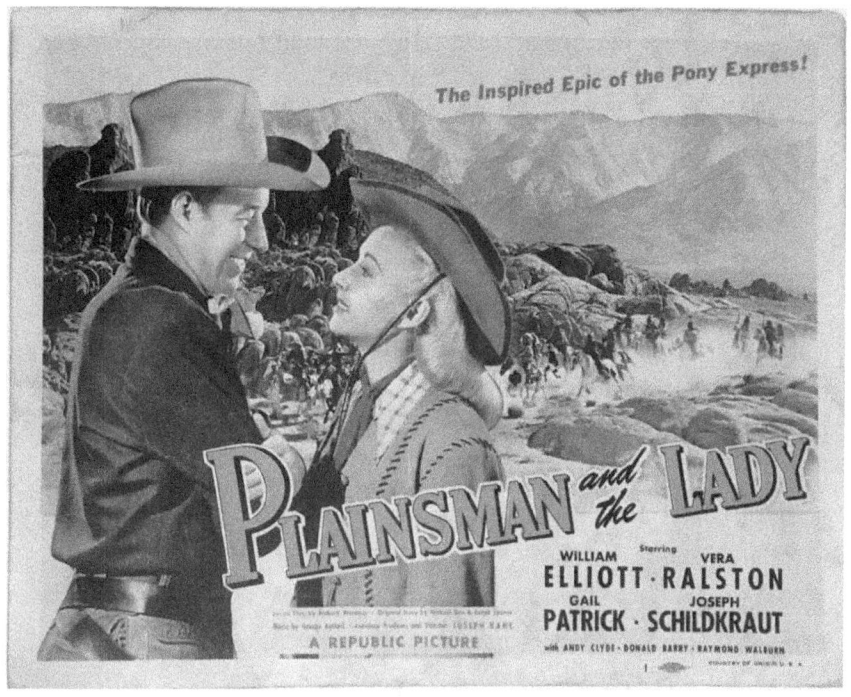

After wrapping up "Red Ryder", Allan Lane, now billed as "Rocky" Lane, entered into a series of somewhat different pictures, in which he was usually a traveling U.S. Marshal who'd wander into a town to save the day. Riding his stallion Black Jack (who'd played Thunder in the "Red Ryder" pictures), he and his sometime sidekick Nugget Clark (Eddy C. Waller) solved problems in pictures like *The Denver Kid* ('48) and *Marshal of Cedar Rock* ('53). Earlier in his career, he'd been a romantic-comedy lead at RKO Radio, before appearing in four Republic serials and then signing with the studio, becoming their top B-Western star when Wild Bill got his promotion. Other Republic cowboys included Sunset Carson in *Call of the Rockies* ('44) and Monte Hale in *California Firebrand* ('48), and the last of the line, Rex Allen, the "Arizona Cowboy", who made 20 B westerns enhanced by his great singing voice. After Republic stopped making Westerns, Rex would go on for years singing and narrating for Walt Disney.

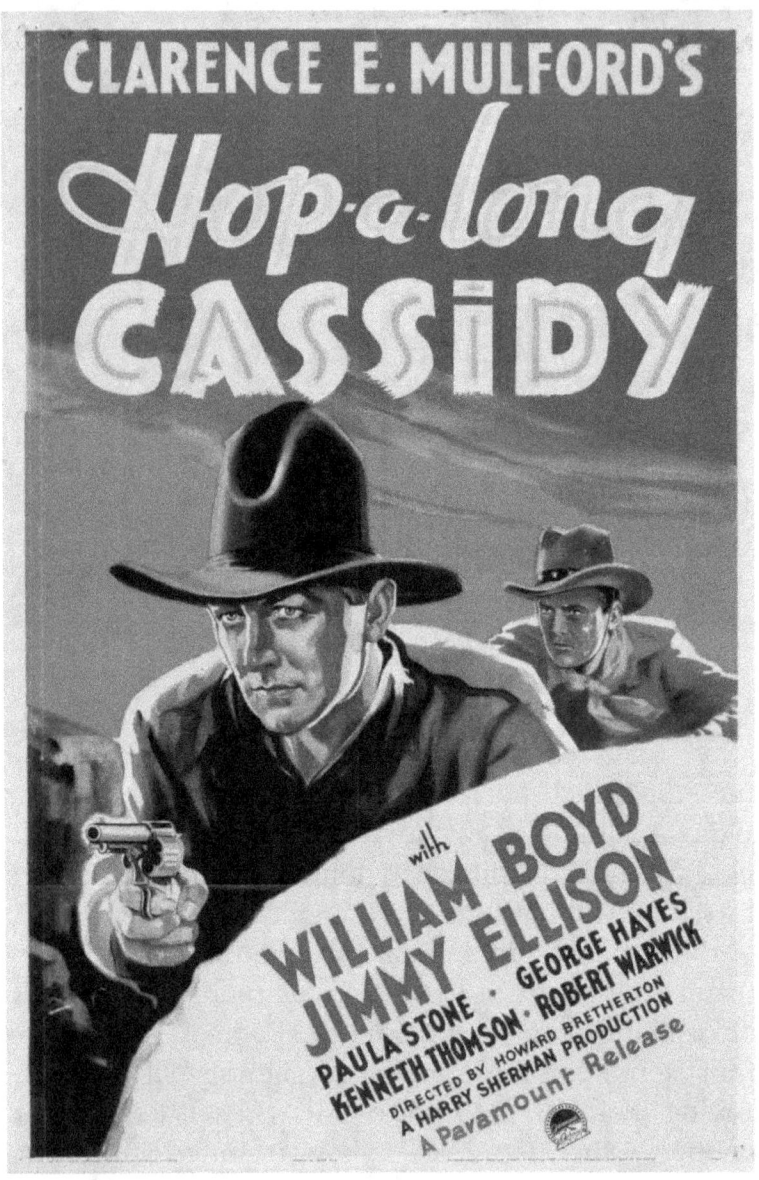

Hopalong Cassidy was a favorite among readers of Western novels. His hard-bitten, realistic adventures, penned by Clarence Mulford, earned his fame. So when Paramount announced a series, adults and kids alike waited to see if they would do their hero justice. The first picture, *Hop-Along Cassidy* (1935) surely did, even to showing the way "Hoppy" was injured, earning his nickname. Later films skewed away, though; Hoppy never limped again, and the rough-hewn cowboy became a sterling, polite champion of justice as played by silver-haired William Boyd. But fans of the books liked the pictures, and even Mulford grudgingly agreed Boyd could keep "his" Hoppy his way. Harry "Pop" Sherman produced the films through *Forty Thieves* (UA '44), after which Boyd made the investment to buy the rights – and all the films – and continued as Cassidy. He later launched a TV series, and started the first video fan craze. Through the careful stewardship of his wife, the former Grace Bradley, Hoppy became a marketing phenomenon on the scale of a Disney promotion, with clothes, lunchboxes, comics, badges, and all sorts of what is now memorabilia. The Hoppy pictures exemplified the "cowboy trio" sub-category, as the older Hoppy always had some young squirt (like James Ellison or Russell Hayden) to be rescued from his own folly, and a comic foil (like "Windy", played by Gabby Hayes, or "California" Carlson, Andy Clyde) to accompany him on his missions of derring-do. Other trios included the Range Busters (*The Range Busters* [Monogram, '40]), the Trail Blazers (*Death Valley Rangers* [Monogram, '43]), and the Rough Riders (*Forbidden Trails* [Monogram, '41]).

But the best of the trios was "The Three Mesquiteers" (a group that included John Wayne, Bob Steele, Tom Tyler, Bob Livingston, Rufe Davis, and Max Terhune over the years), created in print by William Colt McDonald. For a slight change, it was two leading men and a comic sidekick (or two if you counted Elmer Sneezeweed, Terhune's ventriloquist figure who got many of the laughs when Max was part of the group). All three would get mixed up in some kind of trouble, the two leads would jostle for position with the pretty girl, and, often, the boys would be on the wrong side of the law at some point. Originally the trio was composed of Livingston, Crash Corrigan, and Terhune, but the group had many changes in line-up over their eight years: Wayne replaced Livingston when the latter got bumped up to A-Picture status (and then they switched back when Wayne got *Stagecoach* and he became the A-Picture star at Republic). At the end, Bob Steele, Tom Tyler, and Rufe Davis took over, playing the same characters. *The Three Mesquiteers* (1936) set the tone, and later efforts like *Overland Stage Raiders* ('38) and *Wyoming Outlaw* ('39), both with Wayne, carried them through until *Riders of the Rio Grande*, with Steele, Tyler, and Jimmy Dodd, in '43.

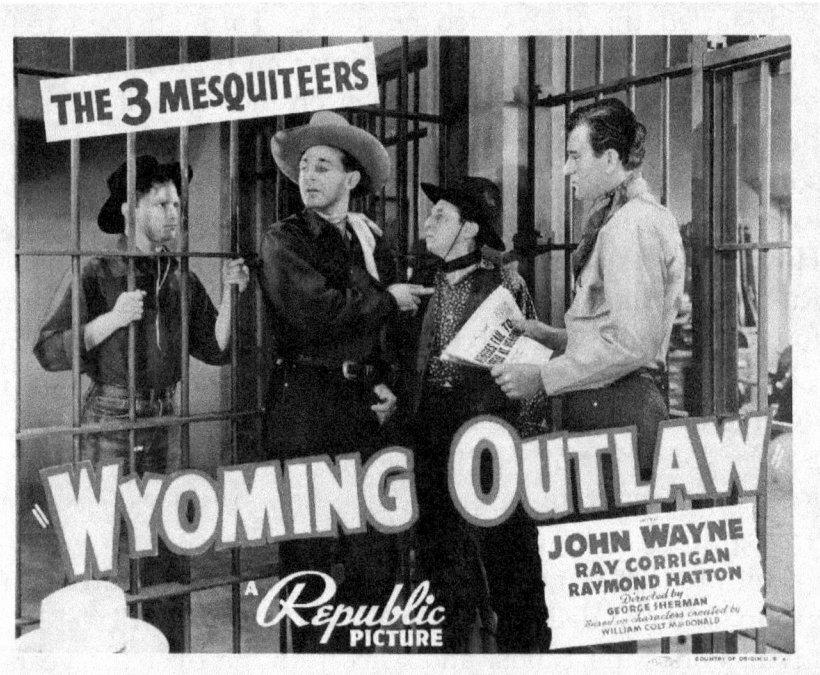

Columbia's other big star was Charles Starrett, who had made dozens of B westerns before *The Durango Kid* (1940), after which he returned to "regular" cowboy duties. A belated follow-up in 1944, *The Return of the Durango Kid*, finally kicked off one of the longest running series in film. Starrett made 63 more pictures after that, and in every one he played the Durango. When the series folded, he retired to a long and peaceful seniority. Clad in black, with a simple bandanna mask, Durango would appear from nowhere on his white horse, Raider, to right the wrong of the moment, and no one ever connected him with two-fisted but less flashy Steve (whose last name would vary from picture to picture) and his horse Bullet (named by fans in a contest!). For a while, the Durango had help from Wild Bill Elliott's old sidekick, "Cannonball" Dub Taylor. But when Smiley Burnette became available, he was quickly signed to be the new comedy relief, with his antics and his wonderful songs, and stayed through the rest of the series, to great kid appeal. Starrett also benefitted from two of the top stunt-doubles for the action: first Edwin Parker, then Jack Mahoney (better known as Jock or Jocko Mahoney) in pictures like *Riders Of The Lone Star* ('47), where Jack could leap into the saddle from a rooftop – in one set-up!

Tim Holt, son of actor Jack Holt, had risen from co-star of George O'Brien pictures to his own series, frequently teamed with singing Ray Whitley and a comic side-kick, usually Eddy C. Waller or Emmett Lynn, but always "Whopper" by name. Interrupted by the Second World War, Tim came back strong in an RKO Radio series that survived the B-picture purge of new owner Howard Hughes. Tim was teamed with Richard Martin (as Chito José Gonzales Bustamonte Rafferty, a Mexican/Irishman character) and the popular team fought and joked through five seasons, beginning with *Thunder Mountain* (RKO Radio, 1947) and continuing with entries like *The Arizona Ranger* ('48), co-starring Tim's dad, '49's *Masked Raiders*, and his last, *Desert Passage*, in '52. Martin had played the "Chito" character in three oaters before Holt returned from War service; he'd also played a contemporary character of that name in RKO Radio's '43 *Bombardier*, perhaps the grandson of his Western character.

George Stevens had a history of great films like the 1939 RKO Radio release *Gunga Din* when he produced and directed *Shane* (Paramount, '53), which starred Alan Ladd as a world-weary retired gunfighter who drifts into a bad situation and tries to make things right. Complicating his task is the friend (Van Heflin) who fears he may lose his wife (Jean Arthur) to the gunman, and the friend's son, who has come to idolize Shane in a way that might cause the boy to grow up to be the thing Shane despises – a gunfighter like himself! And of course, there's the actual trouble, exemplified by Jack Wilson, the scroungy, soulless killing machine masterfully enacted by Jack Palance. The story development, the performances, even the camera angles and the haunting color-palette of the West make this one of the best of the *genre*. And it was in its way an adult response to the B-style cowboy antics that were even then already migrating to television.

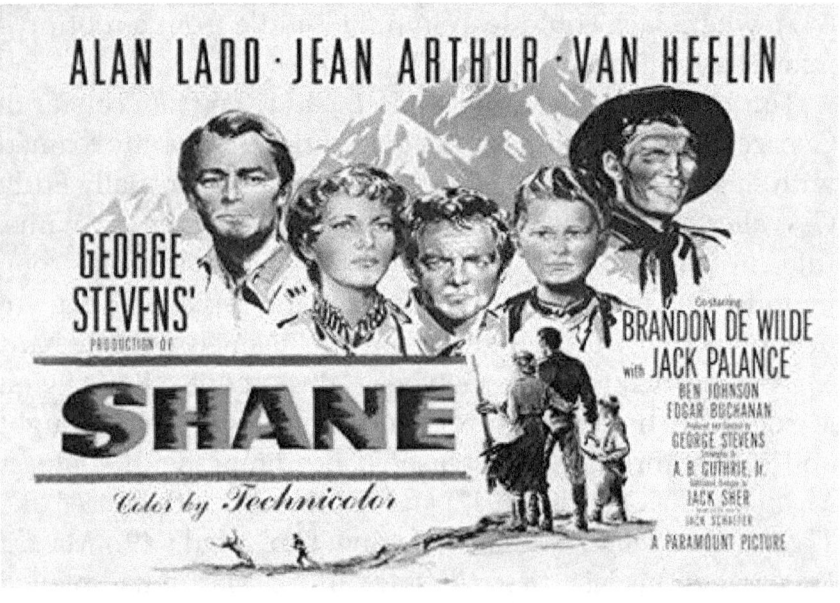

Randolph Scott, an action and dramatic star of long standing, went into partnership with director Budd

Boetticher and producer Harry Joe Brown in the 1950s to film a series of top-notch westerns, beginning with *The Tall T* (Columbia, 1957), but he'd made many oaters before. In *Frontier Marshal* (RKO Radio, '39) he played Wyatt Earp in a version of the Tombstone days that while exciting was rather poor history (despite being based on Stuart N. Lake's book of Earp's reminiscences). In the '50s, a grittier Scott became the old veteran, often tired of the trail but unable to adapt to a new West, such as in *Ride Lonesome* (Columbia, '59), from a script by Burt Kennedy, in which he starred as a bounty hunter. In his last Western, *Ride the High Country* (M-G-M, '62), he teamed with long-time pal Joel McCrea as two old-timers at the apotheosis of the beyond-their-years plotline.

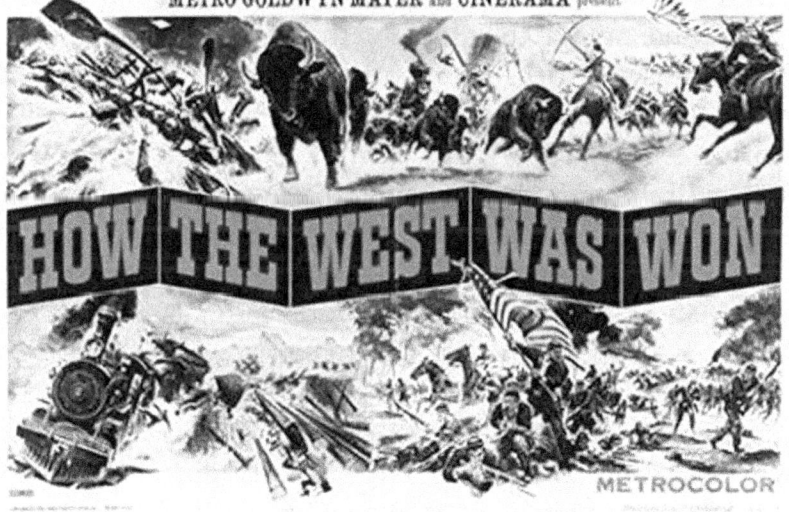

How The West Was Won (Cinerama Releasing, 1962) in a decade of super-duper films, was *The* Western, three screens wide and as far as the eye could see on the Cinerama screen. Divided episodically, it told of the winning of the west through the lives of the Prescott and Rawlins family, beginning with the Prescotts' trip along the Erie Canal and their meeting with mountain man Linus Rawlins (James Stewart), the days of the riverboats and the Civil War, in which Rawlins is killed, and finally the homesteading and the coming of the railroads. It was epic and exciting, with a huge cast including Debbie Reynolds, John Wayne, Henry Fonda, and George Peppard, narrated by Spencer Tracy. A long fight sequence, on a moving logging train, is dynamic as all get-out, but as disturbing visually as it is engaging. The extra-wide screen of Cinerama was never quite as smooth as its inventor had hoped, and the three-strips of film simultaneously projected was soon replaced with a single strip, with a reeeallllly wide image. As impressive as the picture is, its conclusion, in which the West is shown as paved over with freeways – which is considered progress – is a great disappointment.

In the more recent past, Comedy oaters popped up from time to time, though they too had thinned out with the fading of Westerns from the mainstream of the US cinema. Mel Brooks, riding high in a long string of big-picture spoofs of assorted *genres*, brought us *Blazing Saddles* (Warner Brothers, 1974), with himself as crooked and feeble-minded Governor LePetomane, and Cleavon Little and Gene Wilder as the two... well, I guess they must be the heroes, plus Harvey Korman as Hedy Lamarr (oops, sorry; that's *Hedley*!) and Madeline Kahn as the Marlene Dietrich of *chanteuses*, all whipped up into a devastatingly accurate parody of every A Western ever made, from the clichéd townies to the inept owlhoots, stitched together with Brooks' amazing sense of humor, that ranges jokes from the subtle to the downright raunchy and still gets away with it. There's really nothing else like it, but earlier, gentler spoofs of the *genre* included *Along Came Jones* (RKO Radio, '45 [an International Picture]), Bob Hope's *The Paleface* (Paramount, '48) and its remake *The Shakiest Gun in the West* (Universal, '68), *Callaway Went*

Thataway (M-G-M, '51), specifically a nod to the "Hopalong Cassidy" craze, and the Three Stooges picture *The Outlaws is Coming* (Columbia, '65).

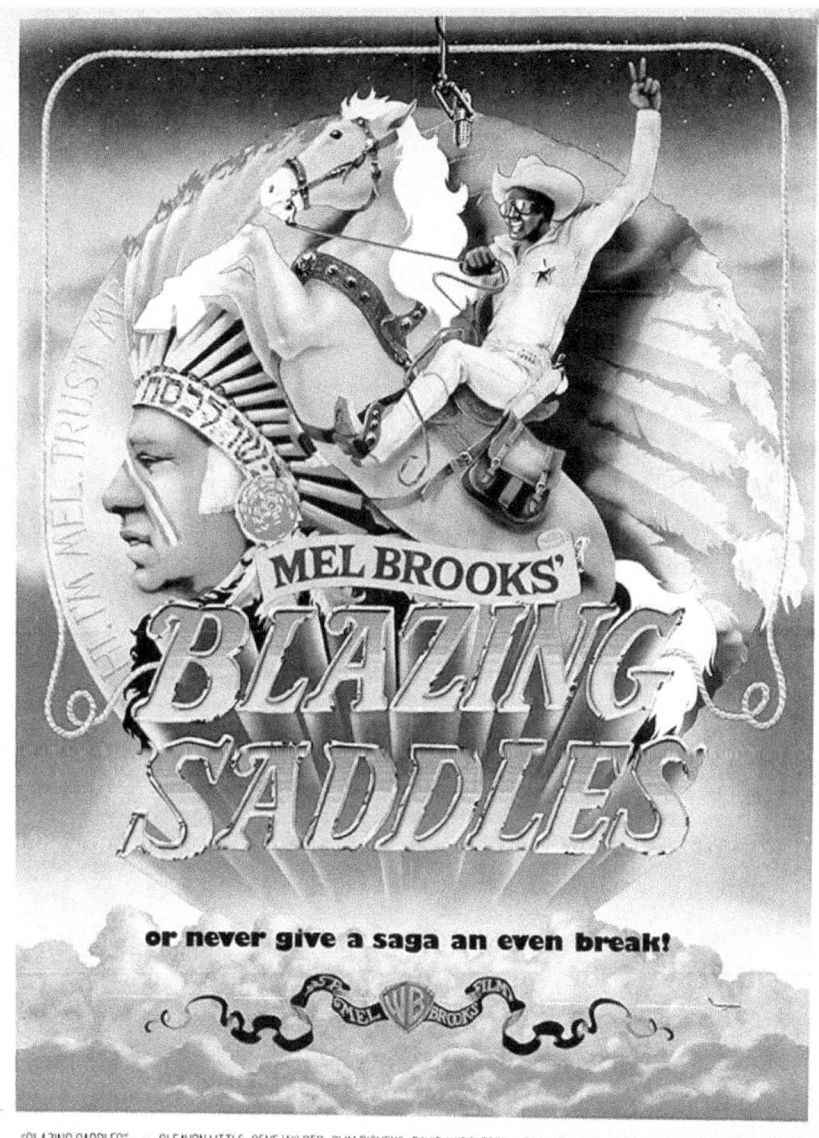

Big Westerns continue to show up, every once in a while.

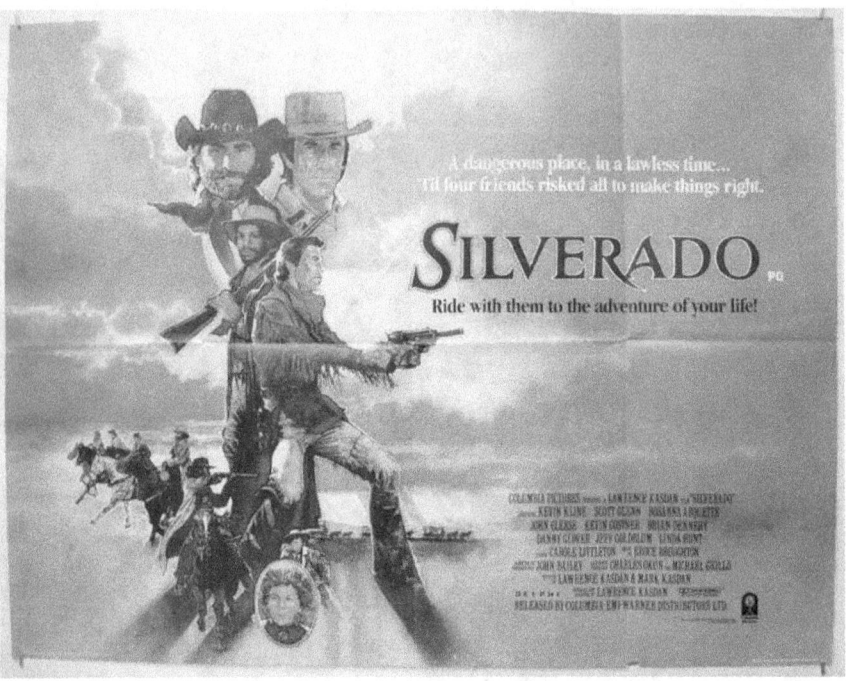

Silverado (Columbia, 1985) was Lawrence Kasdan's knowing tribute to "Three Mesquiteers"-style Bs with an A picture treatment, as not three but *four* cowpokes team up to save a town from tyranny and right a few wrongs. Emmett (Scott Glenn), avoiding an ambush, sets out on his way home. In the middle of a hard-pan desert he meets Paden (Kevin Kline), who's been dry-gulched and left for dead. The two slowly work their way to Silverado, collecting Emmett's brother Jake (Kevin Costner) and returning local Mal (Danny Glover), only to find the town under the thumb of Cobb (Brian Dennehy), who'd once been an owlhoot with Emmett but is now the town marshal. The thrilling story, with just the right amount of humor for leavening, was a knowing and loving look back at the classic Western by a true fan. Great cinematography, a stunning variety of locations from desert to snow-country, and a seasoned cast including Jeff Fahey, Linda Hunt, John

Cleese, Rosanna Arquette, Jeff Goldblum, James Gammon, and cute dance-hall girl Amanda Wyss. The only disappointment in the film is that, at the end, as Jake and Emmett ride off into the sunset, Jake yells, "We'll be back!" – they never were. But the Western lives on.

Many Westerns were influenced in one way or another by the War Between the States, either directly or by casting the opposing forces on opposite sides even years after the conflict had ended. And in the early 1940s, the concurrent world-wide conflict found its way into Westerns, so it's no great leap from the battles of the West to...

CHAPTER TEN: WAR

WAR MAKES CRACKLING good reading, and dynamite cinema – figuratively and literally. The conflicts of Men and States for riches, for power, for land, for hatred provide exciting and thrilling bases for the movies, from the familiar American wars to the historical battles, all the way back to prehistoric times. The wars of Troy and Greece, of Rome and Carthage, of rose-emblemed royalty, bring with them the human drama of the people swept up in them. For war by itself, while action-filled, is just special effects unless it's set against the examination of the lives and fortunes of the men and women who wage, or protest, or try to lead their lives despite the Hell in which they find themselves. This is not a justification of war, these struggles are a fact of our lives and history, and tell in vivid relief the progress of society as it strives to make each war the last one. The American Revolution freed a people from absent bondage, the War Between the States defined the tenets of a nation in relation to its constituents. The World Wars opposed and overcame tyranny, and the conflicts of Korea, Viet Nam, and the holy wars of history record the dangers of fear and mistrust of one society for another. Science fiction brings us wars of the future, but perhaps the lessons of history will yet be heeded, and those wars will forever remain speculative. And these lessons are best taught by motion pictures, to depict not only the heroism but the horrors of war.

THE TROJAN WAR

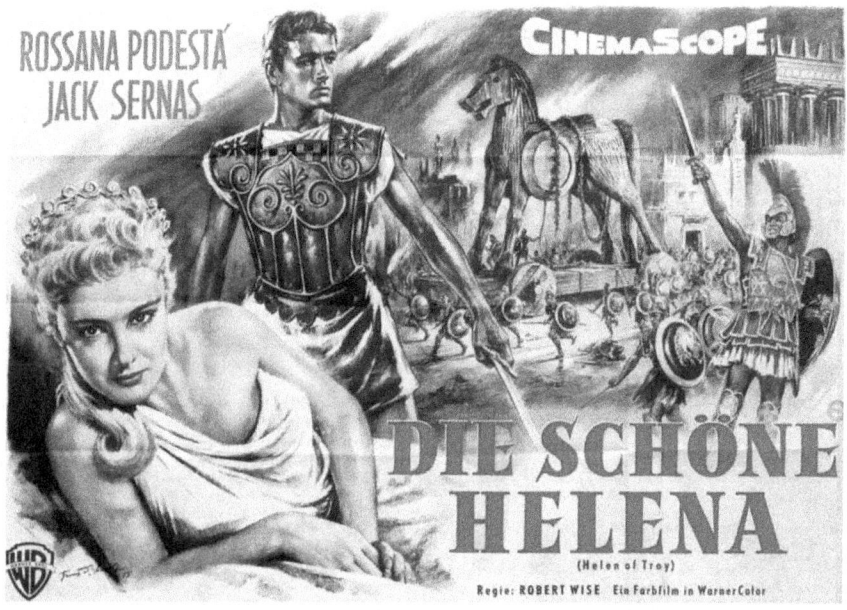

Full of excitement and personal combat, the wars of ancient Greece and Rome provided a change of pace from Westerns, though in the U.S., the same actors worked both types of picture. Produced in Italy with an international cast including Rosanna Podesta as Helen, Sir Cedric Hardwicke as Priam, and Torin Thatcher as Ulysses, *Helen Of Troy* (WB, 1956) provided spectacle in CinemaScope and WarnerColor. Many points of the story are familiar to modern audiences: the rape of beautiful Helen, abducted to the Anatolian coast, the seemingly endless conflict to rescue her, the withdrawal of the Hellenes and their abandonment of the field, leaving behind the tribute of a giant wooden horse, a symbol of the Trojans' matron goddess, Athena – and the squad of warriors secreted within the horse, who, when the Trojans fell exhausted from their victory revels, opened wide the gates of Troy and ushered in the Greek Army, and ushered out the Trojans as a force with which to be reckoned. Most such epics were presented as Adventure or Fantasy, and indeed this particular War may have been the invention of the poet Homer, but its presentation in this film is as a War epic.

THE CRUSADES

The quest by the Franks (that is, western Europeans) to free the Holy Land from the Moslems provided many a young nobleman of medieval times with a purpose in life, and much later filmmakers with fodder for their lenses. Producer-director Cecil B. DeMille, whose taste for spectacle was almost

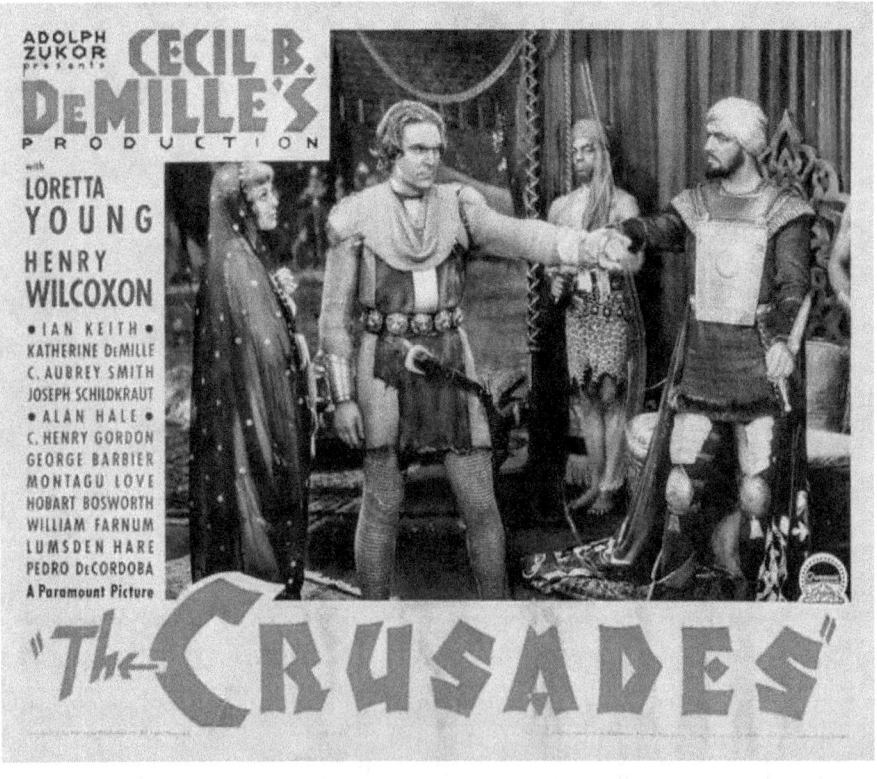

The only one he had, brought us several Biblical and historical epics, including *The Crusades* (Paramount, 1935), a typically overblown but entertaining epic, compressing the several

campaigns of the Crusades into one glorious saga of Richard Lionheart (Henry Wilcoxon, DeMille's protégé) against Saladin (Ian Keith). DeMille always balanced spectacle with quiet moments: Richard, on his way, woos the Princess Berengaria of Navarre (Loretta Young), a royal maid less than excited by the prospect of a husband leaving her to go to War. DeMille's earlier *Cleopatra* (Paramount, '33), with Claudette Colbert, though not a war story but an internecine conflict tale of Roman, is cut from much the same cloth.

THE AMERICAN REVOLUTIONARY WAR

Oppressive taxes, denial of representation, treatment as a mere servant to the King; all these led to a fierce and determined desire among the American colonists to wrest themselves from British control. Names like Washington, Franklin, Adams came to be despised by England but loved by future generations of citizens of the United States of America. Disney's *Johnny Tremain* (BV, 1957), based on the novel by Esther Forbes, showed us the conflict from the point-of-view of a youngster, coming of age with his new nation. Intended as two parts on the "Disneyland" TV series, it received theatrical release before airing. Two other episodes comprised *The Swamp Fox*, starring Leslie Neilson as Francis Marion, hero of the War in the southern swamps.

Kirk Douglas and Burt Lancaster were always big draws at the box office, and their appearance together in *The Devil's Disciple* (UA, 1959) augured top entertainment. In a nod to *A Tale of Two Cities*, a civilian (Kirk Douglas) is mistakenly identified as a local minister (Burt Lancaster) suspected as a traitor, and allows the mistake to go uncorrected, leading to the added complication as the Reverend's wife in admiration of his sacrifice falls in love with him.

A later look at the conflict is *The Patriot* (Sony Entertainment, 2000), in which Mel Gibson, as a veteran of the French and Indian War, has come to shun violence and seeks only to be left alone, but soon finds that there is no solitude for a patriot in times that try Mens' souls.

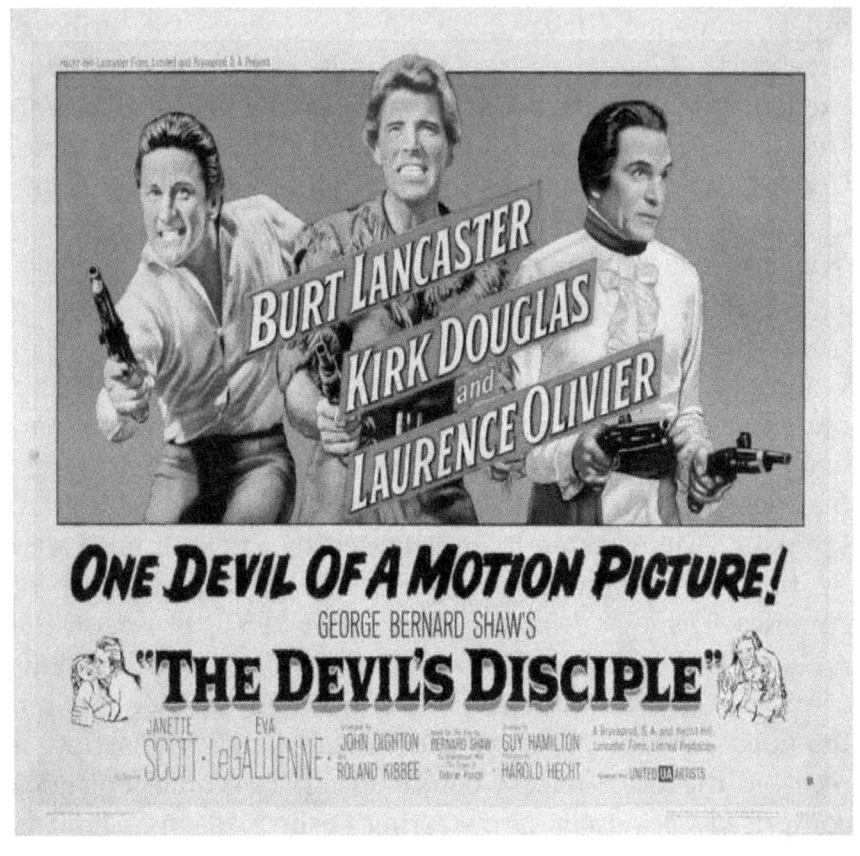

NAPOLEONIC WARS 1805-1815

The Little Corporal spread his domination across Europe after assuming control of France, and only the combined might of the British Empire drove him back. Put down once and exiled to the island of Elba, he was restored to power and redoubled his efforts at conquest until he finally met his Waterloo, creating a phrase that echoes through history and has been used as a term of derogation by Brits ever since. Pioneering filmmaker Abel Gance adapted the saga of the Corsican (Albert Dieudonne) as the basis for *Napoleon*

(Ufa/Filmverlich GmbH, 1927), using a variable-width screen technique that opened up the vistas to a Cinerama-like breadth for the exciting battle scenes. Another look at the conflict is, of course, found in *War and Peace* (Paramount, '56).

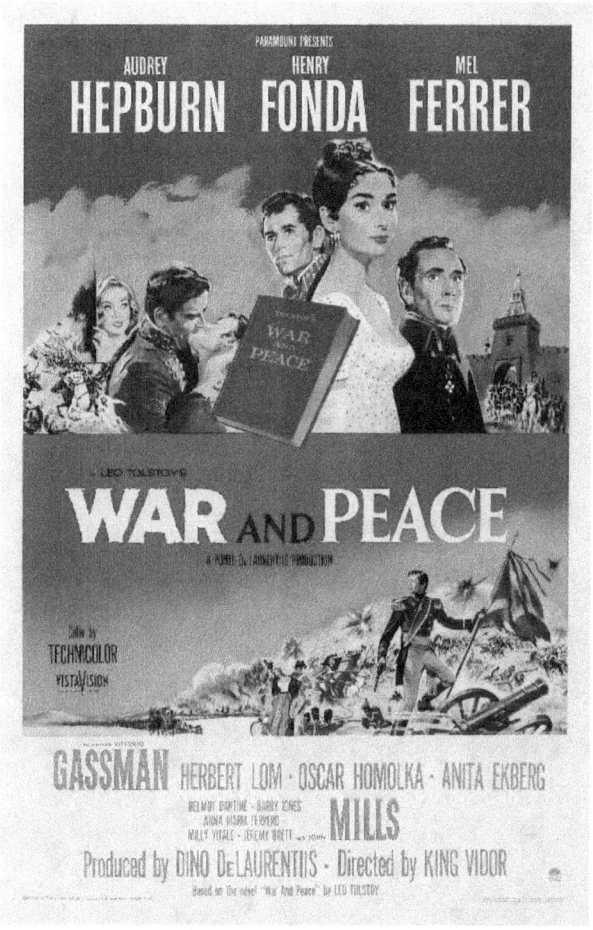

THE WAR OF 1812

Still smarting from the blow of the upstart United "Colonies", and with the scourge of Napoleon behind them (or so they thought) England made a serious attempt to restore order to their wayward sons by re-capturing the

Americans to the Empire. But heroes of the young United States, led by men like Andrew Jackson, battled them back. Seeking to capture New Orleans, only recently acquired by the U.S., British forces ran into an unlikely American ally in pirate Jean LaFitte, as seen in Cecil B. DeMille's *The Buccaneer* (Paramount, 1938), where LaFitte (Fredric March) and his lieutenant Dominique You (Akim Tamiroff) led the guerilla war against the British in the bayous. The 1958 remake, directed by DeMille's son-in-law Anthony Quinn, was an acceptable but lesser effort. The fact that the actual Battle of New Orleans took place *after* the war was concluded is attributable to the poor lines of communication.

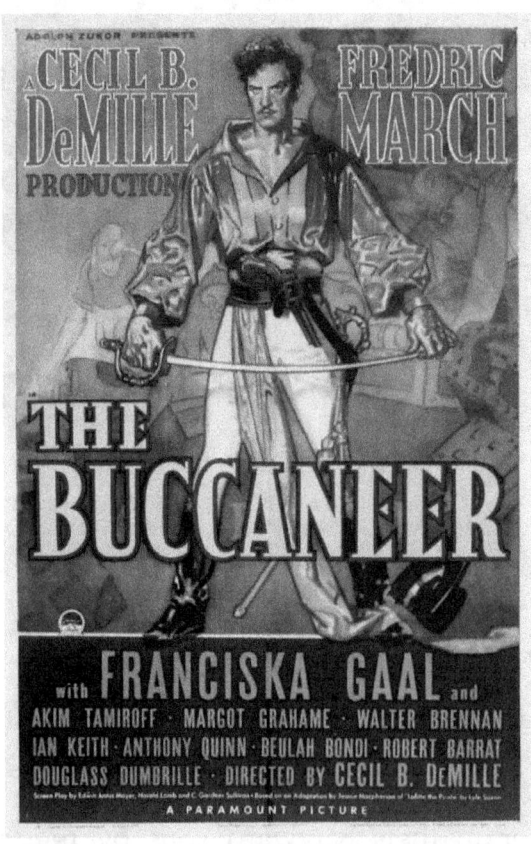

THE CRIMEAN WAR

"Into the Valley of Death rode the Six Hundred..." reads the poem by Alfred Lord Tennyson, praising the dogged spirit of Empire. On film, the disastrous cavalry attack led by Lord Cardigan into the Russian forces during the battle of Balaclava in 1854 formed only the climax of Warner Bros.' 1936 *The Charge Of The Light Brigade*. The earlier British battles in India set the plot in motion, though the picture's chronology is off by a few years, and the villain from the Indian campaign turns up in the Crimea to justify the heroes' transfer to the historic location, the dramatic structure of the film holds the excitement. Michael Curtiz directed, with B. Reeves "Breezy" Eason shooting the charge scenes, which were accompanied by a superb score by Max Steiner, to follow Errol Flynn as he drives home the point of British might even though his attack is doomed to ignominious failure, because he knows that his sacrifice will save the life of his brother (Patric Knowles).

THE AMERICAN CIVIL WAR

The war was long over by the time cinema reached the masses, but movie audiences included people to whom the Recent Unpleasantness was still a memory. Buster Keaton's excellent *The General* (UA, 1927) told a serious story (based on a real incident) with cleverness and humor. Buster, as engineer of the locomotive *The General*, goes through Hell and high water to rescue his beloved train from Union forces, using every trick he can muster. When Union forces pile loose ties across the tracks to stop the train, Buster adapts a tool as old as Archimedes to lever aside the bulwarks to regain the safety of the South and the girl he loves. Disney later remade the story with less humor as *The Great Locomotive Chase* (Buena Vista, '56).

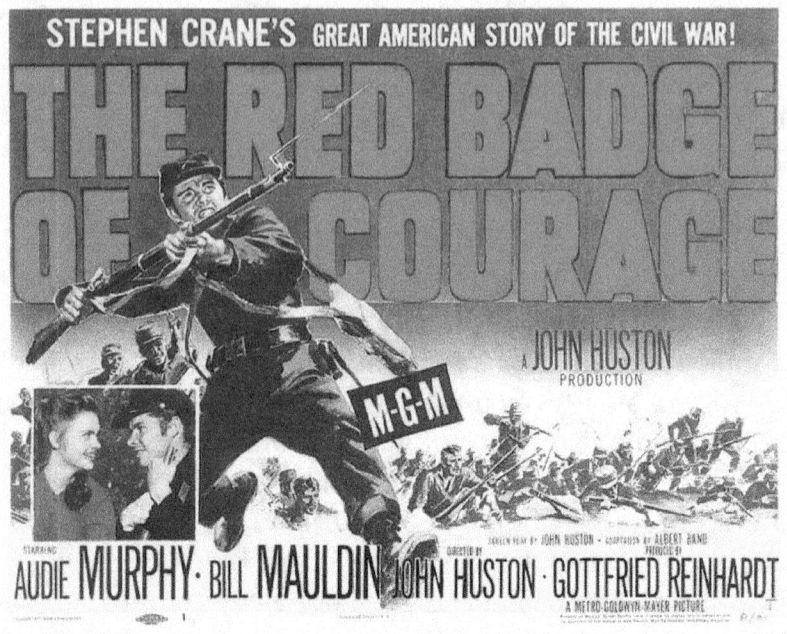

Even with two Wars just passed and another one gearing up in Asia, the American audiences' interest in the War Between the States continued, though heroism might now take a back seat to reality. Stephen Crane's novel was brought to the screen by John Huston as *The Red Badge Of Courage* (M-G-M, 1951), starring Audie Murphy, one of the most decorated soldiers of the Second World War. The film was true to the book in examining the hero's flight before the enemy and his subsequent battle with his conscience over the conflict between bravery and cowardice, as a man must look into his heart in his search for the meaning of life in time of war. The film isn't all it could have been and the story behind it is fascinating, as revealed in Lillian Ross' book, *Picture*.

THE WORLD WAR

It broke out because of misinterpretation, but several governments took advantage of the confusion to bolster their own dreams of conquest. The War to End All Wars was the first to happen after the development of the feature film, and many actors of the pre-talking era had served in the conflict. It was also the first war to be fought from the skies, as dramatized in *Wings*, a 1927 Paramount Picture directed by William A. Wellman. It copped the first Best-Picture Oscar, for despite its drawn-out length, it featured scenes of ærial combat that are still among the best ever filmed. Stars Richard Arlen, "Buddy" Rogers, and Clara Bow headlined the already typical romantic sub-plot on *terra firma*. Wellman, a veteran of

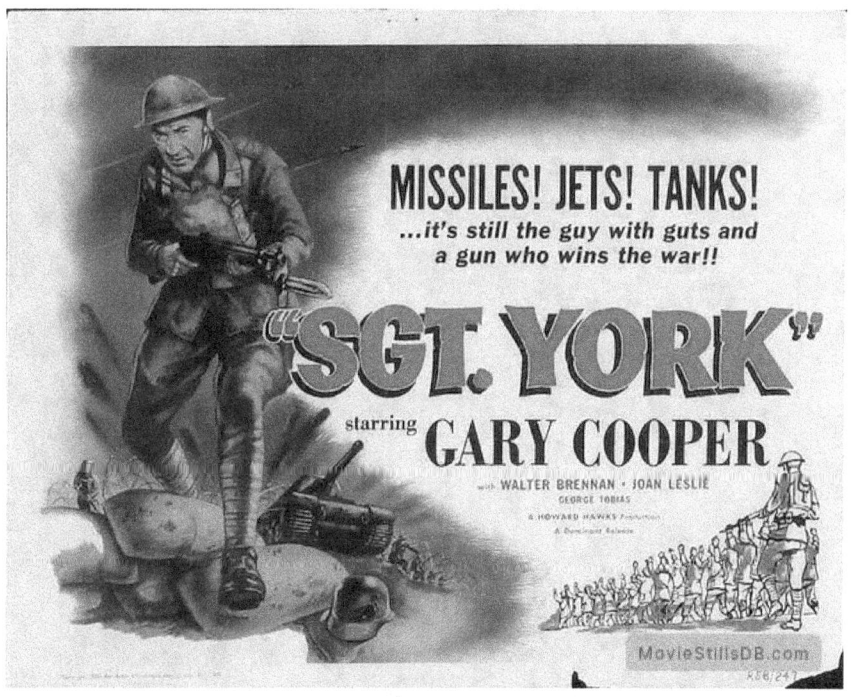

that conflict, later turned his service into the dramatic *Lafayette Escadrille* (WB, '58) starring Tab Hunter, but with Wellman's son portraying his father. War had been raging for some time before American ground forces joined in the fight. One of the great figures of that conflict was young Alvin York, a backwoodsman and pacifist who balked at attacking any of his fellow men. But serve he did, and he learned the need for aggression in extreme cases, yet managed to single-handedly capture the largest contingent of enemy combatants ever taken – without firing a shot or killing a man. When a second World War threatened, Howard Hawks roused sympathy for the cause by filming Alvin's story as *Sergeant York* (WB, 1941) with Gary Cooper and a cast including Walter Brennan, Joan Leslie, and George Tobias. Coop kept Alvin human with his natural folksy performance, and the story included scenes of his life at home to bolster his coming to understand the Aggression and how to deal with it.

THE SECOND WORLD WAR

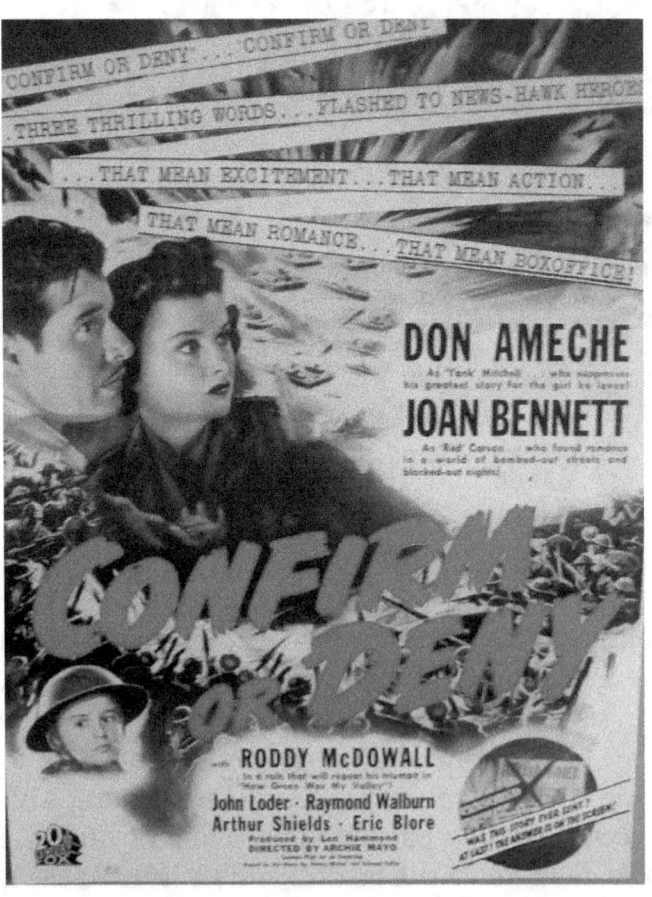

The *blitz* of London was only the opening act of the new world-wide conflict, and it gave U.S. studios exciting backgrounds for what Hollywood did best – love stories. In 20th Century-Fox's 1941 *Confirm Or Deny*, Don Ameche is the London correspondent for a wire news service and Joan Bennett a military driver with whom he falls in love (because that's what happens in stories like this). When a *Nazi* raid demolishes his office and traps them behind tons of rubble with a live bomb, his only means of communication is his direct teletype line to New York. Stories of this sort sought to highlight the steadfast determination of those with whom we'd be allied as America was drawn into the battle.

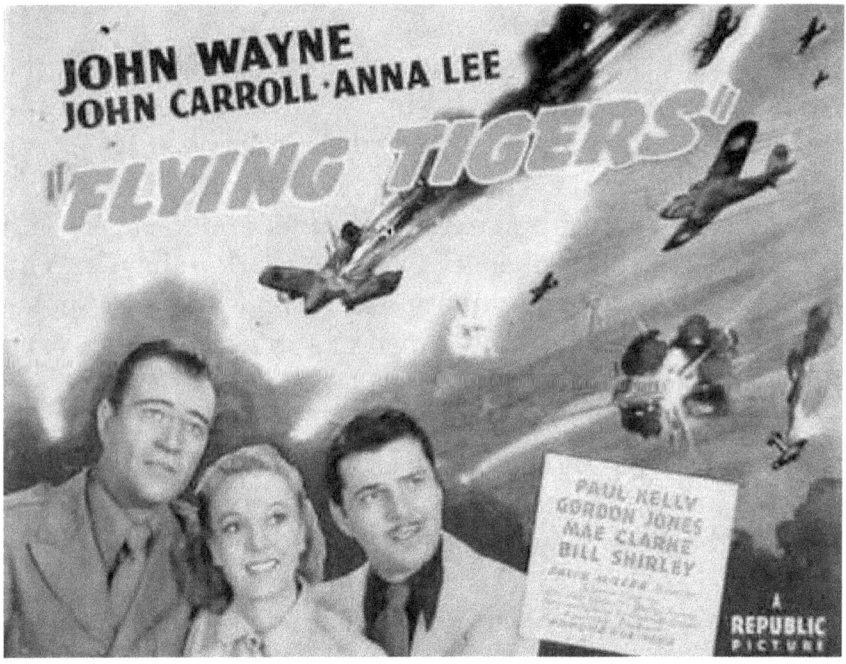

Even before the U.S. entered the new great conflict, American volunteers under the direction of Captain (retired, maybe) Clair Chennault organized a flying wing based in China to combat Japanese assaults on the Asian mainland. In 1942, with the War just declared, Hollywood sought out any suitable subjects for new war pictures, and the valiant work of the AVG, better known as the *Flying Tigers*, made a hit for Republic Pictures. Backed up by stalwarts like John Carroll and Paul Kelly, John Wayne began his career as a one-man Army. The Duke of Westerns had found a second career winning the War, storming beaches, taking islands, and drinking and relaxing with his buddies after a hard day's fight in over a dozen pictures over the years. In Republic's *Sands Of Iwo Jima* ('49) John Wayne, young John Agar, and Forrest Tucker took the fight to the Enemy, but at the end of the film, having successfully conquered Mount Suribachi, Wayne, taking a cigarette break, is killed by enemy fire – just offscreen. But the rest go on; there's still a war to win, to justify the sacrifices of the soldier.

In order to gain desperately needed intelligence for the American bombing raid on Japan, a submarine crew slips into the port city's harbor, their *Destination Tokyo* (WB, 1943). The story, based on real events, of the men who risked their lives was brought to tense and exciting life by Delmer Daves, with typically great performances by Dane Clark, John Garfield, and Cary Grant as the submarine commander, and top-notch model work depicting the dangerous intrusion into Tokyo bay by the submarine *Copperfin*.

While United Nations forces mapped out the Pacific Theatre assaults and planned for the invasion of Fortress *Europa*, individual patriots of their respective homelands harried the Enemy wherever and whenever they could. In *Commandos Strike At Dawn* (Columbia, 1942) Paul Muni starred as a Norwegian ally helping British forces by providing vital intelligence and aiding sabotage to delay *Nazi* projects like the creation of heavy water at the Norsk Hydro plant. Anna Lee, little Ann Carter, Rod Cameron, Richard Derr, and Lillian Gish showed that even the little man could do his bit against the invaders.

Even Edgar Rice Burroughs' apeman got into the fray, when *Nazis* invaded his African paradise, seizing control of the lost city of Pallandria and endangering his friends. In RKO Radio's Edgar Rice Burroughs' *Tarzan Triumphs* (1943), with Jane away in England, Tarzan (Johnny Weissmuller) comes to the aid of beautiful princess Zandra (Frances Gifford, only recently Republic's "Jungle Girl", based on another Burroughs property), when her lost city is threatened by villains Stanley Ridges and frequent *Nazi*-portrayers Sig Ruman and Philip Van Zandt. At first reluctant to involve himself in what he sees as other men's war, he soon finds, as did many Americans, that there are no neutrals when fighting *Nazis*. When Weissmuller cried, "Now Tarzan make war!" kid-audiences must have cheered.

Using the data provided by the heroes depicted in *Destination Tokyo*, General Jimmy Doolittle and his crack team of airmen took the battle to the enemy homeland, as dramatized in *Thirty Seconds Over Tokyo* (M-G-M, 1944). David Thatcher (Robert Walker) and Ted Lawson (Van Johnson) crewmen of the plane "Ruptured Duck", stood with Doolittle (Spencer Tracy), ready for the word their desperate mission could begin. With insufficient fuel for a round trip, the raiders had to continue on in hopes of landing safe somewhere in China, despite the Japanese invasion force in occupation there. Better than average effects shots mixed with actual combat footage to provide top-notch, uplifting entertainment for civilian audiences and our boys in combat zones.

With American and British forces virtually knocking on the door to continental Europe, *Nazi kriegmeisters* knew an invasion was imminent. But where? Calais seemed the most likely, but exact intelligence was vital. In *36 Hours* (M-G-M, 1964) Major Jefferson Pike (James Garner) is kidnapped while on assignment in neutral Portugal and whisked to an especially prepared camp, where he is persuaded that the War is over and he has been in and out of hospitals suffering from the effects of *Nazi* capture. The intent: to get him to "fill in the details" of the Allied invasion – before it has actually taken place. Of course he's fallen in love with his nurse (Eva Marie Saint), and so is crestfallen when he learns of her duplicity. But neither she nor his doctor (Rod Taylor) are whole-heartedly in the scheme, and so – maybe – Pike will be able to reach freedom, taking with him the vital secret.

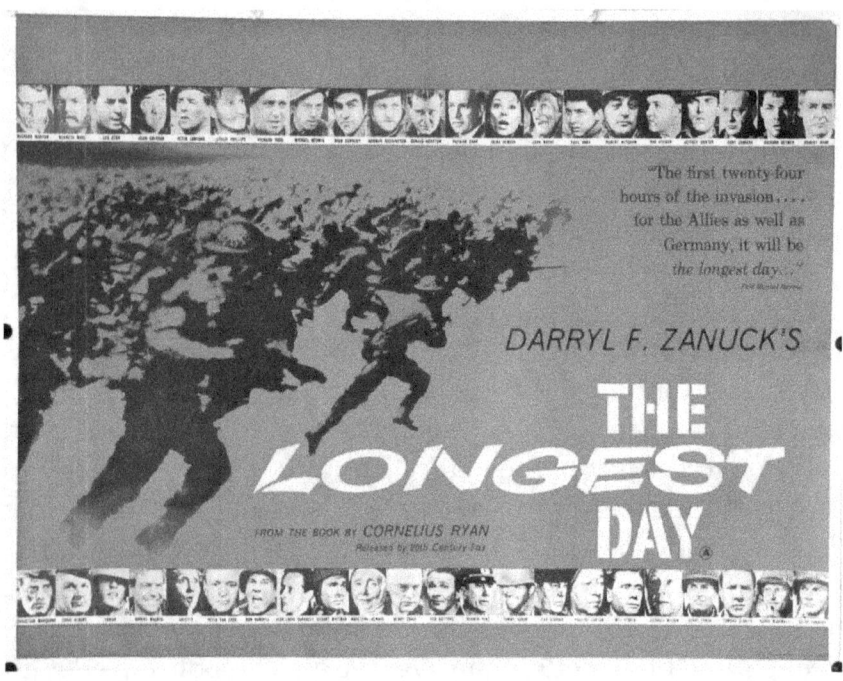

That the *Nazis* were unable to break down Major Pike's will in time is evident in their complete surprise when United Nations forces stormed beachheads in Normandy. Code-named Sword, Gold, Juno, Utah, and especially Omaha, the shores saw some of the bloodiest and most violent fighting in the history of Mankind, as the Allies battered their way through Axis fortifications. Darryl F. Zanuck made his production of *The Longest Day* (20th Century-Fox, 1962) *the* biggest and most explosive war epic ever, with three directors (an appropriate one for each of the three principal languages depicted) and a cast including John Wayne, Robert Ryan, Robert Mitchum, Red Buttons, Richard Burton, Sean

Connery, and Curt Jurgens. In fact, so great was the cast that most stars appeared in little more than extended cameo performances. One additional notable aspect of this terrific film was its score: the theme is first heard being whistled by a GI awaiting the signal to go; from there, the underscoring builds, slowly at first, until in the last reels, it has become an organic part of the film.

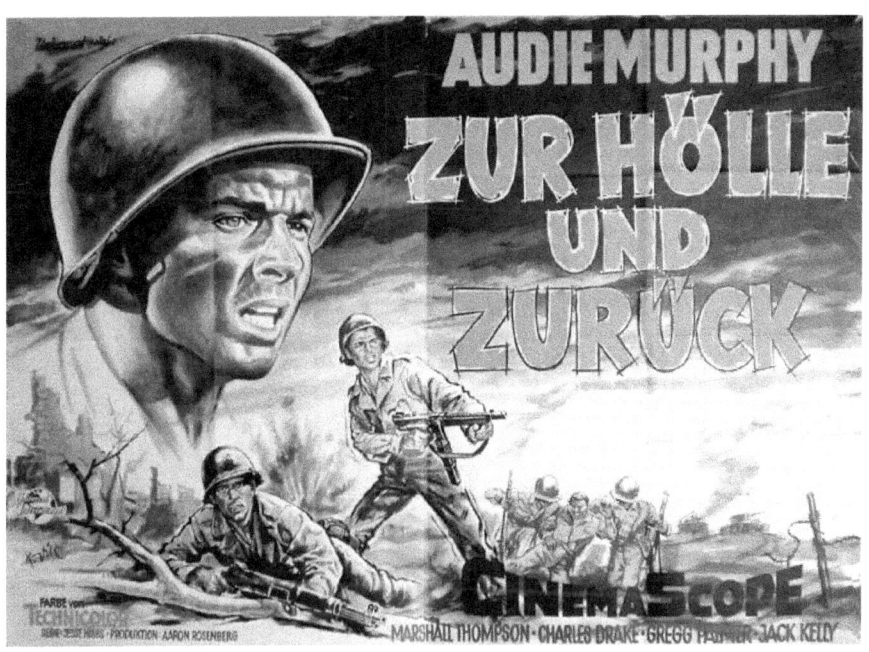

Now an established box-office star and author, Audie Murphy was a sure bet to play himself in *To Hell And Back* (U-I, 1955), based on his autobiography, telling his own story of how he came to be among the most decorated soldiers of the War. Recreating heroic and amazing – but true – vignettes from his own past could not have been easy for the veteran, but fighting war on the back lot is a lot less trouble than the real thing.

Once Allied forces had breeched Fortress *Europa*, death and capture were all but inevitable, and hundreds of American soldiers and airmen found themselves sitting out the fight in

Prisoner-of-War camps like the one depicted in *Stalag 17* (Paramount, 1953), with William Holden under suspicion as a double-agent and Eric von Stroheim as the sadistic camp *Kommandant*. In general, most prisoners did their best to harry and overwork their captors, tying up men and resources that might have made it to the Front, and perhaps even themselves escape to get away to re-join the fight.

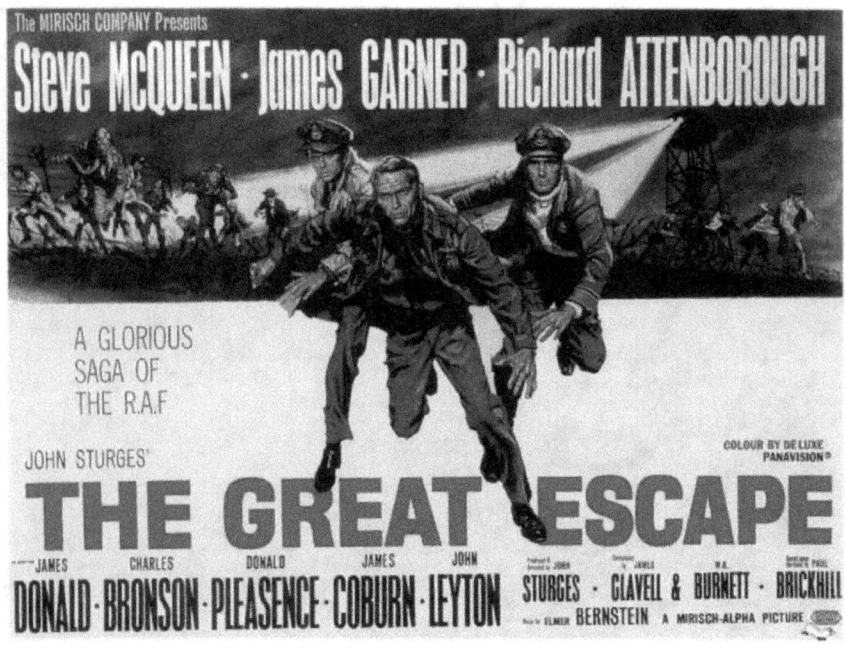

One such ploy for freedom was worked out by the inmates of *Stammlager Luft* III, the biggest break-out ever planned – *The Great Escape* (UA, 1963), a highly fictional dramatization of an actual event, with an international cast. Digging multiple tunnels, the Allied prisoners are ready after their first tunnel had been uncovered, and are able to proceed. The plan, masterminded by "Big X" (Richard Attenborough), sends dozens of men fleeing into the night. As the Germans try to catch them, the soldiers desperately use any means to escape. Hendley "The Scrounger" (James Garner) and Blythe "The Forger" (Donald Pleasence) steal an airplane, and Hilts, the "Cooler King" (Steve McQueen) steals a *Nazi* motorcycle, leading to a thrilling chase sequence in which he tries to jump a barbed-wire fence – twice! The conflict continued to catch the imagination for decades beyond its end. The British picture The *Password is Courage* (M-G-M, '62) included coverage of the same material, and became a template for the later TV series "Hogan's Heroes", which plowed this same field with the addition of a traditional war-era device, ridiculing the Enemy and portraying him as inept, which worked better as contemporary propaganda than as latter-day humor.

THE KOREAN CONFLICT

When our Second World War allies, the USSR and China, had rid themselves of their immediate enemies, each sought to extend its own domination of its neighbors. Russia easily overcame eastern Europe with its power base of East Germany, but the Chinese found the attempt to make Korea a satellite state a more difficult matter, as southern forces, aided by an army provided by the new United Nations Organization, resisted to the point of deadlock, resulting in the two Koreas that exist to this day. In *M A S H* (20th Century-Fox, 1970), scenarist Ring Lardner, Jr., and fledgling director Robert Altman brought to the screen "Richard Hooker's" *memoir* of the darkly comic side of war as experienced by Hawkeye Pierce (Donald Southerland) and Trapper John McIntyre (Elliot Gould). A slightly different edit of the film was issued in 1973, in conjunction with the series ("M*A*S*H") based upon it that became one of television's greatest hits.

THE VIET NAM WAR

The South-east Asian conflict of the 1960s was an unpopular war, with many protesting in the streets and others fleeing the draft to Canada. But it was a war to stop or at least restrain the forces of the dreaded and feared Communism, still trying (this time with some success) to dominate the former Indo-China area. And America's number-one patriot, John Wayne, leapt into the fray as he had a generation earlier, to attempt to win the unwinnable as head of the great fighting force, *The Green Berets* (Warner Bros.-7 Arts, 1968). As a way to make the audience understand the government's position, Wayne as Colonel Mike Kirby tried to explain the importance of the conflict to a doubting journalist, George Beckworth (David Janssen). A famous "goof" – a sunset scene at a beach – often cited by reviewers, is unlikely to be an actual mistake. Viet Nam *does* have a west coast at the far south.

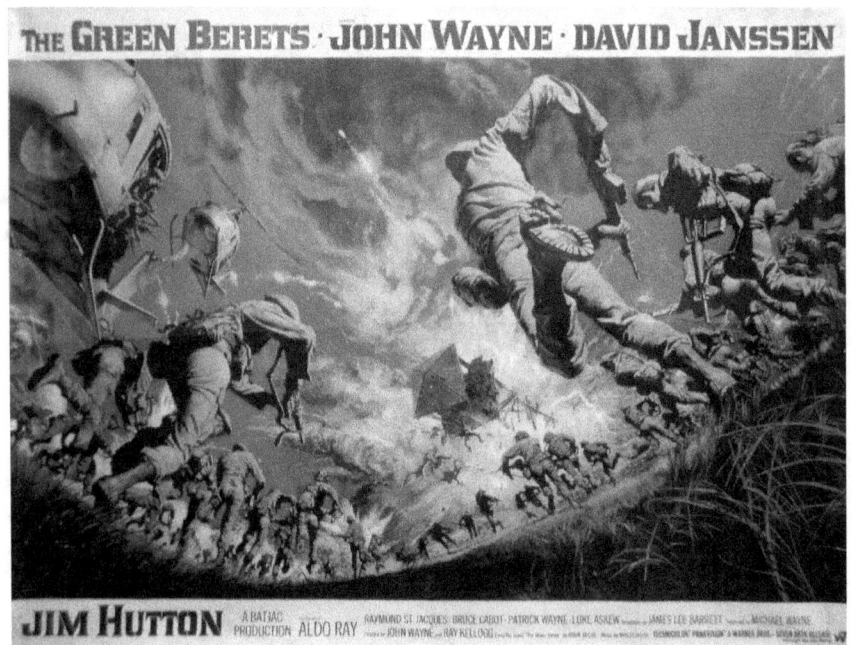

Of course, war did not end with Viet Nam, nor had it started with the Trojans. While some "War" pictures were fact-based, like *To Hell and Back*, incorporating true events in their narratives, others were entirely imaginary. But some were *entirely* factual, part of a *genre* that did, for the most part, tell the truth (with occasional lapses for entertainment's sake). A class of film nonetheless interesting for their reality, they were the...

CHAPTER ELEVEN: DOCUMENTARIES

THESE WERE THE films that told the truth, at least mostly. The "Why We Fight" series brought the Second World War into the lives of those who stayed behind, and did it graphically and powerfully. But there were many other slices of life to be brought to the Masses: recreations of voyages and journeys, examples of other lands and other cultures, reports of explorations successful or doomed, wild animals of land and sea. Films that proved that there was drama – and humor – as much in real life as in fiction. Cinematographers and crews braved heat, cold, sickness, privation, and even death to bring the world a little closer together in a time before airplanes and television made these fabulous journeys, if not accessible to everyone at least more familiar.

South Sir Ernest Shackleford's Epic of the Antarctic (States Rights, 1919; later re-titled *Endurance*) lives up to its sub-title, as Sir Ernest leads an expedition to Antarctica on the ship *Endurance*. The crew, determined to bring knowledge and glory back to England, set out from Buenos Aires in 1914, reaching the Antarctic mainland and beginning their journeys of exploration. Unfortunately, *Endurance* becomes trapped in ice, and all attempts to free her fail. Her hull crushed, the ship never leaves the continent again, and her crew is forced to retreat in the lifeboats, braving a voyage of over 700 nautical miles to South Georgia Island (itself a more hazardous voyage than any Shackleford ever made), eventually returning to a hero's welcome for the discoveries they'd made and the footage they brought back. Shackleford would return to the Antarctic on another expedition, but would die in South Georgia, where, at his wife's request, he was buried. But the record of his explorations fascinated millions.

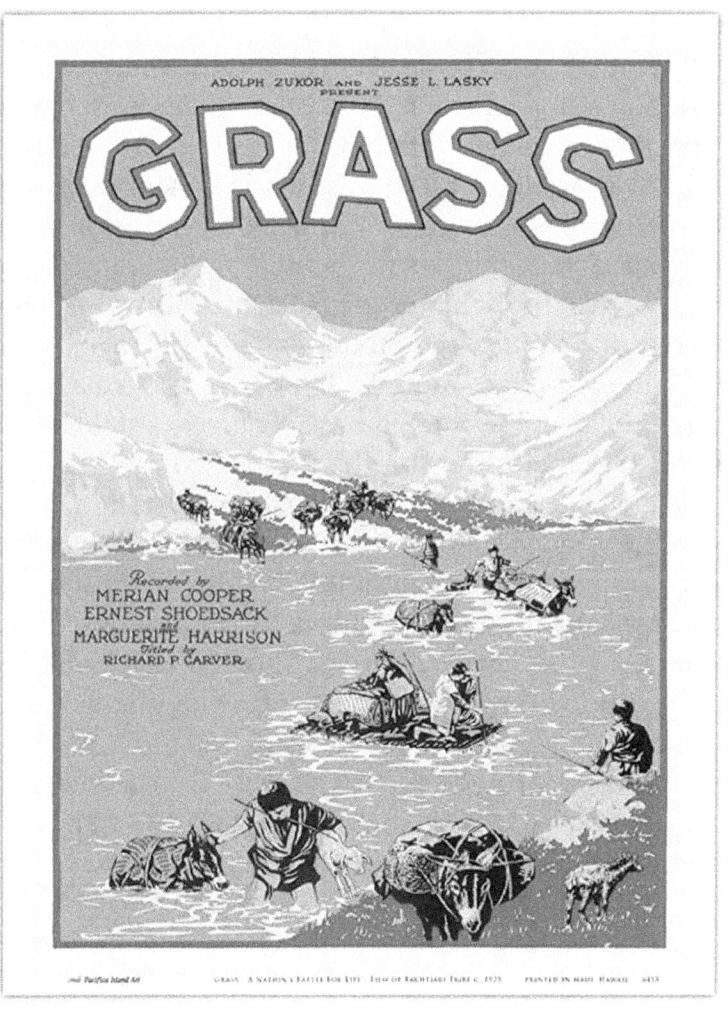

Grass A Nation's Battle for Life (Paramount, 1925). Film-makers Merian C. Cooper and Ernest Schoedsack, who would later bring us *King Kong* (*Q.V. in Adventure*), and Marguerite Harrison journeyed from Angora, Turkey (now Ankara) into the trackless wilds of Persia in this, the first of their spectacular true-life pictures. Traveling with the Bakhtyari people from their camp in western Persia, where pasturing and climate have exhausted the food supply, the crew documented the travails and dangers as the tribe – men, women, children, and livestock – make a desperate crossing of the icy and treacherous Karun River, and, as the inter-titles inform us, the tramp of 100,000 feet and the thunder of half a million hooves echo over 150 miles, including having to summit the highest mountain in the region, to reach the rich green land, the valley of Iran. Authentic footage taken during weeks of hardship shared by the Bakhtyari and the film-makers made this a hit when it premiered in the U.S. Cooper and Schoedsack brought another slice of reality, this one with a bit more drama imposed on the footage, in *Chang* A Drama of the Wilderness (Paramount, '27), where Lao tribesman Kru and his family brave the Siamese jungle to establish a new home. The theme of the story is that the Mighty Jungle will overcome Man's puny efforts to bring civilization, and Kru must resort to his wits in the fight, building his house on stilts and creating a pen to save his animals from predation. But the jungle has an ultimate weapon: a thundering herd of elephants! Once again, the team showed determination in bringing real-life thrills to the audience; though this time they added some showmanship to the mix.

Frank Buck's *Bring 'Em Back Alive* (Radio Pictures, 1932) was the first of the records of the man who "brought 'em back alive" and took a camera crew into the jungles to document his exploits. Generally narrated in Buck's own flat vocal style, and with some scenes staged for humor or excitement, the efforts of the hunter to procure wild creatures for zoos, circuses, and scientific study are still amazing, even after all the years. Buck's style of hunting, and the entire idea of capturing animals to become entertainers for a curious public, have fallen into disfavor, though some captured animals have become the only hope for the preservation of their species. Today, the curious can see films of the animals in their native habitat, or journey to see them in person, but that wasn't an option in Buck's day. He continued with several additional features, and later edited a compilation entitled (and laboriously sub-titled) Frank Buck's *Jungle Cavalcade* from Bring 'Em Back Alive • Wild Cargo • Fang and Claw (RKO Radio '41). Buck occasionally appeared in fiction films, including the '37 Columbia serial release *Jungle Menace*.

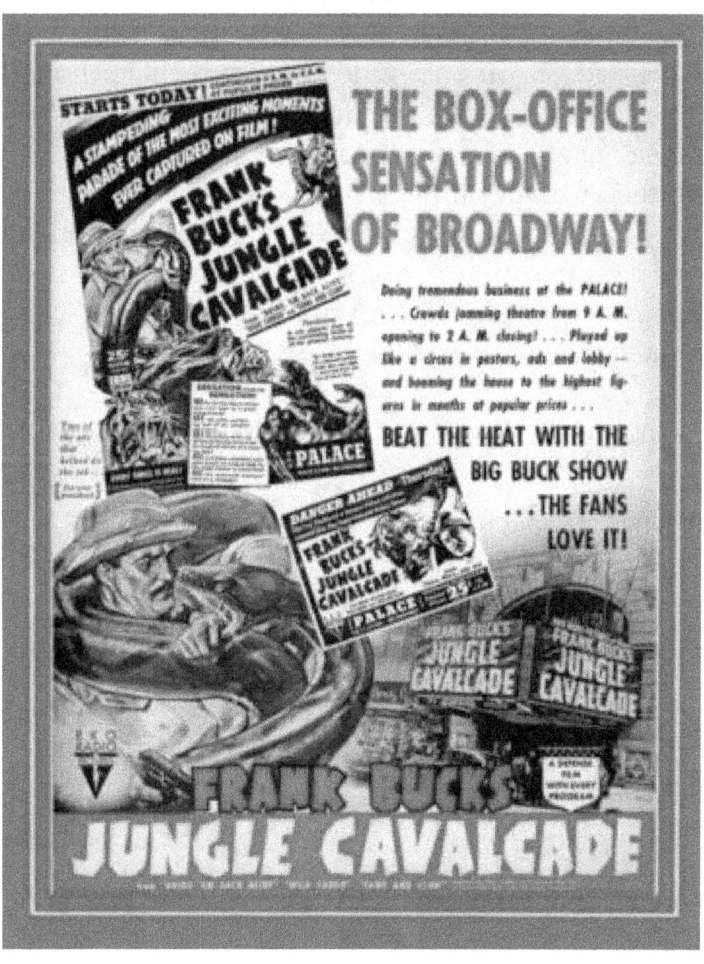

Prelude to War (Office of War Information, Bureau of Motion Pictures and Twentieth Century Fox [theatrical], 1942) was the first of a series of what were effectively propaganda films to inform the American public of the dangers of the Axis and why we should engage in wars that seemed to be limited to Europe and Asia. Narrated by Walter Huston, each of the films explored an aspect of the conflict. Most of the films were supervised by director Frank Capra (of *It's a Wonderful Life* [*Q.V. in fantasy*] and others), who saw the series as a direct response to Leni Riefenstahl's *Triumph des Willens* [*Triumph of the Will*] (Ufa, '35), to show that we were as tough and capable as any *Nazi*. U.S. Army and Navy footage, as well as captured enemy film, was used to show those safe in their neighborhood Bijou or Odeon what their home-town sacrifices contributed to the War Effort. The final installment, *War Comes to America* Information Film #7 (War Activities Committee of the Motion Pictures Industry and RKO Radio Pictures [theatrical] '45) came so late in the conflict as to almost be superfluous. All seven films are available on Youtube, since none was copyrighted, being the "property" of all Americans.

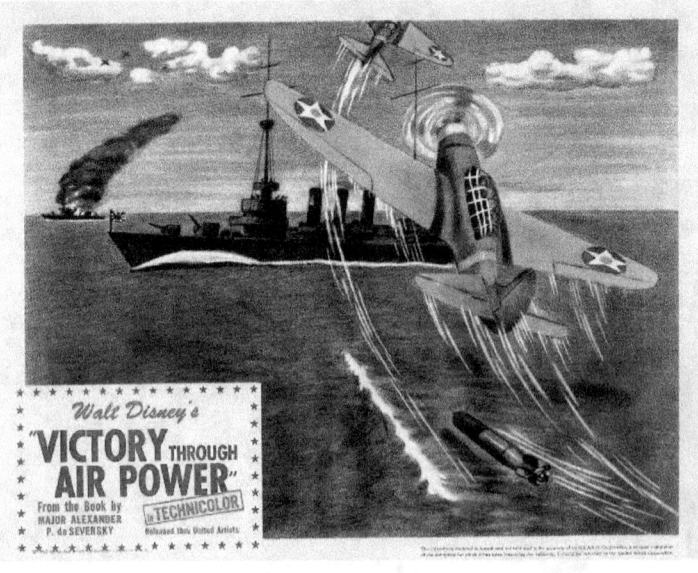

Victory Through Air Power (UA, 1943) was Walt Disney's personal plea to Washington. He'd read Major Alexander P. Seversky's book of the same title, and saw air superiority as the deciding factor in Second World War. With live-action and animation, the film explains and explores the possibilities of aircraft in combat. According to Leonard Maltin in his introduction to the DVD release, "[the film] changed FDR's way of thinking—he agreed that Seversky was right", and devoted men and materiel to the Army Air Corps, soon to become the Army Air Force and then its own branch of our fighting forces. When Disney's distributor took a pass on the film, he financed it himself and released it through his old distributor, United Artists, and spent some two years paying off the debt he incurred. During this period Disney was a primary supplier of product for the government, with animated training films and even nose-art for airplanes.

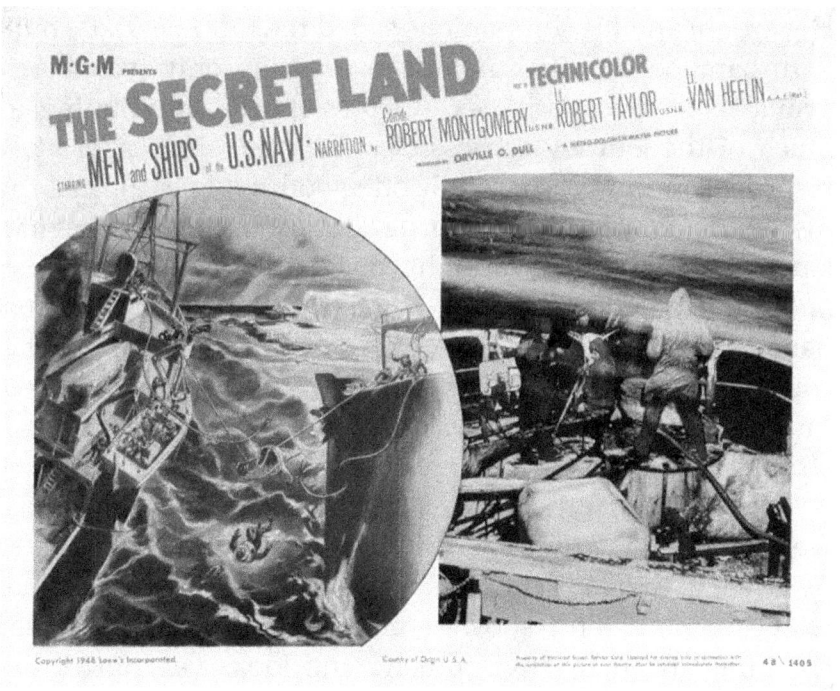

The Secret Land (M-G-M, 1948) details in actual footage shot

251

on location the 1946-'47 expedition to Antarctica, Operation "High Jump", as commanded by Admiral Richard E. Byrd, who'd had some previous experience with the poles. Some 4000 men and a dozen ships made the perilous voyage and flights to the bottom of the world. Given a major publicity campaign, the picture was narrated by three Metro stars, using their service ranks – Commander Robert Montgomery, U.S.N.R.; Lieutenant Robert Taylor, U.S.N.R.; and Lieutenant Van Heflin A.A.F. (Retired) – to promote the military importance of the trip. As often happened in Hollywood, footage from the expedition was later used in fiction films, such as *The Land Unknown* (U-I, '57).

Kon-Tiki (Sandrew-Baumanfilm AB, 1950; RKO Radio, ['51] in US) is not just the proof of Thor Heyerdahl's theory that the South Seas Islands could have been populated by South American natives, but the amazing adventure of a crew of 20th-century men proving the theory by living it. For 101 days, Heyerdahl and his companions sailed the raft *Kon-Tiki* – built with bamboo on a balsa-wood base using only technology available to the aborigines – across the Pacific, filming as much of the journey as possible. Their adventures, crudely recorded on film, include episodes both whimsical, like the discovery many mornings of a new crop of flying fish that had landed on the deck overnight, providing a tasty breakfast; and the frightening, when a whale shark, biggest and most dangerous of fish, begins to frolic around the raft, a toy it could sink on a whim. Well edited, with narration, bits of music, and the sound-effect of ocean waves, *Kon-Tiki* is a striking documentary and testament to Man's ingenuity.

Rachel L. Carson's *The Sea Around Us* (RKO Radio, 1953) was produced and supervised by Irwin Allen (later of "Voyage to the Bottom of the Sea", "Lost In Space" and other television fare) and showed glimpses of the lives of sea creatures and their environment, and looks very good. But Carson was unhappy with the treatment of the material, especially the narration, and declined future requests to adapt her other non-fiction works. Surprisingly, the film ends with concerns about the rising sea temperature, a worry still much on the minds of scientists today.

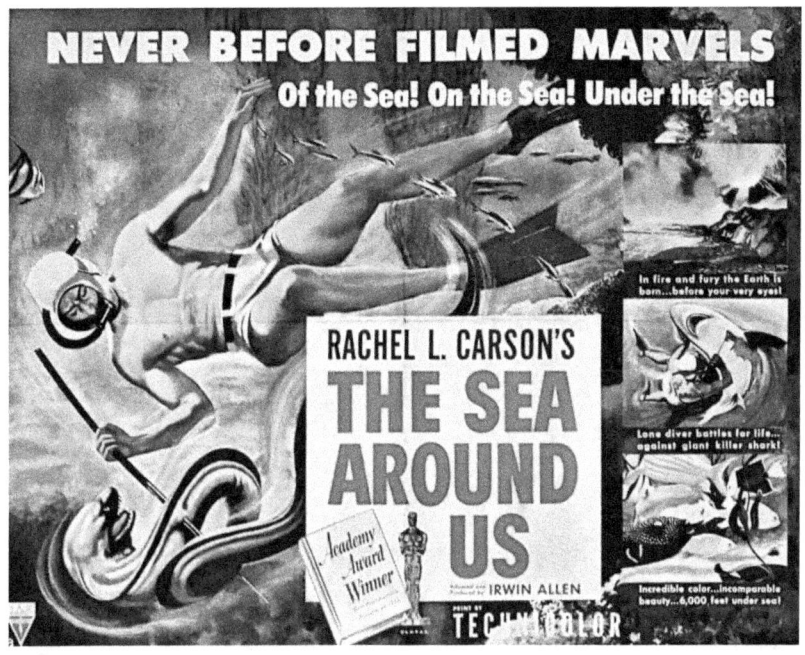

A True-life Adventure *The Living Desert* (BV, 1953), first feature-length installment of a series that had previously been short subjects, caused another rift with distributor RKO Radio, this time causing Walt Disney to open his own distribution company. The film, directed and co-written by James Algar, long-time Disney creator, and narrated by Winston Hibler, gives us glimpses of an area most people thought of as desolate and empty. But here we see lizards, snakes, and other fauna living in harsh conditions. We meet the peccary, the wild pig so tough a group of them can "tree" a bobcat (atop a cactus), and see the "Stingaree", a fanciful sequence of dancing scorpions, achieved by careful editing and reverse-printing of shots to accompany a square-dance tune. (This sequence drew criticism at the time, but is one of the favorites among young audiences.) Disney followed the desert with a whole series, beginning with A True-life Adventure *The Vanishing Prairie* (BV, '54), another Algar picture telling much the same story about the Great Prairie of the mid-west, though concentrating on the past, as the area was by then increasingly being populated by people.

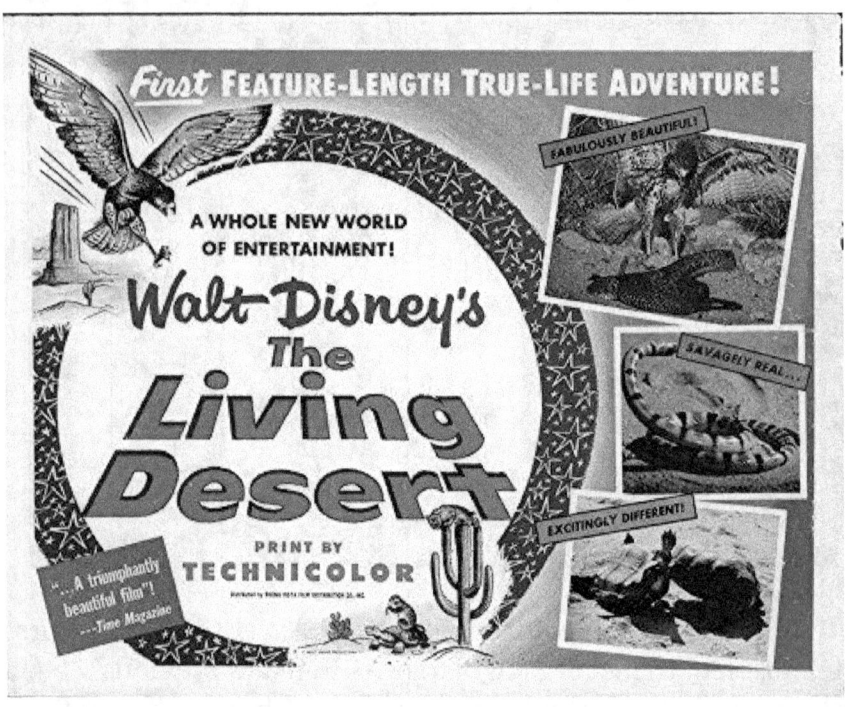

The exploits depicted in these films were as real as the hardships faced by the men and women who made them. Among the Hollywood crowd, these were the adventurers, bringing us real recreations of amazing feats. And (because Hollywood is an economic company town) providing miles of stock footage to enhance the perceived reality of one last *genre* of moving pictures, the heroic tales of...

CHAPTER TWELVE: ADVENTURE

ADVENTURE WAS THE very heart and soul of the movies, taking audiences on fast-paced exploits in faraway lands and times. Literature had already been full of such tales for hundreds of years when the movies brought them to life. *Jivaro* headhunters, the lofty peaks of the Himalaya, Red Indians swarming over a fort, elephant stampedes were all easier – and safer – to see in a movie than in real life. With an elaborate back lot and a good supply of stock footage, a studio could set a film anywhere – Africa, China, the North Pole, even Mars. Policemen, soldiers, spies, scientists and even innocent bystanders could be swept up in excitement, action, the thrill of a lifetime (or, for the series hero, the thrill of the month). The format could enliven stories in other *genres*: *King Kong* is a fabulous adventure. Top directors like Howard Hawks and Alfred Hitchcock produced exciting adventure pictures like –*Only Angels Have Wings* and *Saboteur* in their careers. With continuing characters like Tarzan, Jungle Jim, and Brass Bancroft, and classics like *The Adventures Of Robin Hood* and *Gunga Din*, adventure films were a staple throughout the era of the B-picture, and continued on, thanks in part to the 007 franchise that began in 1962 and continued into the 21st century. Stronghold of stunt-players and special effects, here are just some of the most effective adventure pictures.

PIRATES

The days of the Spanish Main, of cutlasses and belaying pins, of the High Seas and High Adventure, led many a kid to yearn for a pirate's life… as long as they got home in time for supper. Who could resist the sea-faring life, when it was represented by such heroes?

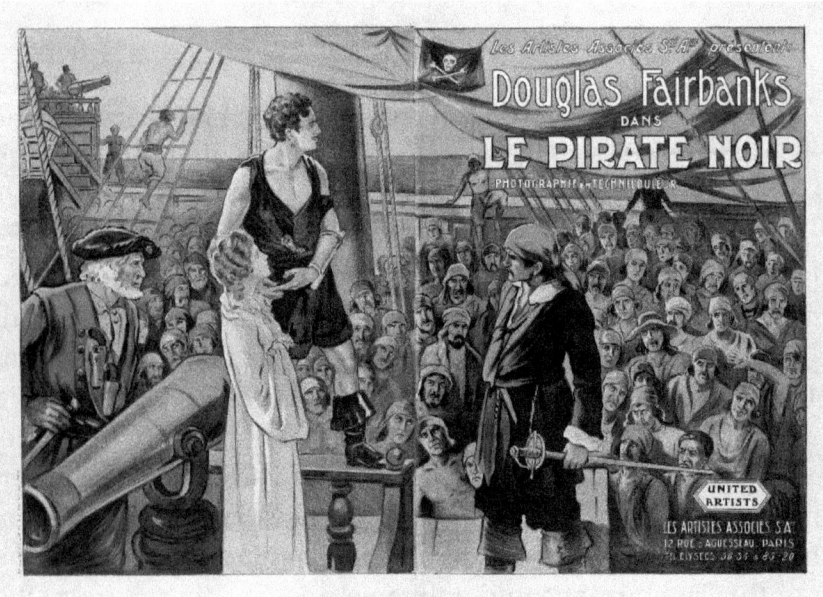

Douglas Fairbanks was king of the swashbucklers in the days of the mute cinema, with *The Black Pirate* as his shining adventure moment, in a two-strip Technicolor 1926 feature (released through his new venture, United Artists) with Billie Dove as the beautiful Princess Isobel. Strikingly well photographed, and with its own musical accompaniment, the film's scenario encompasses less than thirty hours of excitement. After his ship is wrecked and his father killed by pirates, a young man adopts the identity of the "Black Pirate" and joins the pirate band, soon taking control and leading them to their doom in revenge. A complication arises when he captures a ship and takes a beautiful girl, whom he must protect from the pirates while maintaining his masquerade as a ruthless cut-throat. The film breezes along through one adventure after another, as Fairbanks challenges the pirate captain to a duel, as he single-handedly captures an entire merchant ship, as he's found out and forced to walk the plank, and so much more. The chief exponent of high adventure in those days, Big Doug in his *repertoire* included Robin Hood, Zorro, and *The Thief Of Bagdad* (*Q.V.in Fantasy*). Fairbanks often did his own stunts, only occasionally being doubled for some of the most dangerous gags (a fact assiduously concealed for many years).

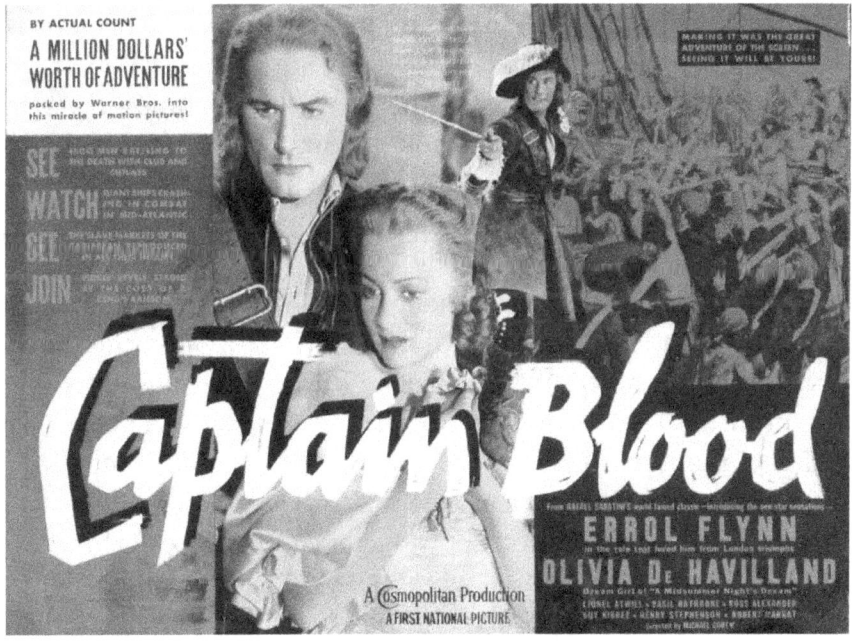

Rafael Sabatini was always a great source for swashbuckling adventure. *Captain Blood* (as provided by Warner Bros. in 1935) gave us Errol Flynn as a physician forced by political intrigue into the role of pirate, roving the Spanish Main while having time to romance Olivia DeHaviland and sword-duel to the death with Basil Rathbone. Michael Curtiz' direction and a masterful score by Erich Wolfgang Korngold re-launched a *genre* and launched Flynn's career: he'd go on to a dozen such epics as *The Sea Hawk* (WB, '40; more Sabatini in spirit than word) and *The Adventures of Robin Hood* (*Q.V.*)

The Black Swan (20th Century-Fox, 1942) was not only a great picture but historical as well. Filmed in magnificent Technicolor, directed by Henry King, and adapted by Ben Hecht and Seton I. Miller, it told the story of how the British solved the problem of the pirate raids of Captain Henry Morgan (Laird Cregar) – by appointing him Governor of Jamaica, to the displeasure of his predecessor (George Zucco). When one of his former captains, Billy Leech (George Sanders) opts to continue his piratin' ways, Morgan is compelled to send trusted Jamie Waring (Tyrone Power) to hunt him down. But along the way, Jamie takes time to romance the former governor's beautiful daughter Lady Margaret Denby (Maureen O'Hara) who furiously repulses his advances. But he's a pirate, after all; he'll chase her from here to Dry Tortuga.

Circus ærialists before their movie-star days, flier Burt Lancaster and his former catcher Nick Cravat punctuated Burt's string of quality dramas with a couple of comic adventures. They followed up *The Flame and the Arrow* (WB, 1950), a medieval Italian romp, with *The Crimson Pirate* (WB, '52), in which Roland Kibbee's script played with pirate conventions and added both science-fiction overtones – nitroglycerine, flame-throwers, even a submarine – and plenty of opportunities for the boys to leap, whirl, tumble, and hurtle through space. Our "hero", a thorough rogue, Captain Vallo (Burt), and first mate Ojo (Nick, whose performance is mute because of his thick accent) engage in all sorts of derring-do, utilizing their acrobatic talents. The period visuals, filmed on location, are engaging, and the performances, especially that of Torin Thatcher as 'Umble Bellows – who, if he can't live like a pirate, will die like one – are appropriately theatrical.

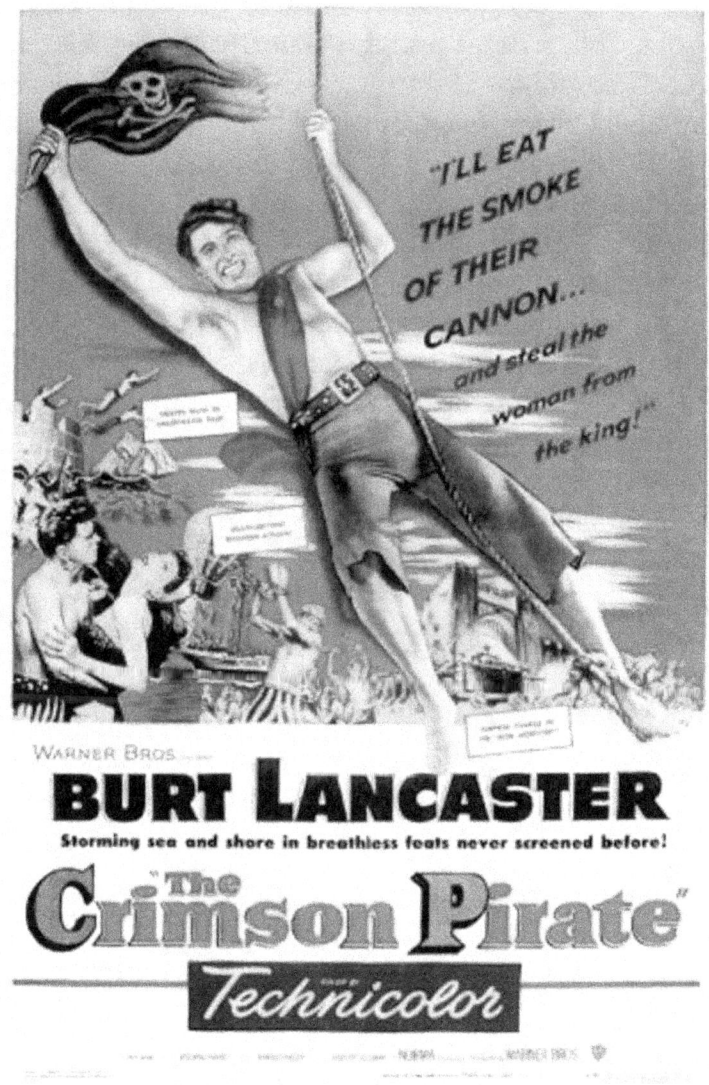

A more recent look at the High Seas was begun with what has proved to be a popular pentalogy (so far): *Pirates Of The*

Caribbean The Curse of the Black Pearl (BV, 2003) filmmaker Gore Verbinski emphasized the fantasy elements that had weaved their way through the plot since Will Turner and Elizabeth Swan first met as children in the wake of the passage of the ghost ship *Black Pearl*. With the doomed crew of the black ship, the involvement of the chained goddess Calypso, and fantastic – and fantastically clever – action, and the "Pearl" somehow a ship in a bottle, the action never lets up. Captains Barbarossa (Geoffery Holden) and Jack Sparrow (Johnny Depp), each having been brought back from the dead, squabble over whose ship the "Pearl" is; Swan (Keira Knightley) has inherited the captaincy of her own pirate ship, in the quest for the heart of Davy Jones, tragic lord of the sea; and young Will Turner (Orlando Bloom) has his own incredible problems. With five pictures so far, the Jolly Roger seems likely to stay aloft yet. Pirates throughout movie history make for crackling good adventure.

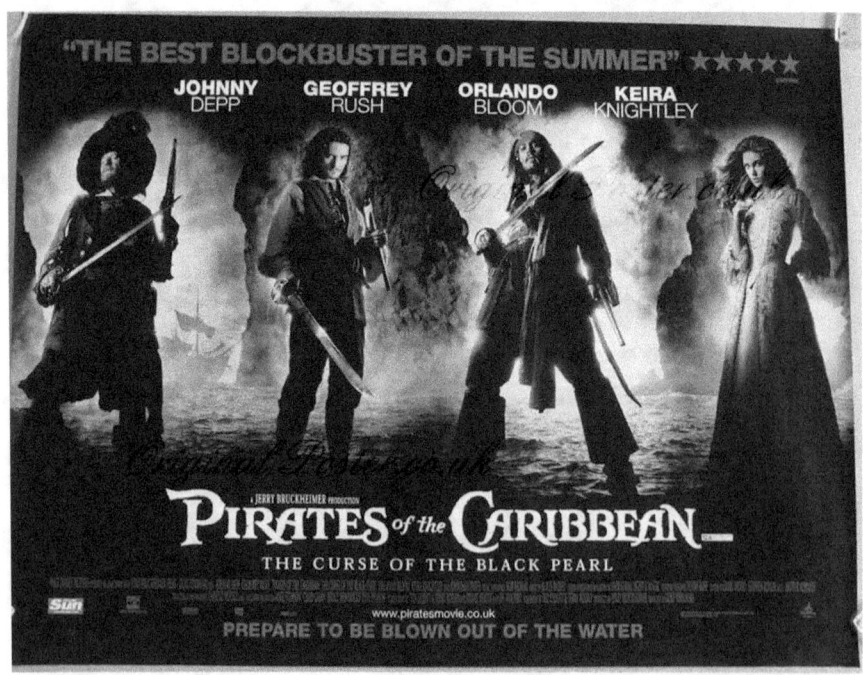

SWASHBUCKLERS

European history, real and invented (and sometimes a combination of both) brought us colorful characters and romantic settings, in pictures like:

Edward Small had done well with his productions of *The Count of Monte Cristo* (UA, 1934) and would again in *The Corsican Brothers* (UA, '41), and he knew there was more to be mined from the Dantes family tree, if only he could invent one. His decision to follow the exploits of the offspring of Edmund Dantes brought variable results. The first and best follow-up was *The Son Of Monte Cristo* (UA, '40), with Louis Hayward as Dantes, Junior, the richest man in Europe in the 1860s. Learning of the evil plans of a certain Gurko Lanen (George Sanders) to seize control of the Ruritanian principality of Lichtenburg through extortion and by marrying the beautiful Princess Zona (Joan Bennett), Dantes pretends to offer financial support while masquerading as "the Torch" and fighting for the underdogs (thank you, Diego Vega). Rand Brooks, Clayton Moore, and Jack Mulhall were among the heroes; top character actor Henry Brandon provided menacing support. Later Dantes appeared in pictures including *The Return of Monte Cristo* (Columbia, '46, with Hayward as another descendant) and *The Wife of Monte Cristo* (PRC, '48, with Martin Kosleck as the original in a supporting role).

Anthony Hope's novel of Ruritanian romance and espionage, *The Prisoner Of Zenda* made a great vehicle for the dashing Ronald Colman, as Rudolph Rassendyll, who bears an uncanny resemblance to his distant cousin Prince Rudolf, missing and believed kidnapped by Raymond Massey as the suspicious Michael (who will become king in Rudolf's absence), and his henchman Rupert of Hentzau (Douglas Fairbanks, Jr.). But when Rudolph assumes the identity for the coronation, he finds he must keep up the pretense even for Rudolf's betrothed, Princess Flavia (Madeleine Carroll).

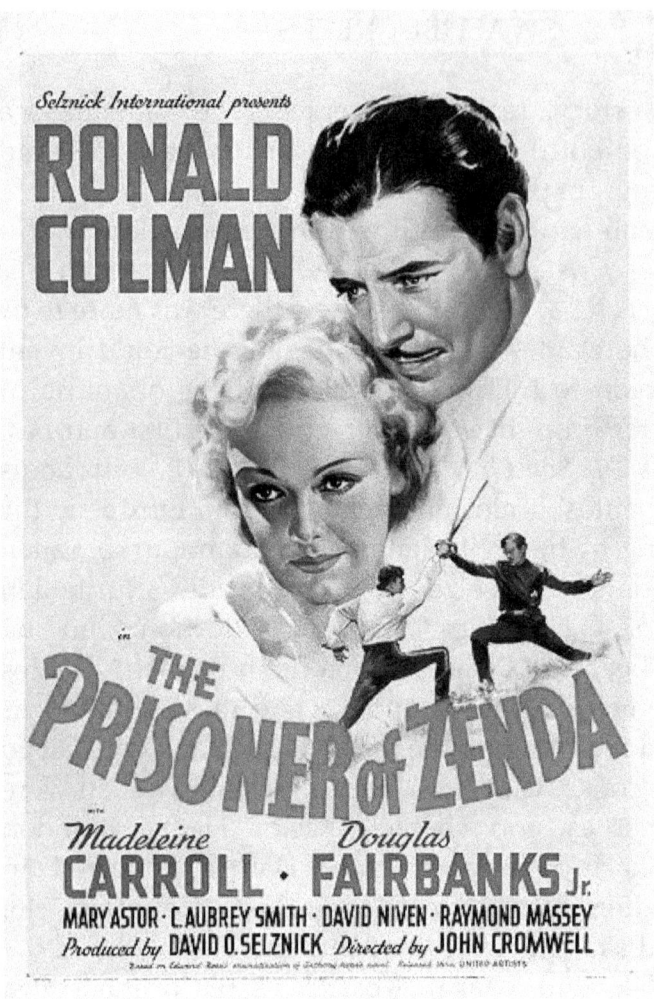

Producer David O. Selznick, who made the picture for United Artists' release in 1937, intended to follow up with a version of the novel's sequel "Rupert of Hentzau", but found the storyline too downbeat and declined to have the story re-written to recast Rupert as a hero. Stewart Granger, Deborah Kerr, and James Mason starred in a 1952 scene-for-scene re-make for M-G-M, in Technicolor but without the same dash.

Sabatini struck again in *Scaramouche* (1952), fashioned by M-G-M as a vehicle for their newest swashbuckling star,

Stewart Granger (a Brit whose real name was James Stewart) as Andre Moreau. Andre, born on the wrong side of the blanket, is drawn into the fight for French equality when his friend is killed in a one-sided duel with the Count de Maynes (Mel Ferrar). Hiding among the comedy players of his friend

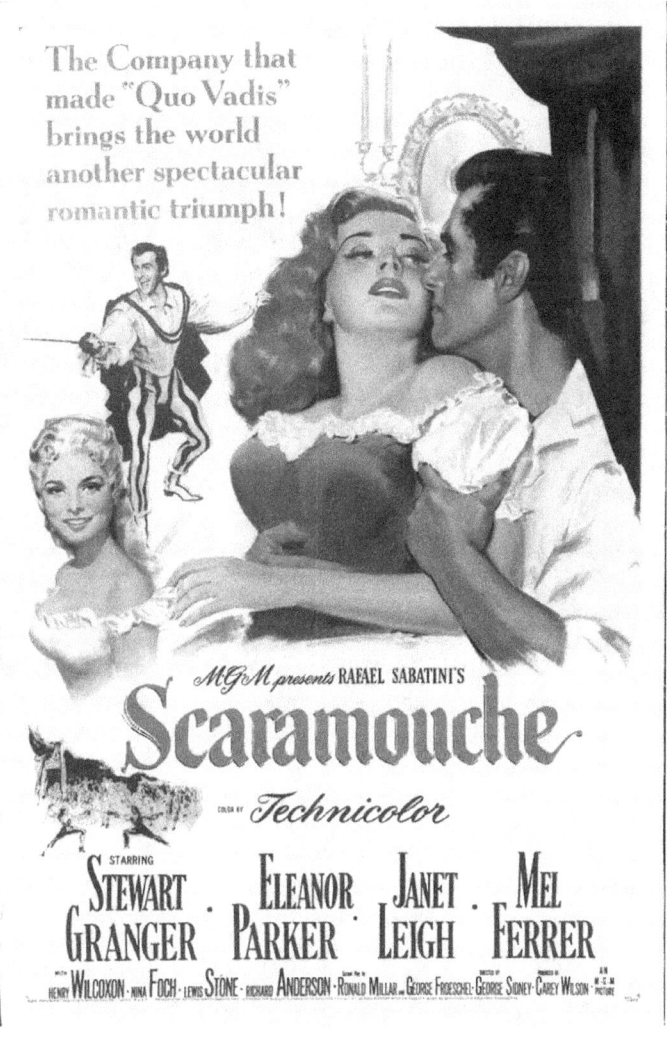

Binet (Robert Coote) and sparring with on-again, off-again lover Lenore (Eleanor Parker), he assumes the character of comic hero Scaramouche, while secretly learning to duel so

that he may avenge his friend and kill de Maynes – but things are never as easy as they seem. Their climactic duel – the longest in pictures, and without any underscore – is thrilling, comic, scary, and breath-taking by turns, and has an incredible ending. The cast also included Janet Leigh, Henry Wilcoxon, Alma Kruger, and Lewis Stone, here playing Georges de Valmorin, a good guy; in the Metro Pictures' 1923 version he'd played the heavy, the Marquis de la Tour d'Azyr.

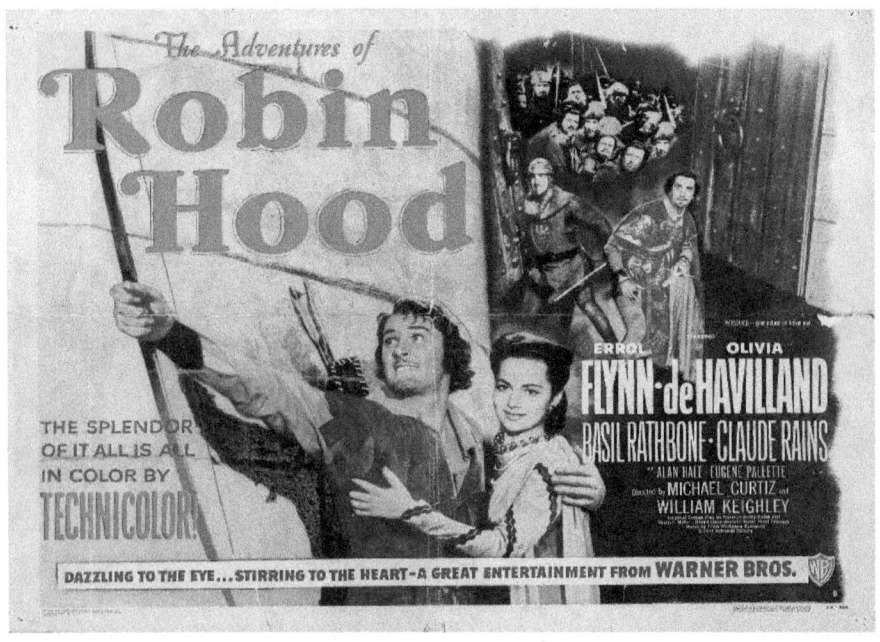

The fun and adventure of Warner Bros.' 1938 Technicolor adventure *The Adventures Of Robin Hood* place it at the top of many lists of favorites. Beautiful photography in the forests of Los Angeles and upstate Chico, a pulse-pounding musical score by Eric Wolfgang Korngold, and outstanding performances by a cast of Hollywood's finest make it a treasure. Retelling the legend of the Englishman who defied the perceived usurper of the throne in the absence of the right ruler Richard Lionheart, the story featured Olivia de Haviland, Alan Hale (Senior), Patric Knowles as good guys, with Claude Rains as John Lackland, taking advantage of Richard's absence to victimize the populace (especially the Saxons). But the film is truly a grudge-match between Robin of Locksley (Errol Flynn, of course) and his best on-screen adversary, Basil Rathbone as Sir Guy of Gisbourne. Their battle of wits and swords ended in a climactic death duel that's hard to beat.

SOLDIERS OF THE KING

The sun hadn't set on the British Empire when the soldiers and policemen of the King patrolled the world. From the East India regiments to the Royal Northwest Mounted, the flag would be upheld.

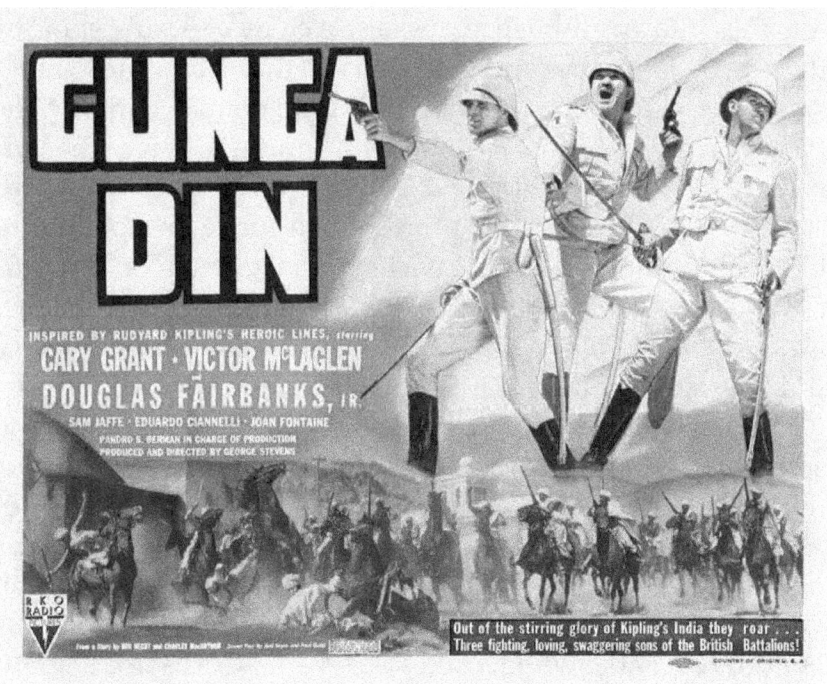

Rudyard Kipling wrote of India under the British *Raj*, when "enlightened" Westerners sought to rescue the heathen from his squalor born of ignorance (and just incidentally exploit these noble and educated peoples for great profit), and his poem of the native beasty who dreamed of joining his Britannic Majesty's forces became the basis for an adventure picture with great spectacle and a load of laughs. In *Gunga Din* (RKO Radio, 1939) producer-director George Stevens expanded upon the original to create a story of dedication, brotherhood, and sacrifice, with Sam Jaffe as Din, and Victor MacLaglen, Douglas Fairbanks, Jr., and Cary Grant as the Sergeants Three, comrades in arms through thick and thin – unless a woman comes along. Grant's refusal to take life seriously, and so to try to thwart his comrade's plans to marry, counterpoints the deadly serious schemes of the Guru (Eduardo Ciannelli) to dispel the foreigner from his land. The thrilling climax, with our heroes, wounded and surrounded at the Thug stronghold, while their regiment all unknowingly marches into an ambush, gives Jaffe a chance to truly shine on the screen. Re-makes and variations on the "Comrades Three" story include *Soldiers Three* (M-G-M, '51) and – with the Rat Pack – *Sergeants Three* (UA, '62) with Sammy Davis in the Jaffe role.

Cecil B. DeMille could pretty much make any picture he liked, and did, creating lavish spectaculars like *Cleopatra* (1934) and *The Crusades* ('35) for Paramount. For his *North West Mounted Police* ('40), he brought in the Mounties, Red Indians, pretty girls, beautiful vistas – and a cowboy! Gary Cooper starred as a Texan – named Dusty Rivers, which is something seen more in Texas than Canada – who comes north on the trail of a bad guy. The fugitive proves to be working with Louis Riel (Francis McDonald) a real historical outlaw who fomented rebellion to create a new state in his White Horse Rebellion. Rivers works with the regulation-bound redcoats, while pretty Louvette Corbeau (Paulette Goddard), sister of Dusty's fugitive, betrays the Mounties to save the life of her beloved policeman-boyfriend Ronnie Logan (Robert Preston). It's all pretty, in Technicolor, and great fun to watch, but does not hold up to critical analysis.

The same events were used in Sam Katzman's serial *Gunfighters of the Northwest* Last of the White Horse Rebels (Coumbia, '53). Other Mountie pictures of interest include *River's End* (WB, '30) with Charles Bickford, remade in 1940

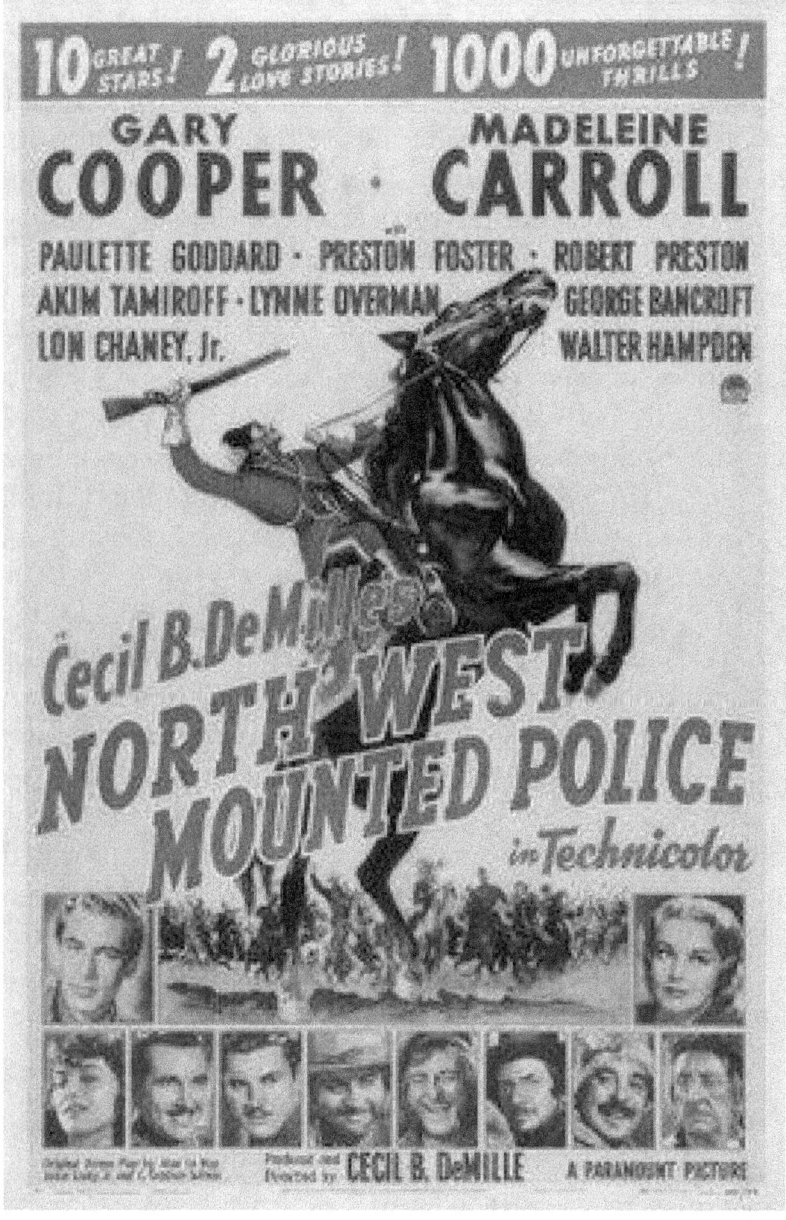

with Dennis Morgan, *Renfrew of the Royal Mounted* (Grand National, '37; first of a series of four), *Saskatchewan* (U-I, '54; re-titled *O'Rourke of the Royal Mounted*), as well as *King of the Royal Mounted* and *King of the Mounties* (Republic, '40 and '42, respectively), serials based on the newspaper character by Stephen Slesinger (under the by-line "Zane Grey").

Captain Hugh "Bulldog" Drummond, like his creator Sapper (Cyril McNeile, who'd chosen the pseudonym from the common name for his unit of engineers), was a veteran of the War to End All Wars, but did his bit for King and Country as a private citizen in a collection of popular novels. Drummond appeared in numerous guises over the years on film; Ronald Colman played him twice, and a generation later Richard Johnson was a revived, jazzed-up Drummond in two spy thrillers in the wake of the Bond Revolution. But in 1937 Paramount began a series of eight programmers beginning with *Bulldog Drummond Escapes* starring Ray Milland. John Howard assumed the role in *Bulldog Drummond Comes Back* and continued through *Bulldog Drummond's Bride* in 1938. Reginald Denny as his pal Algie and E.E. Clive as his dogsbody Tenny (originally "Denny" but changed to avoid confusion with his co-star) appeared in all eight installments. Captain Drummond faced saboteurs, international spies, and war-mongers, frequently coming to the rescue of his *fiancée*, a rare example of a recurring female in this type of series. (The very British nature and popularity of Drummond is indicated by the fact that Alfred Hitchcock intended to make his own Drummond picture, but with the rights encumbered, had had the script re-worked into *The Man Who Knew Too Much* [Gaumont-British, '34; and with modifications Paramount. '56].)

JUNGLE JUSTICE

From the king of the Jungle to mighty maidens of

Mombasa, cheap back-lot action and on-location thrills were box-office gold, because boys – even grown-up ones – flocked to see the latest African adventure.

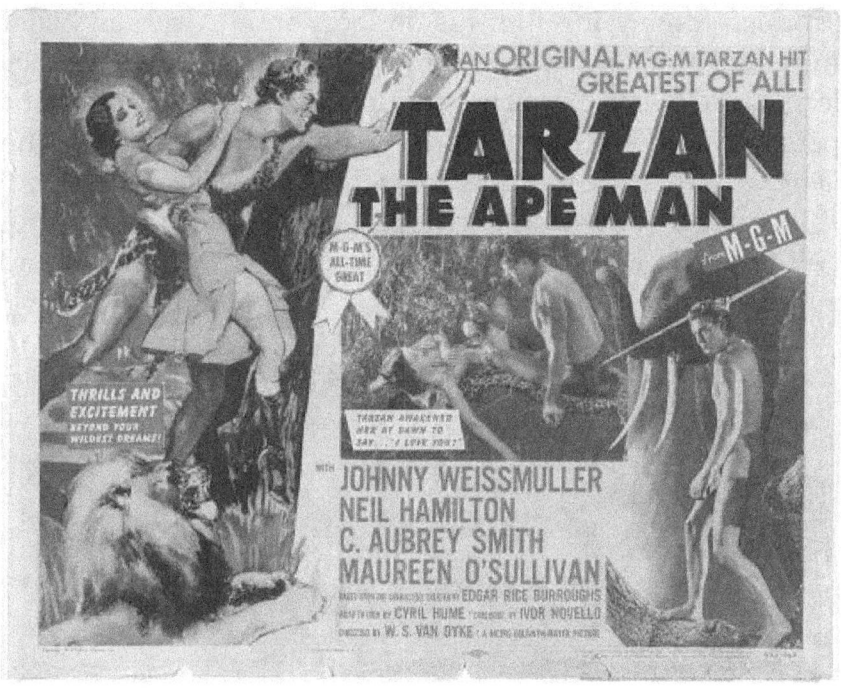

When Metro-Goldwyn-Mayer brought Edgar Rice Burroughs' jungle lord to the big screen, they ignored both the heart of the novels and the activities of several previous mute features and serials, as the well spoken (in English and French) Jack Clayton, Lord Greystoke became the primitive but noble savage in their 1932 hit *Tarzan the Ape Man* with Olympian Johnny Weissmuller and lithe Maureen O'Sullivan as the jungle lovers. Despite attempts by Burroughs and others to display Tarzan as he'd been written, the Metro version overwhelmed, and Weissmuller ruled Africa for 17 years, moving in the '40s to RKO Radio, where he continued in the person of Lex Barker. When producer Sy Weintraub entitled his 1959 Paramount release *Tarzan's Greatest Adventure*, he wasn't kidding. Spectacular location shooting in Africa and a performance by Gordon Scott that pleased both literary and cinema fans of the Ape Man made for an outstanding production. Weintraub had recently taken over the Tarzan reins from Sol Lesser, and worked to upgrade the product, filming installments on location in Africa and later India and Thailand, with stuntman-star Jocko Mahoney in the lead. From there, Tarzan moved to American television, in the person of Ron Ely. More recent versions were created by John Derek (as a vehicle for his wife Bo [for M-G-M in '81]), the oh-so-literary *Greystoke* the Legend of TARZAN Lord of the Apes (WB, '84) and Disney's animated *Tarzan* (BV, '99) feature and subsequent TV series.

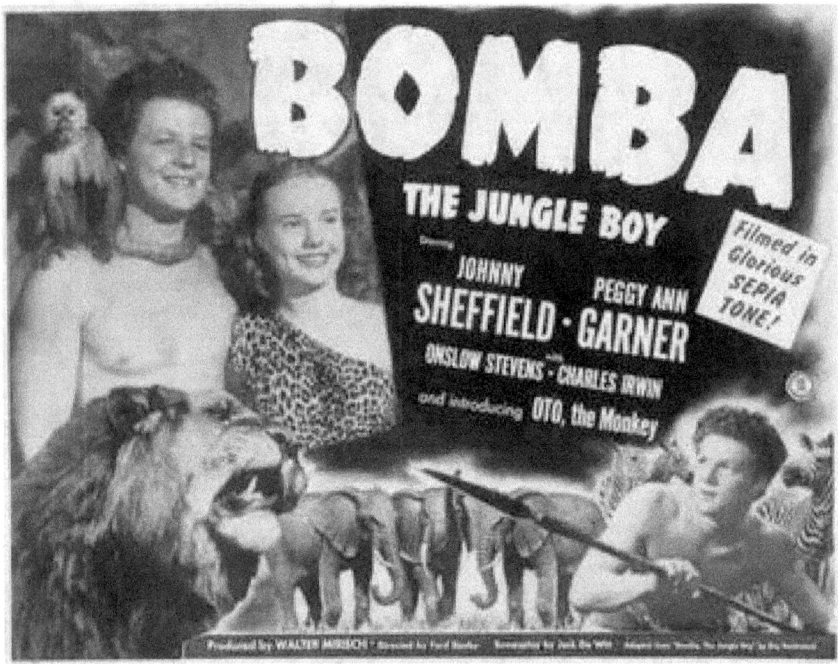

Bomba the Jungle Boy (Monogram, 1949) was the first of a series based on the juvenile-adventure books, about an orphan boy raised in the jungle, by "Roy Rockwood" (a house name at Cupplers and Leon, publishers), brought to movie screens by Walter Mirisch (who would go on to bigger things)

as a vehicle for Johnny Sheffield, who had recently left his role of "Boy" in the "Tarzan" pictures. That the series was aimed at youthful viewers is evident in its casting of youngsters, especially starlets-to-be, like Karen Sharpe, Donna Martell, Barbara Bestar, and Beverly Garland, some of whom went on to long careers. Later installments relied heavily on stock footage from the earlier pictures, scenes taken at the Los Angeles Arboretum, a jungly park in nearby Arcadia. Individual low-budget jungle adventures include *Daughter of the Jungle* (Republic, '49), with stock footage from their 1941 serial *Jungle Girl*, based on a book title by Edgar Rice Burroughs; and for historical value, *Nabonga* Gorilla (PRC, '44) with Julie London, and *Wild Women* (Morris Landre Productions, '51).

While Sheffield had moved on from "Tarzan", Weissmuller had remained, for a while at least, and when he outgrew the role (in girth), Sam Katzman hired him to star in a new series based on a popular Alex Raymond cartoon strip. *Jungle Jim* (Columbia, 1949) began a new set of Jungle adventures for Johnny, who now got to wear clothes and speak in complete sentences. The series pictures, including titles like *Jungle Jim in the Forbidden Land* ('53), were usually entertaining, though not particularly inventive, and when the license from publisher King Features Syndicate expired, Sam just kept making them anyway, merely changing "Jim" to "Johnny Weissmuller", a part he could hardly fail to make his own, in pictures like *Jungle Moon Men* ('55) with pygmies but no aliens. Jim had had one previous film outing, Universal's 1936-'37 serial with Grant Withers.

Filmed primarily on the jungle sets created for *King Kong*, Radio Pictures' *The Most Dangerous Game* (1932) expanded upon the famous Richard Connell short story about a hunter who takes advantage of shipwreck victims to track and kill them – for Man is the most dangerous game. In the film version, Zaroff (Leslie Banks) deliberately lures ships to their doom on the rocky shores of his island, and when he ends up with Joel McCrea and Fay Wray as guests, he enlivens his sport by chasing both together. The story has been filmed a number of times, including as *A Game of Death* (RKO Radio, '45) and *Run for the Sun* (UA, '56).

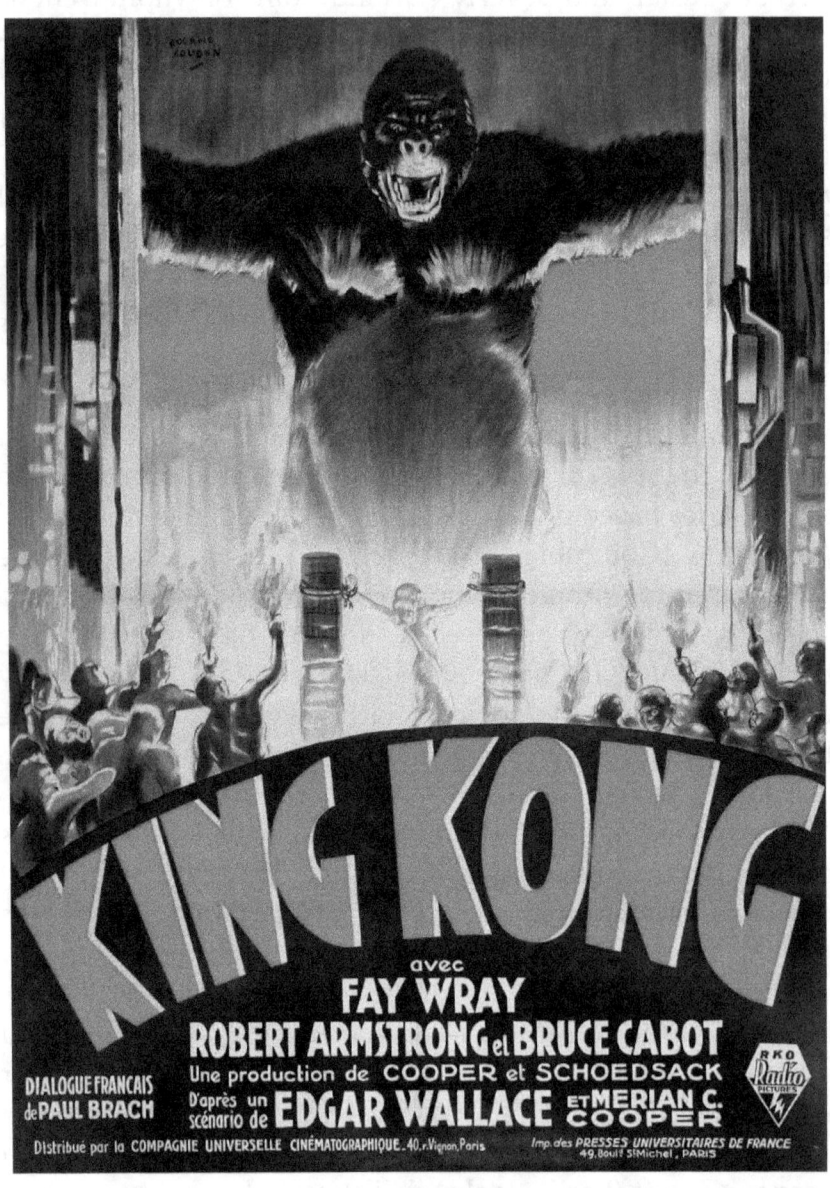

But perhaps the greatest adventure movie of them all

mixed in science fantasy in the person of *King Kong* himself (in the 1933 Radio Pictures release of the same name), an improbably large great ape who holds the natives – and most of the local *fauna* – in a grip of terror on his home, Skull Island, where Ann Darrow (Fay Wray, of course) finds herself nominated as the latest "bride" of Kong (the work of master animator Willis O'Brien). Fortunately for her, the great ape finds her of more interest than the usual native girl left for him, and she's carried off to his mountain-top lair for intimate examination. Also fortunately for Ann, two men will pursue her rescue to Hell and back: Jack Driscoll (Bruce Cabot), who loves her, and Carl Denham (Robert Armstrong), who loves the thrill of the chase and the fame he'll garner for bringing back alive the "Eighth Wonder of the World". Their crusade across the dinosaur-laden landscape of the forbidden island, encounters with a brontosaurus, a triceratops, and other prehistoric creatures balance with Kong's adventures against the modern monsters of New York City, as the great ape flees to his habitual redoubt, the highest point on the island, unaware that creatures mightier than a pterodactyl lurk in the clouds. Remakes, spin-offs – like *Kingu Kongo tai Gojira* (Toho, '62; *King Kong Vs Godzilla* [Universal, '63] in US) – and "re-imaginings" have not tarnished the original.

MYTHOLOGY

Mythology, mixed with history, brought us gods and heroes of yesteryear.

Adventure knew no bounds, and even the master of inexpensive cinema, Roger Corman, whipped out a couple. The most amazing enjoyed the full title *The Saga Of The Viking Women And Their Voyage To The Waters Of The Great Sea Serpent* (A-I-P, 1957), though most marquees just mentioned the two living items. Making their fantastic journey, the Vikings are caught in a surprisingly energetic (considering the budget) storm at sea, as stars Ottar (Jonathan Haze) and Thyra (Betsy

Jones-Moreland) desperately hold their course against the might of the raging ocean, to reach the land of the Great Serpent (but, alas, not the Serpent itself). Abby Dalton (as Desir) and Susan Cabot (as Enger) starred as, well, Viking Women. No classic, but definitely a motion picture.

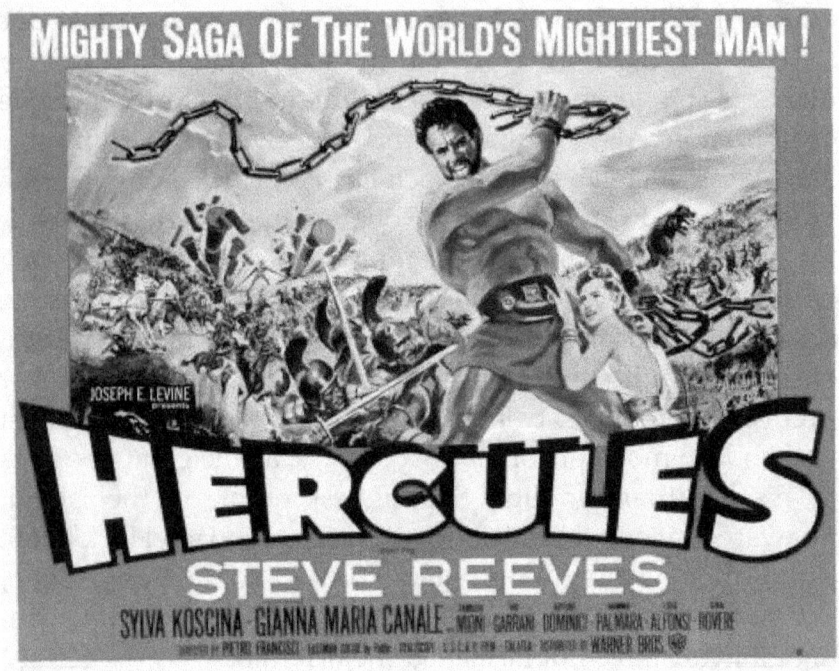

Joseph E. Levine struck movie gold when he acquired the Galatea Pictures production *Le Fatiche di Ercole* (Lux Film, 1958; *Hercules* [Embassy,'59] in US), and made an international star of body-builder Steve Reeves. The story was of the demi-god's twelve labors, and was quickly followed by *Ercole e la regina di Lidia* (Lux Film, 1959; *Hercules Unchained* [Embassy, '60] in US), which opened the flood-gates for literally scores of similar epics for theaters and television, dubbed into clumsy English but watched avidly by fans. *Ercole al centro della Terra Omnia* (Deutsche Film Export, '61; *Hercules in the Haunted World* [Woolner Brothers Pictures Inc., 1964] in US) and a flood of others, mostly released directly to television, followed, many marketed under the umbrella title "Sons of Hercules".

JUST PLAIN GOOD OL' ADVENTURE

...to be found wherever it may raise its exciting flag, in a variety of pictures.

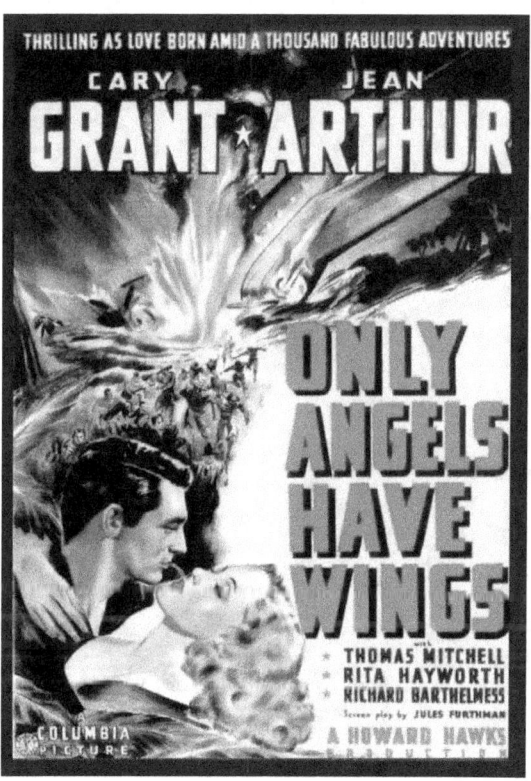

"...Calling Barranca! ...Calling Barranca!" These urgent words, the desperate cry for aid from a plane lost in a high mountain pass through the Andes, crackled across the airwaves in one of the greatest adventure pictures ever. Howard Hawks was a genius of producer-directors, turning out comedies, westerns, dramas, and especially adventures like –*Only Angels Have Wings* (Columbia, 1939), the story of men living lives that might be extinguished at any moment as they strive to deliver the mail by air over the Andes through that dangerous pass. And when women get involved, trouble *really* descends. Cary Grant, Jean Arthur, and Rita Hayworth starred, supported by Thomas Mitchell, Sig Ruman, Allyn Joslyn, and Noah Beery, Jr. As exciting and novel as it seems, it was partially pre-figured by a 1932 M-G-M "all star" vehicle, *Night Flight*, with Clark Gable, Robert Montgomery, and the Barrymore brothers.

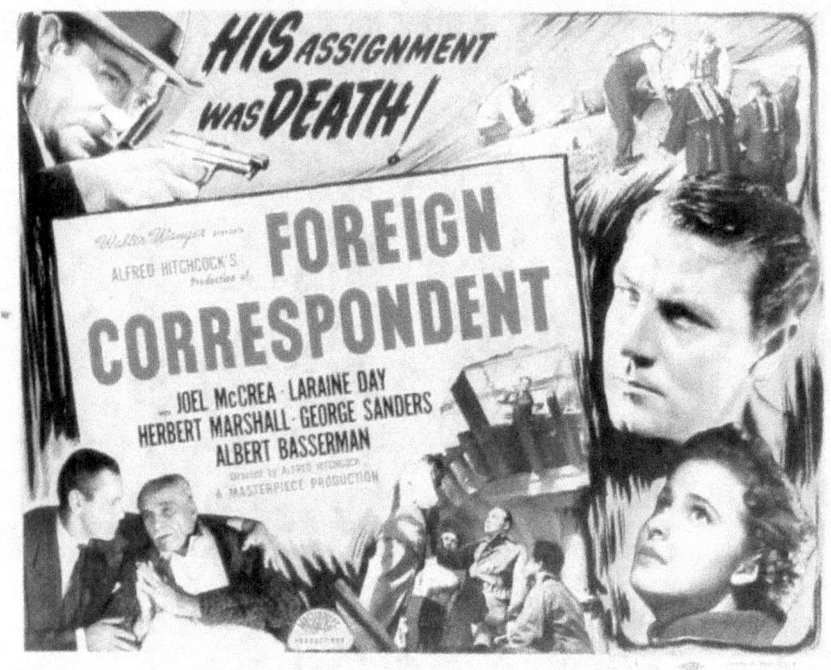

Alfred Hitchcock was already known as the master of the thriller when he started adding patriotic sub-texts to his pictures. His second U.S. film, *Foreign Correspondent* (UA, 1940), is daring in its depiction of obviously Germanic villains, as well as British counter-spies, as Joel McCrea, playing reporter Huntley Haverstock (né Johnny Jones), finds himself in trouble from London to Amsterdam to the mid-

Atlantic. On the track of a great story, searching for a man who may or may not have been assassinated, unknowingly revealing his plans to the man behind the plot, Johnny is nearly captured in a deserted windmill, nearly pushed to his death by a murderer-for-hire, and shot down in a clipper ship over the Atlantic. And all while romancing Larraine Day, whose father may just be a bad guy. Hitch's ability to blend suspense and humor makes this an outstanding picture.

In *Saboteur* (Universal, 1942), Hitch was able to call *Nazis* by name, and show us what the Enemy could do. Defense-plant worker Barry Kane (Robert Cummings), charged with an act of sabotage, escapes and embarks upon a desperate attempt to locate a man named Fry (Norman Lloyd), whom he knows to be the real culprit, finally cornering him at the torch of the statue of Liberty. "3000 miles of terror" cried the one-sheet poster, and the film lived up to its hype. Along the way Barry acquired the requisite girl (Priscilla Lane) and met fifth columnists like Charles Tobin (Otto Kruger), an apparently good American, and Mrs. Sutton (Alma Kruger), a seemingly unimpeachable society matron – Hitch's point being that even the most trustworthy may not be what they seem. Hitchcock would revisit the "man on the run" theme again, in pictures like *North by Northwest* (M-G-M, '59) with Cary Grant.

A Western? Yes, but a *swashbuckling* one: Johnston McCulley's novel *The Curse of Capistrano*, published in 1919 in "The All-story" magazine, had been the source of Big Doug Fairbanks' *The Mark of Zorro* (UA, 1920) with Diego Vega taking up mask and sword to right the wrongs of early California. Fairbanks repeated his role – and that of his own offspring – in the sequel *Don Q Son of Zorro* (UA, '25). In 1940, 20th Century-Fox intended to produce a new version. Because Republic Pictures had already featured the character in serials and a feature (*Q.V. in Chapter Plays*), Darryl F. Zanuck was hesitant to use the character's name in the title, preferring *The Californian*, but common sense won out, and a new *The Mark of Zorro* appeared, starring Tyrone Power, Linda Darnell, and the delightful Basil Rathbone. A major release, it spotlighted the derring-do of the hero and down-played the Western angle of Spanish California, as foppish Diego plays at love with a beautiful *señorita*, saving swordplay for the cruel *Capitan* Esteban Pasquale (Rathbone, essentially reprising his role from "Robin Hood"). Zorro continued to be a popular hero, in many films produced (with and without authorization) in Latin America, a TV series from Walt Disney, and more recent features, including the spoof *Zorro The Gay Blade* (20th Century-Fox, '81) and the light-hearted adventure *The Mask of Zorro* (TriStar Film Distributors, '98).

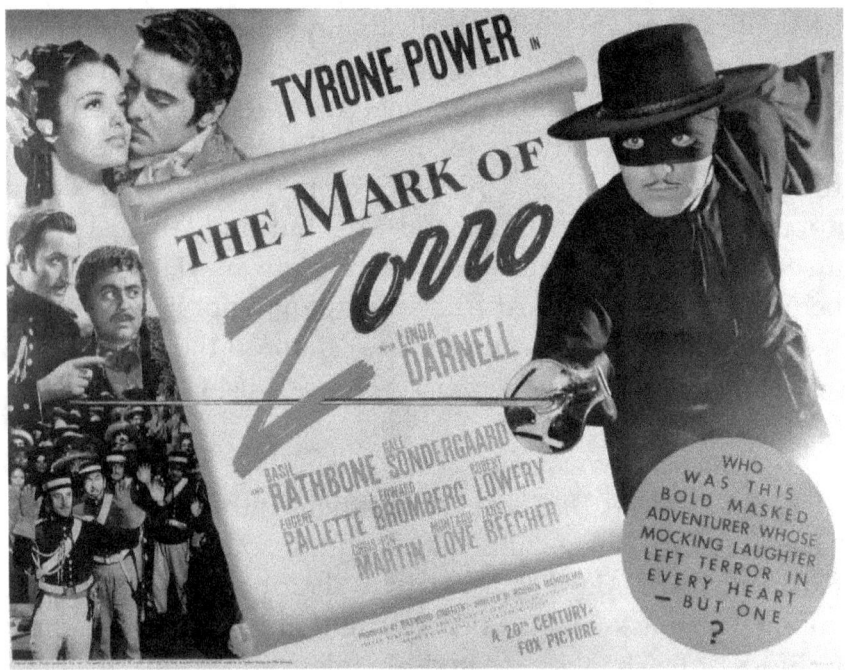

A sort of double feature, two films from different studios and years, told the adventures of Prince Dakkar, better known to literature as Captain Nemo of the submarine boat *Nautilus*, in *20000 Leagues Under the Sea* (BV, 1954) and *Mysterious Island* (Columbia, '62), the former from the genius of the Walt

Disney studio, the latter from the genius of Ray Harryhausen. When shipping is endangered by a strange sea-monster, a whaling ship goes in pursuit, only to become the monster's next victim. But then Ned Land, Professor Arronax, and his man Conseil (Kirk Douglas, Paul Lukas, and Peter Lorre) discover the monster is really an undersea vessel, and are taken aboard by its captain (James Mason), who has sworn to end war by destroying the weapons of war. His captives disagree and bring about his downfall, but years later, while civil war rages in the United States, a group of fleeing prisoners end up on a strange island populated by giant creatures... and Nemo (now Herbert Lom). Science fiction, yes. But also great adventures.

The "Big Picture" of the nineteen sixties was exemplified by movies so long they had intermissions. *Ice Station Zebra* (M-G-M, 1968) told of the mission of USS *Tigerfish* to the Arctic icepack. Rock Hudson (as Commander James Ferraday, a role originally offered to Gregory Peck) is sent to deliver Patrick McGoohan (as a British agent who calls himself David Jones), Ernest Borgnine (as Russian agent Boris Vasilov), and a squad of U.S. Marines to Drift-Ice Station Zebra on a secret mission. Cold-war politics and xenophobia underscored the adventure as our heroes try to head off dirty rotten Commies seeking a fallen orbital camera containing photographs of Soviet installations. Who will succeed? Who is the spy in our ranks? Both reclusive billionaire Howard R. Hughes and TV mogul Ted Turner were said to love this thriller. Other submarine pictures include *Run Silent Run Deep* (UA, '58) and *The Hunt for Red October* (Paramount, '90). And one must needs mention the exciting but ludicrous *Voyage to the Bottom of the Sea* (20th Century-Fox, '62), with its incendiary radiation and sinking icebergs.

Inspired by the actual historical kidnapping of Ion Perdicaris, John Milius' *The Wind And The Lion* (M-G-M, 1975) pulled a little sex-switch, as Candice Bergen made a better victim as Eden Pedecaris, swept away with her children by the lion of the desert Mulay Ahmed Muhamed Raisuli (Sean Connery). The Raisuli soon finds that the wanting of a captive may be more desirable than the having, as the willful woman devils him in ways that no man would dare, and no less than the President of the United States Theodore Roosevelt (Brian Keith) arrays the mighty wind of an entire nation against him. An earlier picture, *Khartoum* (UA, '66), told a similar story in the tragedy of the contest between the British, as represented by General Gordon (Charlton Heston), and the Arabs, following the civilized but determined Mahdi (Laurence Olivier).

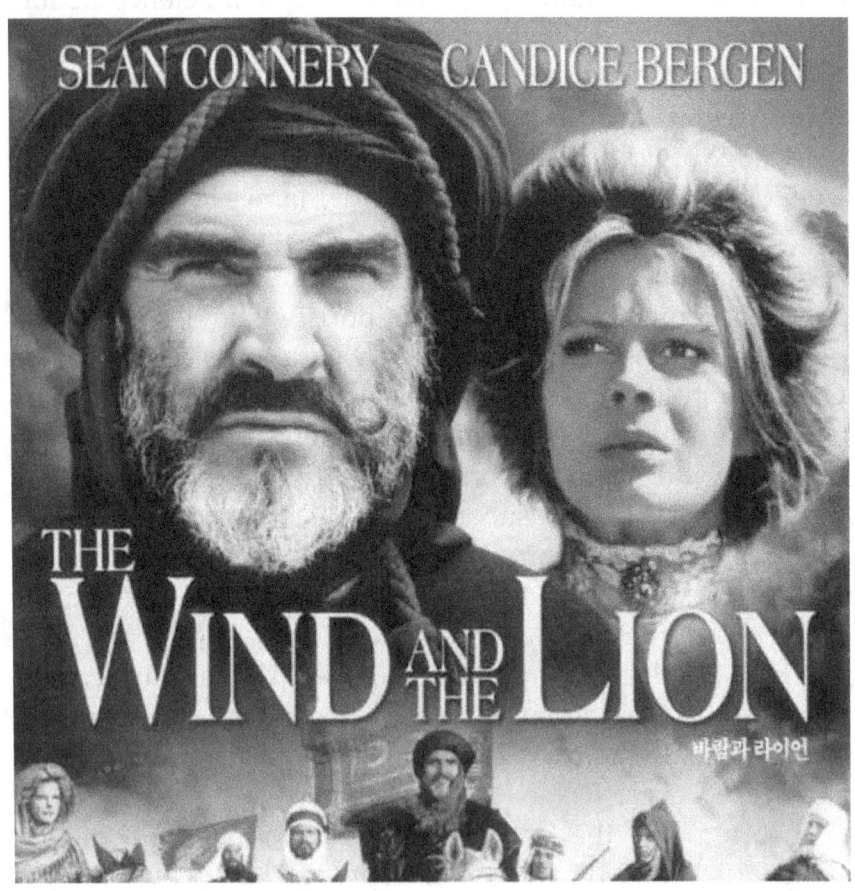

Though *Raiders of the Lost Ark* (Paramount, 1981) and *Indiana Jones and the Last Crusade* (Paramount, '89) were styled as feature versions of serials, with fantastic escapes and diabolical plots, the picture between them – Steven Spielberg's *Indiana Jones And The Temple Of Doom* (Paramount, '84) – was a fantastic adventure film in the classic tradition, though embellished with gruesome sequences. Hero Henry Jones, nominally a university professor, in his quest for rare antiquities finds excitement all over the world, for himself and his companions. Set before "Raiders" (originally so that a character killed in "Raiders" could return as the villain), it was less well received than its predecessor or its follower, and depictions of gruesome sacrifices disturbed younger viewers. After a long hiatus, Indy would return one more time, in Paramount's 2008 *Indiana Jones and the Kingdom of the Crystal Skull*, in which Ford was as good as ever but which somehow failed to match the trilogy's impact, and in 2023, Disney has brought us *Indiana Jones and the Dial of Destiny*, completing at last the original plan for four sequels to "Raiders". Other similar stories over the years are *Tropic Fury* (Universal, '39), one of a series starring Richard Arlen and Andy Devine, and *High Road to China* (WB, '81).

ESPIONAGE AGENTS

But don't let's forget about the spy – the man who, never an adventurer in real life, seems always famous and aggressive in pictures. Don't tell anyone, but here are some great secret agents:

Mister Moto, J.P. Marquand's recondite Japanese spy, who flitted in and out of the novels bearing his name, stepped front and center in a series from the 20th Century-Fox B unit. Though usually lumped in with mysteries (because of its close association with the "Charlie Chan" pictures), the stories are more adventurous than mysterious, as Moto (pleasingly played by Hungarian Peter Lorre) travels the globe to stop killers, thieves, and spies in eight B features from late 1937 to 1939. In the first, *Think Fast, Mr. Moto* (1937), the agent of the "international police" was a man of mystery, but in later pictures he was also a dedicated man of action. All eight are enjoyable, with *Mr. Moto's Gamble* ('38), with Keye Luke as Lee Chan (it was originally a "Charlie Chan" picture, re-written when Warner Oland became ill and died) particularly satisfying, and the last one, *Mr. Moto Takes a Vacation* ('39), with a great mystery and a great villain, among the best. A feeble follow-up, *The Return of Mr. Moto* (Twentieth Century-Fox, '65) starred villain-actor Henry Silva.

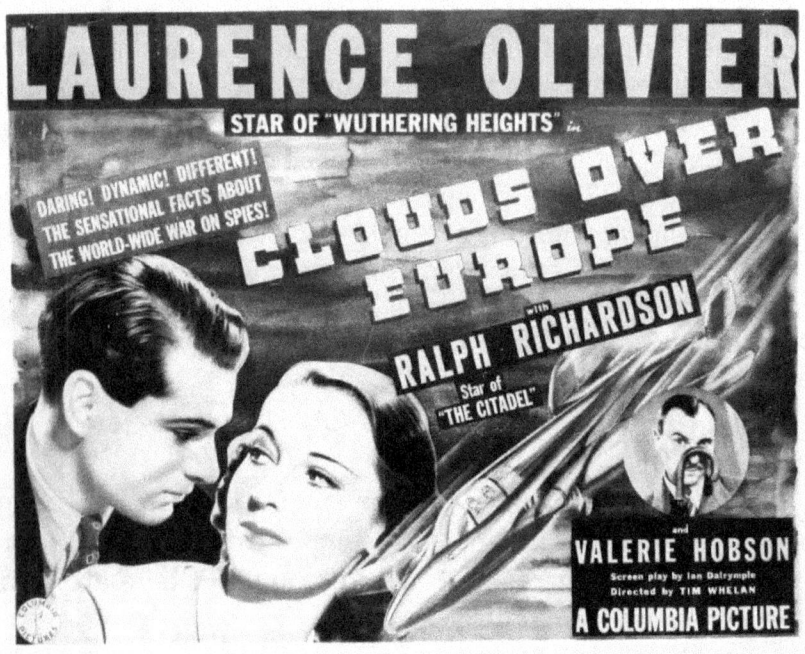

In *Q Planes* (Columbia, 1939; *Clouds Over Europe* in US), Ralph Richardson plays a seemingly ineffectual government pencil pusher, but handily saves the day against a German super-weapon in a low-key thriller laced with humor. Richardson starred as Major Charles Hammond, with Laurence Olivier and Valerie Hobson. A series about the hero would have been most welcome, but spy tactics were about to take a deadly turn in real life.

In the nineteen sixties, the "super-hero" type of spy gained great traction, and serious thrillers were followed by spoofs, both knowing and clumsy. *Our Man Flint* (20th Century-Fox, '66) was the best of these, with James Coburn as the man-catching, lady-killing agent who takes a case reluctantly but comes crashing through, finding the enemy stronghold and turning the villainess Gila (international actress Gila Golan) against her masters. The follow-up, *In Like Flint* (20th Century-Fox, '67), with a plot of women trying to take over the world, tried too hard to be clever and rather missed the mark.

Dean Martin, for reasons unclear, was picked to portray Donald Hamilton's famous character Matt Helm for a quartet of comedy spy pictures, beginning with *The Silencers* (Columbia, '66). But the book Helm was a counter-assassin, and his exploits rather gritty and visceral; the films cast Helm as a playboy/spy/photographer, with Dino laconically waltzing through the stories that bore only a skeletal resemblance to their source but contained sufficient value for the ticket price.

An assortment of similar spy thrillers, foreign and domestic, peppered the cinema for several years, including *Se tutte le donne del mondo... (Operazione Paradiso)* (Columbia, '66; *Kiss the Girls and Make Them Die* [Columbia, '67] in US) starring Mike Conners, Dorothy Provine, and Terry-Thomas, as well as *To Trap a Spy* and *The Spy With My Face* (both M-G-M, '66) along with six other features edited from TV's "The Man from U.N.C.L.E." series (these first two played in U.S. theaters; the rest only in foreign markets). But these were only reflexive presentations.

The most famous "secret" agent of them all, James Bond, British agent 007, the character that started the whole craze, was the creation of author Ian Fleming (himself a former intelligence operator in the Second World War). 007 began his movie career with *Dr. No* (UA, 1962) though he'd previously appeared in a television version of the first novel, *Casino Royale*. With a little help from President John F. Kennedy, a big fan of the book *From Russia, With Love*, Bond had become box-office gold by the release in 1964 of United Artists' *Goldfinger*, one of the best of a series that has continued into the 21st century. A master of the arts of death and of love, Bond dispatches the bad guys without a tear, and dispatches the bad girls with only a wistful glance back after his night with them. Location shooting all over the world and casts of superior actors have kept the series evergreen at the box office. Other superior entries include *From Russia With Love* (UA, '63), *You Only Live Twice* (UA, '67), *On Her Majesty's Secret Service* (UA, '69), *License to Kill* (UA, '89), and *Goldeneye* (UA, '95), as well as the "re-boot" version of *Casino Royale* (UA, 2006), starring Daniel Craig as a grittier Bond who'd continue for the next several pictures in the same vein, a far cry from the lightest Roger Moore entries..

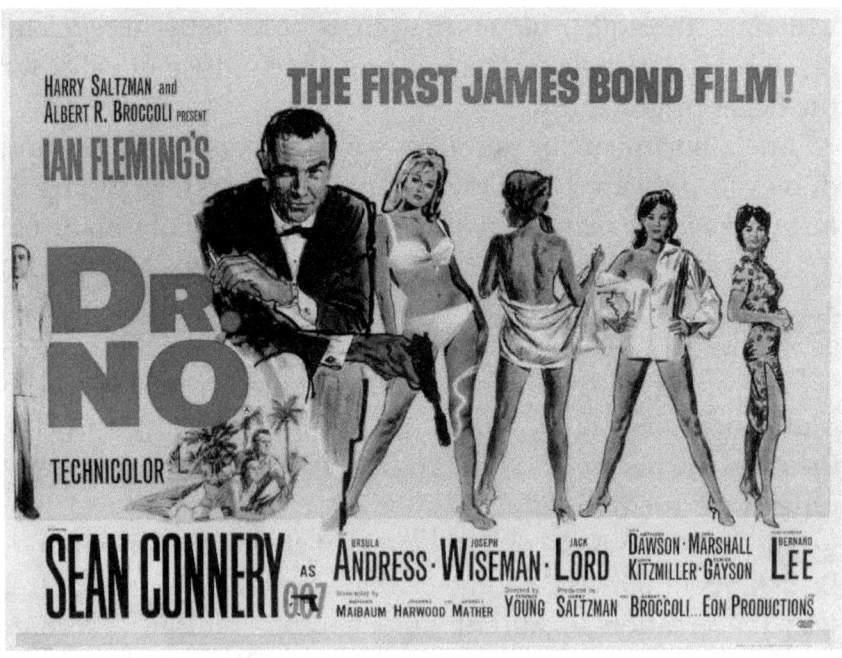

Spies, Jungle Men, Soldiers of Fortune of all types, the Adventure heroes brought audiences back week after week –

really, all the *genres* did, one way or another – to see what might happen. As each *genre* has led into the next, "Adventure" without the excitement cycles us back to Chapter One.

AFTERWORD

THE YEARS OF the double feature – from 1933 to 1962 – have been called the "Golden Age of Hollywood". The pictures of those years entertained and educated countless millions in the United States and across the globe, but the society that both embraced and fostered them is gone, passed by as are eventually all societies and eras of history.

Yes, that era is gone now, but unlike the previous epochs of history, not only has that era of motion pictures left a record of itself, it has left its view of all the ages before. Today's pictures will do the same for today – any age you live through can be a "golden age" in retrospect – and others will come to write of their impact. The years of the double feature encompassed laughter, tears, scares, thrills, delight, joy, and surprise. The factory system assured a rich treasure of films of all kinds, and today those films remain with us, thanks to the many people – professionals and fans – who have worked to preserve them for ages to come.

This book has provided a glimpse into the *genres* and types of films produced in that era, and hopefully has given an indication of the permeable margins of those *genres*. This book is intended as a starting point; many wonderful and famous films have been left out, to be discovered as one delves into the world of the cinema. But once the reader has been given an insight to the world of the motion picture, it will be easy to discover other, similar pictures, including films of more recent vintage, as has been shown in the commentaries above. With this indicator, a search of the Internet can reap a bounty of treasure. And if your interest and curiosity about the "behind the scenes" details of the films hasn't been sated, and you want more, check out Facebook page, CLJII's "Your Best Entertainment" Companion, with more tidbits and ephemera on the motion pictures of the past, at:

https://www.facebook.com/profile.php?id=100081418001578

I hope this look back has enhanced and enlightened your appreciation and understanding of those times and films.

CLJII
Hollywood, 2023

REFERENCES

The primary reference tool in all cases is the film itself, but these sources also contributed:

Interviews and Conversations

Forrest J Ackerman
Kirk Alyn
Donald Barry
William Benedict
Turhan Bey
Henry Brandon
Philip J. Castora
Frank Coghlan, Junior
Donald F. Glut
Dick Foran
Ray Harryhausen
Eric Hoffman
Mark Kausler
Richard Kiel
Bill Mills
Vincent Price
David Sharpe
Curt Siodmak
Tom Steele
Jean Marie Stine
Linda Stirling
Frankie Thomas
Ken Tobey
George D. Wallace
Bill Warren
William Witney

Ephemera

Studio documents, newspaper clippings, notes, and memoranda from the files of the USC Film and Television Library (including the Universal Pictures collection); and from the Fairbanks Center for Film Study, Academy of Motion Picture Arts and Sciences, (including the *New York Times Encyclopedia of Film*); Some still photographs provided by the Ackerman Archives, Eddie Brandt's Saturday Matinee Video and Memorabilia, and the collection of the author.

Magazines

American Cinematographer; various editors and publishers; American Society of Cinematographers, 1920 to present

Famous Monsters of Filmland; Forrest J Ackerman, editor, James Warren, publisher; Warren Publishing, 1958 *et al*

FILMFAX The Magazine of Unusual Film and Television; Michael Stein, editor and publisher; Filmfax, Inc., 1986 to present

Screen Thrills Illustrated; James Warren, editor and publisher; Warren Publishing, 1963 *et al*

Spacemen; Forrest J Ackerman, editor, James Warren, publisher; Warren Publishing, 1961 *et al*

Books

The Columbia Story; Clive Herschhorn; Crown Publishers, 1989

Disney A to Z the updated Official Encyclopedia; Dave Smith; Hyperion Press, 1998

The Films of 20th Century-Fox; Tony Thomas and Aubrey Solomon; Citadel Press, 1979

The Fleischer Story; Leslie Carbaga; Nostalgia Press, 1976

In a Door, into a Fight, Out a Door, Into a Chase Moviemaking remembered by the Guy at the Door; William Witney;

McFarland & Company, 1996

"A Job for Superman"; Kirk Alyn; Kirk Alyn, 1971

Keep Watching the Skies! American Science Fiction Movies of the Fifties; Bill Warren; McFarland &Company, 1982 (Volume I), 1986 (Volume II)

The MGM Story The Complete History of Fifty-seven Roaring Years; John Douglas Eames; Crown Publishers, 1975

Our Gang The Life and Times of the Little Rascals; Leonard Maltin and Richard W. Bann; Crown Publishers, 1977

The Paramount Story; John Douglas Eames; Crown Publishers, 1985

Producers Releasing Corporation A Comprehensive Filmography and History; Wheeler Dixon, editor; McFarland & Company, 1986

Republic Confidential, Volume 1; Jack Mathis; Jack Mathis Advertising, 1992

The RKO Story; Richard B. Jewell and Vernon Harbin; Octopus Books, 1982

Superman: Serial to Cereal; Gary Grossman; Popular Library, 1977

United Artists The Company Built by the Stars; Tino Balio; the University of Wisconsin Press, 1976

The Universal Story; Clive Herschhorn; Crown Publishers, 1983

The Warner Bros. Story; Clive Herschhorn; Crown Publishers, 1979

ABOUT THE AUTHOR

CHARLES LEE JACKSON, II, is a Hollywood-based film scholar, author, and cartoonist, whose study of the era of the American double feature has placed him in the front rank of motion-picture historians. He has written for the Dutch *Orbit Magazine* and *FILMFAX*, and published *Extra Added Attractions*, a magazine dedicated to second features, short subjects, and Hollywood history, as well as several short books on specific films. Mr. Jackson is a frequent guest speaker at film-related conventions, conducts the college-level course "Ephemeral Cinema", shares his extensive knowledge of film in several pages on the social network Facebook, and is preparing a book on the history of the motion-picture serial. Additionally, he produces three popular fiction series, "The Emperor's Secret Files", "Six-gun Westerns", and "Star Service". He is also a recipient of the Forrest J Ackerman Award, presented by the Los Angeles Science Fantasy Society, for lifetime service to science fiction.

12 GOLDEN AGE FILM MYSTERIES ANSWERS?
KNOW THE ANSWERS?

1. Which actor in *Casablanca* (Warner Bros., 1942) utters the famous line, "Play it again, Sam"- Humprey Bogart or Ingrid Bergman?
Neither, this is one of the most misquoted lines in film history. Bergman as Ilsa Lund says, "Play it once, Sam. For old times' sake." A few minutes Bogart as "Rick" Blaine, says, "You played it for her, you can play it for me!" No one says. "Play it again, Sam."

2. How did Universal Pictures explain Sherlock Holmes, consulting detective of the Victorian age, being alive to battling World War Two Nazis?
A written foreword to the first film, *Sherlock Holmes and the Voice of Terror* (1942), asked, "What if Sherlock Holmes were alive today...?" And then on with the story.

3. In *Devil Girl from Mars* (British Lion, 1954) an alien arrives seeking males to help repopulate her dying civilization, but what later film reversed her quest?
Mars Needs Women (American-International TV, 1967).

4. In how many motion pictures did Bela Lugosi portray Dracula?
Only two: the 1931 original, and *Meet Frankenstein* (Universal-International, 1948) with Abbott and Costello.

5. Why did Michael Todd film *Oklahoma!* twice?

It was made simultaneously in both CinemaScope and Todd-AO, incompatible wide-screen formats, for a wider viewing audience.

6. Where does the Laurel and Hardy 1935 M-G-M comedy *Bonnie Scotland* primarily take place? (Hint: it ain't Scotland.)
India, to which their Scottish regiment is dispatched.

7. Who was the animated character who spoke not in words but in sound effects?
Gerald McBoing-boing, from UPA.

8. Why did Republic Pictures promote plainclothes cop Dick Tracy to a G-Man?
For greater breadth of action, and because real-life G-Man Melvis Purvis was intended to star.

10. What box-office star and author appeared as himself in a film version of his war-time autobiography?
Audie Murphy, in *To Hell and Back* (Universal-International, 1955

11. What documentary feature film caused Walt Disney to leave distributor RKO Radio and create his own releasing company?
The Living Desert (Buena Vista, 1953).

In *The Mark of Zorro* (20ᵗʰ Century-Fox, 1940), Eugene Pallette played *Fray* Felipe, a valiant priest. The role was essentially the same as a part Pallette played in what previous adventure film?

The Adventures of Robin Hood (Warner Bros., 1938), where he played Friar Tuck.

www.ingramcontent.com/pod-product-compliance
Lightning Source LLC
Chambersburg PA
CBHW072353290526
45794CB00001B/56